PRAISE FOR PHIL COUSINEAU'S BOOKS

"Every new book by Phil Cousineau is a cultural event, but *Who Stole the Arms of the Venus de Milo?* is the crowning book of Phil Cousineau's literary career. His work here is poetic, allusive, sensuous, and expansive. His Venus is now my Venus, bringing forth the marvels of the Greek spirit and revealing how art might still reveal to us how to live our own lives. This weaving together of art, mythology, travel, and philosophy, reminds me of Wallace Stevens' "Thirteen Ways of Looking at a Blackbird." Read it and you will never look at art in the same way."
> —Alexander Eliot, author of *Three Hundred Years of American Painting*

"It's just marvelous the way you've demonstrated how similar the journeys in mythology are to those in art, literature, movies, and dreams. You've done what all artists and writers must do with what I call the great stuff in myth: You have made it your own."
> —Joseph Campbell, author of *The Hero with a Thousand Faces*

"Regarding Phil Cousineau's *The Accidental Aphorist*, there are writers who can take moments in time and distill from them the purest images: shimmering but steel-like, transitory yet ineffaceable, smoothly perfect as a circle yet sharp-edged as a sword. Give such a writer an hour and you will be engaged for a lifetime. Unlike most of his colleagues today, Cousineau appreciates the treasures of our tongue: Nouns sit proudly in their proper places while the verbs arise and dance. Reading him is a ball."
> —Georgia I. Hesse, travel writer and editor of the *San Francisco Chronicle*

"Phil Cousineau has chronicled a lifetime of pilgrimages, from the depths of lost jungles to the heights of the human soul, always with passion, curiosity, warmth, wisdom, and soul. And in this little golden guide, *The Art of Pilgrimage*, he brings us along with him. This is an experience not to be missed for any reason."
—Mort Rosenblum, author of *The Secret Life of the Seine*

"How few writers realize the gift of the complete freedom of speech and the colossal spiritual gift of poetry. Phil Cousineau's new poems are ingenious, wondrous, and delightful. *Night Train* has stunning glimpses of the world and a cosmic planet citizen appeal."
—Antler, author of *Factory and Last Words* and winner of the Whitman Prize

"The prolific Phil Cousineau has released another book, *The Oldest Story in the World*, about the wonderful world of words. Cousineau recalls stories that enchanted him as a child and stories revealed to him at family gatherings. He is, like all of us, hungry to mine meaning out of the stories he hears and tells. And moving inexorably behind our own quests for meaning is the unfolding story of the evolutionary universe."
—Frederic and Mary Anne Brussat, *Spirituality & Practice* magazine

"Phil Cousineau—part historian, part shaman, part raconteur, part magician—bares the keys to all creation in his new book, *Stoking the Creative Fires*...a sensory journey through creation itself."
—Gerald Nicosia, author of *Memory Babe: A Critical Biography of Jack Kerouac*

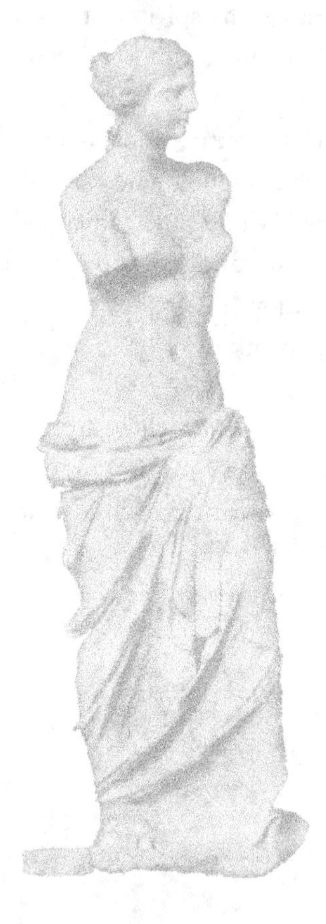

WHO STOLE THE ARMS
OF THE
VENUS DE MILO?

BOOKS BY THE AUTHOR

The Hero's Journey: Joseph Campbell on His Life and Work, 1990

Deadlines: A Rhapsody on a Theme of Famous and Infamous Last Words, 1991

The Soul of the World: A Modern Book of Hours (with Eric Lawton), 1993

Riders on the Storm: My Life with Jim Morrison and the Doors, 1993
    (by John Densmore with Phil Cousineau)

Soul: An Archaeology: Readings from Socrates to Ray Charles, 1994

*Prayers at 3 A.M.: Poems, Songs, Chants, and Prayers for the Middle
    of the Night*, 1995

UFOs: A Mythic Manual for the Millennium, 1995

Design Outlaws: Frontiers of the 21st Century (with Christopher Zelov), 1996

Soul Moments: Marvelous Stories of Synchronicity, 1997

The Art of Pilgrimage: The Seeker's Guide to Making Travel Sacred, 1998

Riddle Me This: A World Treasury of Folk and Literary Puzzles, 1999

The Soul Aflame: A Modern Book of Hours (with Eric Lawton), 2000

The Book of Roads: Travel Stories from Michigan to Marrakesh, 2000

Once and Future Myths: The Power of Ancient Stories in Modern Time, 2001

The Way Things Are: Conversations with Huston Smith, 2003

The Olympic Odyssey: Rekindling the Spirit of the Great Games, 2004

The Blue Museum: Poems, 2004

A Seat at the Table: The Struggle for American Indian Freedom, 2005

Angkor Wat: The Marvelous Enigma (photographs), 2006

Night Train: New Poems, 2007

The Jaguar People: An Amazonian Chronicle (photographs), 2007

Stoking the Creative Fires: 9 Ways to Rekindle Imagination, 2008

Around the World in Eighty Faces (photographs), 2008

Fungoes and Fastballs: Great Moments in Baseball Haiku, 2008

The Meaning of Tea (with Scott Chamberlin Hoyt), 2009

City 21: The Second Enlightenment (with Christopher Zelov), 2009

The Oldest Story in the World: A Mosaic of Meditations, 2009

The Song of the Open Road (photographs), 2010

Wordcatcher: One Man's Odyssey into the World of Words, 2010

Beyond Forgiveness: Reflections on Atonement, 2011

Shadowcatcher (photographs), 2012
The Painted Word: A Treasure Chest of Colorful Word Origins, 2012
And Live Rejoicing: Chapters in a Charmed Life, 2012
     (by Huston Smith with Phil Cousineau)
The Soul and Spirit of Tea (with Scott Chamberlin Hoyt), 2013
Rasa: A Pilgrimage to India (photographs), 2013
Burning the Midnight Oil: Illuminating the Long Night's Journey into Day, 2014
Crepuscular (photographs), 2015
The Book of Roads: A Life Made of Travel (New and Expanded Edition), 2015
Fungoes and Fastballs: Baseball Haiku (New and Expanded Edition), 2016
The Accidental Aphorist: A Curiosity Cabinet of Aphorisms, Maxims...
     and Afterthoughts, 2017
Ay, Cuba! (photographs), 2018
The Lost Notebooks of Sisyphus: A Novel with Commentary, 2020
Who Stole the Arms of the Venus de Milo? 2023
Waiting for Kaline: A Baseball Novel for All Ages [forthcoming]
The Long Conversation: Meetings with Remarkable Mentors [forthcoming]
Cobblestones: New and Collected Poems [forthcoming]

AUDIO BOOKS

The Art of Pilgrimage, 1999
Once and Future Myths, 2002
The Way Things Are, 2004
Wordcatcher, 2010
Beyond Forgiveness, 2011
The Painted Word, 2012
Burning the Midnight Oil, 2014
The Book of Roads, 2016
The Hero's Journey, 2018
Stoking the Creative Fires, 2023

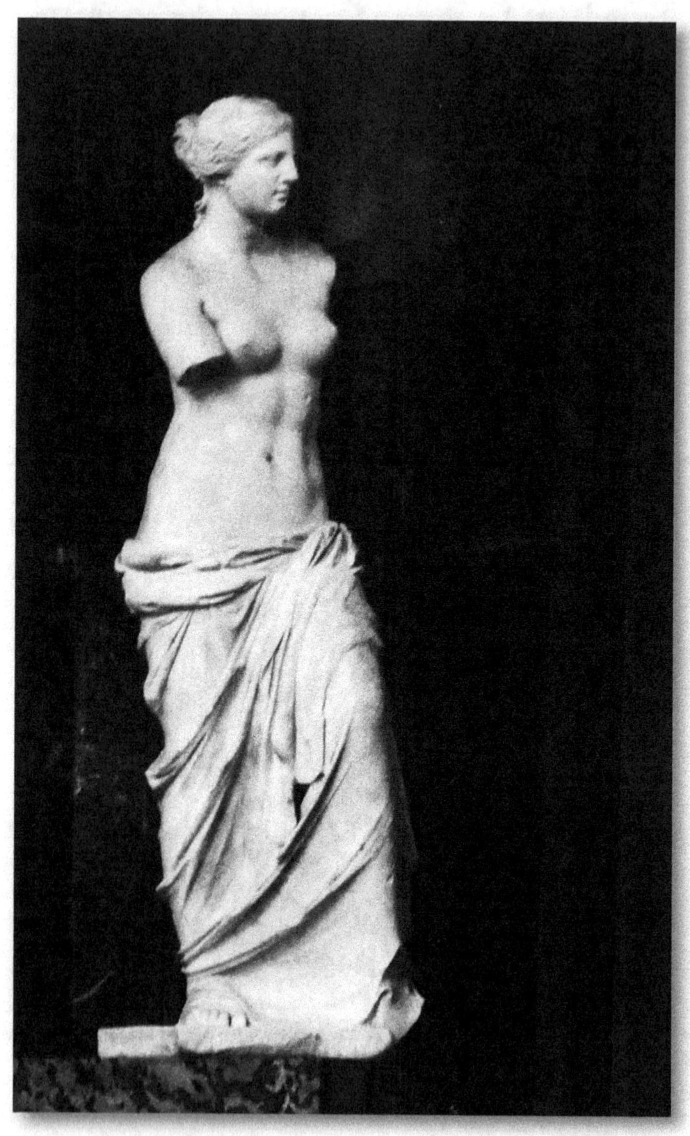

The Venus de Milo, Musée du Louvre, 2010
Infrared photography by Phil Cousineau

WHO STOLE THE ARMS
OF THE
VENUS DE MILO?

A Mosaic of Meditations

On the Eternal Pursuit

Of Love, Beauty, and Happiness

by

Phil Cousineau

with photographs by the author

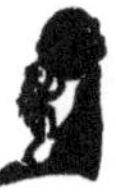

SISYPHUS PRESS
P. O. BOX 330098

SAN FRANCISCO, CALIFORNIA 94133

WHO STOLE THE ARMS OF THE VENUS DE MILO?
The Eternal Pursuit of Love, Beauty, and Happiness

Text © Copyright 2023 by Phil Cousineau
Photography © Copyright 2023 by Phil Cousineau
All rights reserved.

Published in a limited edition of 1000 copies by:
Sisyphus Press
P.O. Box 330098
San Francisco, California 94133
www.philcousineau.com

Library of Congress Control Number (LCCN)
ISBN: 979-8-8689265-8-7 Paperback
ISBN: 979-8-218-34722-2 Hardback

Grateful acknowledgments go to the individuals and organizations that helped make possible the beginning and the completion of this book with a welcome series of writing sabbaticals. The generous souls include Michael and Jeanne Adams for the kind use on several occasions of their guesthouse in Carmel Highlands; Ronnie and Philip Counihan of Renvyle House in Connemara, Ireland; the Bratsera Hotel on Hydra in the Greek islands; Brush Creek Ranch, Wyoming, for my residency; the Thurber House in Columbus, Ohio, while I served as Writer-in-Residence; the Krotona Institute of Theosophy in Ojai, California; the North Beach Garret, courtesy of Mary O'Hara- Deveraux and James Deveraux; and Itha-kana, courtesy of Michelle Neale, in Ithaka, Greece.

Cover and book design by Jim Shubin, the Book Alchemist.
Who Stole the Arms of the Venus de Milo? is typeset in Goudy Old Style

Cover photograph: The Venus de Milo, the Musée du Louvre, 2008, by Phil Cousineau.

All photographs of the sculpture are by Phil Cousineau unless otherwise noted.

Frontispiece photograph: The Infrared Venus, by Phil Cousineau, 2019.

Back cover: Author photo by Jo Beaton Cousineau, 2016.
First edition.
First Printing: April 2024. Second Printing May 2024.
10, 9, 8, 7, 6, 5, 4, 3, 2

To Jo & Jack:
mythic muse,
marvelous son

CONTENTS

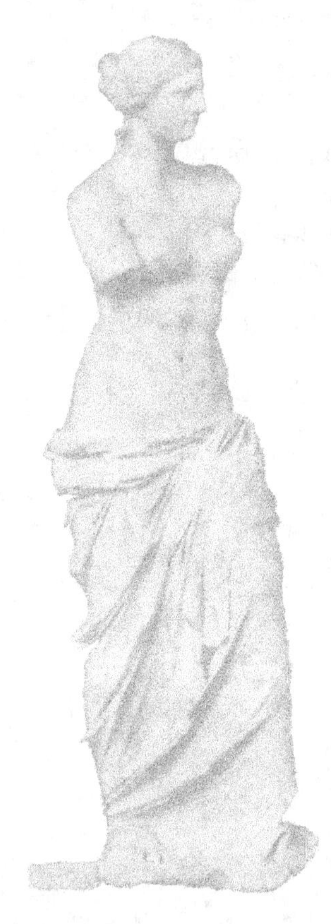

"Beauty—be not caused—It Is—"
—Emily Dickinson

"I am bewildered by the magnificence of your beauty,
and wish to see you with a hundred eyes...
I am in the house of mercy and my heart is a place of prayer."
— Mevlana Rumi

"Where is your Self to be found? Always in the deepest
enchantment that you have experienced."
—Hugo von Hofmannsthal, essayist, playwright

"Any object deeply regarded can be a gateway to the gods."
—James Joyce, *Ulysses*

"To find a form that accommodates the mess,
that is the task of the artist now."
—Samuel Beckett in a 1961 interview

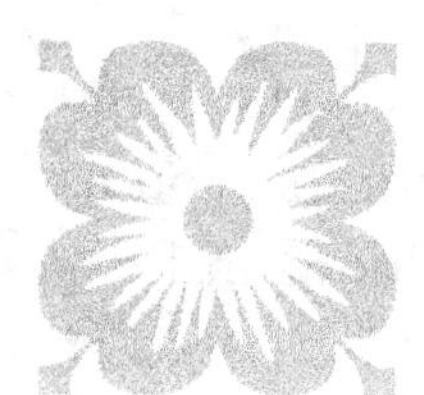

A PARABLE ABOUT BEAUTY

In 1945, the Russian novelist, historian, and activist Alexander Solzhenitsyn was arrested for criticizing Stalin and sentenced to eight years of harsh labor in Siberia. During the brutal forced marches across the freezing tundra, he composed long speeches in his mind on frosty camp evenings, vowing he would someday deliver them to the outside world.

Twenty-five years and several epic books later, in 1970, Solzhenitsyn received a letter from the Nobel Committee in Stockholm. They informed him he had been awarded their Prize for Literature "for the ethical force with which he has pursued the indispensable traditions of Russian literature" and for his commitment to writing the truth, even when it was "not always being presented with pleasure." When Solzhenitsyn stood at the podium and spoke to the august gathering, he only briefly referred to "the millstone of surveillance and distrust" that attendees expected him to expose as the monstrosity of conditions inside the gulag. Instead, Solzhenitsyn stunned the world by citing a passage from Fyodor Dostoevsky's *The Idiot* in which Prince Myshkin, an epileptic Russian nobleman, remarks, "Beauty will save the world."

After this startling reference, Solzhenitsyn paused and asked, "What does that mean?" He paused again and went on, "For a long time, I thought that was just a phrase. How could it be possible? When in our bloodthirsty history did beauty save whom from what? Beauty has ennobled and elevated, yes, but whom has it ever saved?"

For him, the arcane arguments about aesthetics were less important than the ineffable force in art that can "vanquish the lie" that claims culture is useless against the power of political rule. "That is why I think, my friends, that we are capable of helping the world in its agonizing testing hour... One word of truth outweighs the whole world."

Solzhenitsyn did not evade the hard question of how this might happen. "Fortunately," he declared, "there does exist such a means in our world. The means is art. The means is literature." Despite the horrors he witnessed and endured, the author revealed his profound conviction that a secret light is revealed in certain works that are "irrefutably convincing" and which have "scooped up the truth and presented it to us as a living force." Works like these, he stated, have the uncanny capacity to "straighten out the twisted roads of history."

Moreover, Solzhenitsyn insisted, it is the artist's responsibility to create works that are utterly necessary because we need to boldly speak out about injustice.

"One word of truth can outweigh the whole world," he concluded.

If we don't, how will we ever know if beauty can save us?

Save us by luring the truth out of our own souls.

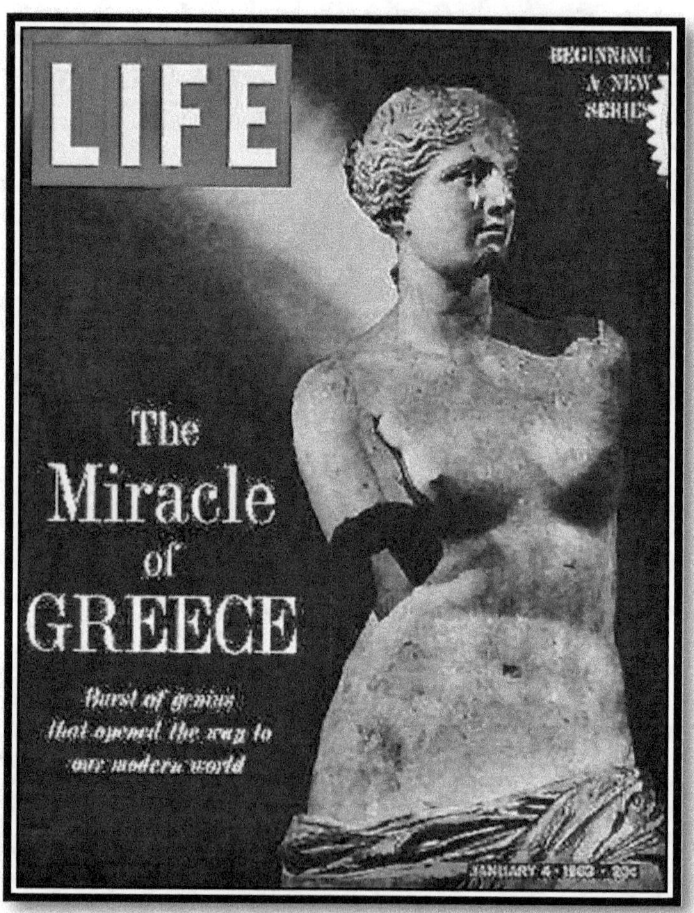

Life magazine, January 4, 1963
Collection of Stanley H. Cousineau
Detroit, Michigan

INTRODUCTION

THE REBIRTH OF BEAUTY

Fall 1997: The Louvre, Paris. For one startling moment, I was alone with the most voluptuous woman in the world. Alone in a room that had been teeming with tourists only moments before.

The Venus de Milo, the Aphrodite of Melos, the White Goddess of Paris, the Ethereal Icon of Beauty and Desire. She has stood sentinel-silent in the Louvre for more than a hundred and seventy years. I had been to the museum myriad times since my first visit in the summer of 1974 on my post-college Grand Tour of Europe, but this was the first time I'd lingered for hours. I am embarrassed to admit that I usually dashed past her like one of humorist Art Buchwald's tourists racing the frenetic "Five-minute Louvre." Not because I thought the statue wasn't worth the effort but because I was convinced that I had known all about her since I was a kid.

Looking back over the tumble of years, it wouldn't be too much to say that I grew up with her or maybe because of her. While baseball and cars may have been my first loves, art and music were close behind. With my father's encouragement, I became an incorrigible ten-year-old fan of museums dragged by the scruff of my neck to Detroit's famous Institute of Arts as well as local galleries and antique shops. Often, I listened to him read out loud from the essays of noted critic Alexander Eliot's ambrosial art reviews in *Time* magazine.

It all began in January 1963, a weekend afternoon when my dad brought in the mail, which included the new issue of *Life* magazine. Smiling in a way I hadn't seen him smile before, he told me to follow him. I had to lengthen my stride to keep up with him as we strode from the living room (bursting with the pride and joy of his life, leather-bound books), through the kitchen, and down the creaky wooden stairs of the house into the cool vastness of our basement. We passed by the roaring incinerator, the green ping-pong table, and the cardboard spaceship that I had built with my buddies out of an old refrigerator box, and on to his silver-painted workbench.

Ceremoniously, he pulled out of his back pocket the rolled-up magazine, which boasted a sepia-toned photograph of the Venus de Milo on the cover. Of course, I was fascinated by her buxom beauty and took a deep breath. As I did, I braced myself and waited for the inevitable art lecture. None was forthcoming this time. Instead, he gazed affectionately at the cover and reached for a slender black wooden picture frame he had recently bought down at Northside Hardware Store, in my hometown of Wayne, Michigan, outside Detroit. With his usual sense of tender toughness, my father slipped the magazine cover inside the frame. Then he hammered a nail into the cement wall behind the workbench and hung the framed photograph of the Venus de Milo.

Something about that moment has always stayed in my mind.

I love the sheer mystery of it, the unknowable source of his affection, the palpable love of art that has influenced my life, and in the spirit of Solzhenitsyn, maybe even saved it. The time with my father was compressed like all such experiences that wedge into our lives. For the first time, I knew there was beauty in the world. My dad was a devoted Ford man at World Headquarters in Dearborn and an amateur art connoisseur in the original sense of the word—one who loves something for its own sake.

For the next several years, there in the colorful confines of our basement, the gorgeous Venus de Milo waited for me and my hungry gaze. Every time I sought refuge in the basement to fetch his tools or grab my 1962 Al Kaline Wilson baseball glove, I snuck a furtive glance at the radiant Venus on the basement wall. But not only because she was nude, which was a special kind of initiation into a forbidden world for a boy my age. The Venus seemed to hold a secret to the fathomless mysteries of love, desire, and from the looks on my father's face when I caught him staring at her, happiness.

And that is how, as the Bard said, I was first wounded by wonder. By this, I mean that it planted a seed in me that grew into a stoic form of doubt about the way things were, a suspicion that nothing was as it seemed, though the sages told us that it also wasn't otherwise.

Over the years, I have seen a reel of flickering images of the Venus ranging from the reverential to the satirical in art history books, movies, paintings, cartoons, songs, and dances. I am particularly fond of the postcard I found in one of the green metal *bouquinistes'* bookstalls along the Seine in Paris of the seven-foot-tall, 1,700-pound replica of a chocolate Venus de Milo that had been on display at Henri Maillard's "Fine Chocolates and Cocoa" pavilion at the 1893 Chicago World's Fair.

Flickering indeed. Didn't Joseph Conrad write, in *Heart of Darkness*, that we live in the *flicker*, the movement between worlds, the motion that seems to make the world—and us—come alive? And didn't my friend, the sociologist and culture critic Theodore Roszak, write that the flicker was at the heart of the mystery of the movies? Imagining Jean-Luc Godard's description of the miracle—"Cinema is truth twenty-four times a second"—helps me visualize the connection.

For me, the imagery of the Venus has become so phantasmagorical that it has become difficult to see whatever is most *deeply real* about the statue because of the clutch of clichés that casts a cloud of unknowing over her. André Malraux, the French art critic and Minister of Culture, wrote in *Museum Without Walls* that our experience of art changed forever with the rise of mass reproduction, such as prints, postcards, and photographs. The sudden omnipresence of art that gave modern people the sense we have always known certain works that shine from within and stretch our souls, such as Vermeer's *The Milkmaid*, Leonardo's *Portrait of a Man in Red*

Chalk, Michelangelo's *David*, the *Winged Victory of Samothrace*, Kahlo's *The Two Fridas*, Rodin's *The Thinker (Le Penseur)*, the Pyramids of Giza, the Taj Mahal, the Brooklyn Bridge.

The welter of images has made it more difficult to enjoy an encounter with the real thing. I remember the old Ella Fitzgerald commercial where she croons, "Is it live—or is it Memorex?" Today, the question has transmogrified into: "If something I've done isn't on social media, did it really happen?" This doubt is at the heart of our existential crisis: If the world doesn't notice me, do I even exist?

It was spring 1997 in Paris. I'd been meandering the halls of the Louvre, the world's most capacious museum, for hours, getting lost in the nine miles of labyrinthine corridors and frustrated about only seeing a fraction of the thirty-five thousand items on display, feeling what curators now call "museum fatigue."

On the learned advice of the legendary Alexander Eliot, the same art critic my dad admired enough to read every week while I was growing up, I had decided to visit only one work of art today—this one, the Venus de Milo, in the belief that if I focused on one work, it might reveal the entire world to me.

So, I was there to see the Venus with my own eyes, the secret of all museum-going. According to the probing art critic John Berger, the impulse to encounter significant art is the deep desire *to have seen*. To be clear, I was also there because I didn't *really* see her on that first visit, being too young and callow. Over the years, I had become vastly disappointed in myself for missing the mystery. It's weak tea to know that most of us are moving too fast to comprehend what we're looking at before bolting away to see the next thing. Then the next. A way of looking in the world that has culminated in the scourge of the selfie stick, which encourages us to see *ourselves* rather than seeing the things themselves. With my traditional orange French Clairefontaine sketchbook in one hand and my Olympus II single-lens reflex camera in the other, I walked around her again, not unlike a pilgrim circumambulating a holy temple, a pitcher striding around the mound. Turning around the statue, it felt like I was winding myself into reverie, which is why I didn't notice a mother with her young daughter entering the gallery.

The silence snapped in half. The room crackled with laughter. The statue gleamed.

The darling little girl came skipping up next to me and stared at the Venus while her willowy mother shuffled right behind, whispering to her in a lilting Irish accent, "Shush, love. Don't disturb the nice lad." When the girl looked closer at the imposing statue that loomed before her, she stopped, as if a large pane of glass had suddenly appeared between her and the Venus. She spun around and asked her mother in the wispiest of voices: "Where are her arms, Mama?"

Her mother responded in a bemused tone, "Let's be quiet, shall we, sweetheart?" Tenderly, she put her forefinger to the girl's lips and added, "We're in a *museum*."

A smile sauntered across my face, an instinctive response to the girl's utter joy that brightened up the room. Her sweet insistence on the delight of beauty touched me, while her mother's unusual pronunciation of *museum* delighted me. Her emphasis on the first syllable—*muse*—brought home the origin of the word like none I'd heard before. I detected in her voice an echo of its original meaning, the "house of the muses," those winsome goddesses who happened to be the nine daughters of Mnemosyne, the personification of memory. Within the word *muse*, I heard the ancient Greek *mu*, which originally meant "closed lips." It referred to the silence of initiates in the ancient mysteries as well as *myth*, which I have come to think of as the "mother story."

Uncanny, I think. The Irishwoman's dulcet tones transported me back to a time when it was believed that museums housed the nine goddesses—the nine forces of nature believed to personify and inspire the arts. For those gifts, the ancient Greeks believed, we should act accordingly, in quietude, so that we might feel some amusement, laughter inspired by the muses about the human adventure.

Well, that has been the ideal anyway. The practice has veered from one extreme to the other, the sacred to the profane, the numinous to the ridiculous, the reverential to the commercial. But the ideal remains that we are *moved* beyond ticking off another box on the list of things to do for tourists and travelers.

To allow the mother and daughter some privacy, I edged away until I reached the rear wall of the gallery, near the niche in the wall that displayed a few of the other marble objects—a mottled forearm, a rough-hewn hand holding a ball or an apple, and two herms of Herakles and Hermes, as my trusty guidebook informed me, which were found alongside the statue when it was discovered in the Greek islands.

The girl frowned and started to pout, crossing her arms and insisting again, "Tell me, Mama, tell me why she's missing her arms?"

Together, mother and daughter came closer to the Venus, unusually respectful, as if approaching an altar in a cathedral. They acted surprised at how imposing she was—all six-foot-eight and 1,984 pounds of her. Then they squinched their faces, as if bothered by an annoying question that I would confront over and over in the coming years: *Hmm, she's interesting, but is she, well, to be blunt, beautiful?*

The Irish lass then broke away from her mother's grasp and danced around the statue, as if it was a maypole, never taking her eyes off it, never losing her delight, her sheer joy. Her mother watched, her emerald eyes blazing with pride. Pulled by the centripetal force of maternal love, the girl soon returned to her mother's side and clasped her hand. The mother turned silent, furrowed her brow, and tilted her head in wonder about the infamously missing arms.

"Mama, who stole them?" the girl insisted, but not petulantly. Her interest was that of a child whose parents encouraged her to express curiosity. "Who stole the arms of the Venus de Milo?"

There it was, the beveled-edge moment with the sacred on one side, the profane on the other. The instant when life could go in either direction. The spark I had been looking for, although I never would have been able to put it that way at that moment. This was the whimsy I needed, the quickening that comes upon me whenever I'm in the presence of any great work of art. Thus moved, my mind swerved to one of my favorite lines in Pablo Neruda's poem, "Horses," where he wrote, "I saw, I saw, and seeing came alive," which expressed so concisely what often happened to me in a museum. The Chilean poet's characteristically humble observation has served as a constant reminder for me to stay alert in museums and every other essential encounter in my life.

Again, that's the ideal.

Finally, the Irish mother shrugged her shoulders, saying, "Sorry, love, I just don't know." Four of the hardest words for any of us to say.

I was impressed by how easily she admitted what she didn't know. It's so much easier to feign knowledge we don't have. Then the girl's mother noticed me noticing them. My scalp prickled, my throat constricted. What was happening? I felt ashamed that I didn't know something that I thought I knew, or should have known, the Venus' origin story.

Then the Irishwoman surprised me by the earnestness with which she admitted to her daughter, "I don't think anybody *stole* them, sweetheart." In the spirit of her storytelling ancestors, she paused and stated with an assurance that velveted her voice, "Still, I think she's beautiful, don't you? Even without her arms, she's beautiful *anyway*."

A whole world swung on that adverb, the world of my fascination and this book.

The girl squirmed, suggesting, "Maybe she *lost* them, Mama!"

I could feel the Irish woman's eyes probing me, waiting for a saving response. My mind went as blank as a newly stretched canvas, my legs turned as weak as a runner stumbling at the finish line.

There was a problem. Since I was a kid, I had taken it for granted that I knew a fair amount about the Venus de Milo because my dad talked about her so often. The summer of '62 was especially magical because he helped me build a go-kart so I could compete in the local Soap Box Derby. While pounding nails, he pounded art history lessons into my thick skull. Years later, I recalled how the image of the statue's looming presence ran through my mind like a ticker tape, providing me with the oddments of art history and history's arcane facts that he loved to pass on to me. Mostly, it was nostalgia for the gossamer moments we spent together.

But the facts were less important, he liked to say, than the *feeling* conveyed by a work.

I have found some company, even solace, in the observations of the melancholic essayist Cyril Connolly, especially in his classic, *The Unquiet Grave*. There he explores a series of great works of literature, from Horace's *Odes* to the essays of Montaigne, and the *Illuminations* of Baudelaire, concluding, "In feeling...masterpieces contain the maximum of emotion with a classical sense of form." What is common in their thought, he asks. "Love of life and nature." I wonder if Connolly was aware of the personal comment made by the painter Paul Cezanne, "A work which did not begin in emotion is not art"? Or if he ever heard Ella Fitzgerald perform "Feelings," where she goes fathoms deep in her painful excavation of love: "For all my life I feel it. I wish I'd never met you boy..."

I gaze on, trying to recapture what originally captivated me about the Venus. I remember being mystified by the held-breath expression on her face, the thousand-yard stare, the moonstruck look of love layered with the subtlest sense of dread. I believed then and now that her look held the answers to the mysteries of the universe.

A vain urge rises in me to say that I and I alone know what happened to her arms. But I am chastened by the memory of reading about the notorious sniping in the *Journals* of the Goncourt Brothers, published in the

1890s, about the paintings in the Louvre having to endure an endless array of boorish remarks from bored tourists.

So, chastened by my own literary memories, I turned silent as the stars.

As I did, a stream of gauzy memories rose from the deep like the bubbles from a diver's scuba tank. I vaguely remembered that she was discovered by a French soldier in the early nineteenth century on the Greek island of Melos. On the heels of that image came a memory of my staunchly proud French-Canadian father regaling me about the art war that broke out when the statue was found. I remembered it as a sultry summer night. We were working in the basement, measuring the wood for my go-kart, sawing and nailing it together. As usual, he veered off into a rambling story about the chance discovery of the Venus de Milo and then its delivery to the Louvre, which allowed the French to boast that they now possessed the most famous work from antiquity.

None of that arcane knowledge helped me now, not in this decisive moment, this determining test of knowledge and memory. I didn't have a clue about what happened to the infamously missing arms of the Venus de Milo, but I couldn't bring myself to admit it. Not knowing what to say felt like a lash of humiliation. But I did feel a momentary reprieve when I recalled the words of Oklahoma's favorite son, the humorist Will Rogers, to his niece the day they saw the Venus together at the Louvre: "See what will happen if you don't stop biting your fingernails?" Or the New Yorker cartoon that portrayed the Venus pleading with a passing visitor, "Sir, can you please scratch my nose for me?"

A plangent silence hung over the gallery.

The Irishwoman and I gaze awkwardly at each other.

In turn, I was stricken with the feeling that she was hoping I might say something that would satisfy her daughter's curiosity.

"What do *you* think?" she asks me quietly.

I felt my cheeks redden with embarrassment, feeling as mute as the statues standing in the nearby Greek, Etruscan, and Roman sculpture galleries, the dazzling accumulation of centuries of discovery, looting, preservation, and culture wars.

Shaking my head and shrugging my shoulders, a pitiful admission of my ignorance, I turned my attention back to the statue, at once mystifying and numbingly familiar. I like to think it was the little girl's use of the word *missing* that made my mind move orthogonally back to an early comment Geoffrey Grigson made in his winsome book about Aphrodite/ Venus and her son, Eros. The very word *Venus*, he wrote, originally meant "lacking or missing," Venus meaning the "desire for what is missing." What this unexpected etymology tells me is that for the Greeks, the personification of love came from a realization that what is missing longs to be filled in.

Missing. A word that haunts me. It always visits me when museum-roaming. Curiously, I think of the Irish author James Joyce, and the case of the missing words in the original 1922 edition of his masterpiece, *Ulysses.* When the revised Gabler Edition was finally published in 1984, there were corrections of more than six thousand errors, including entire passages that had been ignored or deleted. Missing. The most dramatic is the haunting exchange between the young hero Stephen Dedalus and his mother on her deathbed.

As she lay dying, she whispered, "You sang that song to me: Love's bitter mystery."

To which Dedalus replies, "Tell me, Mother, if you know now, the word known to all men."

"Love, yes, the word known to all men," his mother answered.

At that moment, I had what I will risk calling an epiphany, a word Joyce himself restored to the language in his short story, *The Dead.* A flash of light, an illumination, a breakthrough. Gazing at the space where the statue's arms had once reached out, I thought *Something is always missing.*

That's life; that's what the people say. That's art: its function, its power. That's the gap that lurks between what is there and what is left out. The music playing in the space between the notes.

I swivel around to look again at the Venus and remembered a few of her familiar attributes. Scholars described her powers as a goddess, such as love, beauty, desire, and happiness on one side, and jealousy, envy, and lust on the other. The act of naming these qualities helps us appreciate the utter vastness of what we are reaching for, showing us that Venus personifies not only our passion but our longing to fill in the void between love and loneliness, fairness and justice, happiness and discontent, immanence and transcendence.

She embodies both sheer absence and utter presence. How does the absence get filled with presence? I turn to the physicist Sir Arthur Eddington, who wrote, "Matter is simply ghostly, empty space," which leaves plenty of room for something ineffable, like spirit, the vital force, the élan vital, or genius, to enter in and fill a work to the brim. In turn, this suggests that the Venus de Milo's missing arms are only more ghostly than the rest of her. After all, there is far more to a sculpture than stone or wood, more to a story than words and structure, more to art than canvas and paint. What's more is spirit, the ineffable vital force that an artist infuses into stone, ink, or canvas. The lived life is imbued with a transcendent quality that makes paint lift off canvas, that brings truth back to beauty, beauty back to art, art back to ordinary people.

According to the English essayist and art critic Walter Pater, there is a vital force lurking in the Venus de Milo, as if some spirit seems to be on the verge of breaking out. This is an attempt at examining the metaphysics of art, a glimpse of the myth-making that has been evolving for at least twenty-five hundred years—that there is something alive dying to get out. In his magnificent journals, the prescient essayist Ralph Waldo Emerson described the uncanny power of any myth as being the story that reveals truths deeper than fact. Our great myths consist of stories and images that describe things that cannot be told any other way, personifying as they do the titanic forces of nature and the phenomenal powers of human emotion. Myths help us understand how much we are in the world and how much the world is in us.

The peculiar loneliness of beauty, a surprising attribute, lingers there like marble dust, raising "a lump in the throat," which just so happens to be Robert Frost's definition of poetry, and so by extrapolation suggests beauty is a special kind of poetry.

I turned slowly again around the statue, gazing at the voluptuous goddess. I was overwhelmed by a lifetime of memories and emotions, all compacted into what John Updike called "eternally ramifying moments." Or what Molly Bloom murmured at the end of *Ulysses*: "Yes, I said yes, I will. Yes." This is what is required of us—affirmation. Viktor Frankl tells us in *Yes to Life: In Spite of Everything* that the prisoners at Buchenwald sang that phrase in defiance of the death all around them to help them survive: "We still want to say, 'Yes to Life!'"

Turning back to the Irishwoman, I echoed her own words, "Beautiful *anyway*."

Our brief conversation hovered above us like a word balloon, attached to me like a wall caption to a painting, an inscription carved in old stone. The little Irish girl danced back to her mother, held her hand, tilted her head, and stared at the statue that had awoken from the slumber of the centuries.

Sweetly, she said, "Maybe, Mama, but I *still* miss them."

The moments were unfolding like a parable.

I was thrilled by the girl's gentling words and gazed around the gallery at the oak-and-glass vitrines containing a few scattered items that were collected when the Venus was discovered in the early eighteenth century on the island of Melos. Savoring every turn, I peered into the nearby Hall of Greek and Roman Sculpture, which featured such masterpieces as the

Kauffman Head of Venus, the Crouching Aphrodite, the Ares Borghese, and Hermes Fastening his Sandal. I shook my head in wonder about the lack of progress since these works were created, remembering Picasso's unusually humble comment after visiting the cave art in Lascaux: "They invented everything; we've invented nothing."

The splendid sight split off into a memory of something resembling the art historian Walter Benjamin's insight, written after a visit to the Louvre: "For what one has lived," he observed, "is at best comparable to a beautiful statue which has had all its limbs knocked off in transit and now yields nothing but the precious block out of which the image of one's future must be hewn."

What I hear him saying is that whatever is missing in a work of art can be compared to what is missing in our own lives, and with a bold act of imagination, we can take what *moves* us in art to help us envision a new life. Surely not due to any meek theory of art as compensation but as a dynamic contribution to the sum of all things. Next, moving around the Venus, I felt the need to explore the enigma of this mysterious work of art that combined the sublime and the beautiful, the ancient and the modern.

I reeled away into reverie.

Gazing at the stumps of her shoulders provoked me into thinking about the missing poetry of Sappho, whom Socrates called the Tenth Muse, and the startling fact that only one complete poem of hers has been found—in an ancient rubbish heap in Oxyrhynchus, Egypt. The other poems are fragments and provide a tantalizing hint of her genius. I thought about the centuries-long search for the lost letters and original manuscripts of Shakespeare, the mystery of Leonardo's half-completed paintings, the pang of knowing we only had two recordings by the Delta blues singer Mattie Delaney.

Something is always missing.

No life is ever complete. No person. No work of art. No soul. No era, no epoch.

We are all broken, which tells me why so many of us have come to love shattered statues, cracked paintings, ruined temples, ripped-apart books, even broken artists such as Caravaggio, Käthe Kollwitz, Van Gogh, Amy Winehouse. We are all members of what U. S. Poet Laureate Ada Limon calls "the hurting kind," which may be why we can identify with the Venus.

After all, isn't this one of the main things art is *for*? To heal the agonizing gaps in life, fill in the void, assuage the loneliness, console us in our cruelest moments? We have art, literature, theater, dance, and music to complete us. With so many arrows in our quiver, we needn't feel alone in our incompleteness, loneliness, or meaninglessness. The greatest works, our masterpieces, do more than entertain us. They help and at times even heal us. As Alexander Eliot wrote in his luminous collection of art essays, *Sight and Insight*, the spiritual struggle endured by artists is inescapable. "A masterpiece has spiritual significance...and is meant to be experienced... taken into the depths of consciousness and re-created there. It shines in the dark chamber of the heart."

Still, I am haunted by this struggle for reasons that reason cannot know, to paraphrase the philosopher-mathematician Pascal, who ardently believed in the primacy of the heart over the mind and solitude over community. I suspect that if we are in the right place at the right time and the right mood, the arts can reveal what is missing in our everyday lives and add immeasurably to it, acting as a counterforce to the Second Law of Thermodynamics, as Buckminster Fuller pointed out in 1973 in a lecture to my architecture class in a beautiful wooden amphitheater at the University of Detroit. The universe is constantly breaking down and losing energy, Bucky told us, always devolving into chaos. But there is one thing that builds the universe back up again, and that thing is art. Whether a masterwork like those that surrounded me in the Louvre or even an abandoned manuscript in an old steamer trunk, forgotten in your grandparent's attic, they offer existential proof that it is human effort that restores, reenergizes, revitalizes the world.

Suddenly, I was alone again.

I took a deep breath and looked around the gallery for the Irish mother and daughter. They were nowhere to be seen. They vanished without saying goodbye. If they did, I never heard them, lost in the tumult of my thoughts. I felt relieved to have another moment to myself with the Venus before the invading hordes returned, but another part of me wanted to run after the Irishwoman and ask her, "What did you mean when you said, 'Beautiful *anyway?*'"

She had vanished, along with her story. I have been trying to articulate a response to her ghost ever since. Now it occurs to me that to explain this enigma might help explain the mystery of the Venus de Milo—not just the power of beauty itself but the mystery of why it *moves* us, and possibly my own mystery. Why I have *come so far for beauty*, as Leonard Cohen named his last tour. Why I need to explore why great works seem to *look back* at us and make us feel—for an infinite moment, as the ancients called it—that we have found ourselves at the center of the universe. I need to know how it is that art is presence by absence, why we love some things for what they are and others for what they aren't. I have come this far to know one work well—*this work*—in the hope of explaining to myself one of art history's great mysteries and possibly what has been missing in my own life. Such as why a mere week after graduating from college, I fled the mean streets of violence-riddled Detroit, the clutches of my college girlfriend (a raven-haired Cherokee beauty named Sagata), and my divorce-ravaged parents and went chasing after an antidote to the corrosive ugliness of my life growing up in the ruins-in-the-making environs of Detroit by visiting famous and infamous places all around the world. Famous and beautiful places that cultivate and celebrate the joy and beauty of life.

"Desire is the reaching out [*orexis*] toward what is sweet," wrote Aristotle. Out of the soul-ravaging experiences in the hellhole of Buchenwald, Viktor Frankl wrote, "In times of crisis, people reach for meaning." Then there is the soulful and bluesy atmosphere of Detroit, where Levi Stubbs of the Four Tops sang in his breathtaking baritone, "When you're feeling lost, and about to give up, and your best just ain't good enough, darlin', reach out, reach out for me..." And most likely the first quote I consciously ever wrote down and memorized, in Miss Belfiore's seventh-grade English class, was Robert Browning's "Man's reach should exceed his grasp, or what's a heaven for?"

Am I overreaching? Stretching the story to fit my fantasies? So, I reach. So what? That's what storytelling is for—reaching for some semblance of the meaning of our very lives. I contain multitudes, as Whitman remarked, which means I am also riddled with contradictions. We reach or we retract, shrivel, diminish. Reaching makes us human. It's a small wonder when we don't. If we don't reach, if we don't stretch, why are we here? We reach for meaning. We reach for beauty to balance the terror. We reach for the infinite in our painfully finite lives. We grasp for and sometimes touch the timeless parts of ourselves. I have come to agree with the Italian physicist Carlo Rovelli, who wrote in *The Order of Time*, "To understand ourselves means to understand time; but to understand time, we need to reflect on ourselves."

We reach for the essence, the real thing, what the Greeks called To *ti esti*, the *thisness* of a thing, which is what the thirteenth-century Irish philosopher Duns Scotus called *haeccity*, and what the culture critic Hannah Arendt intensified by making it a kind of ethical command, "Life is about grasping a thing in its *thisness*." Photographer Walker Evans spent a career trying to capture *it*, and when asked about the search said, "If the thing is there, well, there it is." The anti-hero in the cult hit, *The Adventures of Buck-*

eroo Banzai, riffed on the tricky truism, "When you get to where you're going, well, there you are."

These expressions are pithy and poignant, but my favorite remains the hip expression that I heard from my friend and teammate, Al Berard, star runner on my high school track team and the anchor of our record-setting mile relay team in the late Sixties. As we practiced our handoffs for the final meet of the year at the famed University of Michigan running track, he stared at me and growled, "What it is, Cousineau, what it is!" Fifty years later, I asked him if he remembered that moment. Not only did he recall the time and place, he updated his street wisdom. "Yeah, I said that, and I was surprised you *got* it. I was trying to share with you *the what it is of all that is.* Frankly, I'm still trying to do that now with my son."

Take that, Aristotle.

If I was hearing my running mate right, he was describing the heart and soul of the *lived moment,* what the French philosopher Henri Bergson deftly called *la durée,* the duration, or more intensely, *deeply lived time.* The idea underscores a theory of time and consciousness about awareness of the *moment* we are measuring the *moment.* Time that is deeply experienced.

Or, as we used to say on the streets of Detroit, *the real deal.*

In turn, by virtue of our grasping, we reach for the meaning of the missing arms of the Venus de Milo because it appears so dramatically to us that she once reached out but can reach no more. But for what? If I can figure that out, then I'll know why the arms were or weren't important. Why is she turning, why was she reaching, what was she gazing at with such tender wonder?

And yet, and yet... I can't forget that Charlie Chaplin got it right when he concluded, "Life is a desire, not a meaning."

Clearly, there is a story here crying out to be restored. Stories respond to our curiosity. Not unlike the scholar who is determined to figure out why the Mona Lisa is smiling. Or the artist who is dying to know what Vermeer's *Woman in Blue* is thinking. Or the film critic who asked Truffaut again and again what was on the mind of his young hero gazing out over the ocean in the infamous freeze-frame shot that ended *Les quatre cents coups, The 400 Blows?*

The art is always in the surprise. That's the beauty of it.

SHADOWPLAY Four years later, on the night of September 10, 2001, I took a redeye flight from San Francisco to New York to begin a twenty-one-city national book tour for *Once and Future Myths*, which was scheduled to begin at eleven the next morning at Rizzoli Bookstore inside the World Trade Center. The wheels touched down on the LaGuardia Airport tarmac at precisely 8:50 a.m., and seconds later came the screams of the flight attendants and a few of my fellow passengers who were seated on the left side. I looked over the shoulder of one of them and saw a bright flash and thought it was a flare of sunlight on the windows. A held-breath minute later, a passenger bellowed out that a small plane had crashed into the World Trade Center. To this day, I hear in my head, usually late at night, the cries of "Terrorists!" and the phrases "Seven planes still in the air!" and "They're heading to the airport!" from those who had turned on their cellphones while we taxied down the runway.

As soon as I arrived at the terminal, I dashed like a halfback around the passengers in front of me toward the luggage carousel, grabbed my luggage, and ran outside to the horseshoe drive in front of the main terminal just in time to see the bright white flash, the enormous asterisk of fire and light coming from Manhattan, as the second plane crashed into the second tower. No one around me moved. The traffic on the freeway below us slowed to a crawl. Even the airport police around me were paralyzed with fear, staring into the distance, unmoving. Silent. The moment felt like swimming underwater. I tried to talk to a few strangers, but my voice seemed to echo through a long tube out of which came only the feeblest of words. Finally, I caught the eye of a tall young fellow with a briefcase. He was weeping. I approached him carefully, and he said, "This was supposed to be my first day on the job at the Cantor Fitzgerald law firm. By the looks of it, everyone in our office was just killed."

Sudden as a rapid movie cut, a hotel van pulled up. Crammed, frantic, frightened, I forced my way on board, turned, and beckoned for him to join me. When we arrived at the national chain hotel where it was bound, we learned that it was full, so we forced our way onto another bus. I remember my fingers on the rubber strips of the accordion-like doors, prying them apart so we could leap on. When we arrived at an old, funky hotel near Shea Stadium, I spent the next twelve hours glued to the cheap hotel television, numb and torpid, watching the news.

For the next few anxious hours, it felt as if the entire country was under a savage attack right out of *The Day the Earth Stood Still*. On the hotel television, I watched in horror as rapid-fire reports came in about the attack on the Pentagon, in Washington, D. C., and the hijacking of Flight 93 in Somerset County, Pennsylvania. Over and over, 1 I tried to call home on my cellphone, but the lines had been knocked out when the Twin Towers fell. I had wanted desperately to reach my wife to allay her fears that I might have arrived early at the bookstore in the first tower when it fell, but the telephone lines were dead all evening. Far from home, cut off with no means of communication, and unsure where to turn, I felt desolate, sickened by the carnage. It was terrifying to be in the dark, not knowing what had happened or why. But I was alive.

The next morning, my publisher, Michael J. Fine, who had created special editions of *Once and Future Myths* and *The Art of Pilgrimage*, dispatched a town car to pick me up and meet him downtown at a restaurant near Ground Zero. We spent the afternoon talking about the mythological implications of what had just occurred. At the end of our lunch, we parted ways, and I walked the four short blocks to where the Twin Towers had stood just the day before, passing cars and trucks powdered with a strange snow of pulverized cement, crushed bone, and toxic dust. It was shocking to see ash-covered people walking like phantoms down the nearly abandoned streets past boarded-up buildings. I saw bravery when I watched and listened to dozens of police officers and firefighters enter and return from the smoking, smoldering ruins, and I saw cruelty as a small mob spray-painted the combustible word VENGEANCE on the sides of buildings, written by angry fingers into the ash-covered windshields of several nearby parked cars and trucks.

By the time I returned to my hotel, long after midnight, I watched, numb, as the workers and their rescue dogs dug in vain through the rubble for survivors. The number of casualties rose; hope fell. It was impossible to turn away and impossible to comprehend. I could not wrap my head or heart around this. Not knowing what else to do, the next morning I walked back to Ground Zero, but this time could only stay for a short while. I spoke with one dust-covered, yellow-jacketed, helmeted rescue worker who was holding the leash of his rescue dog. The poor guy was being harassed by a handful of sensation-seeking television reporters. One after the other asked him about what it felt like to be a hero. The fireman was livid and turned away in time to catch my eye, and held it, saying to me alone, chillingly, "Not trying to be a hero, man. This is what I do. This is what I am. This is what the moment demands of me. I'm telling ya, I ain't no hero. Neither are you."

Turning away, stifling the tears, I stormed off, past buildings shouting out with MISSING signs. I walked in a stupor down Broadway toward Central Park and beyond before realizing that in a strange and wonderful way, I was walking to the Met, or it was pulling me in the way that art critic Elaine Scarry wrote in her classic essay *On Beauty* that some art sometimes *calls* to us. In that brilliant essay, she offers an incisive analysis of what she calls the four qualities of beauty. First, that it is *sacred*, second, that it is *unprecedented*, third, that it is a *surprise*, and finally, that *it compels us to desire a copy of it*, such as by writing, sketching, singing, or miming. When we see somebody or something we desire, we want, even if it's unconscious, to copy it, to make it part of us. Hence the desire to paint or sculpt beautiful or even strange people and places, or act like somebody we deeply identify with.

The question soon became *What will our response be?* A submerged part of me seemed to be sending up a message of how to heal from the horror and the cruelty, which wasn't to deny it but to balance it if that's the right word, and not too self-indulgently but with awe and wonder. I needed to do something irrational but indispensable or see something uplifting, a reminder of the transcendent side of life. Specifically, some art at the Metropolitan Art Museum. Not to indulge in any escapism or to be precious or noble, I needed a burst of art, a tonic of beauty. My heart required a jolt of something outside of the tormented moment, similar to what Elaine Scarry described as one of the surprising attributes of beauty—that it is *lifesaving*, as startling as that may sound.

To this day, I'm not sure where that inner command came from except that I craved the real thing. I wasn't looking for anything soft or sentimental, pretty or trendy, mysterious or fashionable. Stunned is what I wanted to be by works of art that took my breath away, that reminded me how good it was to be alive. Not impressed—transported. I needed to experience what one of the poets who has sustained me the most, Jack Gilbert, once wrote in "A Brief for the Defense"—that there is "Sorrow everywhere. Slaughter everywhere... We must risk delight. We can do without pleasure, / but not delight. Not enjoyment. We must have / the stubbornness to accept our gladness in the ruthless / furnace of this world."

But how, but how? Later, he suggested, in "The Abnormal is not Courage," of his desire to experience "a magnitude of beauty that gives me no peace / the beauty that is of many days."

A magnitude of beauty. That's what the man said. It ain't an option is what he meant.

I needed to stand in front of a few works as humbly and chastened as the shipwrecked Odysseus when he was discovered on the beach by the Phaeacian princess Nausicaa and was filled with wonder at the sight of her young beauty. Or when the astronaut Edgar Mitchell floated in space for five minutes with nothing to do but gaze at the big blue marble of our planet, saying to himself only, "Beautiful." Or when the primatologist Jane Goodall observed the family of chimps she had been studying doing somersaults of joy underneath a rainbow-striped waterfall. Years later, in San Francisco, she described this jubilant vision to a small group at the Asian Art Museum: "What a beautiful moment that was in my life. A decisive one. A threshold moment."

As she spoke, I felt the hair rising on my own arms, as if in solidarity.

It helped that I was in a mood to be astonished.

I would settle for nothing less in the shadow-stricken hours after the attacks. I needed to be touched, moved, reminded that life was sacred, reconnected to the presence of whatever is good about our benighted human race. I needed to be reminded of who I was and needed some medicine for my soul. I didn't need art in the abstract. I longed for intimate encounters with real things. And then out of the mystic blue of memory, I heard the voice of my mother when I was a boy when she wished me good night and then whispered, "Be good." A phrase, a consolation, a hope that has never left me.

On my walk uptown, the sun was blotted out by the smoke. Twenty summers rolled past. By the time I passed the great stone lions, Patience and Fortitude, that flank the entrance to the Metropolitan Art Museum, I was eager to encounter Rothko's exquisite panels, which he regarded as his "doors and windows." I was ready to lose myself in the mystery of Jacques-Louis David's *Death of Socrates*, Antonio Canova's *Venus Italica*, Mary Cassatt's *Young Woman Sewing in the Garden*, and especially Vermeer's vision of *The Milkmaid*, the luminous painting I'd loved since I first saw a reproduction in one of my father's art books. I needed to walk around and around the statues in the Greek and Roman sculpture galleries, works in whose presence I feel vitally alive. I had to stand in front of works of art that greeted me and said in no uncertain terms that life is real, life is sacred. After the agonizing life-negation of the terrorist attacks, I needed life-affirmation, art being one of the oldest forms of consolation. Where better to get that jolt than in the House of the Muses? I'd craved it all my life but felt desperate without it now, my spirit crushed by the sheer ugliness of the world.

"The truth isn't always beauty," novelist Nadine Gordimer wrote, "but the hunger for it is."

It is so easy to forget that we are sensory creatures, easy to lose touch with ourselves, easy to forget the ancient willingness, as art historian Elizabeth Prettejohn put it, "to take pleasure in the beautiful." I am reminded of the seventy-seven aphorisms engraved into the lintels of the Temple of Apollo in Delphi, especially this one: "Happiness is the pleasure of sages, pleasure the happiness of men."

Yes, the world may be studded with beautiful people and places, but do we take pleasure in it as often as we should? Wondering about this years later, I reconsidered what was missing and what was present in my own life, the life around me. I mulled over what the journalist Janet Malcolm called, in *Forty-One False Starts*, the "politically correct anti-pleasure school of art people." Instead of losing my faith in the human race, the combustible events of September 11 convinced me that Dostoevsky's declaration about the saving nature of beauty was truer than ever, that we make art so as not to die of the truth about our darker nature. We have always taken journeys across town and even across the world to savor beauty—what's beautiful in museums, national parks, and remote sanctuaries—so we might remind ourselves of our better natures.

To gird my loins, as my father used to say, I have collected a Cabinet of Curiosity quotes that has helped me in mysterious ways in this struggle to believe in beauty.

"Art is longing," said artist Anselm Kiefer. "You never arrive but keep going in the hope that you will."

"Ah, *this* is happiness," gasped Shen T'ang, the seventeenth-century Chinese sage, who made a list in the throes of a terrible plague of thirty-three things that brought him happiness. Thirty-three. The number thrills me. How many things could I name that have made me happy?

The poet-monk, Robert Lax, wrote in a clipped cadence that sounds to me like the waves lapping on the shores of Patmos, where he lived for forty years: "live always / (my friend) / as if you / had world / as if you / had world / enough / and time."

As if.

Witnessing the second plane hit the second tower and spending time with New York's finest and several film crews, and then watching hours of images showing the terrorist attacks, had numbed me, sending me spiraling down into a wrenching depression. Over and over, I heard rumors about more planes on their way, more terrorist attacks, more devastation to come. I was devastated—but I was alive. As I gazed into the abyss of the ruins, I kept thinking of something my Grandma Dora used to say, not in warning but in gratitude *There but for the grace of God go I.* If the attacks had happened a couple of hours later, I would have been in the building signing copies of my book. It was an eerie feeling, but I knew then and there that thousands of other New Yorkers were thinking the same thing. Grandma also said, "A word to the wise, Philip," a phrase I've never forgotten due to the gravitas in her voice. "Become who you are meant to be. It's a matter for you to wonder long and hard about. There is a reason God gave you big shoulders..."

Long past midnight, the stench and sorrow, the unrelenting black and white snowfall, evidence of the slaughter, were too much to bear. I began the long walk back to the new and sleek hotel that my publisher had provided for me. Walking up Broadway, passing many fences that were already being turned into chain-link announcement boards covered with MISSING posters, I realized I needed a surge of life-affirmation, the love potion of art, a visible reminder of the transcendence that our most sublime art offers us. When I arrived at the hotel, where I couldn't bear to turn on the news, I stared out the window, immobilized by the terrorist attacks. It was a dim source of solace to watch long lines of ambulances and fire trucks roaring up and down the streets below, their sirens wailing deep into the night.

Around dawn, I opened the beer-and-coffee-stained leather travel journal I had been carrying in my road-burnished leather knapsack. As if in a trance, I began to write. All I could manage were swirling lines of nonsense, pitiful descriptions of the calamity that had befallen the world around me.

To this day, I wonder where I went when I wrote that night. To decipher the mystery of creativity, it helps me to think by analogy, which is why I was startled by Tom Stoppard's insight in his play "Voyages." There, he tried to name the ineffable process of moving from inspiration to creation by conjuring up the loosely autobiographical character of a poet named Vissarian Belinsky. Stoppard describes his poet's moment of creation as transpiring as he holds his pen in his hand while leaning across his desk. Motionless, absorbed, obsessed. Then in a flash something *happens* to the poet. But what?

"A poem can't be written by an act of will," Stoppard says. "When the rest of us are trying to be present, a real poet goes absent. We can watch him in the moment of creation; there he sits with the pen in his hand, not moving. When it moves, we've missed it. Where did he go in that moment?" Stoppard asks. "*The meaning of art lies in the answer to that question* [my italics]."

The meaning of the Venus de Milo lurks there in those shadows.

So, where did *I* go? I have no idea. But go I did. I dared to write. I'm still wondering why but do not need an answer. I like to think it was a callow but honest attempt to balance the terror with wonder, the grief with beauty. Then something unexpected veered into my mind. I saw the framed photograph of the Venus de Milo above my father's workbench. In response, I began walking around her in my mind and then on paper until her presence filled the hotel room. I wrote through the sirens and the screaming and the snowfall of pulverized cement and bone covering the windowsill of my hotel room. I wrote in a fever dream, not stopping until the first rays of mottled sun lit up the hotel room. I was falling asleep with my journal in my lap, dreaming about being back in the Louvre where I walked around and around the Venus de Milo, winding myself up, as my Grandma Dora used to say, like an eight-day clock.

Writing that night saved my soul.

In some mysterious way, I am afraid I will never fully fathom, I finally comprehended Solzhenitsyn's bold declaration about the life-saving power of art, but in a way, I never would have understood otherwise. I spent that withering day back at Ground Zero, and at my publisher's request left the next morning in a rental car he had arranged because all flights had been suspended. After my first scheduled stop in Buffalo, I carried on to Detroit, Ann Arbor, Chicago, Milwaukee, Minneapolis, St. Louis. Twenty-one bookstores in twenty-one cities in twenty-one days. I gave brief talks about my new book and then spoke about the mythic implications of what I had just witnessed.

Without confronting the mystery of the tremulous presence of the Vermeers and the boldness of the Greek sculptures at the Met the day after the terrorist attacks, I could never have faced the overflow crowds in all those bookstores, never spoken about how art and beauty are not indulgences but necessities to help guide us through the dark night of the soul by embracing the *redeeming beauty of art* and affirming art's role in showing us ways to become human. While viewing art, being redeemed by it, I recalled the journalist Lawrence Weschler's wrenching 1999 essay in *The New Yorker* about the Serbian War Crimes Tribunal in the Netherlands. One day he asked the famed Italian jurist, Antonio Cassese, how he managed to listen to the grisly stories about the war day after day after day. The widely respected judge said, "You see, as often as possible I make my way over to the Mauritshuis museum in the center of town so as to spend a little time with the Vermeers." Weschler speculates that Vermeer was able to paint *despite* his personal sorrows because he "*felt the absence* of [his era's] pressure of violence...amid the horrors of his age, asserting and *inventing* the very idea of peace."

Rather than being ashamed by beauty, Camus scathingly wrote in his 1955 essay, "Helen's Exile": "[We] cannot do without beauty, and this is what our era pretends to want and to disregard."

I am trying to get at the heart of a great thing. We make art so we might know ourselves. I need to say something deeply real about the thing that has haunted me all my life. Call it the loneliness of the long-distance writer reflecting on a work of *inner necessity*. So, I say now that what we love *becomes* beautiful, at least to ourselves.

To do so, I need to return what has been missing for millennia. I am trying to piece things back together. I thought I was alone in this painstaking process until I read Edith Wharton's description of the way she grasped for the essence of her stories: "I had the story bit by bit, and as generally happens in such cases, each time it was a different story."

Fragment by fragment, shard by shard, insight by insight.

Over time, I've come to believe that history is a fistful of silence that needs to be pried open if we are to ever hear what she has to say. Her fingers need to be coaxed open so that the past does not come down on us like a closed fist but rather like a caress, or as Napoleon said of the vagaries of history, it is at best "a fable agreed upon." To accomplish this, I need to do more than write another dry-as-marble-dust historical account. I need to offer a way to view her story the way many have seen it over the centuries. All at once. In the round.

In this book, we will try to see her as Rodin did in 1902, spending entire days at the Louvre. Turning around and around her, trying to *resolve* her. Eight years later, he wrote an essay for a New York newspaper about his experience under the title: "I Will Walk Around You." Wallace Stevens "Thirteen Ways of Looking at a Blackbird" also comes to mind. A wondrous circumambulation of observation, poetic fragments he later described as sensations intended to evoke fresh feelings and new perspectives.

Now it's my turn to saunter, to turn around in my mind the tantalizing insight of the scholar Michael Finley about Homer when he wrote, tantalizingly, that "once he made the gods into man, man learned to know himself." The thought continues to haunt me as I carry on with my meandering explorations in myth and art. All of this was playing in my mind as I turned around the statue, feeling as if the gods had spun an old-fashioned zoetrope to see how the single images gathered into one movement.

Finally, I can contemplate what I smile to think of as the quiddity of her nudity. If we can't play with the language of art and beauty, what's the point? The point is to be reminded as often as possible if we are serious about being playful about the game of life. I think of the English novelist Joyce Cary's declaration in *Art and Reality* that "everything contemplated in its essence is said to be beautiful." While acknowledging the profound need to make sense of what led to the horrors, I felt the tremor and the tumult of something truly beautiful. As in life-affirming, soul-saving, and expansive. And slowly, over the years that followed, I learned to understand what Edith Hamilton wrote in *The Greek Way* about the priority in classical times of turning "suffering into praise."

Hence the plays of Aeschylus, the oratory of Pericles and Aspasia, the science of Aristotle, the philosophy of Socrates, and the sculpture of the mysterious artist from Antioch who carved the Venus de Milo, who we know and don't know. For reasons reason does not know, to paraphrase the philosopher, I need to know who carved her and why. As I reread these pages in the middle of the pandemic, this forty-fourth or so draft of the book, I am in hell, wondering if I will ever write again, or if anyone will care. And so I have a curious need to understand more about my own gnarled process by understanding the process of her sculptor, whose identity was for centuries a stone riddle wrapped inside an aesthetic mystery and carved within a political enigma.

Who was the genius behind the Venus? Where did the vision come from to create a bridge between the Paleolithic and the monolithic? How did he learn to make marble breathe?

So, I ask again, where do we go when we *make* something—*poesis*, the very heart of art—and where do go when we encounter it?

As a comic once cracked, "I told you that story so I could tell you this one." One that is meant to pierce your heart. One that is intended to help you understand why art and myth exist. One that helps me explain the origin and purpose of this book, which arises out of an ardent belief in the possibilities of art to balance the terror with wonder, the horror with beauty.

The Polish-Lithuanian poet Czeslaw Milosz, who lived through the destruction of Vilnius, described "the praise of art as a remedy of the cruelties of life." My exploration of the Venus de Milo is intended to be a celebration, an act of praise-singing that derives from an avid hope that the great works of art and literature, music and sculpture can help us balance the terror with wonder, the cruelty with kindness, the hate with love. A stone hymn to love and beauty.

An echo of the insight I learned years ago when I was filming in Italy and learned that Federico Fellini coined the phrase *la dolce vita*, the sweet life, not as a tourist poster slogan but as an echo of a hard-earned piece of wisdom: "Life can be cruel and violent, but if we look closer, we can glean what is sweet and good out of it."

Only half-joking, the Irish wag Oscar Wilde said, "Love and not German philosophy is what gives our lives meaning." So much for mere theories of beauty, ideas about what is and what isn't beautiful. Writing this, I hear in my third ear the sonorous voice of Seamus Heaney intoning "The Given Note," his haunting poem about the piper who returned from the Blasket Islands playing an otherworldly tune: "So whether he calls it spirit music / Or not," Heaney writes, "I don't care."

I don't detect indifference in that phrase. I hear bedrock conviction. I smell sea salt in his phrasing. Heaney cares, utterly. Instead, I share his unassailable belief in the effable, the encounter more than the theory, the real deal. Heaney wants the melody, the transport, the enchantment. What we love we find beautiful. Not art alone, but our love of it and the wisps of meaning, the hints of happiness that it brings. If we lose the thread of love, we lose our way, or worse, our soul.

Twenty-five years. Call it an obsession; file it under fascination. Consider it an enchantment or think of it as literary detective work. When I think about my motivation for spending so much time trying to get to the truth of this project, my mind moves sideways to the beautiful words of the Icelandic novelist Halldor Laxness: "Learning gladdens the heart."

If I have indeed learned anything chasing the truth about this single statue, it's that it is possible to transcend our sorrows through the beautiful things of the world. This book reflects not only what I've gladly learned but what I needed to *unlearn*, in the sense of Lawrence Durrell's line in his poem "On Ithaca Standing" where he asks himself, "How long will the Unlearning take?" When will we make an art of forgetting to take seriously the glut of information? When will ever learn to unlearn the trivial, and relearn how to revel in the beautiful?

I've been looking for portals all my life in art, literature, music, nature, love. I step through them whenever possible. To lose myself, to *transport* myself. To fully fathom the mystery of life itself. Mostly, to feel more alive.

Recently, I found a note I wrote in 2012 on Crete, a crisp insight into what it takes to finish a book that I discovered in an interview with novelist James Salter for *The Paris Review*. He wrote about a famous solo climber who he had asked about how he conquered fear on the face of the mountain. Calmly, the climber replied that he pretended he was only two feet off the ground. To complete this book, I sometimes pretended that I was holding the manuscript two feet off my desk to see if it could, well, float. To do so, I needed to let go if I was going to unsee it, to move beyond the research. This mind-ruse is familiar to all storytellers.

"Learn, unlearn, learn again." Let's call it the three-act structure of soul-making. Live first, then speculate, then don't forget to live again.

May we never cease learning to see the invisible realm, training ourselves to see the unseen, nudging ourselves to feel more, no matter how painful.

Writing about the discovery of the long-immured Venus de Milo, fifteen hundred years after her beauty was lost, I think of another of Joyce's poetic insights: "Any object deeply regarded can be a gateway to the gods." To do her justice, one of the more mysterious qualities of beauty, I realized early on that I needed a new form if I was going to convey a more complete view of the Venus de Milo, arguably the most famous statue in the world. Something was calling to me as I began writing, and then after many years when I took up the cause again, which called for this book to be a mosaic of art history, aesthetics, poetry, anecdotes, dreams.

I think now of the urgency behind what the Pulitzer Prize-winning poet Stephen Dunn called "the insistence of beauty." Not the luxury or the indulgence. The insistence, the persistence. The ineffable need to connect with my ancestors.

Consider the marvel of looking at the Venus de Milo.

Two blocks of glistening marble quarried from the island of Paros twenty-one-hundred years ago that an obscure young sculptor breathed life into and which somehow, against all odds, still moves us now?

Are you not astonished? I am. I'm lost in radical astonishment and proud of it.

At a 1906 exhibition of the work of Cezanne, who had boldly announced that he wanted to "astonish Paris with my apples," the German poet Rainer Marie Rilke wrote in admittedly astonished tones to his wife Clara about the "conflagration of color" he had seen in the master's work. "It's as if every part were aware of all the others."

This is an act of witnessing. The deepening of looking into seeing, seeing into feeling.

"So it happens," wrote Nobel Prize-winning poet Wislawa Szymborska, "that I look and I am." So, too, with Joseph Conrad: "My task, which I am trying to achieve, is by the power of the written word to make you hear, to make you feel—it is, before all, to make you see."

I know, I know, I tell myself every waking hour. Look, then look again, until you *see*.

I am horrified to the point of shame when I look back over my life and realize how often I was guilty of lazy-looking, or worse, *overlooking*, when I should have been paying attention. My father, dying of a nerve disease, whose health woes I didn't take seriously enough. My film partner, Gary Rhine, who died before I could tell him that working with him had changed my life, maybe even saved it.

These withering confessions have been a surprising source of embarrassment, but I found a great deal of solace one night at a poetry reading at Cody's Bookstore in Berkeley when I heard Robert Haas, the Poet

Laureate of the United States, describe the true function of poetry as "a raid on the inarticulate."

The phrase cuts me to the core. *A raid on the inarticulate.* After witnessing that performance, it felt vain and indulgent to think of myself as all alone in feeling how impossible it is to plumb the depths of my experiences—and then describe them.

"Consider this, consider this," as Michael Stipes of REM sings in "Losing My Religion." And so we do because of the aching conviction.

One night, when I was about twelve, I was brooding at home over a stinging rebuke from Sister Marie Walter, one of the sterner nuns at Wayne St. Mary's. When I stomped past my father in our living room, he noticed and was annoyed by my moodiness. Who knows why? Gripping me by the shoulder, he led me into the backyard, grabbing a flashlight and a beach towel from the toolshed he had built with his own hands. We walked out into the darkness where I basked in the smells of his rosebushes and the crabapple tree and giant maple tree he had planted. Then he spread an old towel imprinted with "Stroh's Beer" on the lawn, plopped down on his back, thumped his fist on the ground in a signal for me to join him, and crossed his arms behind his head so he could scan the constellations. Lying on our backs, we gazed at the night sky, which inspired some of our earliest stories, stitching together our imaginations and stretching our souls.

"Look, buddy," he said calmly, an unusual tone for him. "Forget it. What do those penguins know, anyway? C'mon, toughen up. Look up at the stars. Look at all the beauty in the night sky. It just goes to show you, everything depends on how we look at life. Up, down, sideways."

I craned my neck and followed the crisscrossing beam of his flashlight, which led me on a tour of the night sky. Slowly, he named the ancient configurations for me: Orion, the Plough, the Pleiades, Ursa Major and Minor, and the Milky Way. I listened, not unaware of how he seemed happiest when teaching me something about worlds far beyond ours.

"Son," he said out of the dark blue, "do you know the origins of the word *consider*? It means to think about something 'under the stars.' That's what we're doing right now. Thinking. Wondering. I did this with my father and my grandfather every summer on Lake Nipissing. They taught me how to name the wonders of the world. They weren't school-educated, buddy, but they knew the beauty of the natural world, son, and I want you to learn it too."

The stellar furnaces above us roared and blazed as we craned our necks and gazed in glorious silence. Fifty-some summers have passed by since that night when he reminded me of what the poet-astronomer Rebecca Elson elegantly called our "responsibility of awe."

Writing this now, my mind, the invisible editor in my soul, makes a jump-cut to my first night in Athens in the summer of 1975. The Greek army's tanks rolled into Syntagma Square to thwart the gathering protestors. With all the hotels and hostels closed in response to the fury of protestors, I wandered up to the Acropolis with my backpack and sleeping bag and a copy of Henry Miller's *The Colossus of Maroussi*. Under a full moon, my Spanish bota bag full of Greek wine, I wandered into the open ruins of the Parthenon. The nearly fifty-year-long restoration wouldn't begin for another few months, in July 1975. No guards, no fences, no watchdogs, no other midnight visitors. Spreading out my sleeping bag on the rough stones of the floor of the mighty temple, I felt the stillness of the world, the heartbeat of the universe, as I read, to my utter delight and sheer surprise, that Miller had felt the same cosmic pulse when he visited the grand amphitheater at Epidaurus. The heartbeat of the world. Now, I had the Parthenon all to myself. I remember the moonlight gleaming on the marble columns around me, the shadows flickering on the roughhewn stone floor, fallen pediments, and slivers of ancient statues. Considering the round-the-clock security nowadays that swirls around that ancient holy ground, it seems incomprehensible that no one was there to chase me away. But it's true: The gods smiled on me that night and left me alone with the shadows of ancient peace.

Alone. In a rapture. The love of life returning after the horrors of home. Hoping to stretch the moment from here to infinity. Staring up at the miraculous marble columns of Athena's temple, gleaming with moonlight, I thought back to only the summer before when I was working the night shift at Industrial and Automotive Fasteners in Detroit, taking my coffee breaks outside in the grimy parking lot next to the Michigan Central railroad tracks. The same moon blinked down on the empty boxcars, the sleeping forklifts, and police cars sneaking past us, looking for burglars. I wondered how the moon above me at that haloed moment could have possibly been the same moon I saw halfway around the world, back in Detroit, where my heart pounded for far different reasons, out of fear, when I worked the nightshift at the steel factory.

Lying on my back on the time-gnarled stones of what used to be the smooth marble floor of the Parthenon, my heart was pounding out of wonder, not fear, and I felt a transcendent shiver, a surge of love for my life.

I was seized by joy.

There it is, the secret strength of beauty, which has the capacity to bring us back from the deadening, the numbing, the torpor of our unlived lives. We go to art, architecture, literature, and music as we used to go to church, to remind us that we are capable of more than savage acts of destruction, to help us recall that we are capable of acts of creativity worthy of the gods. To help feel the joy of life, however blurry or indefinable, through art, music, poetry, or nature, even though we have considered the cruel history that surrounds everything we have ever created. I am completing this book as we emerge out of the fourth wave of the pandemic. I have lost five friends and family members to the scourge. I keep turning to my favorite art, music, poems, movies, and ocean views in a modest effort to balance the terror with wonder, the grief with joy, the sorrow with beauty.

So, yes, more than ever, I align myself with those who feel and embrace the joy. Despite the despair. Regardless of the wreckage. I don't need to solve the historical battles over the origins and power plays of art; I don't need to solve the battle between the sexes. I do need to respond to the insistence of beauty, the persistence of desire, the compulsion to *make something out of nothing*, which is the true meaning of *poesis*, poetry. The real thing is the making of something the world has never seen before, original and world-bridging." Desire, as Aristotle said twenty-five-hundred years ago, is the reaching out for the sweet. *Orexis* was the word he used, Greek for "longing, desire, from *orégo*, "I reach, stretch." That is what the Venus de Milo was doing when her arms were intact. She was reaching, stretching, grasping, as she is doing now in my imagination. But why and for what? That is what we will explore in these pages.

The real thing is outside of time and space; the real thing is inside.

This book is in pursuit of a deceptively simple question. Why has this one statue stoked so much delight in our hearts over the last two hundred years she has been displayed at the Louvre? How is it that we can sense it shivering to life? Can our response be merely patriarchal propaganda or bourgeois hegemony in the world of the arts, or a conspiracy to torment us with unreal ideals? Or is there more to her, a glimpse of transcendence, a hint of the very source of human desire, an offer of what the poets called the promise of happiness? Is there in the Venus de Milo a recognition of what the ancient Greeks called *pothos*, a word gleaned from the god of sexual longing and a potent symbol for the loneliness at the core of life? I believe we can detect it if we reconsider her thousand-yard stare, so can we determine what or who she is gazing at? If so, I want to hear the ancient spirits in her.

Slow looking, slow feeling, slow gratitude. These are needed to appreciate the pulsating heart of what is "truly, madly, deeply" marvelous about all masterpieces, along with the practice of what I like to think of as "radical astonishment," along with "radical praise," in the spirit of the Sufi poet Rumi, who wrote nine hundred years ago that lives on today, that those who do not praise daily are thieves. Self-styled cynics who rob us of what is beautiful, life-affirming, and true. If we want to discover who stole the arms of the Venus de Milo, we can start there.

So, yes, the Venus is beautiful *anyway*. But why should we still care after two thousand years? Do we really have a responsibility to feel awe and wonder? Yes and no.

That's the beauty of it.

Phil Cousineau
New York-San Francisco-Paris-Clifden-Ithaka
2001-2023

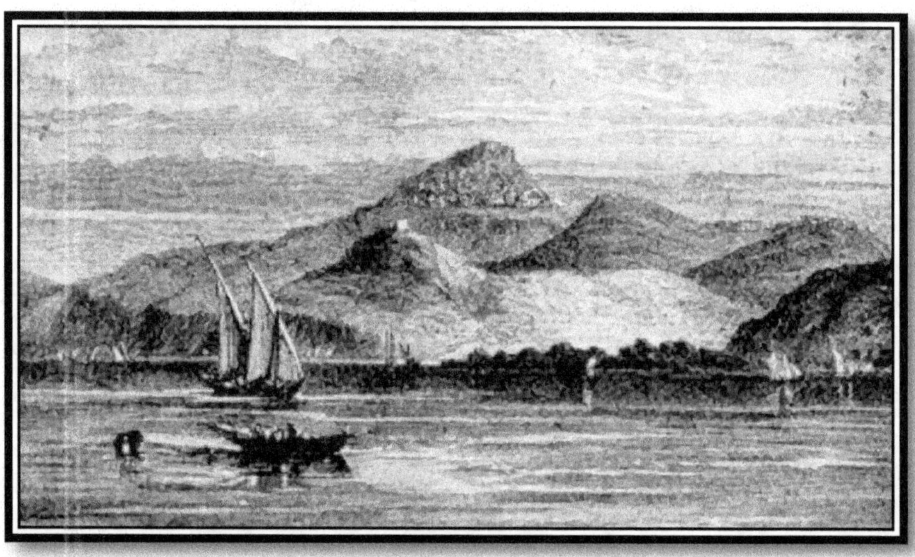

The Island of Melos in The Cyclades
Where the famous "Venus of Milo' was found.
From *Century Magazine*, 1881

I.

THE DISCOVERY OF BEAUTY

N APRIL 8, 1820, ON THE VOLCANIC ISLAND OF MELOS IN THE HEART of the Greek archipelago, a peasant farmer named Yorgos Kentrotas [Konstantinos] was searching in his rumpled field for stones. For years, the farmer had used his own land as a quarry, carting away volcanic rock, chunks of granite, bits of fractured bricks, even old millstones, to repair the walls of his house, as his ancestors had done for centuries.

Wandering along the Vale of Klima, a small stretch of flat land where the ancient capital of the island had flourished for centuries, the farmer followed the tumbledown walls just below the scumbled remains of the old market, the glinting ruins of the marble Roman theater, and a few stumps of columns and far-strewn marble capitals from the old temple. Coming to a small clearing near his grove of gnarled olive trees, he noticed, as if for the first time, the roughhewn stones of a high wall set into the hillside. Because Yorgos needed a few stones to fill in the gaps in the ramshackle house where he lived with his mother, he made an auspicious decision. Although he had passed the time-thickened wall every day of his life, this time he stopped. On a hunch, he pulled out his shovel, wedged it in between two large stones, and yanked hard.

Stone after stone fell away, followed by a *whoosh* of cool air.

The jagged hole revealed a long-sealed cave.

Startled, Yorgos stared into the dank darkness and noticed something strange. A partially buried piece of marble, nearly four feet long, was lying on its side as if it had been resting there for a very long time. His heart leapt like one of the capering goats on the nearby hillside. He pulled on several more stones, which fell to the hardscrabble dirt floor inside the cave. Clouds of dust swirled in the air, making him gasp for breath.

When the craggy opening was large enough for him to step through, he entered the cave. Kneeling next to the stone, he scraped off some dirt that had formed a crust. A bright ray of sunlight needled through the hole in the wall and struck the stone. It came to life, as marble sometimes does in the right light.

Slowly, a serene face emerged. He brushed away the dirt until he could see swirls of woven hair, a sinuous neck, graceful breasts. Her muscular left shoulder was no more than a stump, but enough remained to suggest by its position that the missing arm had once reached out to someone or something. Her sensuously sloping belly ended suddenly at the waist as if she'd been sawed in half. She radiated beauty, glowed with erotic power, flickered with desire. The peasant felt a rush of astonishment. Seconds later, a shiver of panic shot through him. What if someone saw him? In those days, it was dangerous to discover ancient artifacts.

Yorgos began to rebury her, marvelous or not.

No one had seen beauty like this for fifteen hundred years.

Against all odds, the Venus de Milo had survived inside the cave as if she had been waiting until she could be appreciated again. Reappearing now, she seemed to be "a gift from the gods," as Aristotle defined beauty. Or more recently, the Venus "proves that great art transcends its time and place," as Gregory Curtis observes in *Disarmed*.

The statue was a vision from the invisible realm, the unseen world. Whoever laid eyes on her, in her time, would have said she was divine. What infused her was as real as rain, as true as sunlight. To the farmer, she must have been a source of deep delight, far more than a convenient source of stone to fill the gap in his wall.

Confused, Yorgos considered giving up on the stone because it was too awkwardly shaped to be set into the gaps of the crumbling walls of his dirt-floored home. It appeared it would be too much work to take a hammer and chisel to it to make it easier to drop it into his marble kiln to make whitewash for the walls of his humble home. Strange to say, he was suspicious that the statue might be important, even valuable, which made it dangerous.

No doubt, Yorgos had heard stories that flew about the island on the wings of Ossa, better known as Rumor, the infamous goddess who sowed gossip, such as when someone stumbled upon a trove of treasure in their field. Old coins from the royal mint in Athens and Syracuse, broken potsherds from his own island's legendary potters, amphorae half-filled with ancient wine resin, a bronze charioteer hauled up from the sea floor by sponge divers whose arms are still stretched out, as if holding onto leather reins that once looped over the straining necks of racehorses. Word was that treasures had been sold for princely sums to the wandering merchants and travelers who now crisscrossed the island. Small fortunes had been made; dangerous conspiracies hatched. But amateur archaeologists and treasure hunters had to be careful. In the early nineteenth century, the backs of Greek people still bowed under the 450-year-long tyrannical rule of the Turkish Empire. The sultan's law about antiquities was as clear as it was severe, as dangerous as it was unfair. All antiquities were to be turned over to local representatives, who shipped anything valuable to Istanbul. Anyone caught hoarding antiquities would be fined, imprisoned, or worse. Remembering this, the poor farmer hesitated, weighing the chances of becoming a rich man overnight against the possibility that terrified local officials might turn him over to the sultan's authorities on the island.

Yorgos leaned against his shovel in the shadow-fretted cave and weighed the risks of being caught against the chances of becoming rich.

Like many others on Melos, he was concerned that local informants might turn him over to the sultan's authorities on the island, either for reward money or out of fear of reprisals, if it was learned that he had discovered something and said nothing.

Slowly, the realization flared in him that he needed advice. Legend on the island has it to this day that at that very moment, Yorgos heard footsteps outside, and he saw a strange shadow flickering on the walls of the cave.

Nothing is as beautiful as it seems, nor is it otherwise. Nothing is as wise as it seems unless it's beautiful, or so it seems.

FORTUNE Every treasure costs a fortune. Each gift requires a sacrifice. The odds are that this one would never have been found without some blind luck, an ordinary word with extraordinary power. *Luck* has artesian depths. It hails from the fifteenth-century Middle English *lukken*, to happen fortunately, to chance upon, which suggests that we can make our own luck, but only if we take a chance. Luck, then, is a kind of happenstance in which chance meets circumstance and forges our fortune. Luck is fate that has come around in our favor on Fortune's Wheel, as personified by Tyche, Greek Goddess of Good Luck and Prosperity, Chance, and Fate, known in Roman times as *Fortuna*. If your number rolls around on her Wheel of Fortune, says the whirligigging myth, your fate has arrived. That is what the poor farmer was banking on. With any luck, we might consider this encounter a radiant example of how art and beauty lure the imagination, making lone viewers and entire cultures reel under its power. It was an extraordinary bit of luck that the man who stumbled upon this long-lost statue had such a keen eye. Fortunately, but by no means inevitably, Venus's story turned out the way it did.

To understand this chance encounter and the skein of events that followed, which took her from Melos to Paris, we need to tease out the story thread by thread, moment by moment, stone by stone. Detail by divine detail, as Vladimir Nabokov described what distinguishes art and literature, lepidopterology and archaeology. This makes me wonder, as all stories should, why some art endures while other art fades away, and beauty often feels timeless. I say history is a fistful of silence that often needs her fingers pried open. I hear the question begging: Why do some things endure while others fade away, or worse, disappear?

One night while driving across the country I stopped at a Texaco gas station outside Tucson and heard the radio crackling from inside the office. I clicked off the gas pump to better hear the smooth baritone of Canadian folk legend Gordon Lightfoot singing, "At times, I just don't know / How you could be anything but beautiful." Why do I remember the moment so clearly, the loneliness of the all-night drive, the scratching sound of tumbleweed on the highway, the smell of gasoline, the precision of Lightfoot's melancholy that echoed my own that night? Why remember and save the memory in the nearby truck stop diner? Why save paintings, manuscripts, sculptures? Out of a noble desire to pass down our grandest accomplishments or out of a morbid fear of change? Or because we don't want to forget what it means to feel alive?

In his sepulchral masterpiece *The Unquiet Grave*, Cyril Connolly, writing under the pseudonym Palinurus, recounts an ancient wisdom story that helps him explore the nature of grief: "There was once a man (reputed to be the wisest sage in the world) who, although living to an untold age, confined his teaching to one word of advice: 'Endure!' At length, a rival arose and challenged him to a debate, which took place before a large assembly. 'You say 'Endure!'' cried the rival sage, 'but I don't want to endure. I wish to love and be loved, to conquer and create. I wish to know what is right, then do it and be happy.' There was no reply from his opponent, and, on looking more closely at the old creature, his adversary found him to consist of an odd-shaped rock on which had taken root a battered thorn that presented, by an optical illusion, the impression of hair and a beard. Triumphantly, he pointed out the mistake to the authorities, but they were not concerned. 'Man or rock,' they answered, 'what does it matter?' And at that moment the wind, reverberating through the sage's moss-grown orifice, repeated with a hollow sound: 'Endure!'"

Endure, endurable, endurance. All this begins to explain the phenomenon of the Venus de Milo.

Strange how memory works, zigging and zagging in and out of time and space, collapsing old worlds, creating new ones, tripping the light fantastic. According to the poet Robert Duncan, that is the movement of myth, the release of "the force of the real." His utter conviction about the power of the invisible world is not unlike that of my fellow Detroiter, poet Philip Levine, who wrote in words as strong as Detroit steel, "There is only one reason to write a poem—to change the world." I wonder if that's something the creator of the Venus thought about. Because he did change the world, though it took nineteen hundred years to do so. To change the world, the Venus de Milo had to endure long enough to be rediscovered. But how does art change the way things are? Can it be because there is a component in great art that transcends time, nature, even history? The possibility has haunted me for years.

At the beginning of my quest for her missing story, I felt I needed to know what happened to her arms. Eventually, I came to be intrigued by her thousand-yard stare. Why is she gazing into the infinite distance? What or who is she looking at? Why so wistful? Does it add or subtract from her legendary beauty? In antiquity, the various Venuses were associated with divinity, which might be problematic for modern viewers. Not unlike Leonardo, who painted the inexhaustibly mysterious portrait of Mona, wife of Francesco del Giocondo, whose smile stirs us to this day.

And then my focus changed to the mysterious identity of the sculptor of the Venus who was merely described away as "Anonymous" or diminished as "Unknown" on the placard in her galley at the Louvre.

The sculptor of the Venus de Milo, whose identity was long a mystery hiding in plain view, created an incalculably beautiful marble statue of the goddess who was known throughout antiquity as the personification of love, desire, beauty, and happiness, as well as their shadows, lust, disgust, and terror. Glimpses of all these emotions lie at the heart of art and soul of myth. Bring them together in a sublime work of art and one might be able to experience what the ancients called *the infinite moment*. This notion brings us closer to the secret strength of the Venus whose story is a Greek puzzle box. The rediscovery of the Venus revealed how every treasure costs a fortune. Each gift requires a sacrifice. The odds are that this one would never have been found without some blind luck.

"Beauty endures only for as long as it can be seen," wrote the fifth-century poet Sappho. "Goodness, beautiful today, will remain so tomorrow." Horace wrote, "Seek, suffer, endure."

Still, we need to ask, *Why bother?* Out of a morbid fear—or desire—for change? Or maybe a need to transcend the ravages of time? Changing the way we see the world is one of the oldest reasons to create anything. Change. In a strange stroke of synesthesia, I *see* Sam Cooke's voice stippling the blue air with black notes as he sings "A Change is Gonna Come." As the New Zealand reggae group, Fat Freddy's Drop, pleads, "What's the world with no soul?" The Irish bard Van Morrison moans, "We're goin' out in the country to get down to the real soul, / I mean the real soul, people, I'm talking 'bout the real soul."

This edges us closer to what I'm looking for in the masterpiece of Melos, which provoked Hesiod to write, "Without Venus, there is no joy in the world."

As for me, I write to stop catastrophizing. I write to see the world. I write to see myself. I write for the lump in the throat. I write to be redeemed. I write to find eternity in the moment. I write to enjoy my life.

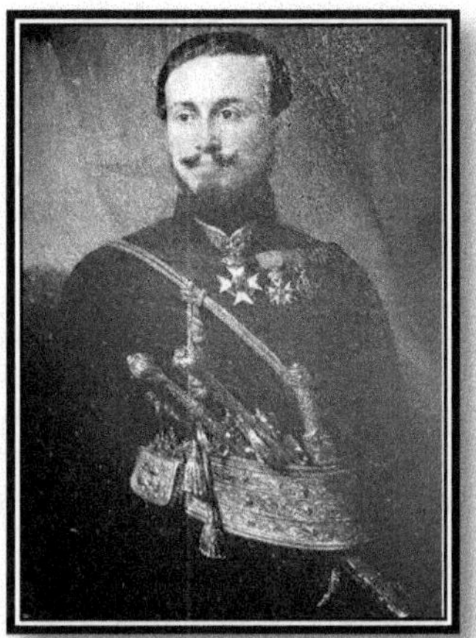

Captain Olivier Voutier,
portrayed as a colonel in Greek army
Unknown painter

THE SOLDIER-SCHOLAR

The blue enamel sky shimmered. The sun threw jewels of light across the wine-dark sea. On the other side of the crescent-shaped island of Melos, in the most magnificent harbor in the Aegean, a squadron of three French naval schooners, the *Estafette, Lionne,* and *L'Esperance,* which had cast their clanking anchors there a few weeks earlier, floated on the aquamarine sea.

March 4, 1820 was an auspicious morning. A twenty-three-year-old ensign first class who bore a jaunty mustache and a melodic name, Olivier Voutier, set out with two younger sailors from the *Estafette* for a long hike around the island. While waiting for his ship to resume its diplomatic mission in ports around the Mediterranean, the young naval officer had been exploring the island, enjoying his meandering walks along the cliffs and around the ancient ruins. Not just for exercise or as an escape from boredom but for the thrill of the chase, the search for lost treasure, a chance to glimpse the glory of ancient Greece. Chance, not worthiness, the ancients believed, was the way the gods allotted their gifts.

As the Irish peasant poet Patrick Kavanagh wrote about his own rambles around the wild Irish countryside, Voutier was entering a world of long-lost secrets.

Throughout the eighteenth and nineteenth centuries, French explorers saw themselves as the proud descendants of the Enlightenment, the movement that apotheosized the pursuit of knowledge and reason. Out of their ardent belief in the nobility of learning for learning's sake arose what the French called *un grand desir*, the great desire, to explore distant lands, notably the Greco-Roman world. When Napoleon invaded Egypt in 1798, he took forty thousand soldiers and ten thousand sailors, but he also brought along nearly two hundred savants, artists, botanists, geologists, physicists, and engineers to record their scientific discoveries and bring home some beautiful artifacts. All to add to *la gloire de France*, the glory of the motherland, the edification of his fellow French citizens.

When he was a young man, Voutier had been inspired by an insatiable desire to travel to see with his own eyes the far-flung marvels of the ancient world. Now that he was in the Aegean, he was going to take advantage of the opportunity. Learn about those who came before us, he was taught at the Sorbonne. Take notes, draw sketches, find evidence. Be rational. Reason your way through life. Pursue philosophy for the love of wisdom. Chase down arcane marvels in manuscripts, art, and architecture. Discover what made those seminal cultures flourish so that we, the French, might revive our own, which might, in turn, ignite a New Renaissance. Not unlike the way Arab scholars sparked the first cultural rebirth in Seville and the Medicis stoked the embers of classical knowledge in Florence.

Such a cultural transformation could only begin with the French genius for observation, their passion for noticing the world and making sense of the enigmas that still riddle the universe. *Noticing* being the operative word, rooted in the Greek word *gnosis*, special *knowledge* of the mysteries, as the psychologist James Hillman pointed out to me at, of all places, Greta Garbo's old mansion in the hills overlooking Santa Barbara.

"We look," he said with a rare twinkle in his eyes, "but the soul *notices.*"

When the *Estafette's* lifeboat swished onto the sandy beach of Adamas, the horseshoe-shaped harbor town on Melos, Voutier followed another impulse, to explore the island. Fascinated by the history of the Mediterranean world, he led his two young shipmates on a languorous search for antiquities, as he had done every Sunday for nearly a month. Together, the soldiers carried shovels and picks over the humpbacked hill up to the modern capital, the much-disdained backwater town of Kastro, perched like an aerie that overlooked the island. Then they slowly descended the southern slope of the island to the grounds of the long-abandoned ancient capital of Klima, which once teemed with thousands of people and had been the hub of trade in the Aegean for centuries. The landscape was riddled with silence.

The sailors meandered around the sparse ruins of a second-century Greek temple magniloquently named the Palace of Melos. Now only a few sickly green bushes could be seen pushing through the scattered stones and the basins of old fountains that had once gushed from freshwater springs, and the litter of broken columns and crumbled statuary. Over the centuries, this temple, the glory that was Greece had been obliterated by invading troops, zealous monks, villagers who used it as a quarry, and wealthy antiquarians who wanted its marble for an architectural folly or two in the gardens of their villas. At the sight of the motley remains, the sailors became dispirited. They wandered the grounds, lazily stuffing a few stone fragments into the burlap bags they had carried with them from the ship.

On the grounds of the old temple, the French soldiers discovered more scattered architectural fragments before shuffling down the efficiently laid paving stones of the ancient Roman road that led past the last remnants of the once colossal city walls. There remained but one tower, a thirty-foot high section of volcanic rock battlements of the Eastern gate, designed to thwart enemy attacks. Nearby were the Early Christian catacombs that had been carved out of the native tufa rock, subterranean chambers that the native Melians believed were haunted by nymphs and nereids, the pagan spirits of the ancients. Further on down the road, they saw across the long flat field that ended precipitously at the cliff's edge. Voutier and his team must have wondered why the locals would have taken the time and trouble to clear such a long stretch of land. Although they had no way of knowing what function the cleared land had served, its purpose held the key to the statue they were about to discover.

Climbing down a series of tessellated steps overgrown with brambles that flanked the narrow field, they walked on until they took one of those random *swerves* that unexpectedly change everything. They had happened upon Yorgos's field, the small clearing with the bower of wild olive trees and the high wall of roughhewn stones. What are the odds? Astronomical, which should make us wonder.

There, they took a short break from the wilting heat before lethargically resuming their treasure hunt in a cooler place, where it would be easier to ponder the evidence of fallen civilizations and enjoyed the susurrus of silence where the voices of politicians, pirates, priests, soldiers, athletes, and farmers once rang out.

Suddenly, Sunday church bells chimed. The islanders climbed the steep hill to the church on the other side of the island. The pealing was crystal clear. Cleansing. We know from myriad sources that the soldiers were leisurely looking for antiquities. But what were they *really* searching for? Surely not just artifacts. That would be far too prosaic. I believe they were looking for something far more interesting than loot. They believed in marvels, and that's what they found.

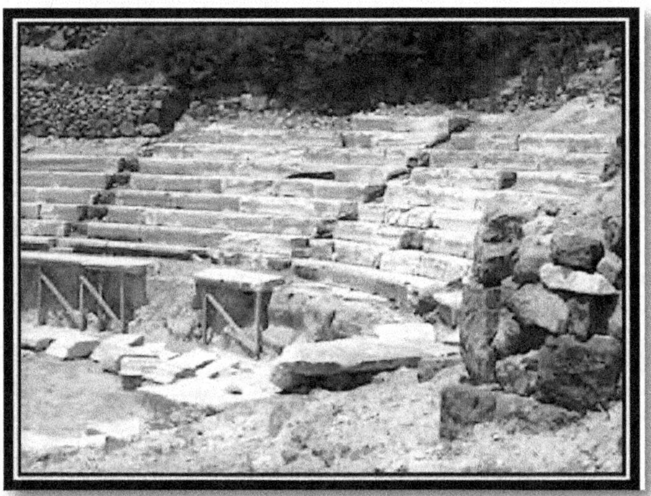

Roman Theater, Melos, Greece, first century
Photography by Phil Cousineau

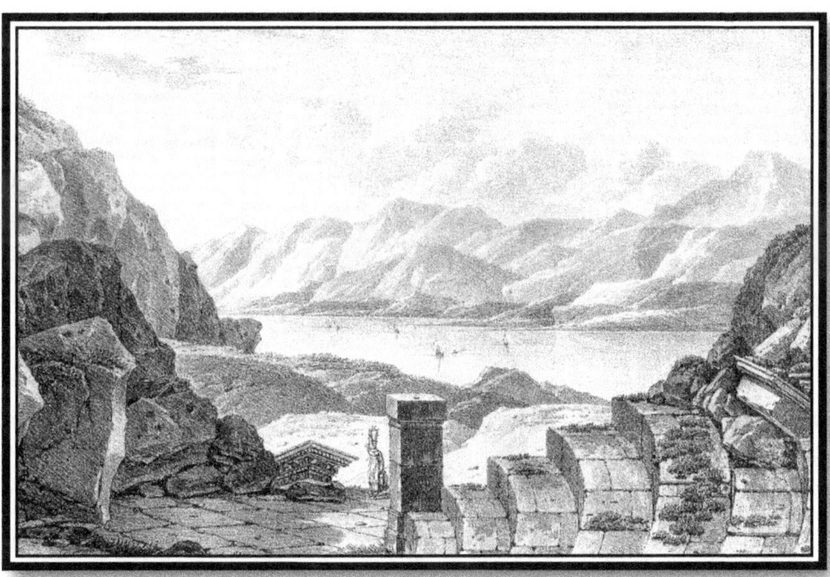

Anonymous engraving of the ancient Roman theater of Melos,
below the village of Tripiti, almost fifty years after Yorgos and Voutier
discovered the Venus nearby, 1869

CONSIDER THE MARVEL

"I confess. I confirm. I learn from. I marvel," wrote Georgio Vasari, the dean of European art criticism, in his massive study, published in 1550, *The Lives of the Artists*. His use of the word *marvel*, which was first recorded two centuries earlier, refers to a miracle or a wonderful tale, deriving as it does from the Latin *miribilia*, strange or wonderful, from *mirari*, to wonder. The marvel is a miracle of seeing, a wonder of language. It stands out as an uncanny blend of the strange and the beautiful. Writing these words, I hear, as if from a faraway radio, the voice of Van Morrison, aching for love: "It's a marvelous night for a moondance / with the stars up above your eyes…" I think of the myriad marvels of the world's mysterious beauty: the flickering bands of the aurora borealis, the twisted horn of the narwhal (which gave rise to the legend of the unicorn), Rembrandt's penumbral *Self-Portraits*, the Curiosity Cabinets of Peter the Great, the glittering blue frozen inside the glaciers near Zermatt.

Recalling them, I think of my own marvelous moments, especially the birth of our son Jack, the startling sight of my memory-tormented mother suddenly snapping back to attention with memories of her child-hood, and the glistening images of the endless Michigan summer when I turned sixteen and hopped freight trains, feeling the cry of freedom in my growing heart. Mornings at Le Select in Paris, with nothing but my journal, a crackling fresh copy of the *International Herald-Tribune*, and fresher words gushing out of my pen. The moonlight on Easter Island when I trekked out to see the *moai* glistening on the hillside overlooking the Pacific and placed my hand on the stone chest of one so that I might feel the pulse of the ancestors. Marvels all, marveling in me to this day, a wellspring of joy.

If you pushed me, I would venture to say the mightiest mystery of all is that we don't marvel more. It occurs to me this might be why we wander outside the moment and wonder about history—what went before us—and why we take pilgrimages to ancient *ruins* to remind ourselves of what our ancestors wondered about. It is marvelous to forge ahead and necessary to know when to turn, as Voutier did that day more than two hundred years ago in the dank cave on Melos, swerving at the last moment until he experienced what the ancient Greeks called *anagnorisis*, the thrill of recognition that changes the course of a single life, a drama, even history. He had been prepared for such an encounter as he was steeped in the marvels, which some call the classics, like all recipients of a proper Sorbonne education. He was armed with knowledge and an uncanny belief in the possibility of endurance in a world of painful transience.

Recently, I read in a passage by one of the literary lions in San Francisco's North Beach, Evan Connell, Jr., from his mosaic of a masterpiece, *Points on a Compass Rose,* "What I am trying to explain is that the past and the present / and future are all stuffed with marvels—events, sights, / Odors and sounds eluding the feeble grasp of our senses." In 1782, the Comte de Choiseul-Gouffier wrote, "When I left Paris, in order to visit Greece, I simply wanted to satisfy the passion I felt in my youth for the most famous lands of antiquity. I was propelled by a consuming curiosity, which I could satisfy with marvels; I could taste in advance the pleasure of crossing this famous and beautiful region with Homer and Herodotus in my hands. At last, I was promising myself a state of permanent intoxication in a land where the smallest rock appears to the imagination to be inhabited by gods and heroes."

I meander. So what? My subject is labyrinthine. So am I.

It is tantalizing to think about the estimated three thousand unexcavated Greek or Roman cities—in a word, *missing,* and believed to be immured in the ground around the Mediterranean. Also missing are the library of Aristotle, the estimated two hundred lost plays of Aeschylus, Sophocles, and Euripides, the near-complete *achillizing* or aching absence of a single Greek painting, and all but one complete poem by Sappho. Fortunately, the latter is her "Hymn to Aphrodite," that reappeared in the nineteenth century. In the poet Anne Carson's translation, "Deathless Aphrodite of the spangled mind, / child of Zeus, who twists lures, I beg you / do not break my heart."

No wonder Emerson remarked, "Man is a god in ruins." And no wonder T. S. Eliot wrote in *The Waste Land*, "These are the fragments I shore against my ruins." It's also no wonder we swoon over melancholic stones. The Sufi poet Rumi provides a clue: "Where there is ruin, there is hope for treasure."

As lovely as these declarations sound, they barely touch on the sepulchral mystery of the dreams I've endured a few times a year since I left the Detroit steel factory where I worked to put myself through college and support my family. In the sepia-tinted dream, a late-night earthquake rocks my hometown, bringing down the walls and the roaring machines of Industrial and Automotive Fasteners, burying me in rubble up to my neck. I always wake up alone. My fellow factory rats are immured in the steel and concrete. Always, I waken in wonder at the beauty of the ruins, as if Piranesi had engraved my dream. Always, I am stricken by a strange form of guilt at my soul's effort to forge beauty out of the terror of growing up in Detroit. Not for nothing did the phrase *ruin-haunting* arise thousands of years ago.

Wonders above, wonders below. Will wonders never cease, as Grandma Dora used to ponder. Writing these words now, I hear the voice of the historian of religions, Huston Smith, who used to chide audiences with this deceptively simple question: "Why bother?" I think the trickster in him was asking us to ask ourselves why we take the time and trouble to explore the imponderables, the great mysteries of life. After a long, sly pause, he sighed, "Longing." Once, at the end of a public event with him at UCLA, I suggested, "We long to find personal answers to universal questions." The wizened professor smiled and nodded, which was enough for me to feel vindicated. Since then, I have often heard Huston's voice in my head: "Why are you *bothering* to explore the story of the Venus de Milo? Why, why, why? To see what's missing in your own life?" No, Huston, I would say if he were still with us. That is too pat, too facile of an answer. It's the search. The search makes me feel more alive. Not just for whatever happened to her arms but for the answer to what she is looking at with that thousand-yard stare.

When asked by a sports reporter about the impossibility of thinking and swinging the bat at the same time, Hall of Fame catcher Yogi Berra said, "There are deep depths there." We are here to plunge the depths.

Art is here to make life worth living, help us endure the absurdities of life, and reveal a scintilla of meaning. That's the beauty of it.

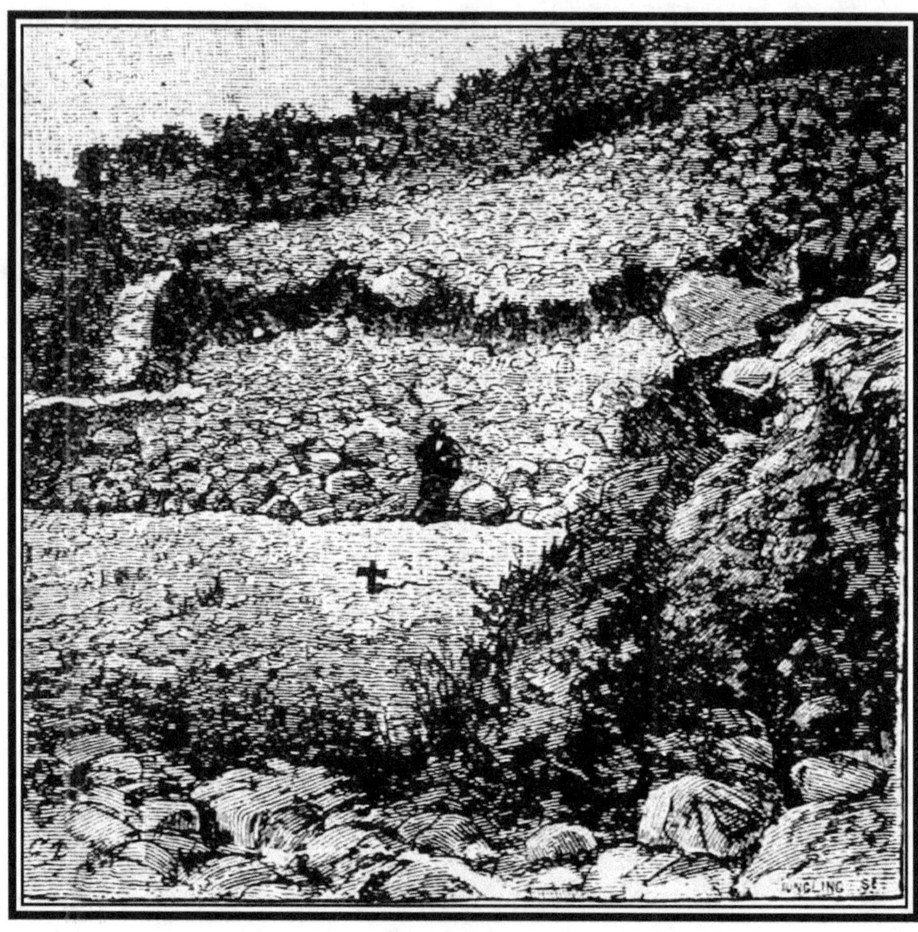

The cross marks the spot in Yorgos's field, where the Venus was discovered. *Century Magazine*, 1888.

A BEYOND OF STONE

For more than a thousand years, Klima had flourished as the center of the island's civic life. For thirteen thousand years, the island had been one of the ancient world's main sources of razor-sharp obsidian, the mining of which brought the island great wealth and renown. The famous poet and sophist Diagoras lived there in the fifth century BCE. With its spectacular harbor, Melos became a vital center of the shipping trade. Its buildings, boats, and women were known for their great beauty. In 416 BCE, the island's leaders met in Klima, as Herodotus wrote, to discuss demands to pay the annual tribute exacted by Athens. When they refused to surrender to Athens' egregious demands, all the men and boys of the island were summarily executed. Two hundred and fifty years later, the Romans occupied the island and built the spectacular marble amphitheater with its equally stunning statuary, including an inspiring one of the trident-bear sea god Poseidon, now on display in the National Archaeological Museum in Athens, and a colossal statue of the quicksilver messenger boy Hermes. By the time Voutier arrived, a lethal mix of earthquakes, wars, pirate raids, and local politics had decimated the island.

Uncannily, Yorgos and Voutier were digging within a stone's throw of each other. They were in a haunt of ancient peace, a portal into another time, a gateway into another dimension. The modern and the ancient worlds were about to bump into each other. Otherwise, we would never have learned that one of the most remarkable statues ever sculpted had been hidden behind a wall for nearly fifteen hundred years. If it had been discovered earlier, let's say by any other farmer or a soldier unschooled in the arts, it likely would have ended up, in the best scenario, as a "folly" in the garden of a Roman aristocrat, or in the worst, melted down in a lime kiln for whitewash, the fate of hundreds of thousands of other marble statues.

The hinges of history swing both ways.

Above the soldier and the farmer trembled the azure sky. Below them were the long-abandoned grounds of an ancient sanctuary. They felt a wisp of wind through their hair, heard a tinkle of bells from stray goats, smelled the salt wafting up from the sea.

Suddenly, Voutier heard the loud *clanking* of a shovel striking stone about fifty meters away. He stood bolt upright and decided to investigate. Approaching the ancient wall, he saw a newly gouged opening that made the entire hillside look as if it were staring open-mouthed back at him. He peered into what he later described as a *"trou,"* a hole or a cave, an oval-shaped, cut-stone chamber with a high arching roof that was painted a faint rose—the color, Greeks believed, of the Goddess of Love and Beauty.

The cave contained whirls within worlds, runes within ruins, parables within stories.

Inside the cave, Yorgos knelt next to the half-buried statue. When the farmer heard the footsteps of the approaching intruder, he got nervous and began to cover the statue with dirt. He knew that if he sold the statue he would be set for life, even earn a flicker of fame. His longing to bask in the sculpture's reflected glory was not very different from Voutier's.

For a clutch of centuries, fifteen in all, no one who chanced upon that high stone wall that flanked Yorgos's field had any idea what they were looking at. It had taken that long for the island to slowly surrender its myriad mysteries, anticipating the modern realization that the world is rarely as it seems. The early Christian-era catacombs in the nearby hills wouldn't be discovered for another fifty years, not until the 1870s. The marmoreal wonders of the statues of Poseidon, Hermes, and Asclepius wouldn't be dug up in the ruins of the nearby Roman theatre until the 1890s. The stunning Bronze Age Minoan murals of flying blue fish wouldn't turn up until 1977, during digs at Phylakopi on the far side of the island.

While Yorgos was reburying the statue, Voutier slipped through the jagged opening of the cave. The young officer could scarcely believe his luck. He had been scrabbling around the island for a month looking for ancient artifacts, and now he had stumbled on something unexpected, even dazzling. A face destined for the ages. Neither disdainful nor expressionless, as author Gregory Curtis says, she is "completely absorbed," an admirable phrase. Underneath her cool surface, Voutier detected a smoldering passion, "a noble beauty," that stunned him into silence for a moment—a glimpse of the hidden beauty of the world, a shiver from the *mana* still lurking inside it.

After nearly two hundred years, the story that informs this adventure is likewise in ruins, broken up like the fragments of a painted vase lying in a barren field. With luck, the story can be restored like a scattered mosaic, tile by tile, each jagged piece picked out of the sands of time and reset for ours. Maybe then we might be able to understand and even appreciate that this one statue has attracted meaning like floating filaments drawn by a magnet. There's the statue, then there's the gaze. One leads us on, the other leads us in.

What we are saying when we say that we're looking for adventure is that we are hungry for marvels. I think of the time when I was on the island of Rhodes in 1990 and found a dusty pamphlet in an old bookstore that purported to tell the story of the Antikythera Mechanism. I had never heard of it. By the looks of it, few others had either. In an hour, I was able to learn about the discovery, hauled up in a fisherman's net in 1899 from the seafloor, of a rusted first-century bronze box that is now recognized as the oldest known calculator. Today the staggeringly beautiful and strangely anachronistic device has its own gallery in the National Archaeological Museum in Athens. I think too of the thrill of finding hundreds of scraps of

Sappho's poetry in a garbage dump outside the pharaonic Egyptian town of Oxyrhynchus, or the original grooved slab of marble that served as the starting line at Olympia for more than fifteen centuries. So, remind me what we are searching for when we comb the past.

While ruins can be "hallucinatory experiences," as Michel de Montaigne described them in his *Essays*, they are also strong, tensile metaphors, which are sometimes more real than facts, in this case signifying, as Christopher Warren writes in his book, *In Ruins*, "decay and resurrection and decrepitude." The irrepressible Victorian traveler Dame Rose Macaulay writes in her masterpiece, *The Pleasure of Ruins*: "All this makes for that melancholy delight so eagerly sought, so gratefully treasured, by man in his brief passage down the corridor of time, from which, looking this way and that, he may observe such enchanting chambers of the past. Ruins are all we shall ever know of immortality." Likewise, Czeslaw Milosz stated that his task in life was to forge the full force of the words from which he wrote poetry out of the ruins of his war-torn Poland and Lithuania.

During the eighteenth and nineteenth centuries, Europeans developed what the French essayist Marguerite Yourcenar called a "taste for ruins." With piercing grace, she described the phenomenal popularity of Giovanni Battista Piranesi's engravings of Roman moldering buildings as "seething" and "lugubrious." What provoked travelers to go great distances to meditate among the ruins was the feeling that we are living in an impenetrable drama in which "the protagonist is Time." It can be edifying to read Piranesi's own reflections on what he was trying to accomplish because they can shed light on our scene on Melos. "I realized that in Rome," he wrote, "the majority of the ancient monuments were lying forsaken in fields or gardens, or even now serving as a quarry for new structures." Piranesi presented an odd paradox. On one hand, his fever dream engravings help us imagine the last of the glories that were Rome; on the other hand, he was involved in projects that reconstructed ruined statues, slapping arms, legs, hands, and heads onto time's mutilated monuments. Mythically speaking, creation and destruction closer than we would like to admit.

As a boy, I didn't have to go far to romp around in ruins, which may be why I became attracted to or at least sensitized to them. One day in the early Sixties (where were you in '62?), my father took me on a tour with my best friends Mark and Steve around Ford's River Rouge plant, as close as I'll ever come to visiting Vulcan's underground furnaces and forges. Afterward, he took us to shake hands with the inventor and futurist Buckminster Fuller, who he was going to lead around the plant. I'll never forget the thickness of his Coke bottle-lensed glasses or his Blakean-like riff on the thrill of seeing the future. Fuller, who was nicknamed the American Leonardo da Vinci, called himself a "comprehensivist" in contrast to a "specialist," believing as he did in the miracle of technology, so what sparked his imagination at the Ford plant was the sheer genius of automation and engineering. But I remember seeing something far different: the dark beauty of the furnaces spewing lava streams of iron ore. While the tour group gathered around my father, listening to his every word, gasping at the miracle of watching a complete car built in less than a minute before their very eyes, my eyes saw the factory ruins of the future in the Stygian darkness of a Ford assembly plant. I found the factory beautiful *anyway*, which turned out to be a preview of the challenges in front of me for the rest of my life. The memory is scorched into me because it was, as Mircea Eliade confided in his memoirs, the first hint that "part of my destiny demanded that I live paradoxically, in contradiction with myself and my era."

There are countless ways to forget that we need a daily dose of the beautiful as there are so many habits to unlearn, including the habit of accepting the ugliness and depravity around us. In 1991, a few nights after American rockets swarmed like wasps over the skies of Baghdad in the first Iraq War, I watched the blue-eyed, white-haired San Francisco poet Lawrence Ferlinghetti give a spellbinding reading before a standing-room-only crowd at the old Italian Opera House, Club Fugazi, in North Beach. Not unlike an Old Testament prophet, he intoned, "I am waiting, I am waiting, I am waiting...for a rebirth of wonder." The Monotones sang, "And I wonder, wonder, wonder, wonder, who wrote the book of love?" No wonder, no beauty, no wonder, no love. No love, no life. I wonder what or who the Venus is looking at, don't you?

"Stop!" cried a frantic voice in last night's dream. "You might find yourself!"

I read, I live, I read again. Tell me again. Remind me what I am looking for. That's the beauty of it. We are here to help each other find it, again and again.

There are travels, and then there are travels. One of my most memorable road moments took place in Cappadocia, Turkey, in 2015. I was leading a tour and added a last-minute surprise: a visit to Özkonak Yeralti Sehri, one of Cappadocia's vaunted and vaulted underground cities. Sahan, our sad-eyed but savvy Turkish guide, led us down several floors dug out of the ground as a refuge from the invading hordes, a subterranean community that housed upwards of ten thousand people at a time. It was replete with a cistern, elaborate ventilation system, winery, schoolrooms, and sliding boulders that served as doors. Emerging out of the oxygen-deprived Özkonak Underground City in Cappadocia, I invited my Canadian cousin, Raymond Guy, to join me for a cup of Turkish mint tea. By sheer coincidence, as if there is such a thing, I chose a simple one-table café. "*Mirhaba!*" ("Hello!"), I said to the man with the red-and-white scarf, who happened to be the owner. He was washing out a plastic jug. His head was covered with a scarf. His features were vulpine, sharp, alert. Out of the blue, his son appeared and welcomed us, telling us, "This is my father, Latif Acar. I am so proud. In 1972, he discovered the caves you just visited."

While offering us a copy of the guidebook for sale in their gift shop, his father gave an elegant bow, pride suffusing his face. His son went on to tell us how his father had been concerned about a strange loss of water from his fields and went searching for the cause. Curiously, one of his stray goats fell into a hole, and when his father followed the sound of its bleating, he felt a cool whoosh of air. When he peered down, he saw a strange sight, an underground room. When the authorities excavated, they discovered more than a room. They found a long-abandoned underground city beneath their feet, ten floors designed to house and protect sixty thousand people for three to six months. The shepherd said a few words in Turkish to his son, his forehead wrinkling wonderfully as he spoke, which his son translated.

"My good father wants me to tell you that he hopes, Praise God, that you enjoyed your exploration. He dropped down into the hole in the ground and was stunned by the sight of another world." His father inserted a closing thought in his native Turkish, which the son translated for me. "He wants you to know that he is happy that his goat got close. Now the whole world comes here to appreciate how beautiful our land and history are. When he first explored the caves, he found ten floors. But the authorities only allow visitors to see nine. We like to think that the tenth floor is like the intentional imperfection that is left in every Turkish carpet because only God is perfect."

RUNES WITHIN THE RUINS

Late one night at one of the best used bookstores in the world, Green Apple in San Francisco, I came across a tattered copy of a hundred-year-old book: *The Venus of Milo*, written in the early 1900s by the obscure German American author Paul Carus, a believer in panpsychism, a philosophy that dates to Thales and Spinoza. I riffled through a few pages and came across the engraving of the stone wall that festoons this section of our story on the peasant Yorgos's land and was as shocked as if I had come across an original line drawing of the original walls of Troy. There must be a word for the shock of recognition upon seeing something you never thought existed, for the reification, the making real, of what was previously unreal and unimaginable, which is exactly what happened then and there. Nonetheless, it helped me to finally visualize what happened next.

I've come around to the idea that art is a soulful response to an awareness of *deep time*. Likewise, I've become fascinated by Tolstoy's startling insight that beauty is not a thing or a theory or a craft but the *transmission* of a *feeling*. Not just any feeling but one that an artist cannot keep to him or herself. The visionary sculptor who carved the Venus de Milo must have sensed something in stone's capacity to suggest the human spirit, the ability to convey vitality, joy, even desire. These qualities lie at the heart of art.

This was a distant echo of what I felt in front of my father's workbench when I couldn't keep myself from staring at his framed magazine cover of the Venus de Milo. I felt an exquisite sense of peace during my visit to MOMA the day after the Towers fell in New York, similar to my preternatural calm on my pilgrimage to the Rothko Chapel in Houston, and the quiet night when I rocked my son to sleep in the old family rocking chair, basking in the moonlight. Both infused me with a newfound love for life.

Lately, I have been musing over the legend of the eighth-century Chinese artist Wu Daozi, who was commissioned by Emperor Xuanzong to paint a mist-shrouded landscape festooned with exotic flowers and fauna on the walls of the palace. With a flourish, the artist obeyed and then painted an ominous cave at the foot of a distant mountain that seemed to appear and then disappear. When the ruler asked about the strange apparition, Wu Daozi said a spirit lived there, and so there was more to the painting than he could see with his ordinary eyes. Then he spun away from the emperor, clapped his hands, walked into the painting, and entered the dark cave that he had created. Astonished, the emperor tried to follow. But he was thwarted on the threshold because when he stepped forward, the painting vanished.

The legends speak to the spiritual dimension of art, what the Hartford life insurance agent-turned-modernist poet Wallace Stevens revealed as the utter mystery of presence-within-absence in his poem, "The Snow Man," as the moment of beholding the "nothing that is not there and the nothing that is." *The nothing that is not there and the nothing that is.* A poetic way of describing the mysterious power of the missing arms of the Venus de Milo.

In her masterpiece *Eros the Bittersweet*, Anne Carson writes about Franz Kafka's short story "The Top," which she is convinced revolves around why we love to fall in love. "Beauty spins and the mind moves," she concludes. "To catch beauty would be to understand how that impertinent stability in vertigo is possible."

My aim here is to catch a glimpse of the face of beauty "Here, There and Everywhere," as the Beatles sang. Or my son's face as I held him for the first time. Or my mother's eyes as she lay dying after a crippling stroke. Or the face of the moon the night I wandered around the ancient *moai* on Easter Island, fifteen hundred miles from the nearest land. Or my own bloated and bruised face, after surgery on my front teeth, the result of years of being bashed in the mouth by flying elbows on the basketball court. Or the face of God, which I was told by parents, priests, and nuns I would soon see but never did. But Sappho did, writing in her "Ode to Aphrodite" in Rosamund van Wingerden's translation:

> Soon they arrived, and you, blessed one,
> with a smile on your immortal face,
> asked me what had happened now and
> why I had called you…

How can this move us twenty-five hundred years after it was written on the island of Lesbos? Jorge Borges, who learned reams of poetry by heart, wrote in *Everything and Nothing*: "The poems of a foreign language have a prestige they do not enjoy in their own language … we think of the beauty, of the power, or simply of the strangeness of them." *Panta rhei*, wrote Heraclitus, the Obscure Philosopher, in the library of marmoreal-minded Ephesus. *Everything flows.* The endless cycle of up and down, air into fire, creation into destruction, the ugly into the beautiful. Everything turning into something else, a constant becoming something else. Perhaps we can call it the *moving* moment. The phenomenon that the South African writer Laurens van der Post poignantly called "not-yet-now." If it isn't beautiful now, it will be, which will be *jouissance*, an exquisite delight.

Despite all we have lost, I find some comfort in knowing there are clues about the meaning of beauty that were detected long ago by our ancestors, evidence we can use now to better understand what happened next in the cave on Melos. But the comfort soon leads to a kind of vertigo, as if I am rising too quickly from the depths.

I am drawing with words the negative space around the Venus de Milo so she might emerge in all her glory. As I've been trying to do all my life, ever since I first felt the void, as all kids eventually do, with the death of my Grandfather Sydney, then the terror of the '67 Detroit Riots, then the terrible truth of the murder of my college girlfriend's mother. In my experience, the sketching of that space is only possible if I can find, and even better, *cultivate* a sense of beauty. I think now of the silver spotlight of the moon the night I wandered around my great-grandfather Charlemagne Cousineau's farmhouse on Lake Nipissing, in Ontario. The sight of the glowing red lava flow on the cliffs of Oahu, the volcano explosion on Stromboli, the glint of light on the green paint on the bleacher seats of Old Tiger Stadium. Echoes perhaps of the face of God I was told by parents, priests, and nuns I would one day see, which I prefer to think of as the revelation of the numinous, the nod of the gods. As Diane Krall suggested in her silky-smooth version of "The Look of Love":

> The look of love is in your eyes
> a look your smile can't disguise...
> It's saying so much more than just words could ever say
> And what my heart has heard, well, it takes my breath away.

Strange and beautiful are these memory turns, these turns of the kaleidoscope of imagination. For the French ensign to recognize the beautiful but time-pummeled statue, there had to be something as beautiful in him, a formula described long ago by the third-century poet Asclepiades of Samos, when he wrote these enflamed words. "Love found a way to mix beauty with beauty."

We have a few hints across the abyss of time about what happened next.

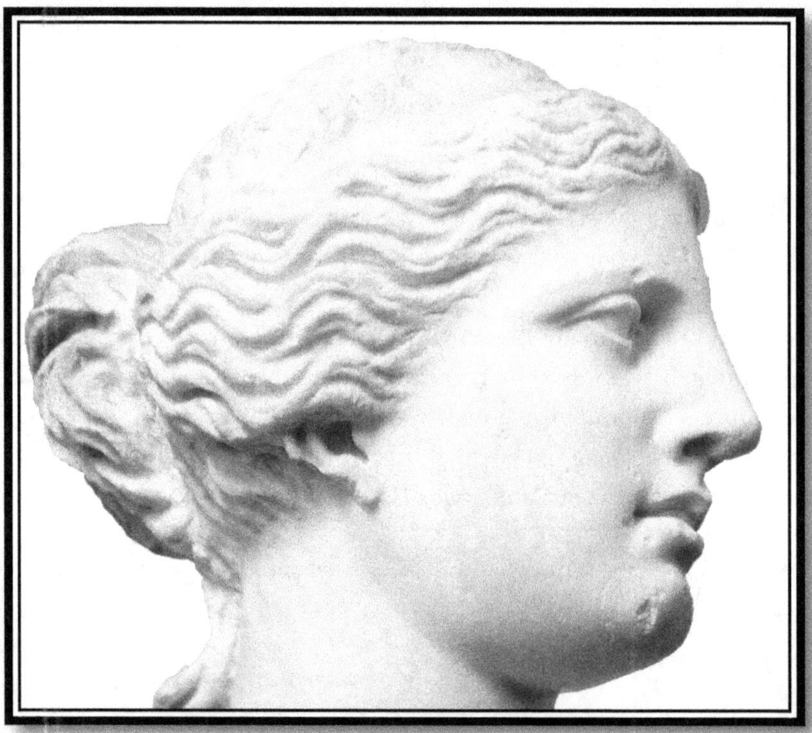

The Face of Venus
Musée du Louvre

ART IS WHAT TAKES YOUR BREATH AWAY

First, Voutier's eyes fell over the Venus's beautiful face, then her sensuous breasts and gently sloping shoulders, which ended in crude stumps. When the ensign recovered from his reverie, he asked Yorgos to keep digging. That's the moment that the farmer suspected his hunch was right. The oddly shaped stone had to be valuable. The stranger was acting like one of those young lovers who came courting from nearby islands, eager to woo one of Melos's famously beautiful girls. The moment unfolded like a parable. The naturalist-author Robert McFarland resorted to an old Celtic phrase that birders still use, *the jizz*, to describe the uncanny, non-intellectual, *instantaneous* reading of an observation. The thrill of recognition, as art lovers love to say.

Boldly, the peasant asked for a few *piasters*, roughly the price of a goat.

To his surprise, Voutier was moved by Yorgos's simple plea. He glanced back at the beautiful face and fell under her trance. In 1860, a full forty years after the encounter in the cave, Voutier described the offer in his memoirs as "*balski*," local Turkish slang for *baksheesh*, a small but not insignificant offer. Decades later, in 1939, Voutier's biographer, Jean-Paul Alaux, described in *The Discovery of the Venus de Milo*, how the French ensign agreed to pay a *pourboire*, an old French word for a tip.

As Yorgos's descendants tell it to this day on Melos, Voutier offered to compensate him fairly the moment he set eyes on the statue, which they are proud to say is a far cry from the outright theft of the Parthenon Marbles by Thomas Bruce, the Seventh Lord of Elgin. Voutier's payoff was downright honest compared to the bribes doled out by rapacious looters to the guards at Angkor Wat so they might look away while nightcrawlling thieves lopped off the stone heads of thousand-year-old Khmer sculptures of dancing goddesses.

Instead, the Greek nation has always recognized the French claim to the statue as legitimate because a payment was offered and accepted, and they have made it clear ever since that the deal was in dramatic contrast to the English claim to the Parthenon Marbles. The original frieze had been an offering to the goddess herself, one islander told me, nearly two hundred years after it happened. The farmer's descendants on the island are proud to recount that the officer offered something far more personable. Georg Vihos, a Greek American painter from Melos who lived in Detroit for many years, told me the traditional story he grew up with. Yorgos's family offered to barter a warm coat and hat for the statue, he said, which everyone agreed was more important than the money because of the cold winters on the island.

Often while musing about the Venus, I fall down the centaur hole into a netherworld where everything seems upside down but somehow still connected to everything else. On my most recent visit to Melos in the summer of 2008, I asked around the island and was fascinated to hear dozens of different versions of stories from local fishermen, waiters, bakers, hotel owners, sailors, the docent from the island's museum, and even tourists. Wildly varying as they were, the stories were told to me in a *sotto voce*, as if the locals were gossiping about a girls-gone-wild beach party.

"They say she lost her arms when the farmer pushed her down the hill to the harbor," a rental car owner in Adamas told me, miffed as if it had happened yesterday. "She broke the donkey's back that tried to carry her," the baker's daughter told me with a wink. "And when she bucked, the Venus went flying off the wagon and broke her arms off." "The Turks stole her arms. They hoped to ransom them for money. Curses on them," a local fisherman who owned the Blue Dolphin boat snarled. The owner of the Hotel Aphrodite was proud to confide to me that the French officer caught the local farmer just as he was trying to push the statue into his kiln so that she, like thousands of other marble statues, could be melted down for lime and later used to make the whitewash for the island's traditional houses. "Just think," he said wistfully, "of all the *Venuses* that were crushed to create white paint for our houses."

With the extra incentive, Yorgos spaded the dirt around the statue until Voutier joined in and helped him lift it out of the ground and stand it upright. Only then, as the dust motes caught fire inside the cave, could they see the statue's nearly perfect upper body, which appeared at first glance to be that of a gorgeous woman, maybe a goddess. If Voutier noticed that the arms were missing, he is not on record saying so. Nobody had stolen them unless you count the greatest thief of all, time itself. And yet, as with lost time, we miss them, time being painful to contemplate and voids being full of dread.

Make way for the enchantress. There is a bevy of beauties in sculpture and painting and films we call Venus or Aphrodite, and they fill the halls of our museums, galleries, movie theaters, villas, palaces, and museums. According to the art scholar Kenneth Clark, an estimated two hundred thousand Venus statues have survived the ravages of time. We are fortunate that a workman on an archaeological dig in Austria found the hand-sized, twenty-five-thousand-year-old Venus of Willendorf figurine. What a beautiful statue! Sculpted in the round out of oolitic limestone, it seems to signify fertility and childbirth, perhaps even the miracle of creation itself. Similar fortune smiled on us with the discovery of the eighteen-inch-high, red-ochre bas relief called the Venus of Laussel from the Upper Paleolithic culture, as well as the nymph-like Venus of Allianoi, found near Bergama, Turkey. In classical times, the coy Aphrodite of Knidos carved by Praxiteles is widely recognized as the first life-sized nude of a woman or goddess, a sculpture so lifelike there were rumors that the Athenian sculptor must have surreptitiously spied on the goddess herself.

More recently, the Capitoline Venus in Rome has caught the world's attention, as have Canova's demur but ultimately sentimental Venus and Jim Dine's iconic modern version of the Venus de Milo in all its lime-green patinaed glory, displayed in downtown Manhattan in a sculpture garden alongside an Aphrodite statue. There are innumerable canvases, too, including Botticelli's immortalizing "The Birth of Venus," Titian's voluptuous "Venus of Urbino," Raphael's "Creation of the World," Dali's "The Hallucinogenic Toreador" (which contains twenty-eight reproductions of the Venus), and Andy Warhol's 1984 radical rendition of Botticelli's "Birth of Venus, a vibrant screen print that has become a modern icon.

Clearly, the world has long been delighted with the Goddess of Desire, Love, Happiness, and Beauty, even to the point of obsession, which isn't necessarily a bad thing. The original meaning was rooted in "besieged," an unwilling intrusion upon our will, but it also refers to *single-minded*, which is necessary for the completion of a difficult task, as opposed to *compulsion*, which refers to repetitive behavior with no goal in mind. The Western world has been fascinated by Aphrodite/Venus for some three thousand years as we try to figure out why we are consumed by desire.

The music world hasn't shied away from the goddess either. Our neon-striped jukeboxes are jammed with tributes to the Goddess of Love, which makes sense if you consider the real purpose of pop music. An internet search reveals there are nearly six thousand songs that refer to Venus or Aphrodite and dozens of songs based on her enchanting beauty. Who hasn't danced or sung along to Shocking Blue's "Venus (was her name)," Frankie Avalon's pop tribute, "Venus," Sam Cooke's "Venus," Bjork's "Venus as a Boy," Miles Davis's trumpet-blasting "Venus de Milo," Paul McCartney's "Kiss of Venus," Lady Gaga's "Venus," or the slightly sado-masochistic "Venus in Furs" by Lou Reed and The Velvet Underground.

Let's not forget the Venus of the poets, from Sappho to Lucretius, Ovid to Dante and Shakespeare, Ruben Dario to Rita Dove. Other writers singing her praises include the Japanese singer-songwriter Hiroshi Sato, contemporary Syrian poet Adonis, and African American poet Henrietta Cordelia Ray. Then there are the radiant Venuses of the silver screen, from Marlena Dietrich's "Blue Venus" to Woody Allen's "Mighty Aphrodite." And for as long as we have had marketing and publicity campaigns, we have been confronted with commercialized and bowdlerized Venuses. Her name is emblazoned on beauty salons, massage parlors, perfume bottles, and satin negligees.

The very word *Venus* has become a touchstone for beauty and desire, sometimes life-affirming but occasionally life-negating. At its most invidious, beauty is a euphemism, as Naomi Wolf writes, for the "dark vein of self-hatred [and] physical obsession," or as she quotes Germaine Greer, a "masquerade" for anything more substantial. So many Venuses, so little time to appreciate them all. Still, there is only one Venus de Milo, whom the Greeks refer to as the Aphrodite de Melos. Why so singular? She reveals a quality, a force, that none of the others possess: sensuality intertwined with spirituality like the two snakes twisted around the herald's wand. And more—an elusive trait that makes her instantly recognizable.

In the early 2000s, I was enjoying a scintillating conversation about the importance of the Venus with former Time magazine critic Alexander Eliot over breakfast at the Figtree Café in Venice, California.

"It has to do with *significance*," he said. "Venus shows us *how to live*."

"Significance?" Alex, that sounds too intellectual," I dared to challenge him. "We're talking about the impact of a great work of art on us. How about describing how much it *moves* us?"

"What's the difference?" he shot back before catching himself, tugging at his sea captain's white beard, then winking affectionately. "Everything in the *mythosphere* moves our souls."

"How's that? Surely, there is a great story at work here. She is focused on someone or something offstage. And she seems to be gasping as if she knows the whole world hangs in the balance."

"It's up to us to decide what she's gazing at. Maybe me, maybe you, maybe eternity."

"I always feel conflicted by great works of art," I suggested, "like Hopper's *Woman in the Sun*, which feels like a provocation to be living ... brighter."

"Well, maybe," he growled. "I like *Early Sunday Morning* better. Out of his eight hundred or so paintings, Hopper told me that was his own favorite. What you're suggesting could be the difference between sight and insight."

If we don't know the context, the story, that imbues a work, we are first exhilarated and then emptied of all feeling, which may be the best explanation for "museum fatigue" ever offered, and by doing so, as Joyce, the first movie theater operator in Dublin, punned, we can "reel away the real world." Speaking of reeling, I recall something the film director Joseph Strick once told me in Paris: "I'm convinced Joyce wrote *Ulysses* as a movie script more than a novel."

Art has always allowed us to see—and *feel*—things we would not have been able to experience otherwise. Invisible things. Life that is seen with the heart and felt with the soul.

The beautiful that is observable through the sorrowful.

The Spanish-American philosopher George Santayana said in his 1896 Harvard lectures, later published as *The Spirit of Beauty*, that life without beauty may not be literally ugly, but it would be "lamentable and degrading." All that would be missing, he said, would be the *pleasure* of life that deep beauty brings. In a lecture that calls out to me like one of our foghorns in San Francisco Bay, the wisely skeptical and aesthetic thinker delivered a single astonishing line: "*Beauty is pleasure regarded as the quality of the thing.*"

It is so easy to forget that we are sensorial creatures, easy to lose touch with ourselves, easy to forget the ancient willingness, as Elizabeth Prettejean has written, "to take pleasure in the beautiful." I wonder if she knows that one of the seventy-seven aphorisms engraved into the lintels of the Temple of Apollo in Delphi was this one, as reported by Pausanius, the world's first travel writer, "Happiness is the pleasure of sages, pleasure the happiness of fools." I am happy to further report that happiness and pleasure are two of the myriad attributes of Venus/Aphrodite, which is another way of saying an interest in her is inevitable, unavoidable, delectable, and dare I suggest, beautiful to contemplate—and sometimes dangerous to encounter because it has the power to make us weak in the knees. Then again beauty and danger, personified by the Greeks as Aphrodite and Ares, and by the Romans as Venus and Mars, have long endured a combustible relationship. But I digress, happily.

Let us say it again. Beauty gives us pleasure. This time with *feeling*, as if we're enjoying it. Why is this so difficult to understand or accept? No pleasure, no beauty; no beauty, no joy; no joy, no meaning. If we are still wondering who "stole" the arms of the Venus, we need look no further than the baffling Puritan bias against pleasure, beauty, and the sensuous life. Every generation needs to breathe new life into its notions of beauty. What doubles the significance of Voutier's rediscovery is how it evokes our own rediscovery of the beautiful throughout our lives. Every time our senses are alerted by a well-kept garden, a streak of sunset, a well-wrought piece of furniture, a sleek car, a beaming child, an evocative fashion show, or the dramatic cinematography of a moody film noir, we rediscover beauty no less dramatically than that red-letter day on Melos when the Venus de Milo resurfaced.

But I digress, happily.

THE GAZING

Together, Voutier and Yorgos, farmer and soldier, Frenchman and Greek, gazed at the long-lost beauty. They sensed the charge of sensuality and the surge of erotic fascination that followed the goddess in the great round of myths, exhibiting what the French novelist Jean Giono would later ebulliently call "the joy of man's desiring," the elusive quality that the long-dead sculptor had somehow infused into the stone that they could sense centuries later.

Of all the soldiers in all the world who could have stumbled upon this statue, Olivier Voutier was one of the few who was capable of recognizing what he was looking at. I like to think he gasped—a reflexive sign, I learned in a private talk with psychologist James Hillman, that is the body's natural response to something so beautiful it takes your breath away. Our very word for the study of beauty, "aesthetics," derives from *aesthesis*, ancient Greek for constriction in the lungs, panting, gasping, a sudden loss of breath. If it doesn't take your breath away, it ain't art. If it doesn't catch your breath, it ain't beautiful. If it ain't beautiful, don't bother. When Ensign Voutier first came upon her, he had no way of knowing who had made her.

Soon, he did.

What Voutier knew was that he was in the presence of a very old sculpture of the Goddess of Love, Beauty, and Desire whom the Greeks knew as Aphrodite. But being French, he knew her as Venus, the name adopted by early Roman scholars. This is how the world came to know her as the Venus de Milo, sometimes called the Eighth Wonder of the Ancient World, always regarded as being emblematic of beauty and desire but also lust and vanity. However, Voutier did not write about his encounter with the statue for another forty years, near the end of his life, when he was living in the south of France. By then, he was a retired war hero. On

March 3, 1860, Voutier wrote to the Comte de Marcellus, who was the French ambassador to the sultan at the time of the discovery. I learned of this while reading Alaux's *The Discovery of the Venus de Milo*. I had to blink twice before realizing I was reading an account of Voutier's discovery *in his own words*. Although there are some discrepancies about where and when Voutier stumbled upon Yorgos, the essential story remains electrifying:

> *En 1820, j'etais attaché a la station du Levant sur la goelette l'Estafette...* In 1820, I was assigned to the Levant [the Mediterranean] on the Estafette schooner. During a call to port in Melos, I learned that a peasant farmer, while searching for stones for a small construction [at his home], had just found a fragment of a statue. When I arrived on the scene, I found that the gentleman, after pulling out the stones that he needed, had thrown back the unfortunate [*malheursement*] statue into its hole in the ground and had already covered it with rubble. With a slight effort he brought her up again ... *Quelle stupefaction!*

"*Quelle stupefaction!*" Today we might say "I was *stupefied*" if we are trying to say we are more than surprised and closer to exultant, dumbstruck, even stunned.

With those exclamatory words, the young naval officer condensed centuries of defining and theorizing about the many effects that great art can have on us. Voutier's well-carved phrase reminds us how visceral the real thing is because it stuns us and then promises something we may not know we have been longing for. You can call it "God" or "the gods" or "inspiration," but appear it does throughout the ages. For Voutier, the soldier-scholar, the discovery was so "stupefying," he had to seize the *moment*. I never dreamed such a letter existed, something that made moribund history bounce to life. I had stumbled across it so serendipitously. It was during the ensign's attempt to clear up the confusion about what happened that sun-spangled day on Melos in 1820 when he happened upon the cave of forgotten beauty. What is rediscovered is loved in new ways; what is resurrected is revered. There was something, then nothing, then something again.

"First there is a mountain," sang Donovan, "then there is no mountain, then there is."

Two hundred years before, Rene Descartes said, "Reading is like talking to people of other centuries." Reading Voutier's letter moves me in a similar way with a curious sense of transport because I can finally see how moved he was by the statue's beauty.

Last words, lost thoughts, missing farewells that fly to us across time and space when they are rediscovered, translated, read. The whole world is there in a single note of music, a glint of light in a child's eye, the sinuous grain of green snaking through marble. You can scarcely believe you are seeing something that approaches infinity. When we are stupefied, our spirit turns bruised-boxer blue. If our wind hasn't been knocked out of us, it can be interesting, but it isn't what we are looking for. It just so happens that soul and breath are synonymous in cultures throughout the world. What is animated is alive; what is alive *breathes*. Stone that seems to breathe animates those who look at it. Stone doing what stone does, inspiring us with their very *stoneness*. That is what occurred to me today while gazing out over the six billion years old boulders in Brush Creek Ranch, Wyoming, near the log cabin where I am writing these words. I gaze at them and sense this is as close as I will ever come to a glimpse of timelessness.

I know this is so.

Knowing this, I feel a strange comfort in the knowledge that in the third century BCE an obscure Greek scholar by the name of Posidippus of Pella wrote a series of sixty epigrammatic poems about the contemporary sculptors he most admired, including this observation that could have been written by Auguste Rodin, Barbara Hepworth, or Louise Nevelson: "The day will come when people will infuse statues with life." Our first art critic goes on to observe:

> This bronze, in every way the counterpart of Philitas, modeled by Hekataios in perfect precision down to the fingernails...*resembles someone who is about to speak*...so much is he imbued with the colors of his character, so alive is he, and yet the old man is made of bronze.

This long-hidden insight helps me nudge my way closer to the mystery of the Venus de Milo, though it exposes my vulnerability—why I have cared so deeply about her myriad mysteries for so long, which is how what is visible stone can reveal what is invisible to the naked eye. Recently, I discovered the singular writings of John B. Flannagan, a sculptor who hailed from Fargo, North Dakota, and lived in both New York and Connemara, Ireland. Flannagan brings this notion of the invisible forces home for me when he describes his own *stony quest for art*, "We communicate something of the human spirit."

Emboldened, I allow my mind to wander. I saunter through my memories back to the late 1980s, when I lived in Paris for a year, courtesy of George Whitman of Shakespeare and Company. A few times a week, I walked the mile or so from the bookstore to the Lipchitz Sculpture Garden. I had a year's pass to all 127 museums in the city, so it was free, and I could eat a light lunch, sketch, and consider sculpture unbothered by crowds or guards. I was especially moved by Lipchitz's rendering of Van Gogh, midstride, his easel strapped to his back. It was there that I first understood how a work of sculpture, if carved with an *enspiriting* hand, might bring us back to life if we learn the lost art of sitting quietly, doing nothing, in its presence.

Animate, ensoul, invigorate, resuscitate, revivify.

This is how the world comes alive. How I came back from the dead, my torpid youth in Detroit, *enlivened* by new life in Paris, by the beauty of the city, by the bookstores, the art, the live jazz in the *caveaux*, the exhilarating conversations in the cafes.

The poet Posidippus was prophetic but a little late to the art show when he wrote glowing tributes to the genius sculptors of his time, such as Praxiteles, Lysippus, and Phidias. What I hear when I read his epigrammatic writing about stone coming alive under the chisel of a great artist is that the acclaimed work in his own time may have been technically accomplished but to his remarkable sensibility was *lifeless*. Impressive but not lifelike enough. I read into his collected musings on art that he was vividly anticipating what some unborn sculptor might accomplish in the future. Or vice-versa. Classical Greece was a small world, even if they believed it was the entire world. If it is likely that her creator, whoever that may have been, would have seen copies or casts of the greatest sculptures of his era, it is not a stretch that he could have read the work of the greatest commentaries about his fellow stone-carvers.

In Greece, every mountain, every island, and every cave has its story. To every traveler, an epiphany. A flaring forth of divine light, the sudden appearance of a god or goddess who urges us on, an unveiling of a mystery, a privileged moment. That's the beauty of it. That's what's beautiful. The moment you feel what the artist felt.

Years ago, I took my mother Rosemary, a florist, to Bonfante Gardens in Gilroy, California. Besides the flamboyant gardens, she "took a fancy" to the Circus Trees, or as the placard said, "The World's Strangest Trees." In 1947, the owner, Axel Erlandson, began his curious project of shaping, pleaching, and grafting tree branches to form letters of the alphabet, archways, zigzags, hearts, and curious geometric shapes. I wondered out loud how he was able to perform these small miracles, and my mom scoffed, "Oh, Philip, isn't it obvious? He *talks* to them." An hour later, I read in the park brochure that the wily old man was often asked, mostly by schoolchildren, how he sculpted the trees. He was fond of telling them, "Oh, I talk to them."

What Ensign Voutier saw in the Venus de Milo that day was a glimpse of the secret strength of art. Stupefaction, not theory-mongering. Praise-singing, not fault-finding. The quest for meaning in art rather than claiming exclusive rights to it. The power of *presence*, not obsession with absence.

Searching for her hidden secrets, I find my own. Rediscovering long-lost images, buried words, undeveloped dreams. Struggling to find meaning in her beauty, the significance of the deep ache, the unfathomable emptiness that transcendent art and transportive words fill in.

Sometimes momentarily, sometimes over a lifetime. Is this compulsion or obsession, passion or impassion, diversion or fascination? None—and all the above. I live for paradoxes. I live for the thing itself, nothing but the thing. The thing called *love*.

Once true, still true. In the Irish novelist Roddy Doyle's 2020 book, aptly titled *Love*, one of his two main characters, a dissolute but lovable taxi driver, confides to the other, "She's beautiful. She shines. I don't know why I think that. She shines. She was real. Everything she did, she said, was real." Call it *deep beauty*, the real thing, the shining thing. Not the spurious one that creates impossible, often cruel standards; not the wounding one that is impossible to achieve. No, *deep* beauty, which we must describe by way of word-work, the profound love of real words.

Art has always allowed us to see things we would never have seen otherwise. Invisible things like the fire through the smoke, the beautiful through the sorrowful. From Melos to Konya, Provence to Liverpool and beyond, people the world over search for the real thing, the face that moves us, the face that is outside of time and space. Sappho wrote, "I say the most beautiful sight in the world is the face of the one you love." The moment the Sufi poet Rumi was alluding to when he wrote, "All of my life I have been searching for your face. And today I have found it." James Salter's young American hero in *A Sport and a Pastime* says to the young French-woman he has fallen hopelessly in love with, "When I see her, my knees go weak." At his buoyant best, Paul McCartney sings with foot-tapping joy in the Beatles' "I've Just Seen a Face," unabashedly admitting hers is one "I can't forget."

BEAUTY AS TRANSPORT

I know beauty when I see it. I feel the force of the beautiful. So do you. So did Olivier Voutier. What has perplexed me for a long time is how he recognized the Venus when he first encountered her. How could he name it and start the ball rolling in transporting her 1,389 miles from Melos to Paris? And then it hit me: He must have known her story, the one that inspired her creator. The story that happened to be one of the most influential stories in Western culture.

Thinking about it now, my mind wanders back to the Louvre and a 1636 painting by Rubens: *The Judgment of Paris*. One of the most influential stories of all-time. I remember focusing on her shoulder then her extended arm, torqued to hold the apple she had just been awarded by Paris, born a Prince of Troy. Fated to grow up a lonely shepherd but a well-respected judge in local athletic competitions. He was "fair," it was said. That said, he was also vulnerable to offers that might change his life.

The complimentary story resides in the negative space around the statue of Aphrodite in the center of her gaze, the hint of her gift. Come closer. You can see him in her eyes; you can detect her own desire in the turn of her hips. You can imagine the *infinite moment* in the ancient story that inspired her creator to capture the miracle of the Venus' gasp during her encounter with the Prince of Troy on the slopes of Mount Ida.

The conflicted moment of pride and pity was rendered into what would become the most famous sculpture in the world.

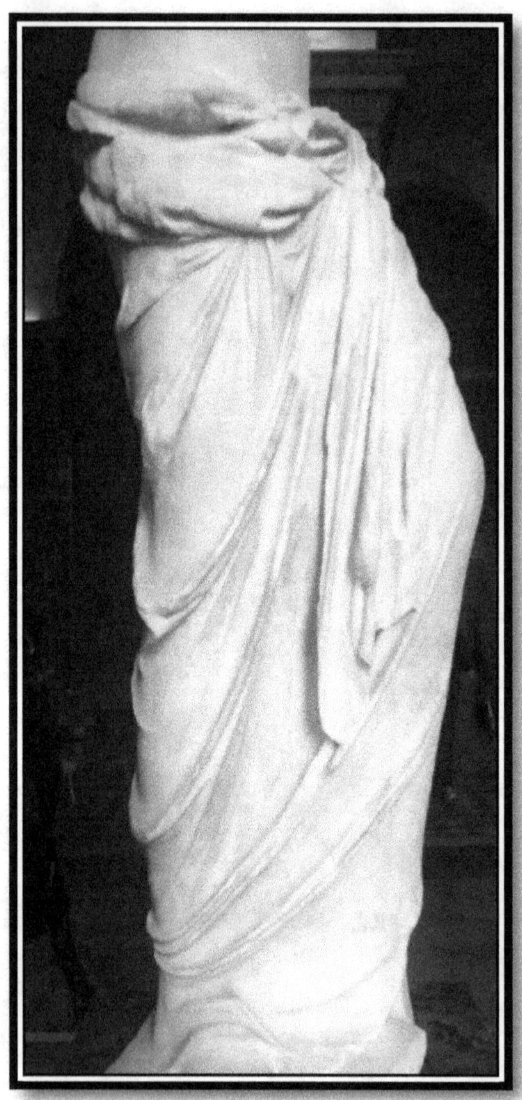

Lower Half of the Venus.
Musée du Louvre, 2010.

WE ARE ALWAYS SEARCHING FOR OUR MISSING HALF

In 1994, scientists discovered 37,000-year-old cave paintings in Chauvet, France. Sixteen years later, in 2010, German filmmaker Werner Herzog entered the ancient cave temple for the opening scene of *Cave of Forgotten Dreams*, noting that a rockslide that providentially corked up the entrance to the cave, preserving the paleolithic masterpieces within. Wending his way past the staggering artwork on the cave walls—capering gazelles, bird-beaked shamans, and shambling mastodons—Herzog whispers to the camera, "It is as if the modern soul was invented here."

Call me an irredeemable romantic or even a sentimental fool, but I like to think that Voutier felt a similar rush of awe the moment he slipped into Melos's equivalent of a paleolithic cave and discovered how the Greeks arrived at their concept of soul, such as Plato's notion of it as "the winged thing."

Soon after Voutier paid Yorgos to keep searching for the lower half, the farmer discovered the sinuously shaped lower half of the statue. Voutier was impressed with the curving drapery of her robe and the way her left knee jutted out and her hips twisted sensuously as if she were about to slip under the sheets with a wanton lover.

Despite the setup, the story didn't add up.

Something was missing, broken until reassembled.

Together with his two shipmates, who had followed him into the cave, Voutier helped Yorgos lift the heavy upper torso and fit it onto the lower half of the statue. It wobbled; it teetered.

"When superimposed, it didn't fit," he later wrote, rather cinematically.

Over the fourteen hundred years or so since it had disappeared from public view in the fourth century, the Venus had been gouged and chipped, and she lost her arms, one foot, and no small amount of pride. Insulted by the jeers of time. Fragments had fallen off her torso like eggshell bits. When Voutier and Yorgos rediscovered the two halves, they slipped them together like the last two pieces of a giant jigsaw puzzle, and now she was intact for the first time in centuries. Thinking about her now, I recall a proverb from Egypt, only a day's sailing from Melos: "A beautiful thing is never perfect."

Gazing at her now in the museum or in illustrations, we can't help but wonder, *what is beauty*, or perhaps even more important, *what is beautiful?*

The New Yorker art critic Peter Schjeldahl writes in his 2003 essay, "Regarding Beauty," "Beauty isn't articulate. Beauty isn't nice. Beauty isn't fair...to state it is mysterious isn't enough."

Then what *is* enough to state or observe about beauty or the beautiful? What can possibly be enough to compel generation after generation to visit our icons of beauty, to copy, revise, inspire, remind us of our divinity?

Over the last thousand years, one of the most influential definitions comes from theologian Thomas Aquinas, who concluded that beauty is a mixture of three qualities: proportion, harmony, and radiance. This profoundly influenced Renaissance architect Leon Battista Alberti, who observed that it is the "harmony and concord of all the parts." Eminently logical but a little bloodless. I vastly prefer the four qualities observed by Elaine Scarry, an essayist and Professor of Aesthetics at Harvard, who concluded that beauty is sacred, unprecedented, surprising, and lifesaving. A subtler observation comes from the quietist painter Pierre Bonnard, who calmly called beauty "the satisfaction of vision." This insight from someone active in the field confirms my suspicion that beauty is a *force*, not a thing, a response, not a quality, a necessity rather than an indulgence.

The mythic proof is the long-held story that love is born from her, in the form of her son Eros, and happiness is the fleeting result. The ability or capacity of these qualities helps make us breathtakingly human. In turn, tell me what takes your breath away and I'll tell you, or at least take a good guess, what you *feel* is beautiful as opposed to what you *think* is beautiful.

This is the only way to grasp the spiritual essence of art—its animating quality, which in turn is what allows us to sense what the artist intended. To my utter delight, I found this sensibility in the work of John B. Flannagan, one of the first practitioners of direct carving, who described the stone-cutter's process as working with a "chisel that thinks and feels" and said that he worked under the assumption that a work "should always be in the state of *becoming* rather than being."

Now there is a description with some bite in it.

According to Voutier's letter, he felt a shock of recognition that led to one of the most poetic insights and descriptions ever made about a work of art. For the first time in fifteen centuries, the Venus de Milo was standing on her own two feet, fully herself, no longer divided, no longer hidden away. Standing there in front of it, seeing her in all her true glory, his memory was sparked, and he struggled for a moment until just the right words came to him. He wrote: "After thorough searching, we discovered the intermediary section, and she was revealed as a true goddess."

Gazing at the resurrected Venus, who some later believed to be no more than an aristocratic woman of great breeding, Voutier saw *something* in her that told him she was divine. We know this because a learned phrase came to him from his knowledge of Virgil's *Aeneid*, where the poet described an appearance of Venus as "*Vera incessu patuit dea.*" This may be translated as: "By her gait, she was revealed as a true goddess."

Voutier didn't write anything as banal as "She looked *like* a goddess." No, he said she *was* one. An otherworldly, dreamy, ethereal being. This may sound anachronistic now, or even superstitious, unsophisticated, uninformed, or a little too impassioned for our modern taste. Yet, whenever we are tectonically moved by life, we reach for mythic language.

Consider George Harrison's wonderful ballad, "Something," which opens with an echo of the age-old belief in the preternatural power of attraction, from *attract*, to "draw near, allure." "Something in the way she moves," he sings, "attracts me like no other lover." Think about Anais Nin's remark about Henry Miller: "He moved me in every imaginable way." Dwell on the description of "The Divine Sarah Bernhardt," on stage in 1890s Paris, or the way that *The Film Dictionary* apotheosized Greta Garbo as the "dream princess of eternity." Or more recently, the way *Le Monde* reviewed Marion Cotillard, the actress who played the lead in *Edith Piaf* as "ethereal" for the way she conjured up the Goddess of Love and Desire. Wistfully, I remember Shelley Winters' reference to Marilyn Monroe as "the angel of love" when they worked together on *The Misfits*.

To keep up with my motile metaphor, I am stirred by these descriptions, reminded that they are rhapsodies on the theme of being moved by beauty and desire, reminding me, in turn, of the Arabian proverb: "All mankind is divided into three classes: those who are immovable, those who are movable, and those who move."

By her "gait," Voutier meant that she appeared to move. In fact, she evoked an early version of the movies. What moves has life, has spirit, has soul, has the capacity to fascinate us. "She came at me in sections," cracked Fred Astaire, of Cyd Charisse. "She was enchantment embodied," Nureyev said of Fonteyn.

So, what is it that moves around and through us if not love itself, the power, as Dante wrote in his immortalizing lines, "that moves the sun, the moon, and the stars."

We're still reaching for just the right metaphors to describe the indescribable, to *move* in with the right words for what *moves* us, the right name for what moves in us, the unexpected swerve in our lives. The rogueries of language save us from the dulling of the senses. The California poet Robinson Jeffers called the unexpected excess in art or craft "divinely superfluous beauty" when describing the obsidian tools found in the Paleolithic caves in northern Spain.

Let's all take a breath before going on.

What moves me now is something that moved Voutier that day in the cave on Melos, the result of a languorous shaping of stone by the sculptor to give the illusion of movement in the torque of her hips, the suggestion of reaching, and the intensity of her gaze. In that startling suggestion, *movement* was revealed, as was the artist's genius. Voutier got it. Of course, she doesn't move for everybody or even for you at first glance. It requires time and patience and not a little talent for *trompe l'oeil*. Voutier recognized the exaltation of love, beauty, and desire. The two Latin words he chose concealed a marvel—*patuit dea*. Like so many commentators from historians to philosophers and poets in classical times, the statue had a living, breathing quality, the dream of every sculptor worth his or her chisel.

At the mythic moment of her discovery, there in the cool of the cave, the Venus *was* a goddess, an otherworldly work that had been created as if in the act of stepping forward to reach for something. This is to say the stone appeared to be *moving*, that it was infused with spirit—the *winged thing*, as Plato called it, which is what the classical Greek word *psyche* meant, both soul and butterfly. The soul of art and poetry is what *moves* in it. The subtle suggestion of an illusion of movement cuts to the mystery of the statue and our story and the persistence of vision, which is really the persistence of the life force pouring through our art. Two thousand years earlier, the Greek poet Pindar wrote in an ode to the Colossus of Rhodes:

> The animated figures stand
> Adorning every public street
>
> And seem to breathe in stone, or
> Move their marble feet.

Not only could Pindar write lyrically about stone; he described it with the depth of conviction that comes only from deep observation. "On Aphrodite's festival day," he wrote, Pygmalion "made offerings at her altar and prayed for his ivory to change into a real woman."

At the heart of art is the movement of the spirit from one human being to another; the very essence of the power of art to *inspire* one another is the task of artists everywhere. The miracle of allowing someone else to feel a moment or millennia from what you feel—and can convey—right now. What could be more miraculous than that—to have felt for a moment what the sculptor felt as he carved this miraculous face? Tolstoy went as far as calling the phenomenon an "infection," a disturbing but accurate description that perfectly conveys the transmission of feeling from an artist to an observer, which may very well be the sibilant source of the shiver up the spine.

The British historian Bettany Hughes calls our attention to the female philosopher Diotima in Plato's *Symposium* with bas-relief-like prose. "Aphrodite's influence," she writes, "pushes her son Eros on the path to seek beauty. Desire is a quest for the beautiful—whatever the beautiful might be. Desire is the thing that makes us feel great about the world, therefore be great in it. It is the life force that spurs us on, to do, to be, to think..."

So *that's* why Marsilio Ficino, the Florentine Humanist, advisor to the Medicis, and Godfather of the Renaissance concluded in his *Commentary to Plato's Symposium*, "Love is the desire for beauty." If so, beauty may be, at heart, the desire for love. With those six words, Ficino condensed and compressed three thousand years of belief and devotion to Venus/Aphrodite, as well as the joy of everyday life in classical Greece.

For me, the true work of art is imbued with spirit or soul or love, an old-school way of saying that it appears to be *alive*. This is the secret of art, rendering the inanimate animate. Making paint, ink, stone *move*. Sheer technique is never enough, nor is craft. Aristotle declared, "Motion is the mode in which the future belongs to the present." If that isn't a miracle, what is? On the humorous side is Mae West's quip: "Sex is emotion in motion."

Any art that doesn't *move* us isn't art at all. It might be, the gods forbid, *interesting*; it might even be provocative. Worse, it could be trendy. But it ain't art. A failed Pygmalion is a Frankenstein in disguise. When asked about dancing, Margot Fonteyn said, "If I have learnt anything, it is that life forms no logical patterns. It is haphazard and full of beauties which I try to catch as they fly by, for who knows whether any of them will ever return?" To do that, we need to be alert to the signs around us that there is more than meets the eye but never more than meets the heart. To be moved, we must keep moving, not unlike the divine Sappho:

> Eros seizes and shakes my soul
> like the wind on the mountain
> shaking the ancient oaks.

As old and venerable as those love lyrics are, there are older ones, from Iraq, describing the attraction between a goddess and a shepherd:

> What I tell is the urge you
> Let the weaver weave
> Into song.

The blue-eyed soul singer from West Hampstead, Dusty Springfield, revealed her own exquisite vulnerability to Eros's arrows in a quivering, shivering vibrato that spoke to the universal sense of feelings of loneliness and love:

You don't have to say you love me, just be close at hand,
You don't have to stay forever I will understand,
Believe me, *believe me*, I can't help but love you.

There it is: the winged thing that moves me most about the Venus de Milo. The revelation that the Goddess of Love is herself loved by the one she is gazing at, the focus of her eros. The stone-cold irony that reveals the moment the enchanter herself has been enchanted. The instant, caught in stone, that informs the story of every pair of legendary lovers in history, from Helen and Paris to Abelard and Heloise, Elvis and Priscilla to Burton and Taylor. Despite their greatest efforts at resistance, *they can't help falling in love.* The Venus embodies the birth of the Western mythology of love and romance, the embodiment in stone of the spell of Aphrodite, the haplessness that riddles the heart of desire, the conundrum of the desire of the heart. The swoon-worthy L. A. soul group, The Incredibles, sang, "Bring your fine self on home / I'll make it easy."

When we gaze at her gaze, look inside her look, we see, as with all heart-bursting art, that we are looking into ourselves. The medieval troubadours called it the great "meeting of the eyes." The blues singer Doris Troy sang it this way in the soulful Sixties:

Just one look and I fell so *har-har-hard* / in love with you, oh, oh...
Just one look, hah, that's all it took, / whoa, just one look...

Years ago, I was doing some research in Galway, Ireland, and ventured into the West Country's beloved Kennys Bookshop. Serendipitously, I climbed upstairs into the poetry section on the second floor and pulled out the first volume my eyes landed on, an anthology of Northern Ireland poetry. I riffled the pages and found a passage in Seamus Heaney's introduction that he identified as "The Dublin Triad," a thousand-year-old poem that read: "This is it. / This is the thing. This is what you're up against."

Yes, this is it, this is the thing, this is what we're up against: the look, the surprise, the gasp of a sudden vision of the future. All because of the thing. The thing *felt* but not necessarily seen.

Sure, I am still intrigued by the mystery of the Venus's missing arms, but I'm obsessed by the focus of her gaze, the look of astonishment on her face, and the mystery of how she knows what she knows. Whenever I try to meet that look, in a photograph or reproduction of her in her gallery at the Louvre, I am transported and experience all over again the last look my grandmother gave me just before she passed away. The last look at the house I grew up in before moving into a miserable apartment. The last light of the setting sun on Venice Beach, California, the day I watched its rays turn from yellow to orange to a flash of green—*le rayon vert*, the flare of emerald on the horizon that Jules Verne used for his image of the divine light that hints at the promise of love.

The luminous look that leads to her story.

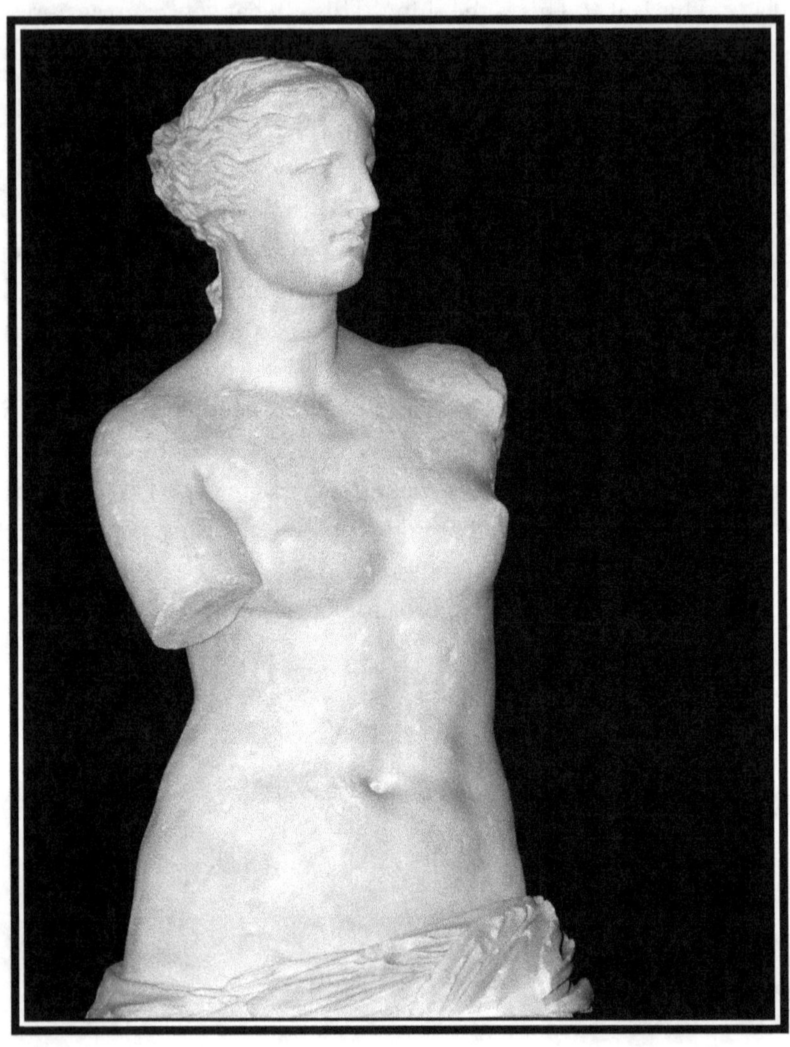

The Gaze that Launched a Thousand Ships
Musée du Louvre, Paris

SOMETIMES THE PAST LOOMS OVER US

Finally, the two halves of gleaming Parian marble fit smoothly back together. The goddess stood up straight and proud for the first time in fifteen hundred centuries. She loomed over the farmer and the soldier, looking good for her age, beautiful for the ages. She was nude from the waist up, and the bulge of her right shoulder and the angle of what remained of her upper right arm suggested that she had been pulling up the falling drapery of her robe that demurely covered her legs, a common theme among Greek sculptors for centuries. She was slightly scarred, with the tip of her nose and tip of her left breast broken off. Several coils of her *chignon*, or bundled hair, had snapped off and were missing. Her torso was scratched, abraded, and bruised, evidence of her fall from grace.

A short distance from her feet lay the base or plinth, which was incised with barely discernible Greek letters, fourteen words when translated into English, that had been nearly rubbed out by the sandpaper of time. Neither the farmer nor the soldier are on record as having mentioned what was carved into the plinth:

> *I, Alexandros of Antioch on the Maender River,*
> *son of Andros, carved this statue.*

Enfin, at last. Finally, we know who sculpted the Venus de Milo.

Together, the etched letters provide a name and a place for the creation of the Venus. Alexandros and Andros, the sculptor and his father, hailed from the ancient city of Antioch, one of the most vital cities in the Seleucid Empire, on the Maender River [later the Meander], on the west coast of what is now Turkey. Founded in 300 BCE by one of Alexander the Great's generals, Antioch reached a population of a half million and became a thriving center for the arts, rivaling Alexandria and Constantinople as the most important city in the Roman Empire and equally renowned for its sculpture and mosaics. Christine Kondoleon, curator of Greek and Roman Art at the Worcester Art Museum, wrote in *Minerva* magazine in 2001:

> The city had been founded only a century earlier, around 250 BCE, and became "the center of worship for holy relics and holy persons ... In many ways, Antioch provides a mirror to our own cities in its diversity of its people, the textures of its material culture, and the complexity of its intellectual and spiritual life. And so these words of Libanius have a special resonance for us today: "If a man had the idea of traveling all over the earth with a concern not to see how cities looked but to learn their individual ways, Antioch would fulfill his purpose and save him journeying. If he sits in our marketplace, he will sample every city; there will be so many people from each place with whom he can talk."

Around twenty-one hundred years ago, in that once noble city, now ravaged by wars and earthquakes, a marble-dusted competitive young man, Alexandros of Antioch, strove to achieve in his sculptor's studio, something new with stone, something unprecedented with the rendering of Aphrodite. Originality, uniqueness, infusion: these are a few of the elusive qualities of what has come to be called genius. It is no accident of language that the Greek phrase for "spirit of place," is *genius loci*. Together, the ancient belief in spirit comes together in marble and myth.

The uncanny ability to infuse his own spirit into the sumptuous curves of her evolving shape, praying in his own way that *her spirit would come alive.* How else could he win the competition against the other great sculptors from the studios of Pergamon, Paros, Naxos, and Athens?

Rereading this passage many years later, I am reminded of Seamus

Heaney's retrieval of the Irish bard's ancient Triad, the mystery declaration that *This is it*. The inscription found at the findspot on Melos reveals the long-lost, long-denied name of the sculptor, as well as his home, the river that runs through it, and the name of his father. But what followed later also reveals what I'm up against in terms of honoring that lineage.

In the brilliant sci-fi film *Arrival*, Ian Donnelly (Jeremy Renner), who plays a physicist, announces, "Here is what we know..." and goes on to deliver an incantatory recitation of the startling science behind the uncanny time-travel abilities of two heptapods, seven-limbed extraterrestrial, first-contact creatures that have descended by spacecraft onto a startled Earth. Together with his partner, the linguist Louise Banks (Amy Adams), he unravels the wondrous creatures' means of communication, palindromic phrases displayed as hypnotically beautiful swirls of inky calligraphy. At first, the scientists believe the messages are meant as a gift, but the translation is tragically misinterpreted by the military as a "weapon." Undeterred, Louise and Ian strive to break the code, unleashing in Banks a series of time-traveling flashbacks, bittersweet premonitions of a daughter who hasn't even been born yet. Eventually, she realizes that the ambiguous communication—their language—is a gift and as she learns it, her experience of linear time is forever altered. In turn, we learn that one person's gift is another's weapon.

So it is with art, including sculptures such as the Venus de Milo.

Once we learn—let's call it the language of stone—our experience of time is stretched, dilated, changed, which is to say the more I have explored this lapidary mystery, the more my perception of time deepens and widens, which have steadily altered the structure of these meditations. Watching this movie a dozen times influenced me with its mosaic-like narrative.

How else can I tell the story of how the Venus was created because of a competition and installed in an ancient Greek gymnasium? Who would have guessed? Only someone who traveled there.

❀

Let's board the Wayback Machine to Ancient Greece, which teemed with competitions in every imaginable endeavor, from athletics and acting to music, art, and sculpture. There were even drinking and kissing competitions. The champions were immortalized in the form of statues, murals, mosaics, poems, songs, and plays. This came about due to the Greek belief that it was human nature to be lazy, so people needed a prod, a goad, a *contest*, which they called an *agon*, to push us to greater heights, even if it was agonizing.

We know that there was a competition for a statue of Aphrodite to fit into one of three niches to be installed in the entrance to the new gymnasium on the island of Melos, which in turn was one of three hundred training sites for athletes and warriors that once stippled the ancient landscape. Sometime around 150 BCE, heralds were dispatched across the empire to announce a sculpture competition, similar to the one that occurred every four years to remind people about the upcoming Olympic Games. While dwelling in Antioch, Alexandros most likely studied at the city's leading school of sculptors, and possibly later, across the sea in Athens. The announcement of the competition on Melos seems to have prompted him to risk something innovative so his piece would stand out above the others, including his predecessors, such as Praxiteles, known for his Knidian Venus, by far the most famous work in the ancient world, and Polyclitus, who achieved fame by sculpting lifelike bronze statues in honor of victors at the Great Games in Olympia. Who knows, maybe Alexandros viewed Phidias's Venus on the frieze on the Parthenon or gazed upon a few of the innumerable mosaics that rendered her image. Perhaps he even read the "Hymn to Aphrodite" to her.

But inspiration only takes us so far.

What interests me far more now is how Alexandros seized the moment of the competition to make one of the most daring leaps forward in the early days of sculpture. While the universally praised Knidian Venus of Praxiteles might have been technically accomplished, burnished, and enticing, she was also demure, coy, and emotionless, closer to Canova than to Michelangelo. For reasons we can't possibly know from such a distance, Alexandros decided to go further, making his version of the Venus far more psychologically true to her role in ancient Greek mythology. By taking such strides, he found the streak of originality required of genius. He depicted the goddess as active not passive, reflective not reflexive, and aware of the paradox that lurks at the heart of such a cruel world, *Ola kala.* Everything that is beautiful. For an infinite moment, the slice of time is immortalized in his statue.

By shaping the moment, Alexandros became a sculptor who sang in stone.

What makes the Venus de Milo a work of genius is the combination of an ideal stillness and self-assurance—the Olympian detachment in the artist's portrayal of her face, shoulders, back, and breasts, with a few daring innovations that art historians call Hellenistic. Her lower torso turns and twists suggestively, yet her upper torso remains preternaturally still. To my eye, the Venus combines the beautiful *and* the sublime, stillness *and* movement, the light of innocence *and* the darkness of desire. She is also infused with the quality Japanese connoisseurs call *sabi,* a beautiful, rusty, worn, even oneiric quality.

My mind swerves again. I don't try to stop it; I trust it. It has a mind of its own.

This time, it moves to the Portuguese poet Fernando Pessoa, who described the role of the invisible forces at work in the world in his aptly named book *Always Astonished:* "Everything is something else, *besides.*" The great San Francisco poet Lawrence Ferlinghetti once told me over lunch at the Steps of Rome café in our North Beach neighborhood that it was his chance discovery of the French poet Antonin Artaud scribbling a simple poem on a napkin at Café de Flor in Paris that inspired him to become a poet. Together with his admiration for Pessoa's words about the role of awe and wonder, he was inspired to write one of his hallmark poems, "I am Waiting." As in: "I am waiting for a rebirth of wonder." Hearing the story from Ferlinghetti himself gave me the courage of my own convictions to intensify and clarify my own sense of amazement with every visit to the Louvre, or any other museum, theater, or seashore.

There is one other pertinent detail about Alexandros. According to ancient chronicles, he won a music contest for playing the lyre or flute. As usual, sources vary. Perhaps that is how he came to give us the equivalent of lyricism in stone. Everything else about him is lost in space and time, including who his model may have been and how he arrived at his vision for the statue.

If we go by the legends of the great Praxiteles or Phidias, he may have combined the features of several models, which was a common practice in classical times. The fourth-century artist Zeuxis was notorious for combining the most winsome features of several different women to achieve his painting of Helen of Troy, often referred to as the "most beautiful woman in the world." Likewise, Praxiteles may have taken the most winsome features from more than one woman to create his ideal of beauty when he sculpted the *Knidian Venus*, considered the first completely nude depiction of a goddess. It was so lifelike that the sculpture became the object of pilgrimages by art lovers from all over the empire. The likeness was considered so divine, the art pilgrims who came to the site spread the news all over the Greek Empire that the goddess herself must have appeared to him. Otherwise, how else could he have possibly made her so lifelike?

The more likely scenario was that Praxiteles hired Phryne, the legendary beauty and enticing courtesan, to pose for the first fully nude statue in ancient Greece. Another possibility is that Alexandros could have employed a courtesan, a *hetaera*, in Greece, or two along the way since they were the most accessible models of the day. Nonetheless, legend has it that the most notorious prostitute of antiquity was the model for some of the most beloved Greek paintings, such as those by the fourth-century Apelles of Kos, as well as statues. Andre Malraux, the French minister of culture, delivered a cross-the-centuries *bon mot* when he said, "Marlene Dietrich is not an actress like Sarah Bernhardt. She is a myth like Phryne."

Posing for artists and sculptures was big business in ancient times. One of the many rewards for winning at the original Olympic Games was being sought out after the competition to serve as a model for the marble and bronze statues of the gods. Virtually every statue of Zeus, Hermes, Ares, Odysseus, and others was inspired by the "fleet-footed" and victorious runners, discus throwers, boxers, and wrestlers. Their mythic proportions, so to speak, were regarded as possessing *kalokagathia*, the beautiful and the good, as befits a god or goddess.

I prefer to think Alexandros was searching for a *shape* to make his own unique version of Venus stand out, as if in bas-relief to the other entries, a shape to speak to the sensibilities of the day. Then he carved the goddess with a confident hand, capturing her held-breath moment, barely able to breathe, stiller than stone itself. What is startling here is that the sculptor surmised—on very little textual proof as most of the ancient commentators were markedly misogynistic—that Venus was moved, touched, in a palpably human way, and vulnerably so.

Consider how the English sculptor Henry Moore described his profession twenty-one centuries later: "A sculptor is a person who is interested in the shape of things, a poet in words, a musician by sounds." Or sculptor John B. Flannagan, who wrote ardently about his task of finding, at all costs, "the image in the rock," which only came to him if he followed "a stirring impulse from the depth of the unconscious."

The names, dates, and dimensions tell us *what* the statue is, but not what it means. Only the swerve into the force field of the Venus de Milo tells us what her eloquent silence signifies.

To me, the Venus de Milo's gaze is to sculpture what the Mona Lisa's smile is to painting and Emily Dickinson's dashes are to poetry. While Leonardo rendered La Gioconda, the daughter of the prince, from her sittings in his Milan studio, Alexandros, the genius behind the Venus de Milo carved an utterly original impression of one of the most beloved myths of his own time—the Judgment of Paris—capturing the essence of the bittersweet gift of the enchantment of love. The gaze of the Venus de Milo probes us while suggesting how we might *actually* live our lives, as all great art does, such as what Bob Dylan said of Woody Guthrie's songs: "You could actually learn how to live."

I would venture to say we make art to save us from a life of abstraction.

Sometimes it is hard to distinguish between losing the thread of a story and following it through the dank corridors of the labyrinth. All those words and images are necessary for us to learn how to live with a little more life. To picture the Venus, it helps to imagine her as a dreamlike character, as the depiction of the origin of our own wild desires. To truly appreciate her—and to imagine the moment Voutier and Yorgos appreciated her—listen to what Ovid wrote in the *Heroides*. Venus says, "I give you the *gift of love*." The operative word is *gift*. The Roman poet conjured such words and sentiments after reading the original Greek texts and presumably from gazing upon the innumerable Roman copies of Venus in Rome before his exile. What he detected was a glimmer of the inspiration that must have fired the heart of the Antioch sculptor of the statue that landed on Melos.

Every detail here matters; each image fits into our story. Each stone props up a nearby stone. The words have been carefully carved and burnished. There are no accidental details. These are the ruins of an abandoned story, so every fragment matters. Every piece is necessary for the cryptic puzzle that is the history of this overfamiliar statue, which needs to be unfamiliarized if we are to see it for what it really is. We are searching for a grander narrative. What remains, remains for a reason. What disappears leaves sometimes for no reason at all unless you count benign neglect or a disdain for the pagan past. You pick up the hints with the tweezers of the imagination, examine them, and see which ones fit into the bigger picture. Some fit; some don't. Some you toss; the rest you use as best you can. But you do have to choose between competing stories. You're trying to make sense out of what's missing by piecing together the fragments that have survived, puzzling out the larger picture, as Teilhard de Chardin wrote about the role of the archaeologist in *Hymn to the Universe*: "Driven by the forces of love, the fragments of the world seek each other so that the world may come to being."

These are the forces that fascinate me. I am digging for the truth which has haunted me for more than fifty years and which haunted the Greeks for more than two thousand. Pieces, bits, shards are what we usually find. Fragments that might shore up the ruins of memory, as Eliot dramatized. If we aren't careful, we can cut ourselves on them. If we're too careful, we never learn to read them.

"Life is one long struggle to disinter oneself," wrote Dame Rose Macaulay in *The Pleasure of Ruins*, "to keep one's head above the accumulations, the ever-deepening layers of objects...which attempt to cover one over, steadily, almost irresistibly, like falling snow." She added, "Nothing, perhaps, is strange once you have accepted life itself, the great strange business which includes all lesser strangeness." I think of Sir Francis Bacon's uncanny perception, "There is no excellent beauty that hath not some strangeness in the proportion." And I feel the courage of my convictions that art is the making of something the world has never seen—or felt—before.

Speaking of the passing strange, in 1995 I was lecturing about the mythology of Mediterranean cultures on the Seabourn Spirit as we sailed from

Athens to Istanbul. One salty morning, I chanced upon a startling photograph on the front page of the English edition of a Greek newspaper in the ship's oak-shelved library. Staring back at me was a weather-wizened fisherman. Above him blared the headline: "ANCIENT SEA GODDESS DISCOVERED." This story turned out to be about a sailor off the coast of Alexandria, Egypt, who had recently hauled up a statue of Aphrodite in his fishing net, which had been underwater for fifteen centuries. The oddest thought occurred to me—that she had been lost, missing, as long as the Venus de Milo had gone missing. "This is why we call her," the fisherman said, referring to the salt-sprayed sea, "the blue museum."

Missing like most of our memories. I think of where I came from, my own myth, which is to say my origin story, the one that provides me with meaning. I think not just of my French-Canadian background but of our basement. The framed photo of the VDM, the ping-pong table that I played on to speed up my reflexes for basketball, the spaceship that led to a lifelong fascination with science-fiction, the dinosaur models from Ford's Disney exhibit at the 1964-65 New York World's Fair. The coal cellar where I stacked canned food in case of a nuclear attack. The incinerator, whose guttural roars kept me awake at night. The hundreds of *National Geographic* magazines my father collected from antique stores.

My father's framed magazine photograph of the Venus cemented my lifelong fascination with Greek myth because it contains the intriguing overlap of art, psychology, and aesthetics, which is to say, the indispensable exploration of the beautiful and my own living out of the ancient dream of walking and circling the things and people I love.

We begin by wandering in search of ourselves and end up walking each other home.

That's the beauty of it.

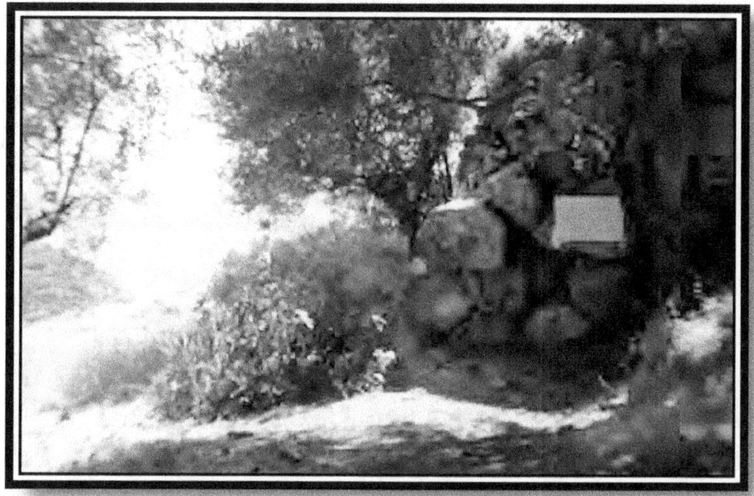

The Findspot of the Venus de Milo and Commemorative Plaque
Melos, Greece, 2004

THE SECRET SIGNS

Melos, August 2004. Late afternoon. The sea calm, the sky a blue shimmer, the wind a cool thrill. I love being back in the Greek islands. I find it easier for my mind to quiet down, my heart softening enough to immerse myself in the elemental beauty.

I bounce across the island on my rented ATV. It feels enlivening to read from the Greek thesaurus of sunlight, which the gods published in many volumes over the millennia, augmented by a single slim scroll devoted to rain. I traveled here on a sea-skimming ferry from Piraeus after attending the Athens Games for ten days in celebration of the publication of my book on the history of the Olympics. I've just enjoyed the sly pleasure of strolling around the Plaka after midnight looking for a cold Mythos beer and noticing several American athletes reading my work while sipping their own beers. During the ten-day celebration, I watched Rulon Gardner, an unheralded farm boy from Utah, take down a Soviet wrestler who hadn't lost a match in twelve years to win the gold medal in heavyweight wrestling. The Lithuanians beat their archrivals, the Russians, in basketball. The Chinese and Koreans waged a fierce battle for the table tennis championship. A fierce water polo match ensued between the British and the Canadians. And the women's twenty-kilometer racewalk was won by Greece's own Athanasia Tsoumeleka, with a grand finish in the Panathenaic Stadium, originally built in 330 BCE by Lycurgus. The Great Games, as the ancients referred to them, had been a deliriously fun celebration of *arête*, excellence, effort, and courage, which overshadowed most of the inevitable commercialism. My love of sports was rekindled, and even more importantly, my belief was restored in the soaring possibilities of living the good life, or better, the *excellent* one.

The past isn't prologue, as the man said; it isn't even past. It's infinite. You can see it in the face of the Venus de Milo if you hold your breath and try to imagine what she's looking at.

Time roars like a lion here. I'm in the mood to visit the site of the discovery of the Venus de Milo, transcendence in stone, in the *findspot*, as archaeologists refer to such sites. To see it for myself. I park on the dirt shoulder of the old Roman road that once ran by the site. There isn't a soul in sight. Nothing but the buzz of insects, the searing heat of the afternoon, the play of light on the silvery green leaves of the nearby olive trees.

A miraculous line from Laurence Durrell's poem, "On Ithaca," comes to mind, words that draw my ever-wandering attention back to the heart of things that hum all around me: "Tread softly, for here you stand / On miracle ground, boy."

All this, as Rose Macaulay put it in *The Pleasure of Ruins*, "makes for that melancholy delight so eagerly sought, so gratefully treasured, by man in his brief passage down the corridor of time, from which, looking this way and that, he may observe such enchanting chambers of the past." That phrase about the melancholy that is "so eagerly sought" slays me, bringing with it a kind of vindication for my own relishing of the blue moods that have come over me all my life.

Slowly wilting in the heat, I pull down the wide brim of my floppy white traveler's hat, faintly reminiscent of the messenger god Hermes's winged hat, or *petasos*, and walk past the last remnants of the ancient city walls that soar twenty feet high. Beyond the dark red volcanic rock walls, I shuffle down an old cobbled Roman road for a few hundred yards. Walking on, I wonder about the millions of visitors who have tramped this road, from peasants to pirates, soldiers to athletes. Did they think the island and sea were *beautiful* in the way we do now?

Peering down a long stretch of unusually flat land, about a few hundred meters long, is where the fates of Voutier and Yorgos came together like the overlapping circles of a Venn diagram. Each of them happened to be searching for stone on the same day in the same place. I feel a swarm of *saudade*, the untranslatable Portuguese word for the strange melancholic longing after something or somebody that may never have existed. An absence so intense it may become the greatest presence in your life. The word arose to describe the yearning of the wives and lovers left behind by their seafaring men during the Age of Exploration. The intensely nostalgic word describes the soul-rattling longing that hits me today while roaming around these ancient ruins, whatever they are.

Somehow this longing is connected to the Venus de Milo, more specifically what she is missing. Or as it occurs to me now, what I am missing in my own life. How strange, this palpable immediacy of the findspot. For the first time, I feel *where it all began*, which is the heart of mythic thinking. I have felt this telltale *frisson* before, while standing before Cezanne's *Mont-Sainte Victoire* at the Louvre, Frida Kahlo's *Self-Portrait*, in Mexico City, and

Matisse's *Jazz* cut-outs at the Detroit Institute of Art. How can I vividly re-member each of these magnetized moments and not remember where I set the car keys in the motel room?

Soulful encounters with stone stir up oneiric images and ancestral memories, reminding us of the peace that still lurks in the heart of the world. For one of the two men, stone was dead, or at best, utilitarian, mere building blocks. For the other, the discovery was a numinous moment. Each needed the other, or we could never have all the posers and postcards and chance placements in movie backgrounds.

"Same, same, but different," as the waiter in Saigon described his in-scrutable menu to my brother Paul and me when we were vagabonding in Southeast Asia too many years ago. Same as it ever was, as the Talking Heads sang. *Plus ca change, plus c'est le meme chose*, as my Great-Grandfather Charlemagne used to repeat again and again on his overstuffed couch in Windsor, Ontario, while rolling a cigarette with one hand, sipping from his scotch glass with the other. *The more things change, the more they stay the same.* Still holding court at 97 about his life as a *voyageur*, when he paddled his birch-bark canoe from Ontario to the Yukon, he told us in a thick-as-custard French-Canadian accent that he traveled as far as necessary to find *"Le grande beauté dieu."*

"God's great beauty," my father later translated for me in the family Ford Falcon as we drove back to Detroit. Looking back, I know now where he learned his habit of sighing *beautiful* when we gazed at the night sky, the autumn colors, or the green grass of Tiger Stadium.

Here on Melos, I need to translate what this icon of ancient art means for us today. I squint in the harshening light and stumble over the long walls that line the hillside, knocking a few stones off and then respectfully replacing them. Then wondering why because it doesn't seem like anyone has visited the site for a while. My heart races. I feel like I've been intimate friends with the Venus for years and writing about her for longer than I want to admit, and now I'm standing on the spot where she was discovered by Voutier, the "accidental archaeologist," and Yorgos, the fortune-favored farmer. My feet tingle, as they often do at sites like this. It might be the prickle of nostalgia or my body's way of detecting a real presence, the numinous force that comes over us when we have a moment of reckoning with the way things always were and still are if we slow down and experience it.

Then again, I may just be a fool for love, the love of old things, the old stories.

Once more, I think about my father. I wish we could have walked together here. He introduced me to Homer and the classics when I was a boy and loved teaching word origins such as *nostalgia*. It was from the Greek, he instructed me, the *nostois*, the coming-home stories of Greek sailors, and *algia*, pain. "Be careful, son," he said in a mock ominous voice. "It hurts too much to be too nostalgic," a phrase that has baffled me ever since.

Today, I am walking around the delightfully named "findspot," which is surrounded by gnarled olive trees that glint silver in the light. I take a few photographs, scribble a few notes, sketch the stones and olive trees in my travel journal. As I record the moment, a reflected truth slams into me, which I read in an essay by Camus: "An artist's task is no more than rediscovering the first one or two images that opened his heart." This robust insight has always moved me, but what occurs to me now is how I found it, in a book sent by my father to me because he was worried that I was throwing my life away while painting those forty-four Victorian houses in San Francisco. It paid the bills for seven years but could also be filed under Procrastination because it meant I wasn't writing anything significant. He was telling me, however obliquely, that I needed to own up to what I loved most as a kid and that I needed to learn to trust those things. Art, books, travel, baseball. He was sending a signal to me that my love of those things would yank me back to the present moment and then hurtle me ahead into the future to encounter my fate somewhere other than a construction site.

Gazing at the very spot where Voutier and Yorgos met, my vision splits in two.

On the scrim of my mind, I see two screens, one here on Melos, the other a montage of beauty. There, I see the Van Gogh self-portrait down at the Detroit Institute of Arts, Vermeer's *The Milkmaid*, the copy of *Moby Dick* with the engravings by Rockwell Kent we read out loud together as a family, the 1962 Topps baseball card of Al Kaline in mid-swing at Old Tiger Stadium.

Each turn of the zoetrope of memory brings an image that transports me far away from the grimoire world of the warzone I grew up in and couldn't escape from fast enough.

I am trying to recover those lost images, like the bronze statues hauled up from the bottom of the sea, slowly, carefully, for fear they will be lost again. I'm trying like hell to open my heart, which may be why I cannot get this statue out of my mind, out of my life. If I can unravel this mystery, I might be able to uncoil the twisted rope of my life, the mirroring of souls being one of the inexplicable strengths of art. To help evoke the atmosphere of the place, I pull out of my thirty-year-old leather satchel a book of modern Greek poetry by Yannis Ritsos, which I bought in a musty gift shop in Ancient Olympia, and read a poem of his called "Working Class Beauty":

Ah, yes, the world is beautiful. A man beneath the trees
wept from the joy of love. He was stranger than death, that man —
which is why we sing...
No one will silence our song. We sing on.
The world is beautiful, we insist
Beautiful, beautiful, beautiful—and we sing on.

The poet's words crisscross time, stun this very place. A part of me resists. My throat clenches. What of the insanity of war, the curse of children born crippled? My mind whips back to Philip Levine, the sure-as-steel, working-class poet from my Detroit, born the same year as my father, who worked in the same Ford factories where my dad led VIP tours for the likes of Gene Kelly, Queen Elizabeth, Van Gogh's nephew, the Japanese ambassador, and the entire Detroit Tigers team. Once Levine escaped the factory hell-holes that I came to learn all too well, he went looking for the "simple bread of truth." I skip through a few more pages and read: "Life is after all so simple. So beautiful." It is not the pretty that distracts but the beautiful that attracts. Pulls us toward the mystery that pervades life, the works that save us from despair. I hear the summons in Ritsos's verses, and feel a need to answer him like a crusty old blues musician with a call-and-response of my own in a poem called "Sleeping Beauties," which later appeared in my collection, *The Blue Museum*:

> The ancient mapmakers warned, "Hic Sunt Dracones,"
> "Here be dragons," and drew sea monsters and serpents,
> basilisks and cannibals, into the uncharted areas of their maps,
> as a way to warn ship captains of potential dangers,
> to be avoided or destroyed. Other cartographers,
> more generous and poetic, imagined the uncharted seas
> as inhabited by "sleeping beauties," mysterious lands
> where glorious creatures were waiting to be
> awakened, embraced, loved.

I reach for the bottle of Zigori water that's dangling from my belt, then reach into my leather satchel for my journal, which is earmarked with a yellowed magazine clipping, a *Time* magazine essay by Roger Rosenblatt dated May 20, 2002. I have underlined a passage in red ink in which he cites

Susan Orlean, author of *The Orchid Thief*:

> I was starting to believe that the reason it matters to care passion-
> ately about something is that it whittles the world to a more man-
> ageable size. It makes the world seem not huge and empty, but
> full of possibility. The exclusionary element of an obsession also
> implies what the obsession includes. In other words, tunnel vision
> takes in the tunnel... I wonder if the heart of the matter isn't the
> heart of the matter—the obsessed one detects a secret hidden in
> the object of his excessive desire, the essence of the Beanie Baby,
> of the orchid, of the girl. And that this secret, once unearthed,
> will tell the obsessor what no one has ever been told...

Why did I snip this passage out of the magazine and then carry it around with me for two years? For that matter, why have I bothered to cut out dozens of newspaper clips and copy quotes from movies and lectures? Why do I cart around my son's boyhood sketch of Alexandros's masterwork, which he nicknamed "The Genius de Milo"?

I need the prompts and can use daily and nightly reminders that stories matter. I need to remember never to forget images that have opened my heart. But I'm human. Too often, I am afraid of forgetting the things that truly matter to me most. I admit I fear that I haven't used the time that's been allotted to me, despite my work ethic, my lifelong tendency to stretch my days out by living on as little sleep and as much work as possible. No one has said it better than Keats: "I fear that I will cease to be before my pen has gleaned my teeming brain."

This is what happens to my pinballing brain when I start thinking about the Venus. My brain teems. My mind gleans. My heart asks why I am still trying to plumb the depths of this one strangely sinuous statue.

Stuffing the poetry book into my back pocket I take a swig of my bottled water and saunter out onto the long flat field, wondering what on earth the statue was doing here, then I dive into my backpack for another book, one by the classicist David L. Miller on the history of the Olympics that makes my hair stand on end. Am I standing in the ruins of an ancient villa that she once decorated, a common use of statuary in both Greek and Roman times? I look over the magnificent sea, two hundred feet below the cliff at the end of the field, catch just a glimpse of the ancient Roman amphitheater, then ponder for a moment over whether this was the site of a nearby temple, since this was often the case in ancient Greek cities.

I am in heaven. Sanctuaries like this make me want to live forever. I think of the stage actress Marian Seldes, who wrote, "Joy has to move, and joy needs a witness," and the powerful Cretan idea of *kefi*, the passionate explosion of joy often rendered in Kazantzakis's novels and poems.

At heart, this search for the Venus brings me such joy.

Back in the whitewashed Nikolas House near the harbor, built by the Mathioudakis family two hundred years ago, only a few years before the Venus was discovered, I play an old Luke Kelly song, "Raglan Road," penned by the Irish poet Patrick Kavanagh, on a battered CD player in the kitchen. A fire flares in my heart. Kelly's whisky-addled voice reverberates in my head. I hear what the old Mississippi blues singers called the *yaarrgghh*, the gut-bucket truth of our sorrow-stricken lives, which are made endurable by flares of love and beauty:

> By dint and tint I never did stint,
> I gave her the secret signs,
> I gave her poems to sing.

Somehow that fits here. The history of the place taunts me, inspiring me to decipher the details and pass them on. Strange, this sense of unrest when one is happy alone as if happiness is only possible with two or more, with the sharing of a moment of glory, a moment when all creation sings to us.

To me, the Venus de Milo is likewise one of the secret signs, a sly wink of fate, a nod of the gods, the original meaning of *numinous*. I am transfixed by her. I want to decipher her myriad meanings and pass them on, like the dark-haired lover in the Kavanagh poem. His biographer reveals how he wandered around Ireland "drunk with beauty, with loneliness and the presence of God," and taught himself how to describe with great simplicity and candor the unearthly beauty of the world. His search never ended because he was "looking for a beauty beyond beauty."

I should be more precise, approximation being the bane of poets. I need to admit that I have come to be more focused on the Venus de Milo's *gaze* than on those damned *missing arms*, and the museum politics of cultural propaganda that turned her into a world icon for beauty, a tool for the ridiculous two-hundred-year-long argument about whether we truly need beauty—or if it is a bourgeoise affectation.

I say this as if we have a choice. A day without beauty is like a day without love. Who would want to live without either one? Show me someone who lives without it, in their home, personal fashion, or choice of art and culture, and I'll show you a lonely, isolated person. I have followed the wistful gaze of the Venus for years hoping against hope that it would lead me to the truth about the spirit that informs her and reforms me every time I look at her looking at me. I have to believe that her gaze, half-wistful, half-mournful, will lead me to the story that inspired her, the myth that scholars say has inspired more art than any other story from ancient times.

DRAWING ON THE BEAUTY OF THE WORLD

In 1939, the illustrious French author Jean-Paul Alaux described in *La Venus de Milo et Olivier Voutier* how the young naval officer had been *frappe*—"struck"—by what he saw. "Well prepared by his studies and by his taste for Greek antiquities," he wrote, "Voutier was moved by the beauty of the torso and sensed that the discovery was going to have great interest for Art."

Moved by the beauty.

Our grand theme. No need to get excited about what is merely pretty or idealized or trendy. If we're honest with ourselves, we want the real thing, the beautiful, the encounter that makes life worthwhile. The real deal makes us tremble, feel a little more tender with the world. It certainly beats the alternative, to feel moribund, half-alive, and cynical about anything uplifting, such as beauty.

The proud and patriotic Alaux pointed out that his fellow countryman, Voutier, was ready, as in educated, to see the statue for what it was and what it was worth. To be educated means more than the accumulation of knowledge. Originally, it held the meaning of being *educare*, drawn out, pulled out of one's isolated self and toward society. Alaux suggests that Voutier was educated enough to recognize genius when he saw it, even though the statue was incomplete, stained, nicked, battered, even mutilated. First identifying it and then attempting to save it, he anticipated the Polish poet Adam Zagajewski by a hundred and sixty or so years, who challenged us to "praise the mutilated world."

Knowing his art history, Voutier recognized that this statue was potentially beautiful enough to replace three of the Louvre's proudest statues, the Venus de Medici, the Apollo Belvedere, and the Laocoon, which the museum had been forced to return to Italy four years before as part of the post-Napoleon peace negotiations among France, Italy, and Belgium. One contemporary visitor remarked that the losses had left the Louvre "bereft."

Years ago, I got a sense of that strange form of cultural loneliness when I visited the National Museum in Sofia, Bulgaria. For three hours, I was the only visitor, wandering around in the near-dark, waking up the only guard in the building, and disappointed in how many vitrines and cabinets were empty. I can sympathize with the visitor at the Louvre whose disappointment at the paucity of art has foreshadowed the ambiguous nature of collectors and curators ever since.

Nothing in the recorded accounts about the moment of the Venus's discovery suggests that the young sailor lusted after the statue for fame or profit. Quite the opposite. Instead, he wanted to present it as a *gift* to his homeland, to France, not in a foppish act of patriotism but in the spirit of *le mission de civilitrice*, the ardent French belief in culture, including all of the arts, the very heart and soul of civilized life. Hence, the image of "the foam-born" goddess embodying a beautiful force from the beyond the visible, described by the surrealist playwright Eugène Ionesco: "Beauty is a precarious trace that eternity causes and is a manifestation of eternity."

The breath of the beautiful keeps us human.

CHASING AFTER BEAUTY

Voutier was spurred to track down someone on the island who had the authority to quickly negotiate for the statue. "He had to act immediately," wrote Alaux. "Without losing an instant, he ran to warn the consular agent, Mr. Brest." Leaving the farmer and his shipmates behind in the cave, Voutier scrambled up the switchback trails to the Kastro, the dirt-laned, whitewashed town perched like a crow's nest on the island's highest hill. When he arrived, he asked around until he found the simple home of the French vice-consul, Louis Brest. Because Brest had minimal duties to perform on the island, it didn't take much cajoling to convince him to accompany Voutier back down the humpbacked hill in the direction of

Yorgos's cave. In a dashing touch, Brest dressed in top hat and tails for what portended to be an important international encounter.

According to Alaux, the ensign Voutier decided to split off when they reached the crossroad outside town and dashed back to the harbor, where he caught a small boat back to the *Estafette*. Once on board, he fetched an album of blank paper and pencil from his cabin then changed, perhaps because he learned of Brest's attire, into similar evening dress, as shown in the engraving [following page]. With his simple sketching tools in hand, Voutier raced back to Yorgos's swatch of land and the cave that had opened like a portal into the past.

Tonight, under a quicksilver moon, I retraced Voutier's footsteps from the Kastro to the Cave and marveled at the soldier's decision to mark the moment, feeling it was equal to the creative urge seen throughout history, from paleolithic cave art to inner-city graffiti. Emily Dickinson's haunting words came to me as I walked along cobbled roads laid down by the Romans in the second century: "Forever—is composed of Nows," an exquisite updating of that ancient Greek observation of "the infinite now."

On the night of April 11, 1820, the day after the discovery, vice-consul Brest was anxiously waiting for Voutier. Barely an hour after the officer had bolted from the cave, he was back again, leading Brest to the marble statue. While the vice-consul contemplated the statue with uncertain eyes and dubious concern, the ensign rustled around in his rucksack for the pad and pencil he'd brought from the ship. Today we might whip out a smartphone, or maybe a single-lens reflex camera. In those days, most educated people knew how to draw because of the widespread belief in the power of the *aide-de-memoire*.

Quickly, Voutier made four simple sketches of the two halves of the

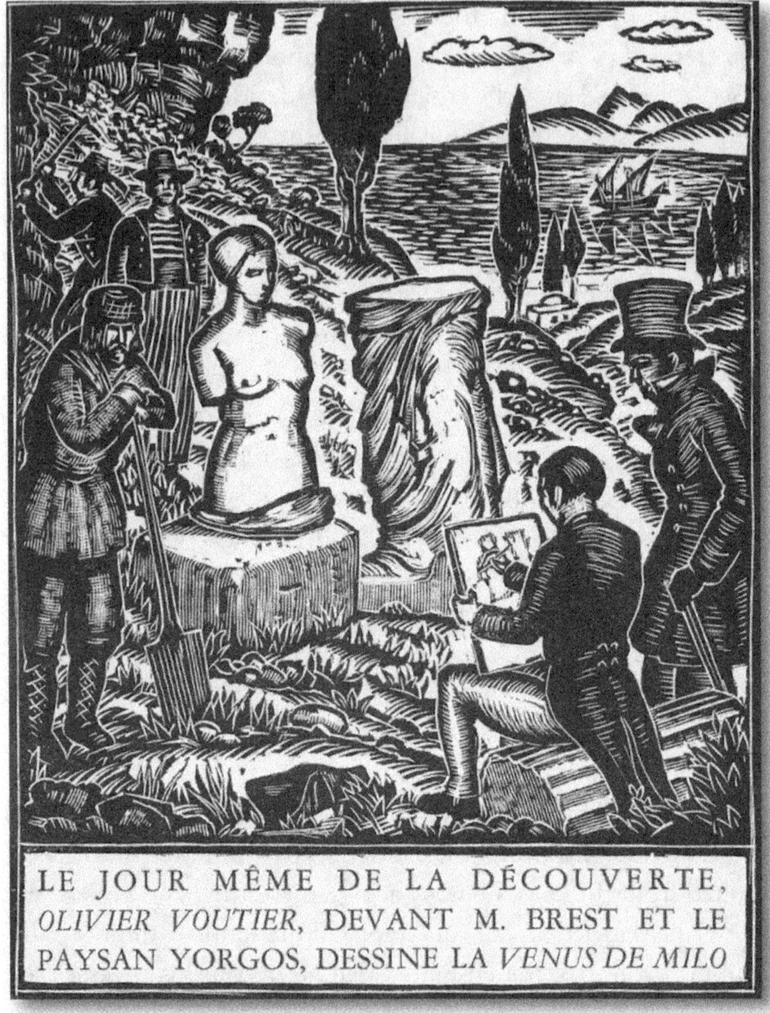

"The day of the discovery. Olivier Voutier, next to Msr. Brest
and the peasant Yorgos, draws the Venus de Milo"
—Jean-Paul Alaux, engraving by Gustave Alaux, 1939

Venus and the herms. His pencil glided across the paper as naturally as a traditional fishing boat moving across the still waters of a harbor. There was inerrant confidence in his rendering. No hesitancy, no self-consciousness. He wasn't trying to be an artist; he was recording the moment, in the original sense of the word *recorder*, to move through the heart. Sometimes in a grand painting, rarely in four simple drawings, is the essence of something revealed, the reality of a thing revealed in the here and now, its *thisness*, the quiddity, essence, or the Berard Brothers' *What it is!*

Consider the observation of English novelist Joyce Cary of *The Horse's Mouth* fame, who wrote in *Art and Reality*, "Everything contemplated in its own essence is said to be beautiful and to give pleasure." Consider, too, that Venus/Aphrodite represented the utter chaos of creation coming together in a beautiful order, expressed by her always bearing a smile, always flush with love. Let's give belated credit to Voutier for his far-from-academic exercise. His drawings are proof of what he saw and what he rescued from oblivion. Here are the contour lines he left behind:

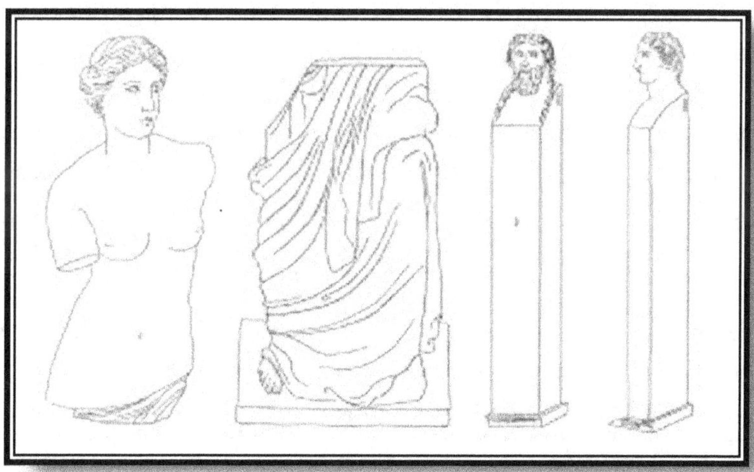

The upper and lower halves of the Venus de Milo
and herms of Herakles and Hermes
Olivier Voutier, April 1820

Voutier's simple four lines are alive. Elegantly simple, evoking for me the elemental lines of Picasso's "Dove of Peace," which became the logo of the United Nations, the grievous power of Kathe Kollwitz's "Home Worker," or Raphael's miraculously simple "Head of a Muse." Who knows what Voutier was thinking; he never wrote about this moment. But he did find enough clarity to sketch her cleanly and swiftly. Four drawings, that's all they are—simple, crisp enough to capture the truth of the moment. But they do capture the truth of the moment. No hesitancy, all conviction. His lines are straight and true. If you look at them again—the very essence of the word *regard*—you see an echo of Paul Klee's impish observation that drawing is no more than taking a line out for a walk. Movement in lieu of immobility, motion instead of inertness. The way Georgia O'Keefe emphasized the dark lines beneath one of her monumental flower paintings, rendered large enough so her viewers "could not ignore its beauty."

So, too, with the French ensign's drawing. His sketches are an easy walk in the country. It's as if the cool clear light of the Greek islands was eyewash for him, freeing him up to render exactly what he saw, which makes it a luxuriant moment. No more, no less—more or less.

Voutier sketched, and as he did, he left ghostly traces of his encounter, evocative for me of the early photographs of subatomic particles. Here one moment, gone the next. Regard Voutier's lines, then look again. His pencil moved quickly and with resolve to reveal what he saw. He was no Leonardo, no Raphael, but who is? No one, nobody. But he did *notice*, which is a holy thing. He imbued something into the sketches that was ineffable, what Matisse called "the desire of the line," a subtle recognition that the pencil and paper often know more than the artist of where the drawing should lead. I'm reminded of the pianist Bill Evans, who described Miles Davis's playing for the classic album, *Kind of Blue*, as *suibokuga*, a reference to the medieval Japanese style of painting that demands uninterrupted strokes with the brush so that the lines won't "break through the parchment" and "erasures or changes" are impossible.

Did Voutier make those drawings because he thought the statue and the nearby herms deserved to be recorded for posterity? Or was it simply a case of the old traveler's reflex to try to preserve a moment, to honor an experience that left a deep impression, the creation of an *aide-de-memoire*, the reason we might pull out a camera today? I think Voutier was counting on Brest being the only person on the island who wielded the legal power to buy it and thought that he might eventually be able to show the sketches to the French ambassador in Constantinople to persuade him to purchase the statue. According to Voutier's recollection, *"Tout en dessinant ces noble debris..."*

> "While drawing the noble fragments, I decided to ask our vice counsel [Brest] to promptly buy them. But the proprietor of the cave [Yorgos] demanded 400 *piasters*, and the good M. Brest asked me hopefully: 'Are you sure I am going to get reimbursed?'"

For the young ensign, drawing wasn't so much an aesthetic exercise as an attempt at artistic persuasion—and a delightful example of synchronicity since Aphrodite is the Goddess of Erotic Persuasion, the personification of the power that compels lovers to change their minds or hearts. On that red-letter day on Melos, in 1820, it was Voutier's task to persuade Brest to act from his intuition and grant his authority to buy the statue from Yorgos outright.

As Voutier drew, he dreamed. The result is oneiric. I think here of an elder of the Wardaman people in Australia, the artist and author Bill Yi-dumduma Harney, who I interviewed along with Stephen Aizenstadt, a dream therapist from the Pacifica Graduate Institute, for *Global Spirit*, a PBS documentary series that I hosted. Harney described his artwork to me as a kind of waking dream but informed by ancestors. "My painting *is* my dreaming, Phil," he said after filming. I feel the same tremor now, writing these words, as I did that day in the studio, and never thought of art the same way.

Dreaming with his eyes wide open, Olivier Voutier left a hypnagogic vision on paper that we can look at now if we wish to relive the excitement of the moment of discovery, capturing, among other things, a hint of the evidence that in works such as the Venus de Milo the Greeks seemed to *suddenly* see beauty everywhere. Her creator, Alexandros of Antioch, was an enchanted realist.

"*Skias onar Anthropos*," wrote Pindar in his last ode, "Man is but a dream of a shadow."

The seventeenth-century Spanish poet Pedro Calderon de la Barca took that oneiric image out for a walk when he wrote, "What is life? An illusion, a shadow, a story. And the greatest good is little enough, for all life is a dream, and dreams themselves are only dreams." And who can forget The Chords' (and later the Crew-Cuts') doo-wop version of "Sh Boom," which croons, "Life is but a dream, sweetheart. / It's what you make it. / Always try to give / Don't ever take it... And I dream of you. / Strange as it seems / All night I see you." And the immortal Emily Dickinson: "We dream—it is good we are dreaming— / It would hurt us—were we awake—" And Christina Rossetti: "I dream of you, to wake: would that I might / Dream of you and not wake but slumber on..."

I am stretching my imagination with these poetry calisthenics. I am trying to understand the secret power of this dreamy sketch, a shadow of the real thing, the lesson that the sculptor was trying to teach with every stroke of his chisel, every burnish of the marble: *Choose me; choose love, choose life.* With only a few deft strokes, Voutier reveals her upper torso in one of her standard poses, turned slightly to the left. A flourish of further strokes renders her coiled hair and a coolly determined face. Her gaze is remote but not indifferent; cool but not cold; elevated but not superior, wistful but not simpering. She is grateful but not surprised, thoughtful but not abstract, self-conscious but not vain. What or who is she looking at? A lover, a prince, a god? The war she unleashed with her spellbinding beauty? A hint of the price we have paid for rushing into love?

When we draw spontaneously, we embark on "a journey of pleasure;" we learn something about ourselves and the world we wouldn't learn any other way. We draw when we are stirred, when we need to remember, and then when we need to forget so that we can finally see for ourselves. I think it would be churlish to point out that Voutier was only preserving the moment on orders from his superior officers, in the great Napoleonic tradition, to record any significant discovery or event. Peter Steinhart persuasively suggests in *The Undressed Art* that we draw *to see for ourselves.* We draw to become aware. To *notice,* from *notitia,* from *gnosis,* which James Hillman once told a group of us at Pacifica Institute, to gain access to the knowledge gained by gazing at the world with the eyes of the soul.

I have to come to think Voutier's remarkably simple sketches give us an idea of how the ancients saw her, as a presence, as a reminder of the larger-than-life powers flowing through us, that spark of fire at the heart of all things. She is desire's own trigger, longing's own model, infused with the desire to ignite love in others, which is to say that *beauty* isn't quite the right word, nor is *eros,* to describe the width and depth of her powers.

Instead, I think of her as embodying a more elusive quality, what I'd like to call *beauteros,* beauty inextricably intertwined with love. The word came to me of its own accord when I encountered great beauties—sultry rock stars, gorgeous movie celebrities, and fashion-burnished models—and noticed that the truly beautiful, as opposed to the mere good-looking, are imbued with eros, which is to say love, passion, avidity, and a tincture of kindness. Beauty alone is a curse, as the actress Halle Berry recently said. Eros on its own gets frisky and dangerous. The rage for "heroin chic" sold a generation on the attractiveness of cadaverous and mindless models, who revived the long, strange connection between love and death, Aphrodite and Ares, Venus and Mars. The early manufacturers of gin in colonial America knew this when they embossed a skull-and-crossbones image onto the bottom of their bottles.

Together, beauty and love move beyond seduction to the joy that makes us foot-tappingly happy. Think of Matisse's paper-cut dancers, simply titled "The Joy of Life"; Gene Kelly dancing in the rain around the lamppost in *Singin' in the Rain*; Ella Fitzgerald's "Summertime"; Adele's "Someone Like You;" Henry Moore's wire mobiles; or Marion (Solveig Dommartin), the ethereal trapeze artist who flourishes feathery wings for her circus performances in Wim Wenders' dreamy movie, *Wings of Desire*.

What moved them then moves us now.

"Beauty comes to us on a wing and a prayer," my Grandma Dora whispered to me the day she fondled her dead baby boy's bronzed shoes. "He was so beautiful, Francis was, he was just beautiful."

"We live everything as it comes, without warning," writes Milan Kundera, "like an actor going on cold. And what can life be worth if the first rehearsal for life is life itself? That is why life is always a sketch. No, sketch is not quite the right word because a sketch is an outline of something, the groundwork for a picture, whereas the sketch that is our life is a sketch of nothing, an outline with no picture."

The sketch is an outline that reveals where the story is hiding. You can do this with any sculpture, painting, poem, song, dance, landscape, building, or body. Look close enough and you can see the whole world. Georgia O'Keefe admitted she hated flowers and only used them because they were the cheapest models and because she had to strip away and forget everything she had been taught. O'Keefe also confessed, "I decided that if

I could paint that flower in a huge scale, you could not ignore its beauty."

All great art signifies the triumph of creativity over destruction, gratitude over sorrow.

Consider Elzéard Bouffier, the wandering peasant in Jean Giono's parable, *The Man Who Planted Trees.* The robust farmer's response to the horrors of the World Wars in France was to plant one hundred thousand oak trees. No asked him to do this. Never did he ask for credit. His selfless attempt to counter the horrors of the wars with the natural beauty of sprawling oak forests reminds us, as the young narrator of the story says, that human beings are capable of things other than destruction. Beautiful things. Giono reminded us how beauty can be the consolation of the world, the affirmation after all the negation.

In his introduction to *The Writer's Brush*, John Updike writes, "The itch to make dark marks on white paper is shared by writers and artists." Likewise, the Italian sculptor Giacometti wrote, "I've been fifty thousand times to the Louvre. I have copied everything in drawing, trying to understand." Delacroix wrote in his ambrosial *Journals*, "Nature is a dictionary. One draws from it." Later, he described how he learned how to draw quickly by imagining a man falling from a window before he hit the ground. For the art critic John Berger, when an artist finds his natural rhythm, he is "riding the drawing," a description that brings a kind of whoopee of joy to me every time I conjure up that image.

There it is: the pith and sinew of our quest. I am drawing, figuratively speaking, on the hard-won truths of the ages to understand the strange appeal of this ancient statue. We copy the thing, and we draw it with some of our own personality slipping in, but it is in service to understanding better what we are looking at as if trying to train our eye to look closer, notice more. I never get tired of seeking ways to see the world anew. Likewise with the passionate pencil and chalks of Van Gogh, so despondent yet so resolute as he produced seven hundred paintings and thousands of drawings in the last ten years of his life. For him, understanding may have been beyond his ken, his ability, so clouded with depression; for him, the act was resurrection. "In spite of everything, I shall rise again: I will take up my pencil, which I have forsaken in my great discouragement, and I will go on with my drawing."

With Voutier's modest sketches, we are allowed to travel back in time to a portal moment that helps explain her importance to the ancients and to the moderns, who have made her one of the two or three most visited works of art in the world. What we see in her moment of enshrinement in world culture is that she is beautiful but far more provocative. She is provoking whoever she looks at, and she is provoking us now.

It's strange to say that to the ancient Greeks, one of the earliest meanings of *kallos*, beauty, was "to provoke," as in to prod, poke, stir, or *move* us, which may very well be the secret of life, the soul of art, the key to love. And the mysterious quality that lines the veins of the Venus de Milo.

RESURRECTION Against this backdrop of the Gallic rediscovery of the Greco-Roman, the Venus de Milo soon became all things for all people. To appreciate the mythopoetics of the moment, we turn to the starkly beautiful woodcut that opens the first chapter of Alaux's book about the discovery of the Venus. The engravings are marvelous and celebratory, sparked by both the Renaissance obsession with decaying buildings and monuments and the surging French pride in being the caretakers of Greco-Roman civilization.

Voutier, the young soldier and amateur archaeologist, sits comfortably on a fallen marble column in front of the two pieces of the Venus, placed side by side on the ground in front of the cave. Remarkably, the sketcher is being sketched; the discovered is being rediscovered.

In Alaux's depiction, Voutier is portrayed as avidly drawing the marble Venus that had been extricated from her crypt only a few hours before.

Standing on Voutier's right, outfitted in a long black coat and a tall stovepipe hat, is Louis Brest, appearing perplexed as he watches the sketch marks flow across the pad of paper. To his left stands the peasant Yorgos, leaning against the shovel he used to pry open the stones that had been blocking the cave; he's dressed in traditional island clothing and looks robust, curious, and pensive. So vivid is the illustration that we are compelled to wonder if he is stirred by the ethereal beauty of the statue or thinking of his reward. By then, the poor peasant detected a sense of urgency in the two Frenchmen and seemed determined to negotiate for a little more than the handful of *piasters* that Voutier had already slipped him. If he could get a few coins to dig up the statue, how many could he get if he sold it? How much is beauty worth?

Two shadowy figures hover in the background. One of them is possibly Yorgos's son, Antonio, who had been summoned there to help his father haul the half-ton upper torso to their cowshed. Next to Antonio is a mysterious character, perhaps one of the two shipmates, who swings his pick against the stone wall, or even a kind of hallucination of Voutier earlier in the day. The illustration dramatically captures the fragile nature of such epic discoveries. The vice-consul's uncertainty is palpable, as is his eagerness to understand the significance of the statue, which is why he is gazing so profoundly at the drawing emerging on Voutier's sketchpad.

Describing his woodcuts, the German painter and printmaker Albert Dürer wrote, "Nature holds the beautiful for the artist who has the insight to extract it. Thus, beauty lies even in humble, perhaps ugly things, and the ideal, which bypasses or improves on nature, may not be truly beautiful in the end." Or as the irrepressible auteur, Federico Fellini remarked, "The bearded lady has her own beauty."

I am inspired by the shadow-strewn engravings of Napoleon's "savants and intellectuals" on his expeditions to Egypt and the Mediterranean, which reveal ruins as the beveled edge of history, the desolation of the past on one side and the inevitable future of all civilizations on the other. Of the scattered remains of the past, poet Derek Walcott wrote, "The sigh of History rises over ruins, not over landscapes, and in the Antilles, there are few ruins to sigh over, apart from the ruins of sugar estates and abandoned forts."

So, what are we looking *for* when we are rambling through ruins?

The way that the past, the present, and the future fit together—or don't. Ruins may be the *memento mori* of art and architecture, the visible hunches of history. The idea that the world is waiting to be discovered is an ancient one, and far more interesting if there is no one out in front of us to tell us where to look. We spend far too much time staring at one thing while thinking of another. Or maybe we don't spend enough time. If you aren't bothered by the stone-hearted behavior of hordes of tourists traveling halfway around the world to see something (usually famous) with their own eyes, only to look for a few seconds and then snap a photograph that they will look at once or twice back home, well, then you can't be bothered. If people are looking more and seeing less, everything we care about is a ruin-in-the-making. And I don't mean merely a picturesque ruin.

Strange how words from one century can help us understand words, images, and deeds from another. What Yorgos and Voutier were looking for in that cave on that remote island in that distant time is what we are looking for. To make the mute world speak in a language we might finally understand. To feel the desire imbued into a work of art that you love or at least want to *save*. Think of the citizens of Florence salvaging five-hundred-year-old manuscripts from flooded libraries or Renaissance-era paintings from collapsing museums and galleries after the 1962 flood. Learn about the Louvre's art curator, forty-year-old Rose Valland who cataloged hundreds of thousands of works stolen by the Nazis so they could be traced down after the war. Imagine the courage of the soldiers who kept out the looters trying to storm the Cairo Museum during the Arab Spring uprising.

We know the true thing by the fire it sets in our hearts, by the heat of the ideas that it ignites, by the clarity that is lit in our minds. In German, Rudolf Steiner reminds us, the words for *beautiful* [schon] and *shine* [schonen] are related. The real beauty shines out there and then in here. In English, to shine means "to shed light, to be radiant." What is beautiful sheds light, radiates something worth living and dying for. Likewise, Patrick Laude writes in his 2010 essay, "Is Not Beauty Its Own Reward?" for *Parabola* magazine: "There is 'something else' of a transcendent order that flows, breathes, or shines through its perfection in a way that makes the latter a mere means to a higher, mysterious end."

Writing this, I think of the night I rediscovered pages of notes I took after a late evening at the venerable Monk's pub in Ballyvaughan, in County Clare, Ireland, with the waggish Irish mystic-poet, John O'Donohue. The fiddle music was joyful in the furious ways of the country Irish. The Guinness was flowing with flair, each pint crowned with a shamrock etched into the creamy foam. When we brought out the manuscripts that we were each working on, it was exhilarating to feel the thrill of synchronicity because we were both polishing books about the same theme: beauty. But as the waiter in Saigon advised me while I stared at the incomprehensible Vietnamese menu, "Same, same, but different; same, same, but different."

"As a priest," John said while savoring a sip from his pint, "I thought if you weren't praying you were abdicating your responsibility to caring for the soul of the world. Now I think if you're not acknowledging the beauty of the world, you're contributing to the cult of cynicism and the dullness of life. I believe it takes courage to admit to your love of beauty and your need for what I think of as the invisible embrace of the world."

I remember another bracing conversation with my old friend Alexander Eliot who often invited me to his home near the boardwalk in Venice, California. One evening, we discussed his fifteen years as an art critic.

Scratching his wild and unruly beard and rubbing his sparkling eyes, he held up a copy of his spellbinding book of art essays *Sight and Insight*, and sighed: "For the first time, I know what love is, what friends are, and what art should be. Love is a seeking for a way of life, the way that cannot be followed alone, the resonance of all spiritual and physical things."

Ultimately, these dots connect. The recovered statue on the remote island was less an ideal of beauty and more the peak of desire. A beckoning, a reminder. Whispering the good news about beauty, desire, happiness. Promising, promising, promising. Is there an overlap between qualities? Yes, and it's called *desire*, from the Latin *desiderare*, "to long or wish for," and it is the mythic force that lurks in the overlap.

Listen. It is nighttime. I'm reading by candlelight: Philip Levine's chapbook of poems about working in Detroit factories in the early Fifties. My family has gone to bed. I'm alone but not lonely. You are never completely alone if you are reading. In a book of interviews called *So Ask*, Levine draws a distinction between two modes of writing poetry. First, John Berryman's, his mentor, which required "a wounding so terrible, he or she could barely survive it." And second, Samuel Coleridge's approach, which was to trust his own genial spirit that allowed him to write "out of his joy in the world and in himself." After mulling this over, I turn to Emerson who startles me with this observation: "We know the missing by the joy."

As often happens with my reading, a kind of soul-adjustment occurred and I saw the Venus de Milo in yet another light, as a challenge to us to be better people, more loving, more joyful versions of ourselves."

On my most recent pilgrimage to the findspot on Melos in 2014, I wondered *What if Ensign Voutier hadn't bothered?* The words keyed off a memory of the tale of the folk artist and epic novelist, Henry Darger, who worked as a janitor in an asylum and wrote and illustrated thousands of pages of strange tales about young women on distant planets. His enormous body of work was discovered in his crowded Chicago apartment by his lone friend in the world the day after Darger was taken away to the same sanitarium he used to mop and clean. When he was asked early in his incarceration about why he hadn't shared his work earlier with the world, he uttered the saddest words in the world: *"Too late now!"*

The negative space between all things teaches what is there and what is missing. So much is missing, how do we know it when we see it? Reading Emerson helps, especially if the news of the day stings like a paper cut: "The poet knows the missing link by the joy that it brings."

What startled the farmer and the soldier startles us now, which is worlds beyond what is usually regarded as beauty. They saw the raw look of desire and how it makes her beautiful and makes us happy to look at her. *The beauty that's a gift that ignites desire and promises happiness.* Seductive comes from *suduire*, Old French for "corrupt, surrender." This depth of beauty asks us to surrender our *real* selves, not the face we have to show the world but the face we show ourselves, late at night, in the mirror before we go to sleep. And if we are reluctant to let go, it may be out of fear, but it may also be out of a suspicion of the dark thread of lust and jealousy that runs through every glimpse of beauty.

Let's repeat this like a chorus singing a refrain.

"The real myth of beauty," writes Nancy Etcoff, a psychology professor at Harvard Medical School, "is that beauty is a myth," a venerable word she uses in the pejorative sense.

"There is another world, but it is inside this one," remarked French surrealist poet Paul Eluard, which is a subtle way to describe one of the most mysterious functions of myth—the revelation of the invisible realm. And, I might add, it's beautiful, even when this one isn't.

The Venus is no longer anonymous, one of a thousand works stored in the cosmic warehouse of art. It was dreamed up and carved out by one man covered in marble dust, working in a simple studio on the banks of the aptly twisting Meander River. Why are we delving into such detail, why are we trying to track her, if not because she is showing us the role of beauty in our troubled world, a powerful attribute, in her cave, whatever it was originally, and ever since at her home in Paris. Still, we need a few clues, or we will lose our way, focusing only on the trendy or the trivial, or as Santayana wrote, the ugly and the degrading.

I imagine that these eternal questions about the role of beauty in a cruel world were on Alexandros's mind when he considered which of the hundreds of versions about Aphrodite's adventures that he must have heard from the wandering rhapsodes and bards of the time he now wanted to retell in stone. His first *move* was to make her *move*, which he accomplished by choosing the contrapposto pose, the subtle shift of weight from her left to her right side, emphasizing her curves and suggesting *movement*. This leap forward in the history of sculpture rendered the infinity in stone.

Sure, something's missing. Something is always missing. In the way we look at things, which is why we are astonished by those who see further and deeper. What's missing if we don't seize it is and always has been the *moment*. That awful truth lies behind the fire in her eyes, the fire that passes between lovers.

"Why do we always go back to childhood?" I asked Ray Bradbury during a break at the Los Angeles Book Fair, in 2004, where he was signing copies of *The Cat's Pajamas*, his one hundred and eleventh book, and I was signing *The Olympic Odyssey*. The notes I scribbled a few minutes later in the Green Room remind me that he went on to say that the search for meaning and order in writing requires "going back to our own personal myth, back to our own root system. It's not just going back to your childhood. Anyone can do that. It's not just your childhood but to all the things that ever gave some meaning to your life that are important." The moment he uttered those words, I was memory-whirred back to my hometown library in Wayne, outside Detroit, when I found his *Martian Chronicles* in the science-fiction section.

In *Unattainable Earth*, Czeslaw Milosz writes, "And we could have been united only by what we have in common: the same nakedness in a garden beyond time, but the moments are short when it seems to me that, at odds with time, we hold each other's hands. And I drink wine and I shake my head and say: 'What man feels and thinks will never be expressed.'" Yet Milosz managed to publish over 70 books, including poetry, essays, and novels. Clearly, he needed to express himself *anyway*. To my mind, after reading much about his war-torn life, what was missing in Milosz's life was peace of mind, and poetry was one way to assuage the myriad losses in his life. How is this humanly possible? Milosz hums with conviction when he writes in *The Witness of Poetry* that true poetry is "the passionate pursuit of the Real."

In dramatic contrast to the ardently real, the spurious thing is vapid, contrived, empty, and tyrannical; the real thing startles and surprises, turns our desires inside out, and *lifts* us, which is why we feel like we are soaring when we sit before our lover's face, the moon through a web of branches, or the heart-pounding beauty of a Giorgio Morandi painting of simple bottles on a brown table. It is so unexpected, it feels like grace and helps us sidle up against something that Friedrich Schiller suggested when he wrote, "Beauty alone confers happiness." Science, too, confers some stature to the claim. In *How Pleasure Works*, psychologist Paul Bloom describes studies that infer that pleasure is an evolutionary force because it leads to happiness. How do we know that? From studies that tell us that partners choose ("the hot choosers," he calls them!) those who make us happy, those who please us, which in turn changes us. This is how we recognize, feel, and absorb it. What I am in pursuit of here is echoed in Bloom's book, where he describes the mystery of "essences" as being at the heart of not only pleasure but beauty and relationships. There is no such thing, he writes, as an objective experience, of either food or art. Instead, there is a train of associations that we bring to the dinner table, a love relationship, or a work of art.

It's said that Picasso once confided to a friend that if he were to connect the dots of his life with his drawing pencil, the result would look like a minotaur. Likewise, I like to think that these stories and reflections are dots that will eventually connect to an image that will look exactly like the Venus de Milo.

SHADOWPLAY One night, at the steel factory, mired in the bowels of Detroit, one of my coworkers, Henry Lemanciewicz, a wiry and lovable old Polish machine operator with a name as long as the part numbers we had to memorize (Locknut #206472801) when we shipped them all over the country, caught me huddling in a corner eating my lunch and reading a volume of William Blake. "Hey, Couz," he grinned, "do you think that shit is going to help you get out of this hellhole?" Smiling to beat the band, not even trying to hide his ghoulishly missing teeth, the wonderfully wrinkled Henry winked at me, signaling he knew that shit would, and then punched me in the shoulder to drive home his point. It did.

Along with the power of the story of her creator, Alexandros, the lyre-playing sculptor from Antioch in ancient Anatolia, I have often conjured an image of him listening one night in his youth to a wandering bard who tells the tale of the Judgment of Paris in such a way that he absorbed it into his very soul. I think of him and the others in the palace or theatre where he heard him, probably hundreds of others, as being overjoyed and grateful for the evening's entertainment. Not unlike the biographer of the Marx Brothers who wrote of their two decades of wandering around the country with their hilarious and dizzying loop-the-loop vaudeville act in a time when "any entertainment was considered a blessing."

Sometimes I feel alone in this desire to make connections, find patterns, forge some sense out of the nonsense. I suspect you do too. But art and literature and music make me feel less alone. You too? Is it an innate inability to sink my anchor into the riverbed of the present moment? Or is it simply the desire to drift to the source of the river, where I can experience again the images and ideas that have moved my life? I can't be persuaded otherwise. When in doubt, leave a mark, as my ancestors did in the Dordogne Valley, near the Lascaux Caves.

This story is my red handprint flaring on the cave wall.

THE WHOLE WORLD HELD IN HER HAND

During Voutier's dash up the hill to fetch the vice-consul, Yorgos felt motivated to keep digging around the cave. Alaux condensed the elaborate drama of the discovery by saying that the farmer was "incentivized by the gratuities [*baksheesh*] and the enthusiasm shown by the young archeologist." He describes the Greek peasant whose land they were exploring as being alert to what else might be in the cave. "Yorgos scrutinized the cave with the utmost care," Alaux added, "which soon revealed two herms [statues or boundary markers]; one was a head of an old man, and the other was the head of a beautiful young man, as well as an inscription, all of which was in a marvelous state of condition."

Named after Hermes himself, the herms were pillars with busts resting on top. Often, they were festooned with an erect penis jutting out from the pillar. These two herms represented the semi-divine Herakles and the messenger god Hermes. Voutier later described them as examples of "excellent workmanship." The farmer's quick search around the cave turned up one treasure after another. He found an inscribed base for the Venus with its inscription intact, a few pieces of delicately folded drapery, a lock of the goddess's hair, and a badly deformed chunk of her left forearm, which he wrote "was impossible to use." Most tantalizing of all was his discovery of a crudely carved left hand holding fast to a time-dimpled round stone object. The hand with the round object had survived intact even after coming loose from the wrist of the infamously missing arm.

Remarkably, Voutier was able to identify it as the infamous "Golden Apple of Discord" episode from the Greek myth of the Judgment of Paris, the fight over the beauty prize episode that launched the Trojan War. This is how we have known ever since that the sculpture is not that of an aristocratic Athenian woman, as some have posited, or Amphitrite, the sea goddess and wife of Poseidon, as others suggest, but Aphrodite/Venus at the very moment she has been awarded the very first beauty prize in history. A mixed blessing, to say the least, the *belli causa* to say the most. The infinite moment enshrined in the Venus de Milo personifies the eternal struggle between love and war, the mythic moment that reveals what led to the war between the Greeks and the Trojans.

The round object depicted in the photograph of the Venus's hand gripping the infamous apple (or ball in some versions) conjures up a keen observation from Anne Carson, who writes in *Eros*, "Lovers who do not wish to run may stand and throw: an apple is the traditional missile in declarations of love. ... The lover's ball, or *sphaira*, is another conventional mechanism of seduction, so often tossed as a love challenge that it has come to emblematize the god himself, as Eros Ballplayer."

A love challenge. Let's remember that phrase.

Curiously, these words conjure up how formal dances came to be known as *balls* until the Middle Ages when simple balls were rolled in the direction of prospective partners in dance halls. Eventually, the gatherings became known simply as *balls*, the place or event where courting took place, where love was tested and found wanted or wanting. The custom lives on in the language: "She's quite a catch" and "He's been trying to catch her for a long time" are distant echoes of this ancient love play. It's all the more insidious that such a playful act of innocent flirtation could be inverted into a game of dangerous beauty. Centuries later, Goethe said, "Happiness is a ball after which we run wherever it rolls, and we push it with our feet when it stops."

Writing about his early days as a poet, Stanley Kunitz, at 96, wrote, "I have only three throws [left] with this great right arm." The philosopher Martin Heidegger used the image of slinging or tossing something to express his insight that every one of us is *thrown into* the world, our family, our community, and a compressed moment of history. The Pulitzer Prize-winning poet and playwright Robert Lowell advised writers, "There is something inside that you have to catch. It's not a feeling, usually, it's some sort of an image or even an abstract image or sequence—and then it's days and different moods tinkering with it."

As if writing one of his spiritual aphorisms, Okakura Kakuz , author of the classic work, *The Book of Tea*, compresses the metaphor. "The art lover catches a glimpse of infinity."

"Put your loving hands out, baby," cried Frankie Valli in "Beggin,'" using a little medieval melisma to evoke his bone-deep misery. "I'm beg...eh...gg...in' you-oo-oo-ou." Sculptor Louise Bourgeois confessed, "I'm not sure what I am, but I am what I do with my hands." One of our throw-away cliches is, "I've got to hand it to you," a reflection of how we touch and are touched, in touch or out of touch.

To catch a myth, you have to think like one.

The mysterious hand and arms of the Venus de Milo, missing for two thousand years, hold the key to her fame and to our story. They can symbolize our longing to reach out for someone or something we care about—or for them to reach out to us. What she is holding holds the key to the mystery of our story. Gazing at it now, in a series of photographs I took at the Louvre in 2010, I wonder why I am not a better man than I am, which is an odd but common response to a work of art.

Surely, art is catharsis and more, a challenge from the artist's soul to ours. Why that is I don't know, but I should. It might have to do with the sheer pleasure of waking up.

Consider the marvel. Apples have been symbols of beauty since the scarlet dawn of time, and as such became synonymous with forbidden fruit, reflecting the ancient temptations of love and desire, or the barely controllable urges of lust and envy. There may be no coincidences in some circles, but *Melos* is Greek for *melon*, a small apple, which just shows to go you, as my Grandpa Sydney used to say. While "love apples" was the moniker for tomatoes when they came from the New World, the ethnobotanist who wrote the definitive study on *soma* and peyote, R. Gordon Wasson, speculated in his book on *entheogens* that apples could have been code for *amarita muscaria*, magic or psychedelic mushrooms, the bite of which created revelatory or transportive states, such as those reported by shamans on soul journeys. To conclude this playful mythic deconstruction, the apple's association with Venus is at once ancient and immediate, hinting at the forbidden fruit of ecstatic love, the transportive powers of sexual desire. If you track it down, sexual desire was the sin, the thing to be feared, in the Garden of Eden. It's the loss of self-control when sexual desire threatens to overwhelm us that has always driven sexual repression, driving love farther and farther away, a remote ideal.

Consider the wonder of Venus's son, Eros. For the ancient Greeks, he was a far deeper force than what was suggested by his Cupid, his Roman counterpart, an insipid god of love. Originally, Eros symbolized the power that created the universe. Love, the poets believed, is older, more powerful, and more dangerous than any other god. Only later did he symbolize the wantontries and coquetries that pass between lovers, usually at the goading of his mother, and he was described by Hesiod as the "limb-loosener and mind-weakener."

An anonymous Greek poet seconded that emotion in Kenneth Rexroth's translation:

> I have two sicknesses: Love
> And Poverty. Poverty
> I can stand, but the fever
> Of Love is unbearable.

Can you feel it, can you feel the mystery, as the Detroit preacher pleaded? Can you hear it in Ella Fitzgerald's bluesy version of "That Old Black Magic"? Her voice turns vertiginous as she sings, "Yes I'm in a spin, I'm loving the spin I'm in / I'm under that old black magic called love."

Enchantment by any other name. The pulsing heart of the matter. The mystery at the spinning core of art that moves us. In case you were wondering, the ancient Greeks called this old black magic *thelgein*, the held-breath enchantment of spellbinding stories or music, the *feel* of being charmed and transported from where we are to where we long to be. Elsewhere. The place where passion is fired, and love burns. I propose a revival of this magical word—thelgein—to bring us closer to the *numinous* power of the Venus de Milo that has mystified me since I was a kid sneaking glances at her in my basement and those who have taken art pilgrimages to see her with their own eyes at the Louvre for the last two centuries. It's the artistic voltage that defies the commercialization and trivialization that has plagued her since at least the Surrealists mocked her with replicas that blindfolded her or riddled her with drawers.

I remember a conversation with the great historian Huston Smith after the murder of his granddaughter, a heinous and tragic act that challenged his belief in the goodness of life. After a long painful pause on the telephone, his response was philosophical and poetic, explaining to me as his voice filled with grief that he hoped we could continue to work on our book, *The Way Things Are*, because, as he sighed, "Life is a vale of sorrows, and we must go on." Then the gentle professor cited Issa, the sixteenth-century haiku master, after the death of his own young daughter:

> So this world of dew
> is a world of dew.
> And yet, and yet...

"Everything passes on," sighed Huston. "So must those we love, and so must we." And so it is in the world of art, and yet, and yet... And yet so much more.

A *cri de coeur* from a sensitive soul in response to an encounter with the beauty and sometimes the terror of the world. A transportation system that carries love and beauty and meaning. The ancients referred to the potency that love has on both gods and mortals as a *daimon magas*, an overwhelming spirit. Intriguingly, it also meant a bittersweet drama, what we still call "the game of love," which helps deepen our theme and is more of a *feeling* than an idea.

Transport is from the Old French *transporter*, to carry away, to overwhelm emotionally. To move or be moved, which is the secret of life, the enigma of art. It's what we long for, in one move or another. I get it. It's what I am leaning in on here, reaching out across the abyss of time and space to get my hands around an ancient mystery and hand it over to you. Can you handle it?

Learning this, I am not embarrassed to say I was astonished.

ASTONISH

If we open the word hoard, we find this pulsating Old Norse word for *stun*, as in being hit with Thor's hammer. Certain art does that: It whacks us over the head. It is astonishing that Voutier and Brest immediately recognized, in the darkness of the cave, the badly mutilated hand and what it represented, and, in turn, who the statue must have represented. How many of us would recognize an ancient work of art if it popped up in our own backyard?

Seventy years after the discovery of the Venus de Milo, Paul Cezanne dramatically announced, "I will astonish Paris with an apple." Sixty years after that, journalist Terry Southern reminded us, "The important thing in writing is the capacity to astonish. Not shock—shock is a worn-out word— but astonish."

What's always missing is love and what is being reached for. "Once you had put the pieces back together," writes novelist Jodi Picoult, "even though you may look intact, you were never quite the same." What goes missing often feels stolen. Missing time. Missing friends. Missing family after they pass on. The more we love them, the more we feel gouged by the gods. "Stolen Moments" is the aptly named album by Oliver Nelson, who squeezed out the sentiment on his gut-bucket saxophone. Gazing at what is incomplete, imperfect, or missing ignites the imagination, which is why my grandfather stopped going to movies when the talkies came in, saying they were too literal to be art. What was missing hinted at what had been, what might be again, in the ancient future. From the very beginning, her imperfections served her perfection. Those missing arms intensify our desire for what we can never have but will always long for.

At first blush, what is the conventional thought on the meaning of romantic love, the bittersweet or sweetbitter presence of the frisky and unpredictable god of love, whose burning arrows of desire pierce every lover's heart? A fragment of Sappho brings this to light: "Eros once again limb-loosener whirls me / sweetbitter, impossible to fight off, / creature stealing up..." Painful as it may be, the poets have always exhorted us to praise the pain of love.

When Zagajewski advised us to try to "praise the mutilated world," many wondered what he meant. Warsaw after the war? I've come to wonder if that is the main task of artists—the sorrow and beauty of it. Praise-singing, anyway, in dramatic contrast to the dirge of mutilation, a harsh word. At least until you read the current tourists' guide to Melos, which states that her arms were "amputated," a lurid word with harsh connotations.

This isn't necessarily a bad thing. Remember that the playwright Lin-Manuel Miranda was asked about the secret of art and said, "Make what's missing." Then there is Willa Cather, in her 1922 review for *The New Republic* of *The Novel Démeublé*," who wrote, "Whatever is felt upon the page without being specifically named there—that, one might say, is created. It is the *inexplicable* presence of the thing not named, of the overtone devised by the ear but heard by it, the verbal mood, the emotional aura of the face or the thing or the deed, that gives high quality to the novel or the drama, as well as to poetry itself."

Let's call it the presence of absence.

Clearly, what's missing can be as vital as what's present. That's what I am trying to do here, to fill in what has long been missing, which is what I was taught to do in journalism school at the University of Detroit. Writing this, my vagabonding mind goes back to the Watergate scandal, which was breaking during my sophomore year. My professor, Judy Serrin, told us how Ben Bradlee, the legendary editor of the *Washington Post*, kept pushing his valiant reporters, Woodward and Bernstein, to get it right, asking again and again, "Where's the goddamn story?" So, yes, I want the story. If I don't have the story, the story that catalyzed the sculptor, I'll never know what that look means. The mirror image of the story that inspired the *Laocoon*, the stone-cold allegory of transforming agony into art. The Venus de Milo is the warm-stone transmutation of love into art. This is another way to say what Dooley Wilson sang at his honky-tonk piano in *Casablanca*: "It's still the same old story, a fight for love and glory." Stories that pierce our soul, stories that make sense out of the nonsense, stories that show us how live.

Missing stories, such as the one about my younger brother, Paul, an officer in the U. S. Air Force who went AWOL in the Philippines in the early Eighties. I searched for him for months until I bumped into him in the boondocks, the mountains of Northern Luzon, where he had been protected by the New People's Army long enough for me to find him. Missing like the young leftist American journalist who was *disappeared*, to use the verb that was in vogue at the time, by the Chilean army in 1973, and never found again. Missing like the 30,000 "disappeared ones," mostly civilians and students, by the Argentine military after the 1976 junta. Missing like the husband and daughter-in-law of a friend of mine, who revealed to me she had been staying at a resort in Southeast Asia, and while sailing with her husband, son, and daughter-in-law, went scuba diving. On her first dive, she stayed underwater for several minutes, and when she rose to the surface, the boat had disappeared. Her family was missing, vanished. Among the thousands washed out to sea, the beach resort obliterated as well, when a violent tsunami came and went without warning or mercy. Missing like the sudden disappearance of enormous numbers of statuary in sixth-century Rome, as reported by Zaccharia—"4,000 bronze statues of emperors and generals, 80 golden and 68 ivory statues of the gods, and innumerable marble statues," which were melted down for the mundane purpose of making lime and whitewash. One thing the world isn't missing is stories about what and who goes missing every minute of every day, which in turn is personified by the poly-fabulous, many-sided story that informs every square inch of the two marble blocks that were sculpted into the Venus de Milo. Missing, as reported by Robert Adams in *Lost Museum*, like the thousands of illuminated manuscripts, tapestries, and marble statuary that vanished from the Forum when the Huns, Vandals, and Goths crossed the Rhine to ransack Rome in the fifth century.

Still, we have the stories. "Tell it!" the GIs told war correspondent Michael Herr when he accompanied them into battle in Vietnam, who honored them by writing the blistering truth about it in *Dispatches*. "Tell us about the sea," the copper miners told Eduardo Galeano when he visited them in remote Uruguay. "Tell it like it is," I heard Aaron Neville sing softly when I hung out with him backstage, sharing a joint, when he was warming up in the greenroom before bouncing onstage as the opening act for the Grateful Dead in Oakland in 1986.

A story that can help, in turn, move us on to the next story, the one that once and forever pierced my heart. Which is what story, the savvy reader might ask, to which I reply with what is sometimes called the greatest couplet written in the history of pop music: "Nature Boy," written by George Aberle, puzzlingly known on the record label as "eden ahbez," who persuaded Nat King Cole to record it and then disappeared, only to be discovered living under the Hollywood sign in the Los Angeles hills. The chorus he wrote, despite his hardscrabble life, could have been written by Alexandros of Antioch, maybe Sappho, and surely Homer: *"The greatest thing you'll ever know / is just to love / and be loved in return."*

All of these stories compress into a single statue, stories we tell ourselves in order to live well, to connect to our ancestors. And now an interlude, another marvel of a word, evoking what happens between the scenes, before and after the major action, from *inter*, between, and *ludus*, play, an intervening or interruptive period—what fills in the gaps of a story and provides context. Or, as my high school basketball and track coach, Mr. Natkowski, used to shout at us whenever we complained about cramps or side stitches during the ferocious workouts that he put us through: "Walk it off, guys. Walk it off." His advice never failed. Since then, I've never doubted the power of walking it off, whether around a running track, a gorgeous statue, or a story that I am trying to unwind. It's the key to the tales that must be understood backwards but lived forwards.

As for me, I am content to live in the mystery, to be surrounded by the unknown. I am content to be a seeker, a pilgrim, a traveler on the road to nowhere. Let us turn now to the story that informs our never-ending search for the secret of the Venus de Milo, the myth of the Judgment of Paris, which some say is the one tale that has inspired more art than any other story in history. It's got it all: love and war, passion and envy, beauty and ugliness.

That's the beauty of it.

INTERLUDE

Once, a long, long time ago, a story came hobbling along an ancient, cobbled road. Eros, the impetuous god of love and desire, became lost in the Underworld and wandered into one of the dank caves sometimes occupied by Hades, the god of death and demise. Disturbed by the Stygian darkness, Eros thought the wisest thing to do was to curl up and sleep till dawn. That was the best time to hunt for vulnerable people on the cusp of love, the beveled edge between night and day. It was the time when Helios stepped into his golden chariot and rode across the cerulean sky, pulling the big ball of sun behind him, and in that way lit up the morning sky.

When Eros felt the first shimmers of warm sun on his face, the mischievous son of Aphrodite, whom some call Venus, awoke and stared through the mouth of the cave and was bone-chilled by the sight of a few wandering ghosts. So distracted was he by the unnerving sight that the Love God reached down through the shadow-fretted cave to the cave floor and grabbed the leather quiver and sharp-tipped arrows. Without looking closer, he bolted from the cave, leaving the arrows behind. Soon after, Hades returned to his earthbound refuge and noticed the strange quiver and arrows left behind by Eros. Thinking they were his, the Dark One carried them back to his dark marbled palace, where he replaced his own collection in the infamous hall of ebony and ivory, shedding, the ancient mythographers wrote, black tears.

And that is why, the ancient troubadours sang, love and death are found in the same quiver.

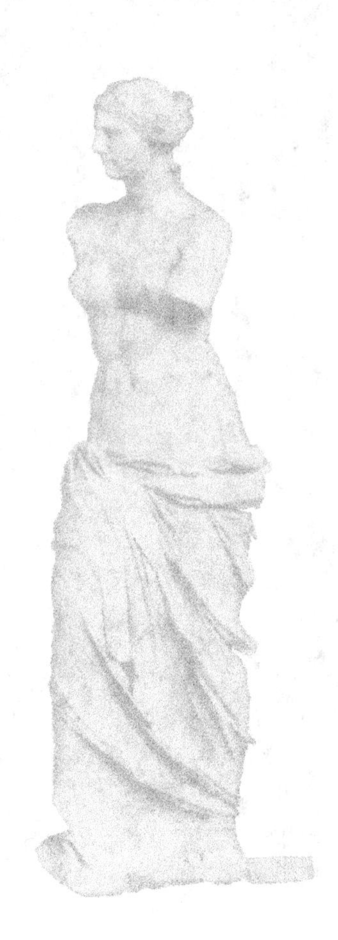

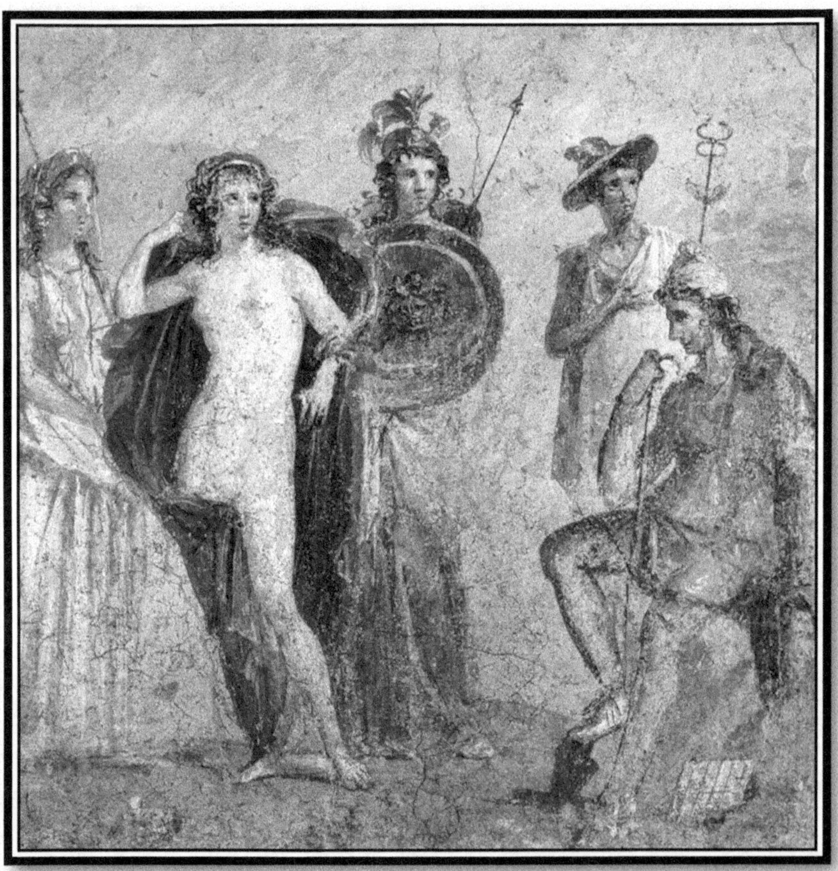

The Judgment of Paris, fresco, House of Jupiter
Pompeii, first century

II.

THE JUDGMENT OF PARIS

N THE TIME BEFORE TIME, DURING THE REALM OF GODS, GODDESSES, strange beasts, and stranger adventures, a grand wedding was held in the marble halls of Mount Olympus. The mortal warrior Peleus, one of Jason's fabled Argonauts who had accompanied him on the search for the Golden Fleece, was to be wed to the sea nymph Thetis, who would later give birth to their son, "swift-footed" Achilles. The trident-bearing sea god Poseidon offered a gift of a wedding couch that was crested with shells inlaid with mother-of-pearl. The leader of the Nine Muses, Apollo, led the wedding parade, playing dulcet tones on his lyre. The heads of the immortals swiveled on their shoulders to gaze upon the beauty of the three voluptuous goddesses in attendance: Hera, Athena, and Aphrodite.

All the immortals were invited to share in the festivities—all but one. Eris, Goddess of Strife and Discord, daughter of Zeus, the Thunder Lord, and Nyx, Dark Goddess of Night. Eris, sister of Ares, God of War and Violence, sister of Deceit and Vanity, mother of Toil and Forgetfulness. The complicated goddess had been deliberately left off the wedding list because her father was embarrassed about her devious nature, certain she would disrupt the wedding.

She did anyway.

Hard-hearted Eris hated to be ignored. When she got the news, she became red-faced with rage and turned hellbent with revenge. A dish usually served cold, vengeance was offered hot as rage. She vowed to rain ruin on all of those who had humiliated her. The hallowed corridors of Olympia's banquet hall were riddled with feuds, but the retribution exacted by Eris for the insult was particularly nefarious. Disguising herself as an old maid, Eris heard that Hephaestus had abandoned his forge for a few hours so he might swill some wine with the revelers. Furtively, she entered his shadow-strewn workshop, which was lit only by the light of golden shields, weapons, toys, and the world's first robots, which the maimed metalworker had created for his fellow Olympians as well as the heroes and heroines and their myriad children in the world below. Eris searched the area and discovered one of the most startling creations by the god of the forge—a solid-gold apple, though some say it was a ball.

Immediately, she knew how it could help her wreak revenge on the revelers.

Quickly leaving the workshop, the Goddess of Discord swooped down through a narrow opening in the storm clouds that gathered over the marble wedding hall on Mount Olympus. There, in the shadows of the mighty palace doors, Eris, the very personification of bitterness, carved a single word—ΚΑΛΛΙΣΤΗΙ—*Kallisti*—with one sword-sharp fingernail into the golden apple that she meant to present as a dangerous prize for beauty. Traditionally, the word has been translated as "for the most fair" and was later written as such on the poisoned apple in the Cinderella fairy tale. But it would be closer to the mark to render it as "for the most *beautiful.*"

With the golden apple in hand, Eris slithered into the hall and hid in the shadows until there was a lull in the celebrations. Stepping into the light, she cackled. Her voice sent slivers of fear into the hearts of the wedding party. Then came a collective gasp as she rolled the apple along the marble floor, which didn't stop rolling until it hit the sandals of Zeus, the Thunder Lord. The mighty god crooked his head and took a glance at the apple, just enough to read the ominous word carved into the golden fruit: "*Kallisti.*"

The beautiful word filled him with ugly thoughts. Not for nothing has it been called ever since the "Apple of Discord." More than a word, the scratched letters were a world-tilting challenge.

A chilling shiver shot down the spine of Zeus, the Cloud Bearer. To decide such a thing was impossible, unthinkable, thankless, hopeless, foolhardy. He dreaded their competitive gazes, especially that of his wife Hera, who he had given great cause for suspicion because of his infidelities. Surely, the two losers would exact their revenge on the one winner, whoever was chosen. The shame would be too much, shame being the operative word, the one that describes what *really* led to the savagery at Troy.

That was just the way, until it wasn't.

The great Roman poet Ovid got the scene right when he adapted it in his *Metamorphosis*: "Judgment of beauty can err, what with the wine and the dark."

The moment was as clear as Santorini mud. A wicked trap had been set for him, as beauty often is. No one claimed judging beauty was ever anything but a risky business. The Thunder Lord hesitated, trying to think of a ruse. The wedding wine swirled in his belly; his mind was rattled. Then, as he feared, the three most powerful goddesses on Olympus—Hera, Athena, and Aphrodite—converged on him. As one, they leaned over his shoulder to examine the apple and read what had been written. Staggering backwards, each of them knew in their own way that the word was a three-syllable challenge to their sense of beauty. All eyes were upon Zeus to decide who was *kallos*, beautiful, but he demurred, waiting to decide on a gambit. The longer he stalled, the more the goddesses shamelessly flirted with him.

It didn't take long for their arguments to turn bitter and petty, as they often do whenever frivolous beauty pageants are staged. Thwarted by his silence, they began to quarrel with each other, which was exactly what Eris had in mind when she plotted how she would avenge the perceived insult. To pit the gods and goddesses against one another was the most, well, discordant trick she could play on them. Seeing them fight over her ruse was a perverse delight for her. As she left, her high-pitched squeals could be heard across the wedding hall because Zeus had been heard repeating the word *kallesteion* to himself, signifying to one and all that the world's first "beauty contest" had been declared. Unwittingly, perhaps, a precedent had been set. If we look a little closer at the word *kallisteion,* we detect that it derives from *kallisti* and *agon,* the agony of the contest, and so we have *the beautiful pain* brought on competitions. The insatiable hunger for glory may increase one's ability to compete, but it also courts the curse of shame among those who don't win are forever regarded as losers.

"Immediately, if not sooner," the goddesses demanded in unison. Turning to Zeus, they bellowed, "You must decide."

As they quarreled, Zeus perversely paused and squinched his mouth, saying to himself, "Hmm, I wonder who *is* the most beautiful of them all?" Then he caught himself and realized it would be sheer madness, even hubris, for him to decide. For once, he erred on the side of caution, knowing that to bow out now was better than to leap into the fray. How could anyone, even a god, judge who was the "fairest," the most beautiful, which suggested the most pulchritudinous, most voluptuous, the one easiest to fall in love with? When we say someone has *winning* looks, is this what we mean? Does that make losers of all the rest? Worst of all, how would you explain your choice to the two goddesses you *didn't* choose, especially when one of them is your own wife? How can you stop the others from seeking revenge? To this day, we still wonder about the merits and demerits of beauty at fairs, carnivals, playhouses, architectural competitions, and beauty pageants. It's an echo of the ancient challenges of beauty that have always asked us to take sides, choices we still struggle with today, which is what makes the tale mythic, timeless, and eternally relevant. Love and beauty, art and literature, the story says, are deeply human ways to bring order to the chaos.

After a short deliberation, Zeus realized he had been set up to be let down.

Looking again at the golden apple that still lay on the floor, Zeus, who possessed the greatest throwing arm in the universe due to thousands of years of hurling thunderbolts, was tempted to toss the apple down the slopes of Olympus to the earth below. No matter which goddess he chose, he was inviting the others' wrath. Quickly, he looked around the hall for a way to get off the hook. Then he spied his wingman, Hermes, God of the Crossroads, who had been lurking in the shadows. Zeus flipped the perilous fruit to him and ordered the psychopomp, or guide of souls, to find an impartial judge, someone who was *fair*. Preferably a mere mortal. A kid. No one would question his judgment or blame him afterward.

The flushed look on the faces of the three radiant goddesses, the flare of their nostrils and the defiant jut of their hips told Zeus he had to make up his snarled mind. At that knotted moment, his divine powers were useless. He couldn't risk their wrath. What he needed was a *fair* judge, someone impartial to decide who was the *fairest* of them all. *Fair*, as in beautiful. Fair, as in impartial. Fair, as in the celebrations on market day. One of the fairest words in our language. Are these false friends, or is there a certain symmetry to their meaning, one that is relevant to our exploration? To be fair, is it ever fair to judge beauty? To be *fair* as a judgment about beauty? To be fair in love and war? To have a fair prince judge a beauty contest *fairly*?

Fair questions or impertinent puns?

Who said there's no justice in the world, or that "all is fair in love and war"? All who are judged, that's who.

"Mirror, mirror, on the wall, who's the *fairest* of them all?" cackles the wicked queen in the *Snow White* fairy tale, which resounds to this day with the echo of Eris. A similar dynamic is played out in the myth and the fairy tale, where we witness the same sleep of human reason, the beauty that inspires envy and retribution, the mirror of vanity, the kiss that breaks the spell, the gasp of joy that takes our breath away. The evergreen story suggests that only the fair can judge the fair. And mythic narratives are our memories of encounters with the numinous, the supreme fiction, the exquisite realization that we can believe in things that lie outside time and space.

Then there is one of the most puzzling of all beauty's attributes, which is *justice*. It has permeated the story from the beginning, the story of a *contest* to decide who was the *fairest* or most beautiful. In the fairest manner, the gods declared. To this day, the fairness of beauty is contested, with many decrying the lack of fairness in its seemingly arbitrary distribution. The myth, the statue, and the story are inextricably connected. You can still see it in the Venus's eyes in paintings and sculptures. She practically invented the look of love, the moment of desire. If you've ever wondered about the uncomfortably close relationship between love and hate, sweet and bitter, push and pull, take a closer look at Venus/Aphrodite. She embodies the moment of desire that the erotic poet, Antipater of Sidon, wrote was stronger than age. Life-in-movement, life engorged, incandescent. The sweet shudder. The bitter savor. This goes as well for the most universal allure of art—sheer *pleasure*, the satisfaction that accompanies an experience of paintings, sculptures, poems, novels, or movies like a dolphin swimming in the wake of a ship. Who knows why they do it other than the pleasure that is signaled by their squeaks of delight and looping leaps in the air?

If you are a dancer or long jumper, you might get an extra thrill out of seeing dolphins capering alongside your ship because such a sight can galvanize a kinetic response in your muscles. So too with the mysterious ways people have responded to the Venus de Milo over the last two hundred years, which proves she is far more than a commercial boon to the Louvre or the result of a long and sordid propaganda campaign.

Instead, if we look closer at the Venus, we can see an ardent example of art to live by—but only if we know its context—the story of the Judgment of Paris that informs its deeper meaning, which is why we are searching for her story. Seen with mythic eyes, she embodies one of the great questions of life: *Do we have a choice, free will, or is everything predetermined by the gods or our DNA, depending on our worldview?* Her creator, the unheralded Alexandros of Antioch, posed her in such a sensuous way that if you gaze at her deeply enough, you are bound to ask more than the obvious "what is it you want?" And I do mean *sensuous*, in art historian Herbert Read's sense in *Letter to a Young Painter*, where he writes that sensuality is a *necessary* quality for greatness in art. I have often thought about the immense focus needed to create her.

Her gaze asks what *you* desire. These are not the same questions. We can want what we don't have and want what we have, but never want what we desire. That longing comes from somewhere else.

In 1995, I co-presented *Ecological Design*, a documentary film, at the Sundance Film Festival. One afternoon, I was invited by an old friend in the film business, Betty Rosen, to attend a sneak preview of a new doc about Brian Wilson, who hadn't performed in public for many years. We gathered around the gleaming black piano and quietly watched the ex-Beach Boy lean into one of his big hits, singing, "Wouldn't it Be Nice" in his aching vibrato, referring to what was missing in his young love life—lovemaking itself. "You know it seems the more we talk about it...it only makes it worse to live without it." What are they talking about? What else? *Love.*

All told, the Judgment of Paris is a rhapsody on the ever-competing themes of love and beauty, sorrow and shame, hope and resignation—a lapidary myth of Aphrodite, Paris, Helen, and the Trojan War. The battlefield, as ever, is the human heart. In a single lambent word, *love*, we find the key to what the Venus de Milo signifies, what she means, why she matters.

THE QUICKSILVER MESSENGER

Hoping to avoid the wrath of the three proud goddesses, Zeus chose Hermes and his quicksilver messenger service to select an impartial judge of beauty. Streaking down the mountain and across the sea, Hermes spied a young shepherd boy, Paris, the exiled son of Priam, King of Troy, brother of fleet Hector, beautiful Endymion, and his sister, the doomsaying Cassandra. Not only did he escape the wrath of his wife when he inevitably made the wrong choice, but the choice made sense because the lad was considered a "fair" judge in local sporting competitions and believed to be the most beautiful of men as Helen was the most beautiful of women.

Who better to judge beauty—if it indeed needed to be judged at all?

According to the favorite son of Mallorca, the raffish poet Robert Graves, this is a largely overlooked detail in the story. The two mortals who now enter our story are also considered preternaturally attractive. Mythically beautiful.

"Paris was of noble birth," Graves writes in *The Greek Myths*, "disclosed by his outstanding beauty, intelligence, and strength...[and] became known for [being] a fair judge." Often, when I ponder the story, the Nat King Cole song "Nature Boy" meanders into my mind, as music is known to do. "There was a boy," he sings, "a very strange, enchanted boy..."

Unfairly, Paris has been much maligned over the centuries. To understand the complexity of his character and his role in the Trojan War, it is vital to know that he had been exiled by his father King Priam. The kindly ruler had sired no less than forty-nine children by the time his wife Hecuba was pregnant with Paris, a birth that provoked a terrible prophesy by the local oracle that the boy would be the destruction of Troy. The comely queen Hecuba had an ominous dream that she was going to bring forth a firebrand, a cursed child who would bring destruction to his parents' house and all of Troy. So, she arranged to have her infant left on the slopes of Mount Ida, exposed to die. Instead, a shepherd took pity on the child and raised him, as one ancient source tells it, to be "the perfection of beautiful manhood." Our fair and lonely lad lived out his youth on the mountain-side, overlooking the plains of Troy, where he was as lonely as a loon on a distant lake. With nothing else to do but tend sheep, he turned himself into a fair athlete and lyre player, which prepared him well to be a fair judge of local sporting and music competitions. Because life is full of tough choices, we can only hope that the scales of justice are weighed evenly, in every matter of competition, from love to war. Our fate often depends on it. The triple play on this ancient word about ideal judgment inspired many an ancient author to refer to the lad as "*Fair* Paris," and a modern author, Bettany Hughes, wrote recently that he was every bit as beautiful as Helen.

And so it was that fair Paris was chosen by the fair Hermes by way of one of those convenient coincidences in myth, the poets describing how he had been respected for the way he was often picked to judge footraces in the lowlands around Mount Ida. Hermes persuaded him to judge, and the other gods ensured him he would be able to resist the offers of the first two goddesses, those of power and fame.

All told, by the time the three goddesses magically appeared before him with the god Hermes under a magnificent oak tree, he was told by the silver-streaking god that Zeus himself had demanded that Paris choose one of the three goddesses gleaming before him to be the most beautiful in all of creation. Before the flummoxed Zeus blinked three times, the three pur-ring goddesses had descended from the heavens determined to use every feminine wile to persuade Paris that *she* was the *fairest* of them all.

Leaning on his shepherd's staff, Paris waited for each goddess to plead her case, and as he listened, he realized what a thankless task it was at best, a dangerous one at worst. It was the choice that was no choice. It worked both ways. The goddesses were as stunned as he was. They hadn't counted on the kid being as handsome as they were beautiful, but also as sly, vain, and vulnerable. This contest was not going to be as easy as they had hoped, which places the story squarely in the middle of the land of myth.

This claim requires some commentary. The British philosopher-linguist Owen Barfield tells us, in *History in English Words*, that *myth* derives from *mu*, to keep silent, and *mu-ein*, an initiate, later gives rise to *mystery* and *muse*. It is the mother of all words, making myth the mother story. There is something in the very sinews of this mythic tale that has been kept silent, even secret, as if only the initiated could hear its message. Myth is an initiation into deeper meanings. As a founding member of The Inklings in Oxford, Barfield persuaded his fellow mythographers J. R. Tolkien, C. S. Lewis, and Charles Williams that myth and metaphor were central forces in literature and language, as well as in the evolution of consciousness.

What about *this* story, *this* myth, and this sculpture, this response?

The Judgment of Paris is at once a colorful story and a cautionary tale about the prizes and perils of judging beauty. We learn or are reminded that great beauty comes at a cost. It is laid out for all to see the rewards and the tragedies that inevitably follow such a decision in such a competition. Here again is a vivid example of the perils of judging, let's say, which of our daughters is most attractive, which actress deserves to be cast in a movie, or in a more inanimate contest, which city is more beautiful than another.

Something else is happening here, something *besides*.

Go ahead—try to be fair, the story says. Look where it gets you. Try to be an impartial judge; just try to be fair. Try to understand what Paris was up against, which is to say, what we are all up against every day, myth being what it is, an image of what is, as James Joyce wrote in *A Portrait of the Artist as a Young Man*, "constant to the human race."

Shuddering is how I imagine Paris the moment the winged god and the fiercely flirtatious goddesses appeared before his very eyes. The original Greek word was *phrisso*, a tremble, a cringe, used to describe Aphrodite's electrifying effect on lovers. Over time, the word evolved into the febrile French word *frisson*, the shiver down the spine that Nabokov used to describe the shock of recognition in a true work of art. Similarly, the ancient Greeks described cosmic desire as the infamous "limb-loosener." And so it was that Eros was considered "the tyrant of men," as Euripides hailed him, but also the most beautiful of creatures, the personification of passionate longing, not only for the beloved but for victory, accomplishment, excellence. This is the Eros who taunts us with the promise and pricks us with the possibility that love may lead to happiness while goading us to risk everything in its name. This may be why we are afraid of it because it takes away our last excuse that we don't have a choice, that all is fated, yesterday by the gods, today by our genes.

What could the lonely young prince have been thinking when the goddesses appeared to him? It is tempting to fantasize that his journals will be found someday, which, in a sense, they have been. In the *Heroides*, the changeling poet, Ovid, reimagines the thoughts of Paris on Mount Ida the morning that Hermes and the three goddesses appeared to him:

My beauty and my vigor of mind, though I seemed from the common folk, were the signs of hidden nobility. There is a place in the woody vales of midmost Ida, far from trodden paths and covered over with pine and ilex, where never grazes the placid sheep, nor the she-goat that loves the cliff, nor the wide-mouthed, slowly moving kine [cows]. From there, reclining against a tree, I was looking forth upon the walls and lofty roofs of the Dardanian city [Troy], and upon the sea, when lo! It seemed to me that the earth trembled beneath the tread of feet—I shall speak true words, though they will scarce have credit for truth—and there appeared and stood before my eyes, propelled on pinions swift, [Hermes], the grandchild of mighty Atlas and Pleione—it was allowed me to see, and may it be allowed to speak of what I saw, and in the fingers of the god was a golden wand.

These are not fey words about a feckless hero nor the secondhand thoughts of a coward or wife thief, names the prince has been slandered with for centuries. He has been condescendingly described as love-struck, moon-struck, selfish, and effete. And yet Homer described him as radiant. Hesiod called him enchanted. Graves focused on his fierce loneliness, and Bettany Hughes described him as doomed by the fury over Helen's beauty. To-gether, these attributes align him even more with the dazzling young woman he fell in love with. How do we reconcile these contradictions?

By looking closer at the Venus de Milo and the story of her creation.

Thousands of years later, we are still pulled inexorably by its irresist-ible centrifugal force. Intuitively, we know that the beautiful is that which simply pleases us, brings us pleasure, inspires and uplifts us—except that it is rarely simple. Instead, it is so infinitely complex, it also confuses, baffles, and upsets us due to its power to ignite love in our hearts, stokes passion in our souls, or, most tantalizingly of all, stirs in us a few fleeting moments of happiness.

What happens next in the myth reveals the mystery of what the Venus de Milo is gazing at and what she was reaching for when she had her arms— and what we are still stretching for twenty-one hundred years later.

CHOOSE ME

According to Robert Graves, who caught the story from Hesiod, the first thing the shepherd-prince asked the goddesses to do was to "disrobe to reveal their true beauty." D. H. Lawrence or Anais Nin might have written that line, but it was Czech novelist Milan Kundera who adapted the mythologem for the opening scene of *The Unbearable Lightness of Being.* His main character, a doctor named Tomas, closes the door to his office in a rural spa, sits down in a chair, and instructs—that is the word—his voluptuous nurse, "Take your clothes off." She appears to be enchanted by his confident tone and earnestness. The steamed-up windows in the clinic suggest what happens next, an acting out of the fine line between seduction and the sacred.

This moment tempts us to succumb to the sin of literalism, which is one more reason we need the universal language of mythology, which helps us *experience* the radiant aspect of beauty, which shines, glows, and reveals spirit.

In the ancient Greek story, Paris's demand would have normally been considered sheer *hubris*, arrogance, and he would have been split asunder by a thunderbolt. But Hermes told Paris not to worry, assuring him that he was under the protection of Zeus. Emboldened, Paris added that he could objectively decide who was, after all, the fairest, the most beautiful, which is to say the most irresistible. But only if they were as naked as blue jays. That was the only way, he reasoned, that he could be sure they weren't hiding anything. Vanity of vanities, confident in their spellbinding beauty, each of the three goddesses agreed, though each took a radically different approach, three different attempts at bribery, so intent were they on securing victory in the beauty contest.

"*Choose me,*" the first two goddesses pleaded with unusual insecurity. *Choose me* signaled the third goddess wordlessly.

Choose me, Geraldine Chaplin asks her lover in the Alan Rudolph movie, *Choose Me*, about bohemians in 1920s Paris. Years ago, the night after I watched the movie at the Castro movie palace in San Francisco, I woke up just before dawn and habitually scribbled a few words from a dream about my wife Jo in a spiral notebook. When I got out of bed an hour later, I glanced at my notebook and read what she had murmured to me in the dream: *Choose me.* And then after a few indecipherable words, I read, *I knew I would be the one.* It was such a vivid line I included it in a poem dedicated to her a few days later.

If myths are public dreams and dreams are private myths, what is the communal dream the Greeks dreamt that became the Judgment of Paris? How is it possible that it speaks to us to this day? Ovid picks up the story in the thoughts of Paris, the exiled prince of Troy. This is not a callow prince, as we've been led to believe. This prince is discriminating, sophisticated, but also under a spell. He turns our story upside down:

> At the same time, three goddesses, Venus [Aphrodite] and Pallas [Athena], and with her, Juno [Hera]—set tender feet upon the sward. I was mute, and chill tremors had raised my hair on end, when 'Lay aside thy fear!' the winged herald [Hermes] said to me; 'thou art the arbiter of beauty; put an end to the strivings of the goddesses; pronounce which one deserves for her beauty to vanquish the other two!' And, lest I should refuse, he laid command on me in the name of Jove [Zeus], and forthwith through the paths of ether betook him toward the stars. My heart was reassured, and of a sudden, I was bold, nor feared to turn my face and observe them each. Of winning all were worthy, and I who was to judge lamented that not all could win.

Singlehandedly, this passage and its equivalents inspired dozens, if not hundreds of painters and poets during the Renaissance and beyond.

What they saw in this episode has rarely been commented on and may have been unconscious in the minds of these myth-besotted artists and writers. But see it they did; moved they were.

What did they see; what moved them? Simply the moment that so many moralists leapt on as the one that sparked the Trojan War, or was there more to it? The beloved myth that *informs* the Venus de Milo is rife with these themes of choosing, deciding, competing. What is implied is as important as what is revealed. The characters off stage—Paris, Helen, Eros, Ares—are like the negative space in a drawing. If you blink and see *outside* the *inside* lines, you can see who is implied in this one-character diorama: a welter of characters.

Often, when I think of the drama unfolding in this single work of art, I think of what Jorge Borges told his student and future culture critic, Alberto Manguel, in Rio de Janeiro many years ago, which Alberto relayed to me at La Rotonde in Paris in 2015, paraphrasing a line from Homer's *Odyssey:* "The gods weave adversity so future generations will have something to sing about."

Listen, we are nudging closer to the moment captured in the Venus de Milo's sublimely sculpted face. Like the chorus in a song, let's hear it one more time. The *story* behind the sculpture helps us understand the held-breath expression on the face of the Venus de Milo—her surprise, her pleasure, her sorrow of being rewarded with the apple of discord and Paris's choice of her, and his choice, perhaps the first in recorded history, of love and happiness over power and glory. Every attribute of Venus, or Aphrodite, gives rise to a mythic moment—our choices about love, desire, and happiness. When they come together, when they merge, the *beautiful* arises like foam on the sea, naturally, wondrously, helping us come full circle to the mythic origins of Aphrodite.

The Venus de Milo enshrines the moment that Aphrodite realizes that Paris has chosen her over the others, chosen love over power and riches.

Hers is the godmother's offer he can't refuse. In the *Hymn to Aphrodite*, attributed to Homer, none could escape the desire for Aphrodite except the martial Athena, the solitudinous Artemis, and the tenebrous Goddess of the Underworld, Hekate. When Aphrodite is in the room, she tells us we have a choice, but we mustn't dither. We must choose. Or else the world decides for us. Choose love, choose passion, choose happiness, choose what appears beautiful to you. Only then, she says in the timeless language of myth, will you find happiness. And even if you don't consciously choose, her son, Eros, might choose for you. A decision that gives rise to Nabokov's famous riddle: "Which arrow flies forever?" His curious answer: "The one that flies forever." The arrow plucked from the quiver that Eros carries over his shoulder that he lets fly; golden arrows aimed at lovers who then quiver from sweet desire. And yet even if it is Eros who releases the arrow, the ancients insisted, it was his mother, Aphrodite, who chose where it landed. Sometimes the chosen lovers are wounded; always they fall, which is why we still say we fall in love.

What is unique, even unprecedented about Eros, son of Aphrodite, is, as Rachel Koussar writes in *Aphrodite and the Gods of Love*, that a romantic dimension is added to desire. In the imagery of mythic love, he puts a face on love and desire as his mother puts a face on beauty and happiness—and a scowl on everything that gets in the way. The evergreen reliable Ovid described him with a pinch of wit: "Love is a naked child: Do you think he has pockets for money?"

Without those faces, life is abstract, cold, calculating, soulless, which is another way to describe why Eros searches for Psyche, the soaring heart longing for the grounding of the soul.

Paris must have found it hard to breathe. He would have heard the stories about the goddesses from the wandering *rhapsodes*, the storytellers who roamed from town to town, palace to palace, and sang of mortals who had been destroyed for seeing a goddess in all her naked splendor. Still, he dared a glance at Hermes, the trickster, the god of the crossroads, who smiled knowingly, as the Renoir painting portrayed him, which is how Paris knew he would be spared, at least for now. The first time wasn't the charm. Nor the second. The third time is the charm, which is to say, the enchantment, the magic spell, the transformation that changes everything. What did they know that we don't? That we need three chances because we rarely get it right the first time, hardly ever the second, sometimes not even the third?

So, all the while that Aphrodite/Venus was gazing at Paris, yearning to be chosen, she wondered how she might persuade him to choose her. This deliberation is behind the puzzling expression you can still see on the face of the Venus de Milo today at the Louvre, a wistful echo of the wonder I saw in the *Life* magazine cover nailed to the wall behind my father's workbench. The look of love I later recognized in the Dusty Springfield song of the same name, which she sang sultry and sensual in a soft bossa nova rhythm.

Choose me, choose love, choose *life*, the goddesses implore him. Or else. Or you will be fated to live your life alone as an exiled shepherd. Out of touch, out of mind, out of love.

The fame of the Venus de Milo began with a shock of recognition. Ensign Voutier saw what few in his position would have recognized in Yorgos's cave on Melos. Inflated by a politically motivated propaganda campaign at the Louvre, it has continued, even intensified, to this day because of her seductively beautiful face. If that look didn't strike the flint in the heart of visitors, they would have long ago abandoned her. If you give her a chance, you might be filled with the ardor that made the anonymous Renaissance poet's heart overflow when he declared that his lover's smile could reveal six paradises.

> I see your face before me
> Crowding my every dream
> There is your face before me
> You are my only theme...

So it is. All these moments, all these expressions, compressed into a single statue, allowing us to see the past in the present, the present in the past.

THREE OFFERS

Three is a magical number in folklore the world over. The ancient Greek Pythagoreans believed it was the first true number, so harmonious it brought wisdom and understanding. Throughout the world, mythology heroes are offered three choices—guesses, tests, or wishes, reinforcing the ancient belief that it takes one or two failures before we learn how to overcome significant ordeals. The genie granted three wishes in the Arabian Nights tales. Three choices are offered to Irish epic heroes who are captured. Travelers encountering the Sphinx were given three guesses to solve its deadly riddle. Batters are allowed three strikes in baseball before they are out. And, you guessed it, Paris was surrounded by three goddesses who offered him the chance to select the most beautiful among them.

"Venus and Juno [Hera], and unadorned Minerva [Athena]," Ovid writes, "more comely had she borne her arms, appeared before you, Paris, to be judged."

HERA'S OFFER OF POWER

Of the three Queens of Heaven, Hera, wife of Zeus, was the first to speak and the first to offer a reward to the shepherd boy. She stepped forward in all her svelte glory, her cheeks dimpled, her cleavage beckoning, promising him the world. She considered her offer to Paris.

"If you choose me," she said, "Not only will I grant you sovereignty and unlimited power as the leader of all Asia, I will also make you the richest man in the world, so wealthy you will make King Croesus look like a pauper."

Strategically, she intensified her argument by insisting that she was most beautiful and should be awarded the golden apple because she was the wife of Zeus, hinting not too subtly that it would be wise to stay on the powerful god's good side. Paris could barely keep his eyes off her sunstormed breasts, but finally, he shrugged. What was money and the leadership of far-flung cities to him, already exiled from his home and hearth on distant Mount Ida?

Unexpectedly thwarted, flabbergasted as only the privileged can feel when they don't get what they feel they deserve, Hera stepped back and tried to look as regal as possible, confident the callow youth would change his mind. When she saw his attention swerve over to Athene, her heart turned to flint as she began to conjure ways to avenge her defeat, knowing the violence she would help unleash.

"Hell hath no fury," observed playwright William Congreve, "like a woman scorned." Lady Antebellum agrees: "There ain't nothing like a woman scorned / There ain't nothing more dangerous than a country girl trading her halo for horns."

ATHENA'S OFFER OF FAME

Next came Athena, the owlish Goddess of Wisdom and War, the founder of civilization, law, and justice, and patron of Athens. Some say that when she heard of the encounter with Paris, she ran a hundred and twenty laps around a nearby gymnasium to look as vigorous as possible. Standing before the young prince, she stood tall and strong, displaying herself in full battle gear, resplendent with a fearsome spear, helmet glinting, shield bulging with Medusa's face. Constantine Cavafy's poem about her speaking to the Senate in Athens can be read as a foreshadowing of what she would say to Paris. Her offer to Paris was a promise of radical change in him if she was chosen—a rapid transformation into both the wisest of philosophers, the most handsome of men, and the greatest of warriors. She argued that she deserved the gold apple because of her stature as a great warrior and protector of Athens, qualities that surely made her more beautiful than all the others. She swore she could guarantee victory on the battlefield.

"Forget Achilles, Odysseus, Ajax, and Hector," she told him. "Your name will be spoken until the end of time. You will outshine them all." His heart raced for a moment at the hint of *kleos*, everlasting fame, but he soon calmed down. The idea of waging war may have tempted his brother, stout-hearted Hector, but Paris had been a lonely shepherd boy for far too long. The thrill of battle was lost on him, the longing for glory, instilled by his brother *Pothos* into the hearts of warriors, was for other young men, not him. He longed only for solitude, to be left alone on his mountain, or so he thought until he was granted a choice.

Their gift offerings were fair enough, thought Paris, but he remained unconvinced. He was even mildly surprised by what they considered to be gifts because he was savvy enough to know there were strings attached, poisonous ones at that, a thought that cancels out the whole idea. A gift must be something the giver is disinterested in, something beneficial only to the recipient. Ancient mythology is rife with references to the dubiousness, the ambiguity, the combustible nature of gifts as the third offer would present.

But something arose that was unanticipated, even to the gods. Paris's indifference produced more than mere spite. The force that arose now was something dark, menacing, the shame that the Greeks called *aidos*. Not rivalry for trade routes nor the evils of the patriarchy, and surely not the winsome beauty of Helen of Sparta, was the root of *Ilios persis*, the Trojan War, which soon followed. The debilitating shame felt by Hera and

Athena, who felt they had "lost" to Aphrodite and been humiliated by the young shepherd boy, curdled into the desire for revenge that was the poison that led to war.

And then there was one.

APHRODITE'S OFFER OF LOVE

The third goddess only needed to offer her beautiful self. Her very being, which the ancients believed was the longing for love, the beauty that promises happiness. Not all beauty does that, which is why not all beauty is beautiful and why hers was irresistible. She embodied what is alluring. She personified the ache of desire. She symbolized the great beguiling.

Aphrodite, our Venus. She, too, tried to persuade the young prince, her offer sounding like beauty but promising so much more. First, she offered her beauty, then she offered the legendary beauty of the Queen of Sparta. Implied in her offer was her fairness and her allure, a noble word that once described calling a falcon back to the falconer's gantlet. It is said that Aphrodite possessed the power to make lovers feel like the falcon called home by the falconer. The goddess did not have to think long about what she might offer the young shepherd that the others couldn't possibly offer, an offer he couldn't refuse. Then she saw something other than the grave threats the oracles had seen, something other than the preening vanity his brothers complained about. What she detected in his young face was an old soul, a loneliness, a longing. In that infinite moment, she knew what she alone could offer him.

Throughout recorded history, stories have revolved around the instant we act on the desire to choose—or not—to actively participate in our own destiny.

"Neither Hera nor Athene looked at their features in the bronze disk mirror," wrote Callimachus, "nor in the diaphanous waters of the nearby Simois River. They were more focused on their social and political and martial powers than their sexual powers. But Cypris [Aphrodite] several times, while gazing into her shining disk [mirror], undid her curls."

Catapulting forward to our own time, this is Greta Garbo, Katherine Hepburn, Marilyn Monroe, Marie Cotillard, or Halle Berry, gazing at their own reflections, using the abacus of a mirror to calculate the effects of their beauty on men, striving to seduce them with a single piercing glance.

Now, radiant Aphrodite approached the callow young Prince of Troy. She moved seductively, her diaphanous garment swirling open in the gentle breezes. *Seductive*, from the Latin *seducer*, to lead away, lead astray, as in persuading a vassal to desert his lord, or in our case to lead away from a cruel fate, a lonely exile. She glowed like dawn, with which she was often compared. Her smile promised eternal happiness. Aphrodite, the Golden One, vowed to herself that she would give him the very thing he secretly longed for, and it was not money or power, the strength of warriors, the cunning of politicians. What is lesser known and rarely acknowledged is how she persuaded him to risk everything for such beauty, and with it, love, and with that, the suggestion of the end of his loneliness. What could have possibly been her lure, the alluring offer?

Not a masquerade but a gift of love. Not an infatuation but a taste of bliss. This is about far more than beauty; it's about how she made him *feel*. The feeling that points to the mysterious power of the Venus de Milo, a power that goes beyond stone.

On this one point, the ancient poets agreed. Aphrodite knew Paris was watching her. She wanted to reinforce the incandescent power of her gift. So, the laughter-loving goddess whispered honey-sweet words into the ear of the lonely shepherd. She revealed her scarcely believable offer, the hand of a mortal woman as beautiful and as passionate as herself and widely regarded as the most beautiful woman in the world: Helen of Sparta, soon to be Helen of Troy.

In this mythologem of the bronze mirror, we can catch the reflection of her vanity as well as her carefully cultivated powers of seduction. The power of this gift that all admired and all dreaded is the reason why Venus/Aphrodite was also called "The Head-Twister" and "The Joy-Giver," even "The Peace-Bringer." These epithets are more than literary affectations. They help us appreciate her grip over us over the last twenty-one centuries.

Her gifts were far from passive; they were active. Her beauty provoked, stimulated, aroused, importuned, persuaded, cajoled, inveigled, incited. *Swayed*, as in *Sway*, the sultry saloon song that I heard on the luxurious Seabourn Spirit where I once danced with my wife as we sailed toward Crete. *Sway* is a song about being infatuated with dancing and your dance partner with lyrics that mimic the rolling waves and rhythms of the side-to-side motion of the Aegean below us: "Sway me smooth, sway me now / Make me thrill as only you know how / Sway me smooth, sway me now."

Swaying that hopes to sway our deepest desires. As Aphrodite did the moment she dropped her robe, her very nakedness signaled many things, including the moment of sexual awakening.

Catching the gaze of the figure just "off-stage," reaching out, as we suspect she does because of the torque of her left shoulder, tells us she is offering a gift or *exchanging* one, which is the greatest gift of all. Ovid pierces the truth of the mystery when he has Venus tell this mystery figure she is offering him the *gift of love*. It was a crisis then, it's a crisis now, as James Hillman vigorously wrote: "Below the ecological crisis lies the deeper crisis of love, that our love has left the world. That the world is loveless results directly from the repression of beauty. If love depends on beauty, then beauty comes first."

The English scholar Nigel Spivey gets in the requisite sweaty mood in *Songs of Bronze* when he describes the goddess: "Aphrodite let the tip of her tongue flicker over his earlobe. Paris shuddered. He knew what desire was. He had desired many women; he desired Hera and Athena. But he had never felt such a seizure as this: as if a hundred hot, hard hammers were hitting on his heart... There was no time to deliberate. He knew he must have what Aphrodite offered him. He must have it as soon as he could, now and forever—whatever it took."

In the ancient Greek formula, beauty follows love, as it was to Renaissance thinkers such as the polymath Marsilio Ficino. "Love is the desire for beauty," wrote the mentor to the Medicis. "Bring your sweet lovin'," sang Sam Cooke. "Bring it on home to me." One of my favorite movie directors, Terrence Malick, the maverick director of *The Thin Red Line*, an excoriating look at World War II, writes, "Who are you? Who are you, really, wanderer? Who are you, who are you, really, stranger? Love—where does it come from? Who put this flame in us? No war can put it out... I was a prisoner. You set me free." The virtuosic Victor Hugo wrote, "The power of a glance has been so much abused in love stories that it has come to be disbelieved in. Few people dare now to say that two beings have fallen in love because they have looked at each other. Yet it is in this way love begins, and in this way only."

But beauty is also a combustible gift.

"Tell the truth and shame the devil," murmurs Veronica Franco, the heroine in the seductive movie, *Dangerous Beauty*. How can beauty be dangerous? "No matter their shape or size...position or wealth," her mother tells her, "[men] all dream of the temptress. The irresistible...unapproachable Venus who quickly turns pliable maiden when they've had a hard day."

A tumult of thoughts surged through Paris's body and soul. The prince paused; he deliberated; he weighed his options as the magnificent goddess approached him. Sinuously, she came nearer, appearing as lonely and isolated as she was beautiful and desirable. But her offer was more alluring than the promise of sexual delight, as assumed by most commentators over the centuries. This is the part of the myth that reveals her as a sorceress of the heart. For she enchants him with the promise of love, with its long association of happiness.

In the ancient language of myth, Venus is saying, *I will enchant the beautiful Helen and I promise that she will want you and love you and together you will be happy.*

This is the godmother offer, the one the young prince cannot and will not refuse. The triple offer of beauty, love, and happiness makes Venus incandescent in his eyes.

This is promising the moon, promising paradise, promising the end of his isolation. Paris is enchanted, which means his fate is momentarily out of his control, controlled by a goddess. Still, he loves the way the story plays out for the most human of reasons. He's been lonely on that mountain slope. Man does not live by sheep alone, not even horny young shepherds. Paris wanted more to live by, so what does he see when he dares to look at Venus? What poets and singers have been crooning about for two thousand years, *the promise of happiness*, the hint of the ecstatic in a humdrum, often disappointing and violent world.

Can you hear in your third ear the swoon-inducing voice of Motown singer Smokey Robinson evoking the sweet ache in his incantatory ballad, "The Love I Saw in You Was Just a Mirage," when he sings, "There you were ... beautiful / the promise of love was written on your face..." And goes on to describe its intensity of his love as being more "than any age or time could destroy."

The intensity of the love spell can make love feel as if it will last forever.

Something enchanting this way comes. The ineffable beauty of her face. In Graves's version, Aphrodite goes beyond offers of power and wealth and promises him, well, *more love*. "Paris," she says in dulcet tones, "it is my heavenly task to arrange the love affairs of gods and men alike. You choose me and I will command my son Eros to guide you to the land of the Spartans, where you will find Helen, the most beautiful mortal woman in the world, as beautiful and as passionate as I am."

What the Radiant One is assuring him is more than the hand and the bed of Helen of Sparta, the most beautiful woman in all the world, which would have been pedestrian in comparison. She says that Helen, "fair, delicate, hatched from the swan's egg, loves hunting and wrestling," will fall truly, in the parlance, truly, madly, deeply, hopelessly in love with you.

Now, what lonely seventeen-year-old anywhere, anytime, can turn down an offer like that?

"Choose me and you choose her," cooed Aphrodite. "Grant me the golden apple and I will grant you her hand *and* her bed. Give me the prize and my promise of happiness will come true."

That was the moment she strategically let down her chiton, that wonderful old word for a transparent nightgown, just long enough to lure him into gazing in wonder upon her naked body, making him even more vulnerable to the desire to see Helen, whose praises the poets had sung and who would be just as beautiful as her.

Paris was now under the spell of beauty. There is the beauty that invites admiration and the beauty that stokes desire. If we fall under its spell, the feeling may be so exhilarating we will risk heaven and hell to be with the one we love because, suddenly, we sense we have never felt so alive. We feel powerless to resist it—and helpless to explain it. But there lies what we might call the paradox of love. We think we have been freely chosen by someone, and that they have freely chosen us—but we know too that we are under an enchantment, so how can we have been free to choose? It's an ancient mystery.

A blind man will not thank you for a mirror, nor will a lonely shepherd boy thank you for the warm bed of a beautiful young queen. We don't know what Paris said at that beveled-edge moment, but we know what he decided.

Smitten with the idea of winning the hand of the most beautiful woman in the world, Paris gripped the golden apple. The fate of his world hung by a thread, a golden one spun for heroes by the Fates. No one says it's easy to find happiness; if it were easy it wouldn't be happiness. With a great sigh of relief, he made his choice and awarded the apple to Aphrodite, which made his heart pound with anticipation but also released the hounds of vengeance for the second time that day—but this time from the two thwarted goddesses, Hera and Athena.

Then Aphrodite doubled down on her offer, increasing the enchantment.

"Sweetly, Venus smiled," writes Ovid in his version of the mythic moment. "Paris, let not these gifts move thee, both full of anxious fear. My gift shall be of love, and beautiful Leda's daughter [Helen], more beautiful than her mother, shall come to thy embrace."

This was in accordance with the ancient Greek belief that beauty follows love, as love follows desire, which was a way of saying we love to desire beauty. To paraphrase Levi Stubbs and the Four Tops, we can't help ourselves. The mythology of love revolves around this kind of circular thinking, and why we feel enchanted when we're in love, which is to say helpless.

To pull off this sleight-of-heart, to coin a mythic phrase, Aphrodite, the capricious chanteuse, promised to lure away Helen's husband, King Menelaus, to Crete, for the funeral of his grandfather, leaving Helen and Paris alone in the Palace of Sparta. She also promised to turn the heart of Paris' father, King Priam, and go against a lifetime of learning the hard way not to antagonize his enemies. If that weren't enough, Aphrodite further vowed to put the idea in the head of the king that when Paris returned to Troy with his newfound bride, he would gather an armada of ships to storm Sparta.

This is the beneficial side of Aphrodite's seductive side, in its original sense, "to draw aside by persuasion," which explains why she was often referred to as the Persuader.

"Her beauty is an active and irresistible grace," adds Rachel Koussar, but it is also occasionally destructive, even dangerous. What she seduced him with is the stuff of myth, a form of magic, a power the Greeks called machlosyne, a useful word revived by the English historian Bettany Hughes to describe "the aura of sexual attraction radiating onto others." According to Homer and scores of other poets and commentators, Paris was so handsome and radiant and vain that Aphrodite found it easy to promise him that she would make certain that Helen of Sparta would find him *irresistible*. The question for the ages—and the source of fierce debate—is whether he was powerless or feckless, enchanted or hypnotized. Were the Greek poets trying to offer up a cautionary tale about the price we pay for vanity and infidelity—or shed light on something far more mysterious, possibly unknowable?

Consider the marvel: Aphrodite was not bribing Paris, as some translators have so ungenerously suggested, but offering the greatest imaginable gift to a seventeen-year-old suitor, *the gift of love* as expressed by Ovid. The poet's nuanced phrasing and deft psychology were lost to the world for centuries while the true power and insight of Aphrodite's gift was transmogrified into a crime that demeaned her, disgraced Helen, and vilified Paris. But as Ovid reflected elsewhere, "Beauty is a fragile gift." The numinous in the luminous. Love is as fierce a force as death. *Amor omnes vincit.* Love conquers all. An aphorism worthy of Shakespeare, whose favorite poet happened to be Ovid. Or Billie Holliday when she sings, "I've got my love to keep me warm."

So be it.

But helpless he was before the charms of Aphrodite and her promise of the hand and the bed of Helen, the most beautiful mortal woman in the world. Emboldened, he handed over the golden ball, the prize for the most beautiful, to Aphrodite. A moment immortalized for all time in the Venus de Milo. And more, the moment all hell broke loose.

One of Robert Graves's great insights into the myth is that Paris was aware of the shadow cast by beauty, the perception of injustice that has accompanied it ever since, writing, "He begs the losers not to be vexed with him."

But Paris's gesture was futile, as Zeus and Hermes and the three competing goddesses knew it would be. No loss of face, which is how the other goddesses interpreted his decision, goes unavenged. This ambiguity is revealed in the face of the Venus de Milo, the complexity of her expression reminiscent of the ability of a great actress to reveal movement from one emotion to another. This mythic moment is enshrined forever in the Venus, a great flaring forth of passion that cannot be rationally explained, only expressed in images, the split second described by the Belgian poet Claire Lejeune: "Beauty alone brings us to our knees."

All of this can be read in the wistful gaze of our statue, the gaze that has obsessed me all my life. All this she saw coming. All this she could have stopped, but she didn't, knowing all too well what it means when love and war sleep together. When Helen and Paris snuck into the Queen of Sparta's bedchamber in the cool halls of Sparta, they came from vastly different worlds but shared one thing in common: they had never loved nor been loved like this before. She had two lovers before Paris, Theseus and Menelaus, both of whom abducted her. So much for young love. Because Paris had been exiled by his parents to a distant mountainside, alone and loveless, he and Helen shared this in common: *They had never been truly loved, nor had they loved.*

It took a spell to make it so; it always does.

Turning back to the *Heroides* and Ovid's mythopoetic imagination, we are afforded a glimpse of Paris's own thoughts, which reveal far more sophistication than he has been generally granted:

> But none the less already then, one of them pleased me more,
> and you might know it was she by whom love is inspired. Great
> is their desire to win; they burn to sway my verdict with won-
> drous gifts. Jove's [Zeus's] consort loudly offers thrones, his
> daughter, might in war; I myself waver and can make no choice
> between power and the valorous heart.
>
> Sweetly, Venus smiled: `Paris, let not these gifts move thee,
> both of them full of anxious fear!' she says; `my gift shall be of
> love, and beautiful Leda's daughter [Helen of Sparta], more
> beautiful than her mother, shall come to thy embrace,' she said,
> and with her gift and beauty equally approved, retraced her way
> victorious to the skies.

In antiquity, Helen was as famous for her voice as for her beauty. Homer
grants her an uncanny gift for mimicry, able to copy the voices of the Greek
soldiers' wives to lure them out of the wooden horse they had secreted
into Troy. If we read between the lines, as myths ask us to do to get us
thinking, beauty itself is a form of mimicry.

If you lose yourself in any work of art, chances are you will come out
on the other side of the canvas, page, or stone either unnerved or invigor-
ated. An anonymous poet wrote the following sensuous words in *Poems
from the Greek Anthology*, which are translated here by Rexroth:

> Let's roll half the garden into the bedroom
> And roll about and moan in unison.

The mythology of love, its enchantment and helplessness, knows no
bounds. To pull off this sleight-of-heart, the capricious chanteuse herself,

Aphrodite, promised to lure away Helen's husband, King Menelaus, to Crete for the funeral of his grandfather, leaving Helen and Paris alone in the palace. She also promised him she would turn the heart of his own father, King Priam, to gather an army and ships that would storm Sparta. This is its beneficent aspect, leading someone away from a cruel life, like a vassal from a cruel king in the original meaning. Seduction in its most mysterious form, the chance for real love and happiness, the sexual drive itself in full force.

"Her beauty is an active and irresistible grace," writes Koussar, but also occasionally destructive, even dangerous. What she seduced him with was the stuff of myth, which is outside of time and space. This is the key to our story. Let's turn it. Turn the moment.

How much are we willing to risk for love, desire, and happiness?

This question is the key we must turn to open our story. The choice to be happy for the first time. It can be seen through like the "*trou*" that Voutier described as the opening to Yorgos's cave. I believe it is the key to the mystery of this statue, and through the power of all works of art. There are arguably more historically important statues of Venus/Aphrodite, and even more *beautiful* ones, such as the Head of Aphrodite, a fragmented Roman copy of Praxiteles' iconic bust from the Aphrodite of Knidos. I saw a marble replica on the desk of the Humanist psychologist Rollo May when I last saw him at his home in Tiburon, California. Again and again, he gazed at his marble replica of the Head of Aphrodite, or the Kaufman Head, as if to ground his comments about the myth of beauty during our three-hour conversation, as tea was served and we mused over long-lost friends.

But there is a more elusive, and dare I say, a more helpful, even illuminating truth to our friend, the Venus de Milo. The spell had been cast, but Venus needed him to drop all his reservations for the spell to work. She needed to leave him naked and vulnerable, which is why she didn't blush when he asked her something awfully rash for a mere mortal.

The fate of Paris is to choose between power and glory or love and happiness to make his own destiny. Her arms may be missing, but we can still approach her and see her if we look hard enough, or is it soft enough, with velvet step and keen eyes, as the keen-eyed French photographer Henri Cartier-Bresson asks? We can't become conscious until we learn how to love *and* how to be loved in return. Or, as the Beatles sang in the last line of the last song they ever recorded, "The love you take is equal…to the love you make." And the story you make, I might add. The looming choice before Paris is what informs the Venus de Milo, the infinite moment that he decided who was going to be awarded the prize of beauty, and the immediate implications in the eternal battle between love and war.

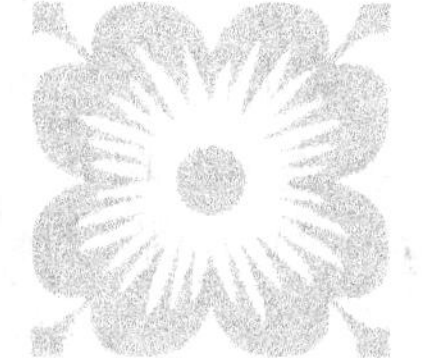

THE CHOICE THAT IS NO CHOICE

The Trojan prince awarded the prize for beauty to Aphrodite, who, in turn, rewarded him with the hand of the most beautiful, most fate-driven woman in the world, Helen of Sparta. It was an ambiguous gift, at best, igniting a conflagration of love, and in its wake, enflaming the most infamous war in ancient history.

This is the infinite moment enshrined by the Venus de Milo.

This splinter of eternity was captured in stone by Alexandros of Antioch.

To underscore our point, Graves adds rather prophetically that Paris was aware of the shadow cast by beauty, the perception of injustice that has accompanied his portrayal by poets and filmmakers ever since. "He begs the losers to not be vexed with him," Graves writes. But his gesture was futile, as Zeus well knew it would be. The three goddesses weren't above being susceptible to bragging rights, and so the notion of a bribe came naturally to them. They were destined to meet and intertwine, like the Goddess of Necessity wrapped around the God of Time, like us, wrapped around our lovers in the dead of night, the light of dawn. The Fates had spoken or whispered seductively. Seeing Venus chosen, in the story and in the gymnasium on Melos, we are inspired to choose love, possibly happiness, so it was promised anyway.

Venus offered more than a gift, less than a bribe. She promised to award him the most magical transformation of all, to love and be loved in return. Often, we offer one or the other, but rarely both. This moment in the myth personifies the beveled edge of love and happiness.

This is the moment that fills the world with hope. She offers Paris a new life, a new *quality* of being. If he accepts her offer, something will *happen*, which is the root of our word *happiness*. It is the unexpected happening in the heart. The marvel in human affairs is that we can't force the feeling; happiness *happens*. And Venus knows this. That is the power of the gift; it is the "agent of change," as Lewis Hyde writes. The gift redounds to the giver, gives twice, blesses. To offer is to receive, to receive to offer. What we are wondering about here is this: What is the *gift* within beauty?

Such is the dulcet desperation of Paris when he awards the golden apple to Venus, who, in turn, offers him Helen's hand. Her response is an encyclopedia of emotion, from awe to guilt, ardor to pride, which can be detected in her face on the statue to this day. Just as Venus is reborn every time she dips into the sacred spring, so too, I like to think, a work of art is reborn every time we dip into it. So much for the search for the fountain of youth. All we need to do is spend time with a great sculpture, a brilliant play, a ravishing book of poetry, and we too can fall in love all over again.

The secret is hinted at in the very word, love, and its counterpart, beauty.

Turning the papyrus page, we find the young prince returning to Troy to seek counsel from his father, King Priam, who likewise was put under the power of the enchantment and, moved by his love-struck son, vowed to ready his ships for safe passage to Sparta. Those boats would be gruesomely described by Homer as "trim freighters of death," redeemed only by later interpreters that Queen Helen of Sparta was so moved by the beauty of Paris and the splendor of his gifts that she asked him to abduct her and take her back to Troy.

Again and again, the myths ask *How much are you willing to risk for love?*

Twenty-five hundred years ago, Plato described encounters with the gods this way: "First a shudder runs through you, and then the old awe creeps over you." That shiver is what we commonly call love at first sight, but with the thermostat turned up, the mercury rising.

Since the very first commentators circulated their opinions about Homeric epics, the more moralistic among them have condemned Paris as a tragic figure: vain, treacherous, oblivious, disdainful of the ancient code of hospitality. But alongside those descriptions have been other readings of the Judgment of Paris, its relationship to the igniting of the Trojan War, and the relationship between fate and free will.

If the old Hays Code-like moralism that demands punishment and blames the world's ills for perceived misconduct can be set aside, it is possible to reimagine Paris so we can conceive of him as being in love with accepting responsibility for his fate. Only then will we come to appreciate the heart-stopping beauty of the expression on the face of the Venus de Milo, her surprise, her wistfulness, her sorrow over what is about to unfold.

Rather than being a disgraced prince, Paris had proved himself a fair judge of animals, and a brilliant athlete, having beaten his more renowned brother, brave Hector, in the funeral games held outside the windy walls of his infamous city. Due to the terrible prophecy that he would grow up to be the downfall of Troy, he had been left to die on a mountainside as an orphan, giving him plenty of reason to feel abandoned and unloved and unwanted. He knew better than most that life was unbearable without love. So, he prayed, and he waited for the imagined goddess to appear to him someday, a sign of the love that the songs about her had promised.

While the gods were plotting, Paris returned to Troy, where Priam learned of his son's existence and planned a series of games in his honor in which the young prince won three laurels for boxing and foot-racing. He then allowed Paris to build a fleet of ships in which to sail to Sparta, replete with a wooden sculpture on the bow of the ship of Aphrodite holding her son Eros in her arms.

THE ETERNAL STRUGGLE

We are within our cultural rights to ask what art and myth teach us about how to live our lives. One place to start is humility, as philosopher Jacob Needleman does when he writes in *The Wisdom of Love*, "We are unknown to ourselves." And then, startlingly, "We are meant to live in two infinities at once—one leading us outward toward action in the world around us, the other calling us to open ourselves to the world within us... When we are in love, we touch moments of pure presence—some call it eternity... In love, we taste a condition of freedom." The good professor insists it is what I see when I gaze upon the Venus de Milo—the wisdom of love. Such are the struggles in the strange land of our souls.

For the Venus de Milo, it is the endlessly ramifying moment when everything was about to happen because she made the *offer he couldn't refuse.* Venus/Aphrodite bribed Paris with the promise of Helen's love and took that apple and the whole world changed. What she knew about what men and women would do for love, what she knew about the power of beauty, what she knew about the promise of happiness is what we still want to know. And why couldn't he refuse? He had been dreaming of her face for a million years. She had been dreaming of escape, real love.

In the story behind and within the story of the Venus de Milo, Paris chooses beauty, chooses love, chooses desire. He prefers love, beauty, and the promise of happiness over power, vainglory, and the uncertainty of fame. His fate is to forge his destiny. What is about to unfold is the only thing that matters in art—the moment, color, shape, form, and pattern that are inexhaustible, that reveal something new to us every time we see it, that changes like the winds over the prairie from second to second, because so do we. And it is always there, but we aren't. If you haven't truly, madly, deeply loved a work of art, your soul is still asleep.

So richly complex and luminously lapidary is the account of the Judgment of Paris that art historian Kenneth Clark has called the single most
popular motif in art history. Virtually hundreds of sculptures, paintings,
poems, and now movies have revolved around the axis of this moment in
mythic history. But repetition does not make meaning. What has been
celebrated in Titian, Watteau, Courbet, Blake, and countless others is the
voluptuousness of the scenario: three gorgeous goddesses preening for the
handsome and horny young shepherd. The truth is more elusive, far more
rewarding, and startlingly relevant for us now, both today and tomorrow.
Love cannot be bought. It must be earned.

Tonight, I find in a scraggly spiral notebook a far-reaching thought
that I wrote on a cross-country motorcycle trip in the winter of 1983: "Any
time not spent on love is wasted." After sleeping on those words, I awaken
the next morning to find in my dream journal an entry from a vision I
don't even remember writing. It's a spectral memory of my wife when we
traveled around Brittany with her looking more beautiful than the morning sunrise and whispering to me, "I knew you would be the one."

I swore there and then to waste no more time.

THE CONSEQUENCES OF BEAUTY

What goes around comes around on the carousel of life and in the myths
of a thousand generations. Listen to Virginia Woolf's description of the
wattage of beauty in her novel, *To the Lighthouse*:

> She bore about with her; she could not help knowing it. The
> torch of beauty; she carried it erect into any room that she en-
> tered; and after all, veil it as she might, and shrink from the
> monotony of bearing that I imposed on her, her beauty was ap-
> parent. She had been admired. She had been loved. She had en-

tered rooms where mourners sat. Tears had flown in her presence. Men, and women too, letting go the multiplicity of things had allowed themselves with her the relief of simplicity.

Together, spellbound, entranced, stupid, sensuality, ecstasy—all these words and more are required to understand this mythic moment, the moment that enshrines that most audacious of human hopes: "the promise of love." This is the very definition of the mythic moment, a situation or condition that never literally happened but is always psychologically happening. Consider that scribes wrote down her alternately triumphant and tragic tale throughout classical times. Her story is told again in the *History of Troy*, by William Caxton, widely considered the first printed book, whose influence washed over Shakespeare and Dante, and along with Ovid's *Metamorphoses*, was a cornucopia of inspiration for art and literature.

The *Iliad* captures this uncanny spirit in the heart-tugging scene on the battlements. The Trojan soldiers look over the plains where they know the final siege will take place the next morning. One of them wonders out loud why they are fighting. Then he and his fellow soldier see Helen as she walks slowly along the far side of the battlements. Wordlessly, they watch her walk, a cameo of grace and serenity and heart-stopping beauty. The soldiers simply nod at each other, seeming to say, "Ah, the beautiful Helen. That's why we are fighting to the death."

Why? Because they were willing to die for beauty.

"Have the courage to love," wrote Euripides in *Hippolytus*. "A god has willed it."

The soul, it has long been said, refuses to give up the struggle.

Then there is the ravishingly beautiful face that launched those 1,136 ships. The first-century B.C. poet Propertius wrote, "Paris himself was said to be undone by love when he saw the Spartan [Helen] naked as she rose from the couch of Menelaus." Her epithets—the names given her by commentators over the millennia—range from radiant and fair to illustrious and golden-haired. Her modern biographer Bettany Hughes writes, "Her history is vexed, brooding, formidable." The Roman writer Lucian wrote in *The Judgment of the Goddesses*, "She is white, as is natural in the daughter of a swan, and delicate, since she was nurtured in an eggshell."

Once again, Ovid, in the *Heroides*, renders her gracefully, having Paris comparing her beauty to that of Aphrodite: "Fame has indeed made great heralding of you, and there is no land that knows not of your beauty; no other among fair women has a name like yours—nowhere in Phrygia, nor from the rising of the sun."

"Undone" is a haunting Robbie Robertson song about being lost without the woman of his dreams, "undone" without his lover. As we all are after love bloodies our hands, our hearts. Are we undone because of real betrayal or unrealistic expectations, disappointed by the broken promise of love? Paris risked everything for that promise, which we have all done at one time or another.

Her fate is alternately cursed and blessed, embodying the mysterious maxim and reflecting the moral of our story: "Where love travels, Eris or strife or deadly conflict, gutsy, delectable, deadly will follow." And yet there is another equally powerful version of events. The differing tales overlap to the point of complementing one another. One version says that Helen is the daughter of King Tyndareus of Sparta, which helps account for her wealth and royal bearing. The other says she is the daughter of Zeus by way of Ananke, Goddess of Necessity, a story that underscores her ethereal beauty and the inevitability of men falling to their knees in submission, stricken with love. In another, discovered on a scrap of papyrus in Egypt and now at the museum in Oxford, Helen is dazzled by how handsome her suitor Paris is and asks him to abduct her and take her back to Troy.

For every commentator who wanted them to burn in hell, there have been ten others who enjoyed the idea of the two of them seducing each other and living for an eternity of love in one night of happiness, no matter what the price. This paradox has been wrestled with for two millennia. Theocritus wrote, "The fleeting pleasure that we pursue makes us suffer because it is mixed with bitter pain."

If love weren't so rare and happiness so fleeting, we would never learn how to risk everything for it. The word *love*, linguists are wont to remind us, comes from the Sanskrit *lubhyat*, which means *desire*. Let's remember that as we imagine Helen spellbound, her heart trampled under the trance of love cast by the original spellbinder herself, Aphrodite. In a word, men were helpless to resist. If so, can they be blamed for the fire in their loins, the treachery in their hearts?

The French poet Paul Valery was blunt in his assessment: "Love is being stupid together." The alarming adjective recalls Voutier's description of the goddess, saying that he was "stupefied," as in stunned, and beside himself, which happens to be the original meaning of *ecstatic*.

There is a moving image in an eleventh century illuminated manuscript from the *Psychomachia of Prudentius* of what appears to be a medieval knight lifting his foot above a bush. It is entitled "Sensuality plunging barefoot into thorns." The very name of the book, which translates as "the battle of the soul," underscores the complexity of the love-trance that Venus cast over Paris and Helen.

Still, Helen felt compelled to rationalize. She told herself that no one, not even the king, had ever loved her like this, and she was willing to risk everything, perhaps because she deserved love after only knowing lust. And, of course, even in his bucolic exile, Paris had heard the voice of the goddess Ossa, the Rumor-Mongerer, on the wind of Helen's legendary beauty. He knew that she was considered the most desired woman in the world, and he had heard that entire phalanxes of men had gone weak in the knees in her presence. Rumor whispered, too, of suicides in Sparta and that Helen was no mere mortal but half-immortal, the daughter of Zeus by Leda. Now it all made perfect sense to Paris. So divine was her beauty, she hardly seemed mortal. Likewise, Paris had never known such love, never felt the "honeyed wound" brought by the arrows of Eros—not coincidentally, Aphrodite's nettlesome son. In the fine moire of Greek myth, the honey that dripped from the arrows of Eros was a sweet substance that brought on desire in mortals and immortals alike and took away some of the pain that comes from being wounded by love.

Now we know why Helen's beauty rendered him speechless, a babbler, so frozen he couldn't breathe. He, too, was hopelessly in love, bewitched by beauty, ensorcelled by the promise of happiness, eternal or otherwise. She stands in for women throughout the ages who symbolized a moment of abandonment, illusion, desire, which is where the notion of terrible beauty is borne, the force that gives rise to desire, which triggers the need to act.

Who hasn't been in his sandals? Whose heart is so cold they can't commiserate. Who hasn't played love's fool and gladly fallen for the myth? This is how the Goddess of Love and Beauty weaves her spells, which is to say she makes mortals and immortals alike *spellbound* by entrancing them. This is how Helen and Paris dissolved like honey in wine into each other's arms for three nights running, then slipped away in silence and stealth in the dead of night on a ship bound for the walls of windy Troy. Helen's story reveals how the divine is brought down to earth. How and why are assumed by all the clichés about faces and ships and vanity and fighting. But a deeper truth is at bay here. Helen is the daughter of the philandering Zeus, who is mightily proud of siring such a stunning beauty and wants all the world to know—all except his wife Hera.

According to Graves, it is Zeus who conspires to ignite the Trojan War. The poet says simply that the reasons must remain forever unknown. We do know, by the lyre of Homer, that Odysseus told Menelaus that it was precisely because Helen was so alluring that he had forced the other princes to take a vow because, sure as snow on Mount Olympus, there would be a slew of suitors drunk on her beauty fighting for her favors.

"Then my advice to you," Graves has him say, "is to insist that all of Helen's suitors swear to defend her chosen husband against whoever resents his good fortune."

The Roman poet Horace described the birth of such crazy-making beauty as "*Ab ovo*," from the egg, referring to the one that hatched Helen. Mythspeak for the birth of beauty with war right behind.

What in heaven's name are the Greeks trying to say about the relationship between love and beauty, desire and war? Philosophers and poets have been wrestling with the issue for centuries and no doubt will tangle with it for more centuries. Few are as eloquent as the barrister Edmund Burke: "By beauty, I mean that quality or those qualities by which they cause *love*, or some *passion* close to it [my italics]." Seen this way, the seemingly insane affair between Helen and Paris becomes an allegory for the relationship between Helen and Paris (both described for their beauty) and Aphrodite (the Goddess of Love). When the three come together a passion is stoked that will set the world on fire.

Does our fair story have to be complicated?

Only if love and beauty were simpler than they are.

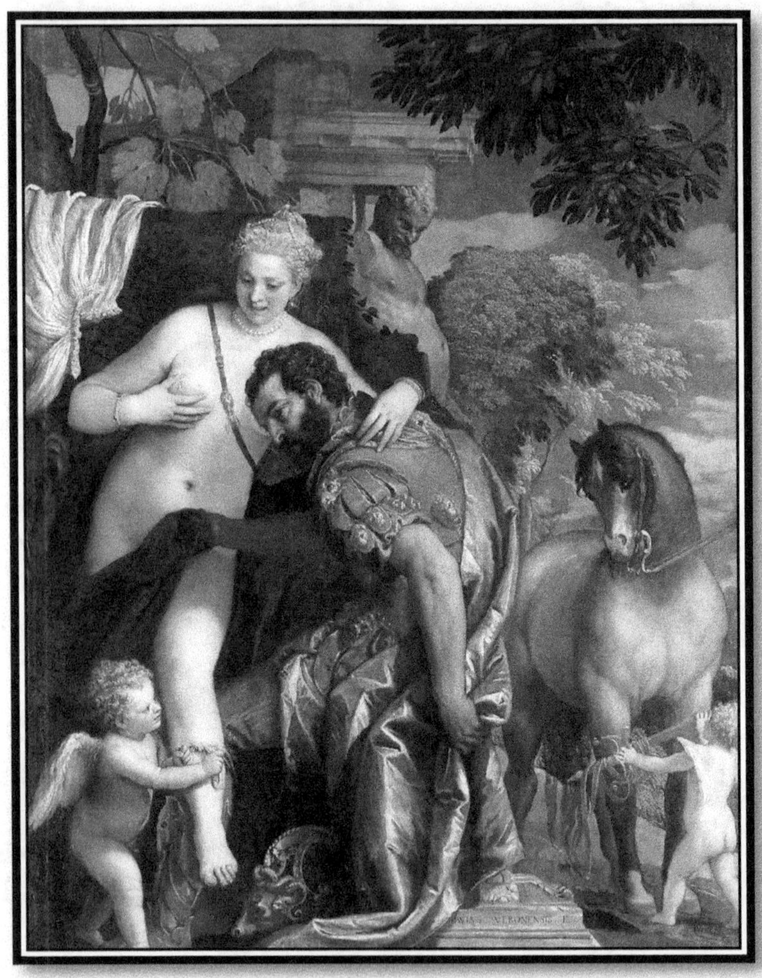

"Mars and Venus United by Love"
Paolo Veronese, 1570
Metropolitan Art Museum, New York

LOVE AND WAR Some say it was Aphrodite's fault, her vanity igniting the spark that lit the fuse in Troy. Others blame Paris for his audacity in breaking the ancient codes of hospitality and carting Helen to his home across the sea. Still others claim it was all Helen—her betrayal, her abandonment of husband and daughter. The great French philosopher Simone Weil compressed and condensed three thousand years of deliberation and called the *Iliad*, which famously describes the last ten days of the ten-year war, as an existential drama, a "poem of force." Written on the eve of World War II, Weil's unflinching analysis "presents a nightmare vision of combat as a machine in which all humanity is lost."

Whether read as a thickly veiled history about the centuries of fighting over sea lanes or the psychodynamics of love and war, the *Iliad* can also be understood as an exploration of the exigencies of enchantment. Aphrodite's offer to Paris was one he couldn't refuse or chose not to. Her enchantment of the young prince and then the young queen surely ignited love's fire, in the bedroom in the palace in Sparta and then in Troy of the high walls. But the real question is what the ancient authors were trying to say allegorically about the nature of the impending war.

No doubt, it was Helen's face that launched a thousand songs, stories, poems, paintings, sculptures, operas, movies, and beauty products, but it was the black-tarred triremes, the fifty-oared ships dispatched by a hundred city-states, whose crews swore to avenge her abduction that made the war infamous.

Once ensconced safely back at Troy, a magnificent wedding was staged, and all Trojans were mesmerized by Helen's beauty and grace and devotion to Paris. It is said that she discovered "a bleeding stone" on the battlements of the famed city, which she recognized as a gift from Aphrodite—an aphrodisiac which, Graves reminds us, she used on Paris "to keep his passion alive." All Trojans fell in love with her, and the good King Priam took an oath never to let her go.

All this passion implied in a single statue. That's the beauty of it.

Every athlete, every soldier, every trainer working out in gymnasiums would have "seen through" the statue, through the story to the backstory that told of how their fellow Greeks had gone to war for beauty and love, just as we might visit the war memorials in Washington, D. C., St. Petersburg, Russia, the Green Fields of France, or Hiroshima and Nagasaki.

Is this myth only a metaphor for tyranny and blood sacrifice, or something even *more real*, sinewy, bloody? The old mythographers regarded Zeus as the one who made Paris the fall guy for the Trojan War. Every battle needs a scapegoat. They claim the Olympian desired battle but loathed peace, wanted credit, and deflected blame, all out of fatherly pride for his daughter, the beautiful Helen, hatched in secret, the result of a chance entwinement with the goddess Nemesis. Out of that commingling of power and need for Helen, famous for her beauty. His wish was to be obscure, in the shadowy background, so as not to make Hera suspicious that he had been resorting again to his bedswerving ways by taking Nemesis as a lover, who, in many variations of the story, becomes Helen's real mother.

My reading of this version is that the old rhapsodes were telling us that it was a Necessity to bring Beauty into the world so we could tolerate the truth of death, a balm so powerful, men and women would gladly die for it.

The contemporary American painter Howard David Johnson rendered the Trojan War by employing a fire-hued distant horizon, a visualization of impending doom, as the King of Mycenae, Agamemnon, leads the Greek charge to the much-vaunted windy walls of Troy and reveals a riff on what the poet Stephen Dunn would call the insistence of beauty. "Beauty isn't nice," he writes. "Beauty isn't fair." Camus claimed that the Greeks died for such beauty. In *The English Patient*, the author Michael Ondaatje has his character, Katharine Clifton (Kristen Scott Thomas) plaintively confides to her lover, László Ede Almásy (Ralph Fiennes), "From this point on...we will either find our love or lose our souls."

I see this as the latest iteration of an age-old belief that love (and beauty) will save us. Think of the so-called Monuments Men who braved the Nazis to save the looted art from the Louvre and braved the rising waters in Florence to save the art from the Uffizi, or the guards who stood in front of the National Museum in Iraq to prevent even worse destruction.

Whose heart is so cold they can never commiserate? Who hasn't played love's fool and gladly fallen for the myth? This is how the Goddess of Love and Beauty wove her spells, entrancing mortals and immortals alike. This is how Helen and Paris dissolved like honey in wine into each other's arms for three nights, the number in folklore that signifies transformation. This is the mood they were in when they slipped away in silence and stealth in the dead of night on a ship bound for Troy of the Windy Walls, King Priam's city, rich in gold. It was said by the ancient mythographers that when they arrived, Paris hated to see Helen's beauty imprisoned behind the walls of Troy.

Today you can visit the rough-hewn ruins of ancient Troy, with stone-wall foundations that must look like giant molars from the sky, but which hold the memories of the millennia. Legend has it that Alexander the Great on his way to India, asked a local landowner to handle the spear of Achilles. Shelley, Keats, Whitman, Gibbons, Piranesi, Macaulay, all loved to ramble through the ruins during the Romantic Age. And now tourists from the world over ramble around the grounds hoping for a glimpse of the glory that crowned ancient Greece.

If we think we invented the past, we only need to read the first-century traveler, Pausanias, a kind of Greek Baedeker. He was downright wistful as he ventured from town to town through ancient Greece, bemoaning the loss of greatness, the demise of glory, the decay of beauty. In the cautionary tale of Aristotle and Phyllis, the old philosopher asks her to make love to him, but later, ashamed, tells the young Alexander who he has been mentoring, "If Eros could prey upon an old man, then a young man must be all the more wary."

This, the mythmakers insist, is the price paid for a moment of bliss, a moment of passion, a moment of happiness. As for war, love and war have been entangled, intertwined, woven together, interconnected since the dawn of time. Every culture has its cautionary tales about the incestuous relationship between the two. Every culture must. Because nothing happened just one time in one place.

PRIAM'S PROMISE

To cast a spell over the hearts of torrid lovers is one thing. To enspell their parents is another, a rigorous task even for the Goddess of Persuasion. For her third spell, she enchanted the noble King Priam, the father of Paris, to send a flotilla of boats and a company of his finest soldiers to accompany his son to his rival, King Menelaus' court in Sparta. As the story progresses in the Trojan War, we come across enchantment after enchantment. This concatenation of coincidences turns the question of free will on its heels, to mix metaphors. All of this was preordained by Alexandros in his award-winning sculpture of the Venus de Milo—her astonishment at being awarded the golden apple and her apprehension that Helen and Paris' love affair will end tragically."

Nine days after he cast his lot with Aphrodite, Paris disembarked from his ship and entered the Palace of Sparta laden with gifts for Helen and Menelaus. As was the custom of *xenia*, the code of hospitality that welcomes all strangers, Paris was honored with nine days of feasting and games. The moment that our heart-in-his-mouth hero entered the palace, he was blindsided by beauty. Not the insipid sort, but what Yeats later called "a terrible beauty," one that presaged war. Enchanted by Aphrodite, Paris was enthralled by Helen, who was as beguiled by the Trojan prince as he was by her. He was held in rapture by the sight of Helen's "beautiful white breasts," as one poet put it, while another would soon write, "I would like to be wind across your breasts." Their three-sided story is a triangulation of ravishing love spells, each enamored with the other with nothing left to chance. Marvelously, Ovid echoes my suspicion of many years. In dramatic contrast to the bribes offered by Hera and Athena, Aphrodite's offer is a gift.

According to Ovid, Aphrodite's persuasive words to Paris were: "My gift shall be of love, and beautiful Leda's daughter [Helen of Sparta], more beautiful than her mother, shall come to thy embrace... with her gift and beauty equally approved."

What Paris is offered is a *choice*: the bribes of power and glory or the gifts of love and beauty. Through them, the myth implies a *chance* at that elusive creature called happiness. As a myth rather than a fairy tale, there is no fatuous promise of Paris and Helen being *happy ever after*, as the old phrase goes. Only a *moment or two of love*, as risky and dangerous and livid as it may be. They are offered, really, all that Aphrodite, or Venus, can offer: a combustible, explosive, dangerous but titillating form of love. Under the double spell of Aphrodite, Paris and Helen curled around each other like acanthus leaves on a temple column. Euripides dared to explain her power in his *Hippolytus*, giving her these lines:

> The power I possess is sex, passion, love, which you mortals,
> in honoring me, celebrate in your diverse ways. I'm not less the
> darling of heaven.
> I am the Goddess Aphrodite.

Still, there was one annoying fact about their assignation. They were canoodling in the palace of King Menelaus, Helen's husband. The "neat-ankled, fair-haired girl whose renown is spread all over the holy earth, the Queen of Sparta, and whose bed was still warm from the body heat of her warrior-husband, could not resist the prince's advances. Her history, as Hughes so vividly describes it, "is vexed, brooding, formidable, born when heaven and earth were in a pugnacious mood."

The mythic lineage is convoluted but worth unraveling for its psychological insights. Zeus, the mythic father of the universe, makes love to the rapturously beautiful Dione, who gives birth to immortal beauty, who we know as Aphrodite or Venus, and later Zeus orders Ananke, Goddess of Necessity, to give birth to Helen, the very personification of mortal beauty. Mythically read, the gods decreed and nature agrees that beauty ignites love and desire, which are necessary to human happiness.

Once Paris enters the palace in Sparta, he becomes helpless the moment he hears the sigh of Helen. Soon, the two lovers are wrapped in each other's arms like the serpents on the staff of Asclepius. However, there was a detail that sticks in the throat. Then the King of Sparta departed for Crete on a diplomatic mission, and he made the fateful decision to ask Paris to watch over his queen.

So besotted was she with the fair prince, she spelled out "I love you" in drops of wine on the oak table that lay between them. Now we know why Helen's beauty rendered him speechless, a babbler, so frozen he couldn't breathe. In a word, he, too, was hopelessly in love, bewitched, ensorcelled. Call it what you will, but don't deny it. Both had been exiled, both lived unloved, and now there was a chance at a better life.

Her two previous lovers, Theseus and Menelaus, had treated her like chattel. She had never known real love, not the kind that "loosens the limbs," or as the ancient Zen masters said, "rectifies the heart." To ever love again, she would have to be swayed, even entranced. This is the power of Aphrodite, a force that lovers around the world have been tapping since Homer's red dawn of time despite the risk of that power to break our hearts. The trance runs deep.

Inspired, he pulled his lyre out of his traveler's satchel and unleashed its dulcet tones, learned in the solitude of the slopes of Mount Ida, softening Helen's resistance.

So armed with Aphrodite's salve, he serves the love potion to his loveless heroine who falls hopelessly in love with him, so much so that he is suffocated with affection, can't get rid of her, and is trapped for the rest of his life by the very love he thought he needed.

It was her story. It was always her story. Now it's yours.

SPELLBOUND

Spellbound. Enchanted. Glamoured. The Venus de Milo's allure was a form of fate, as beauty, love, and desire always are. Paris, like all lovers ever since, was out of his mind, besotted, bowled over, ass-over-tits in love, as my bawdier Irish friends say. An ancient metaphor for being compelled by emotions we cannot control. Mythologically speaking, the apple changes whoever or whatever consumes it. It is *magic*, whether it's an apple or some other variation on the theme of forbidden fruit. Attribute it to hormones or a case of shepherd loneliness, but it's a deep bluesy spell like the one growled by Screamin' Jay Hawkins' "I Put a Spell on You." Hawkins captures the hypnosis, the eroticism, the desire, the transport, the voodoo trance, and the spine-chilling cackles of the real thing, as if someone stuck pins into us, which is the Haitian mythic equivalent of Eros's piercing arrows.

So little, in matters of the heart and the matters of art, has changed over the millennia. Not the willingness to endure the pain for the gain, not the desire to soar, nor the willingness to plunge. As Fleetwood Mac sang in their thumpingly moody "Hypnotized," that "What matters most is the feeling you get when you're hypnotized." In a word, transported. Reveried, to coin a verb. Spellbound.

The lure of Aphrodite's beauty and the promise of love in the legendary Helen's bed was too much to resist for Paris; it was a way out of boredom, a way into his own heart. Helen was Paris's destiny; he was her fate. Seldom considered but entirely possible is the chance that she identified with his lacerating loneliness. He too was alone and forlorn, her only solace being the constant company of her Three Graces, Beauty, Joy, and Radiance. All that is signaled by the shadowy detail in some versions of the story is that Helen's real mother was Nemesis, or Necessity, who had been seduced by Zeus. "Necessity is a hard nurse," goes the old proverb, "but raises hardy children." Leonardo da Vinci, who knew better than most, obsessed as he was by work, said, "Necessity is the mistress and guide of nature."

Regardless of the terms, Paris had been wounded by "love's bloodied work," as he was described by the classical Greek poet Praxiteles.

In *Beauty and the Promise of Happiness*, the Greek-born American philosopher Alexander Nehamas explores the power of beauty is significant is because it is *realistic* and seems possible and carries the possibility of pleasure and joy. Not to have access to the opportunity of happiness is to feel at a loss, as if something vital has been stolen from us.

And so it was that Paris presented Aphrodite with the golden apple, which, it is said in the ancient chronicles, was the possession she coveted above all others. He took a chance because love took a chance on him, threw him his destiny, as suggested in the great old poem by the first-century poet Meleager, from a collection significantly called *Aphrodite's Garden*:

> The loves have me / surrounded
> and don't give me a chance for Beauty, or the Muse,
> or one of the Graces / throws this desire my way—
> What can I say? I'm just burning up.

"Though I lie here for you," cries Sting, "I burn for you." "Fever!" sang the scorching Peggy Lee. "You give me fever, fever in the morning, fever all through the night." And from Billie Holliday: "I say I'll go through fire / And I'll go through fire / As he wants it, so it will be / Crazy he calls me-Sure, I'm crazy / Crazy in love, you see." *Crazy in love.* One of the themes running through the Parian marble of the Venus de Milo. The Imagist poet H. D. [Hilda Dolittle], wrote, "The enchantment held." "I'm crazy," sang Patsy Cline, "for trying and crazy for crying / and I'm crazy for loving you."

The story has come and gone since the time of the Homeric bards, and it goes and goes to this day, as recognizable as any schoolchild romance. What makes the Judgment of Paris so remarkable is that it marks the first time in Western literature that a man chose love over power or fame. This notion helps us understand one of the most influential myths of all time—and the reason for the sculpture in the niche of the old gym. Her presence there is reminiscent of what the depth psychologist James Hillman described as the mythic function of cheerleaders and colorful bunting at sporting events, which is to remind us of the sensuous aspects of sports.

So grateful was the goddess, she took it upon herself to be the personal protectress of the Trojans, at least for the first nine and a half years of that fierce siege. Paris was loathe to admit later on the ramparts of Troy that he had unwittingly incurred the doubled wrath of Hera and Athena, who exacted their revenge for not being chosen and sided with the Greeks, siding with the cruel Mars, which multiplied and magnified what Lincoln would later call during America's Civil War "the awful arithmetic of death."

If you can visualize Venus with arms intact, reaching at the instant, the mythic moment, when she accepts the golden ball from fair Paris, you will know the moment that changed the world and changes it again and again every time we make such a choice.

Why do we need the myths; why bother with these ancient stories? Because the old questions still haunt us. We will never know for certain, but we still need to put a face on this question.

Change—or lack of it—is at the root of drama. Change is the only constant. *Plus ca change.* The heart of metamorphosis. *Ch-ch-ch-changes / Turn and face the stranger*, sings the strutting David Bowie in his anthem about the inevitable effects of time.

The face we have placed on this power for at least the last three thousand years is Venus, the Golden One, the Radiant One, the Goddess of Sweet Shuddering. She is sweet-smiling, a lover of laughter, gold-crowned, awakener of pleasant yearnings in the gods, filling mortal hearts with sweet longing. From her cheeks shone an ambrosial beauty. She has been called quick-blinking, sweet-smiling, and laughter-loving. She is always depicted with a seductive face and has a song that seduces. Her attendants, the Graces—Beauty, Grace, Flowering, Joy, and Radiance—crown her with myrtle and lay rose petals at her feet.

Irony of ironies, Aphrodite herself feels a twinge of desire for forbidden fruit, the charms of a mortal named Anchises. To seduce him without scaring him away with a display of her immortal powers, she disguised herself as a Phrygian princess, the result of their commingling being the birth of the hero Aeneas. "Strong was force, irresistible its power, which brought me to your bed," she purred to him, though immediately after she felt sorrow and remorse.

We dare to say that love leads us to the arts, where we can be healed of the wounds of love. And the one with the beautiful hands is the sister of the sweet-voiced Muses who can heal the pain of love. What do we do with that little tincture of insight from the ancients? What do we do with the words that flow downriver to us from the mountain peaks of past stories? Words that follow, as I heard Johnny Rivers croon one night at the Troubadour Club in L. A., "my wild sweet love."

This is an echo of the ancient Greek code of *xenia*, the rule of hospitality offered to strangers, the promise broken by Paris, but which Helen begged to violate, knowing the risks involved. How could she break such an inviolate code? She had little more than chattel, raped by two famous kings, living a lie. The culture encouraged the ravishing of beautiful women for the reflected glory of their kingdom. This, too, can be seen in the face of the Venus de Milo, questioning all of us who gaze at her: *How much would you risk for love? How far would you go for beauty?* Love isn't always heart-thumpingly wonderful. More often than we would like, it is heartrending, as expressed by Emily Dickinson: "If I can stop one heart from breaking, I shall not live in vain."

Noble as it may be, it is just as often heart-rescuing.

HELEN, QUEEN OF TWO WORLDS

Venus's victory was also Paris's victory in winning the hand of the most beautiful of mortals, Helen of the Thousand Mirrors, destined to enjoy a deadly fame. The Queen of Sparta was a rich landowner, brilliant, clever, and abandoned repeatedly by her husband. But her beauty was a sweet-bitter gift from the gods. Forever in doubt that she was loved for herself and not her spellbinding beauty, she was doubly doomed, enthralled by her king and bewitched by Aphrodite. She had not been consulted in her forced marriage to the mendacious King Menelaus; she resisted being treated like marriage meat. Worse, her first lover, Theseus, abducted and raped her when she was a twelve-year-old princess. Her chieftain husband was away in battle so often the young queen's bed was cold. She longed for love.

When Aphrodite says to Paris, "My gift shall be of love," she is saying that they would both come under her spell. Enchanted, Helen was helpless to resist. This is the Goddess of Persuasion, the personification of her uncanny influence over others, persuasion being one of her innumerable aspects, as echoed in the third-century Orphic Hymns:

> O Persuasion whose joy is in the bed of love,
> secretive, giver of grace
> visible and invisible, lovely tressed daughter of a noble Father…
> With your maddening love-charms you yoke mortals
> and the many races of beasts to unbridled passions.

As described by the brilliant classics scholar Roberto Calasso, "The greatest exploit of Zeus' reign is that of having forced Necessity to bring forth Beauty." To reify this intriguing claim, he tells of a famous statue at Ramnos, which depicted Leda taking Helen to her "real mother," who happens to be the goddess Nemesis, the implications of which are vast.

"What has overcome me?" we ask, astonished, clueless. If doors had ears, they would have heard that Helen would have suspected she was under the spell of the charms of Aphrodite, who it was said presided over "maidenly whispers and smiles and tricks, and over sweet delight and honeyed love."

If we are rendered helpless by love, how do we describe its effect on us? We turn to the arts whose business is the transport of images from ordinary reality into reverie. The mystic monk Thomas Merton said it well: "Art enables us to find ourselves and lose ourselves at the same time." Looking at Rossetti's famous painting of Helen, which his lover, the golden-haired Annie Miller modeled, it is easier to understand what the poet George Nathan meant when he said that art is the sex of the imagination and Mae West's sultry observation that "Sex is emotion in motion."

Revisiting the Rossetti portrait recently at San Francisco's Legion of Honor museum's exhibition of the Pre-Raphaelites, I thought of Van Gogh's plaintive cry to Theo: "Blessed is the man who found his work and a woman to love."

In turn, I remembered Calasso's compressed aphorism, "Only the lover is *entheos*," by which he meant we are full of the gods when we are in love, wildly *enthusiastic* about our sensuous lives. Exuberant. Jubilant. Exhilarated. Jaunty. This has been understood for a long time. We did not invent wild love, no matter how much the internet wishes to suggest we did. The Greeks referred to it as *eratokai thaumatai*, the wound of Eros. Love hurts, as the rock song reminds us. Sometimes ourselves, sometimes others. On some occasions, scores of people suffer because of our decisions in love. Calasso reminds us of one of the hinge moments of the Trojan War when Helen weeps on the battlements at the sight of the slaughter on the plains between Troy and the sea, apologizing to the kind king for being the cause of the bloodshed. "No," Priam reminds her, "you are not the cause of the war. Only the gods are causes."

FROM THE CURIOSITY CABINET OF LOVE AND BEAUTY

"If an act was witless or astonishing," Michael Finley observed in his incisive book, *The World of the Odyssey*, "no doubt a god was involved." Today, we might say that the wiring in our brains went berserk. I prefer the face of a god or goddess to faceless chemistry. This is decidedly not an excuse for aberrant behavior. It is the next step in understanding the astonishment of what is happening in the face of the Venus de Milo.

Mythologically speaking, I think that Calasso and Finley are saying that the *overwhelming* emotions—the ones that reside deep in our shadow side—can cause such irrational human activities as war. This realization prompted Carl Jung to admit in his memoir, *Memories, Dreams, and Reflections*, that even though we long to believe otherwise, we are rarely "masters in our house," hardly ever at home in our own psyches, our very souls.

"How do you *make* somebody love you," asks the twitchy-faced Jim Carrey in the movie *Bruce Almighty*, "without affecting free will?" If the gods bewitch us, are we responsible? We long for change but cry when we are transformed. The myth is trying to resolve this ancient paradox: How is it that we can choose who to love but not who we fall in love with? We long for transformation and to believe that the arrows slung by the impish god will change our lives. Is that so naïve, so selfish?

❈

Trembling far beneath the personal struggle, like the first tremors of an earthquake, is what James Hillman thought was the deepest fear of all—that love itself had disappeared in the world. "That the world is loveless," he writes, "results directly from the repression of beauty. If love depends on beauty, then beauty comes first." This begs the question of the meaning of beauty: What does it mean to say that something or somebody is beautiful? Is it a formula, a theory, or more likely, an experience—an encounter that stirs the soul? Such as an Ojai sunset, a 1937 Bugatti, a Charles Eames chair, an old-fashioned ticker tape with stock reports, the sight of your grandmother dandling your daughter. A deftly turned double play on the diamond. A photo of Saturn's rings from the Hubble space telescope. Footage of chimps doing backflips in the spray of a waterfall. The dazzlement of a flight of fireflies swarming around the pier on Lake Michigan. The smile of an old friend you bump into on the streets in a faraway land, stretching out his hand, remembering things no one else does.

A long time ago I saw a curious rusty sign, riddled with bullet holes, at a drive-in movie theater in Ypsilanti, Michigan. It read: "Let no one say, and / Say it to your shame, / That all was beauty / here, until you came." The sign did its job. Often, when I notice something beautiful, I think of that sign and smile and am able to brace myself for the ugliness of the world.

No need to be somber about this. It might help to smile at the temerity of the question and cite the contrarian reporter Ambrose Bierce, who dared to define it in *Devil's Dictionary*: "*Beauty,* n. The power by which a woman charms a lover and terrifies a husband."

When I met with Rollo May for the third and last time, in the winter

—210—

of 1985, I asked him about this mysterious power, especially in relation to Solzhenitsyn's belief in the power of beauty. "Nothing else seems able to save us," he said ponderously. "One thing is certain: A world that does not have a concern for beauty will not be worth saving."

"Beauty," said Somerset Maugham, "is an ecstasy," which is why we feel "beside" ourselves once under its spell, but not necessarily forever, as George Sand observed. On their bucolic singles track, the whistle-inducing "Groovin'," the Young Rascals sang over a tremulous harmonica, "Life will be ecstasy, you and me endlessly." And here is the French Romantic novelist and essayist George Sand, known to her closest friends as "Aurore," writing from her apartment in Nohant-Vic, outside Paris: "The beauty that addresses itself to the eyes is only the spell of the moment; the eye of the body is not always that of the soul."

As infuriating as it may sound, I think Tolstoy cut through the miasma when he dared to say, "It is amazing how complete the delusion that beauty is goodness." But then again, happiness is less a matter of getting what we want than wanting what we get. And love is less important as a life-preserver than as a soul-preserver. Desire that. In the infinite moment if you can find it. Who's to say what's beautiful? I say it's the face of the one you love.

IS BEAUTY NECESSARY?

How might we imagine Paris, the hapless Trojan prince, at his key moment, the moment of *anagnorisis*, recognition, that was so vital to ancient Greek drama that they coined a word for the moment when a character makes a critical discovery of who they are and what they stand for. The term referred to the hero or heroine's usually sudden awareness of a situation, the realization of things as they stood, and finally, "the hero's insight into a relationship with an antagonistic character in a Greek tragedy."

I am making a case here for the Gaze of Venus as embodying *anagnorisis* as both a moment of mythic recognition and the moment of *the enli-*

vening force of her work and its revival. I detect in the Venus the same instinct followed by prehistoric sculptors, a realization that ultimately the mysterious female power to procreate, to make life itself, has come to represent creativity itself.

After all these years of mulling over the myriad meanings of this story, I like to think of Paris, prince of Troy, arbiter of beauty, saying to himself as he decided who he would name as the winner of the Olympian contest, "I want to astonish Venus with an apple!" Of course, Cezanne had the same thought when he brashly announced, "I am going to astonish Paris with an apple."

And so it was that Paris presented Aphrodite with the golden apple. The ancient chronicles tell us that she coveted this prize above all her other possessions. When he awards the golden apple (or ball, take your pick) to Venus, he has already had contact with it, and it will now be passed on, figuratively, to Helen, making her the New Eve who eats the forbidden fruit.

Call it hormones; think of it as a series of spells or love potions. This is the imaginative way to interpret the sudden piercing of the heart (symbolized by Eros's merciless arrows), the unexpected incursion of passion into a male lover's veins. The prince was, as suggested by one classical Greek poet, Praxiteles, wounded by "love's bloodied work." He felt the heat of the Goddess of Love and saw her bag of seductive tricks, which emerged out of her ethereal beauty, and now he would sail off to be seduced one more time.

Or, as my friend and colleague, the psychologist Robert A. Johnson, pointed out during a lecture we gave together at the Kanuga Conference Center, in North Carolina, Paris was in love with love itself? If so, this is tragically different than being in love with an actual person. Carefully,

Robert pointed out that morning that this is the difference between love and romance, selflessness and selfishness, transcendence and transmogrification. If so, we need to consider that what has been called a "bribe" for millennia was more of an offer, which is no bribe at all but a choice, a cosmic opportunity to rebalance the scales of fate.

The offer of a choice. That is the real mythologem, the kernel of truth, the jewel at the heart of the story. Closer yet, the *provocation* to choose, which is, strangely, at the heart of beauty.

Again and again, I go back to Robert Haas's gorgeous phrase describing the power of poetry as a *raid on the inarticulate* to, in effect, become articulate. This is the task of all artistic expression, especially the attempts to define beauty.

Twenty-five hundred years ago, in the *Hippias* dialogue, Plato imagines beauty this way: "Beauty must be raged or outraged into life, for the lion's cubs are stillborn." The Renaissance scholar and Humanist philosopher Marsilio Ficino tracks the etymology of beauty to *Kallos,* derived from *kaleo,* "provoke." Geoffrey Grigson's derivation and evolution of her Roman equivalent in the Latin *Venus* is similar in the sense that is a force, a compulsion, reflected in its original meaning in the Proto-Indo-European *win*— to strive, want, which he concludes means the *Venus* referred to the "force of achieving a desire." And in a beautiful symmetry of language, we still talk of "winning her hand in marriage" or "he has a winning face." The *Venus de Milo* puts a face on that faceless idea. Not unlike Leonardo painting the Madonna Bonna, the Good Lady, and calling it the *Mona Lisa,* so too did Alexandros sculpt his Venus, the very image of desire.

Beauty, love, happiness are things we *win* in the primal sense of that simple verb because we have *earned* them through deep and honest desire, the competition to be true to ourselves. This is such a reeling, spinning experience, *throwing* us out of ourselves, evoking again the evolutionary leap, that many philosophers and biologists suggest how it feels to fall under a spell. In turn, it isn't passive and banal, after all, but passionate and active, provoking admiration, tears, identification, connection. At least the beautiful does, as opposed to mere beauty. Think of the encounter with the first snowfall each November in Michigan, the white blanket over the green lawn, or shadows doing backflips over the old Roman arched stone bridge across the Seine in Southern France, or the face of the one you love when you wake up in the morning, feeling blessed by the gods that she has graced your life.

Seeing the need for love, desire, and beauty in the world, Venus leaped at the *opportunity* to bring together the two emblems of mortal beauty, the handsome and *fair* prince, Paris, and the deliriously (from the old Latin word *delire*, being out of line) beautiful Helen. Not an arbitrary word choice there either. For the ancients, opportunity was a god. It's a beautiful open-aired word with those two open-armed "o's, which is to say offering a clean chance. It's an old Roman word based on the god of harbors, *Portus*, a marvelous way to describe how every *chance* is an opening, a promise of still waters ahead, safe anchorage. When I was young, that was a golden word. I remember my basketball coach in London mumbling to the rival coach for the U. S. Army team about my intense play that year. "The lad takes advantage of every *opportunity*." That made me wickedly proud. A favorable chance for movement, circumstances for progress, a window for advancement. When the time is fit, the time is favorable, dating back to two late-fourteenth-century words, *ob*, toward, and *Portunas*, Roman god of keys, doors, locks, and harbors (from *portus*, harbor). An *opportunity* is an opening for happy and safe landings versus an *importunate* moment, from the Latin *importunes*, unfit, but originally "having no harbor"—*in*, not, and *portus*, harbor. An importunate moment is an unsafe time to seek harbor. The Roman philosopher Seneca wrote, "Luck is what happens when preparation meets *opportunity*." *Opportunity only knocks once*, as the proverb has it. But where do fortune, love, and necessity intersect? "Chances are..." sings Johnny Mathis. By chance, you say when someone asks how you met the person you married. But take it. The actress Mary

Tyler Moore concurred: "Take chances. Make mistakes. That's how you grow."

So much detail, so little understanding. Some sail safely into the harbor, others sink. Think of Henry Miller's lover, Rachel, confessing to him one afternoon in Paris that she only loved paintings that *looked back at her.* It's in the eyes, she said. Trust the eyes. Think of Edward Hopper saying he never thought of creating masterpieces: "I want to paint light on the side of the house." And he did in the orange-lit "Girl with a Sewing Machine" (1921), which moves me for reasons reason does not know.

Rather than the dissection of analysis in work such as theirs, I prefer the art critic James Elkins' elegant observation, "The beauty of beauty is that it exists."

This begs eternal questions: "Did beauty always exist or was it born? Did it have a beginning? Venus riding ashore on the half-shell? Was the world insufferably ugly until the mighty Aphrodite came into being? Was it beautiful because of her? If so, how so? Tell me again what beauty is supposed to save us from— cruelty, monstrosity, hypocrisy, or grotesqueness, hideousness, soullessness?

Beauty is a start, but what is the finish?

To consider the Venus is to consider the entire pantheon of gods and goddesses, from Zeus, her father, to Eros, her son, Mars, her lover, the Three Graces, her maidens, and on and on. I've never seen a smiling face that wasn't beautiful or a look of love that didn't make me happy.

Still, some of us pretend we don't need it: the anti-beauty crowd, or as essayist Janet Malcolm calls them, the anti-art contingent. Those who resort to posturing about being *beyond* such petit-bourgeois things as beauty—leaving those who pretend to be in a world without beauty to live in a velvet cage of abstraction. A golden apple, a roll of the ball, an incandescent opportunity, a shining, a dangerous risk. The choice you *can't* can't make if you are to find love on the other side of pain and sorrow. Note the double-negative, the *italicized* verb that forces us to focus on the necessary move toward the positive and then go beyond even that. The spark-off-the-flint poet Jack Gilbert did this when he forged a fiery truth from his twenty years in the Greek islands, rendered in the opening verses of "Not Easily":

> When we get beyond beauty and pleasure,
> to the other side of the heart (but short
> of the spirit), we are confused about what
> to do next...

A memorable sculpture, like any significant art, requires that genuine emotion in the story that infuses it, as it did when Alexandros found just the right piece of Parian marble to go with his reinvigorated story. This round of stories humbles us by showing us the limits of our will power, the unlimited power of the gods. If you want to make the gods laugh, tell them who *you* decided to fall in love with.

All this emotion, all these stories, in a single statue, the Venus de Milo, reimagined twenty-one hundred years ago in Antioch, in Asia Minor, by a flute-playing sculptor who made a giant leap forward in his decision to reflect our deepest feelings about love, desire, and happiness and anticipating, in myth's mysterious ways, what we think and feel today.

If there is a secret message to the Venus de Milo, it is like the rays of a lighthouse shining over a dark harbor, a radiance created by a genius who carved a prayer in stone, a bewildering monument to passion and sorrow, vitality, and serenity, the sublime and the beautiful, which just might reveal the hidden springs of love itself.

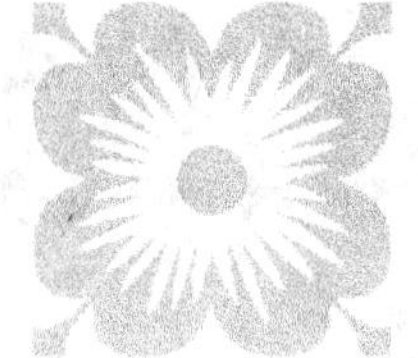

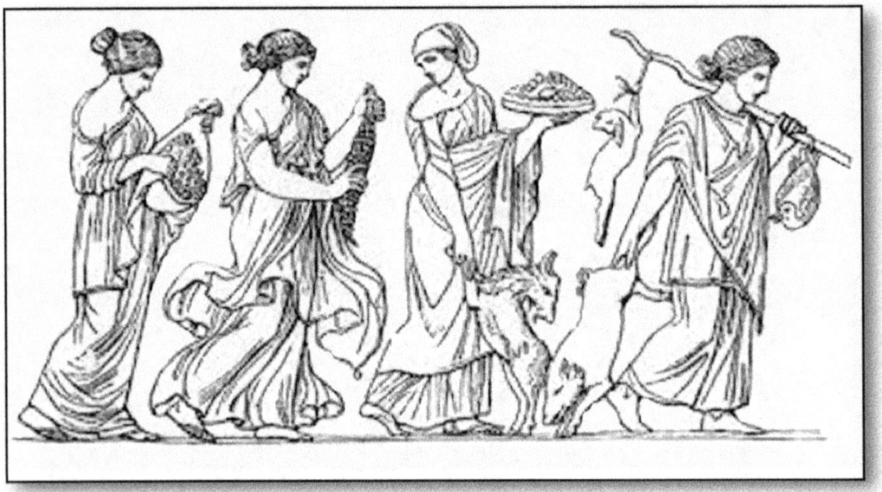

The Horae: Goddesses of the Seasons and the Hours: Eunomia (Order), :
Dike (Justice), Eirene (Peace), who are led by Dionysus.

INSCRIPT

The nearest we can come to the classical Greek words for *beauty* and *beautiful* are *kallos* and *kalos*, respectively. The etymology itself is a thing of beauty. But the soul of beauty is best evoked by *horaios*, the Koine Greek word for "beautiful," which derives from *hora*, meaning "hour." By association, beauty implied "being of one's hour," being on time, in one's own time, in synch with one's fate or destiny. The echoes of this elegant correspondence remain with us today in our belief that it is beautiful to have your finger on the pulse of the times, as when we are encouraged to pick fruit when it is ripe, create a work that speaks to the cultural moment, to be available in the right place at the right time, to make a move in the nick of time, the time of beauty. Beauty as the art of time, time the art of the beautiful. It's about time. That's the beauty of it.

INTERLUDE

fr. Latin, *inter ludus,* "between play,"
a break, timeout, pause, performance

On that propitious spring day in 1820, on the volcanic island of Melos, Ensign Voutier had a remarkable moment as he entered the narrow opening in the wall of Yorgos, the poor peasant, the accidental archaeologist. The Greek playwrights had long called attention to the shock of recognition that changes everything. Instantly, Voutier knew the statue was not only a Venus but *the* Venus of The Judgment of Paris and was worthy of the long journey from Greece to Paris. Now all he had to do was get her home or to her new home in Paris as a gift to the king. It would be a long hard fight to do so. Keep moving until you find what you love, then admire it with all your might. It's the royal road to meaning. As the comic said, I told you that tale in order to tell you this one. It is a rhapsody on the theme of the Transit of Venus, a brief account of what happened to the Venus de Milo on her zigzagging route from Melos to Constantinople to Piraeus to Marseilles, and on to Paris. Once there the journey carried on into the lore of art history, where she has become one of our culture's imponderable masterpieces, though few people can say why.

INSCRIPT

Curious how we have practically banned the word in art and literary circles over the last hundred or so years while remaining utterly obsessed about it in everyday life. The last time I heard a critic hiss between his teeth at the use of the word to describe a painting by De Kooning, I thought back to a conversation I had with a reporter at the International Press Club in Phnom Penh in 1996.

Looking over his shoulder, the nervous writer told me that during the worst of the scything terror of the Khmer Rouge, the monsters in charge of Cambodia banned certain words from use in newspapers and in public discourse, seemingly innocuous but ultimately combustible words, especially ones suggesting emotional bonds, such as the words for *love, comfort, happiness, radio, thanks, sorry.*

And *beauty.*

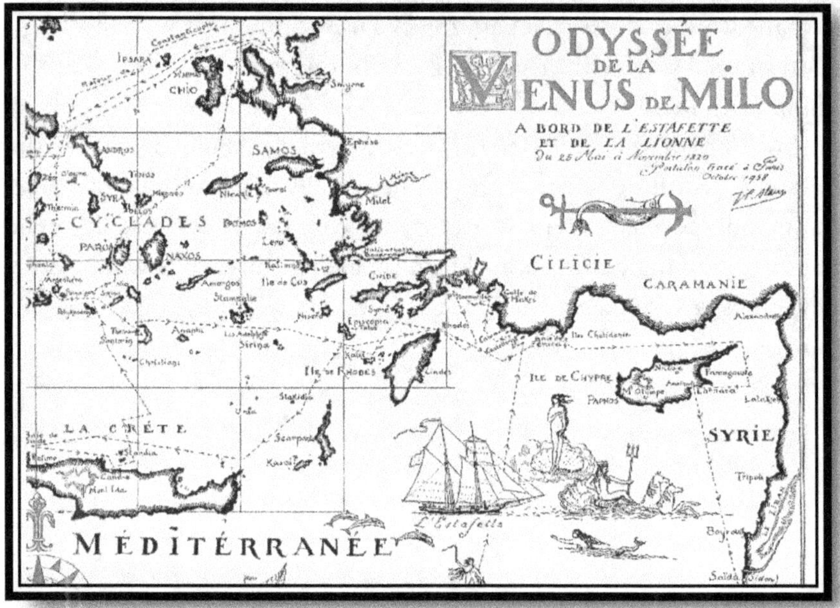

Nineteenth-century map depicting the long and winding sea road
sailed by the Venus de Milo

THE BATTLE FOR BEAUTY

Listen, I know this isn't the story you thought it was going to be. A worthwhile story rarely is. The best ones surprise us. As I tried to do for those eight languorous days spent at the Louvre in the fall of 2010, walking around and around her until I finally saw what was there and what wasn't, then what wasn't there and what was. Walking around with pen, paper, and camera, looking for myself and something more intangible. Beauty, not in the abstract, not in the academic sense, but in the tangibility of living life to the hilt. Generation after generation, we tell and retell these tales to deny our nothingness and to confirm our 'somethingness,' to transform absence into presence, and to turn meaninglessness into meaning.

And so it was that on April 9, 1820, the day after the discovery of the Venus de Milo, that events accelerated faster than a hundred-oared Greek trireme surging across the wine-dark waves. The serendipitous encounter between Ensign Voutier and Farmer Yorgos happened a full fifteen hundred years after the Venus had been abandoned in her cave, probably due to the wanton demolition of ancient sites under the barbaric directive of Theodosius in 393 CE. Eleven days was all it took to complete the negotiations over her price and destination. In turn, the zigzagging voyage from Melos to Paris required a year.

The ancient Greeks believed that the moment that Kairos, God of Sacred Time and Synchronicity, appeared, one must *seize him swiftly*. Soon after his discovery, Voutier did just that. As noted, he scrambled uphill to the Kastro, where he alerted the local vice-consul, Louis Brest, about the Venus and persuaded him to follow him to the findspot so he could see her for himself. While there, he dispatched a messenger to invite Captain Robert of the *Estafette* and Captain Duval d'Ailly of the *Lionne* to join them. The three Frenchmen gathered at the cave entrance, exclaiming: "*Magnifique... Merveilleux... Une splendide œuvre d'art!*" Magnificent... Marvelous... A splendid work of art!

Swayed by her beauty and their diplomatic responsibilities, Captain Robert encouraged Brest to notify Pierre David, French consul and secretary to the Sublime Porte, seat of the Ottoman Empire, in Constantinople. Brest's letter reveals his learned observation of the Venus as representing the Judgment of Paris. "*Venus tenant la pomme de discorde dans sa main,*" he wrote. "Venus holding the apple of discord in her hand." The next day, April 10, two other French vessels, the *Bonite* and the *Emulation*, arrived in the harbor of Melos. Quickly, Brest met with their commanders and led them likewise across the island so that they too could view the Venus. On the following day, the commander of the *Bonite*, Captain Dauriac, recognized the cultural significance as well as the looming diplomatic issues, so dispatched a letter to Pierre David. Dauriac's report is significant as it was the first written description of the circumstances behind the discovery:

> Three days ago, a peasant who was digging in his field [on the island of Melos] found a white marble statue representing Venus receiving the apple of Paris. She is larger than life-size. At the moment we have only the bust down to the waist. I have been to see her. The head appears well conserved to me as well as the hair. The end of one of the breasts is broken. The peasant was told that the discovery that he made was of great value and he believes it now because there are people who have already offered him one thousand piasters. M. Brest ... asked me for advice about the statue, but I am not able to give him any, not knowing anything about the subject.

Seven days later, on April 17, Voutier departed on the *Estafette* for Smyrna [modern Izmir], while the *Emulation* and *Bonite* sailed for France. Brest met with local officials to persuade them not to allow Yorgos to sell the Venus until word came back from his superiors in Constantinople. Later that day, a fourth ship, the *Chevrette*, arrived in the harbor. Aboard was the raffish Jules-Sébastien-César Dumont d'Urville, a scientist, classicist, and self-mythologizing world explorer. D'Urville and his superior officer, Lieutenant Amable Matterer, met with Brest and expressed their curiosity about the sculpture. The vice-consul led them to Yorgos' land, where the farmer and his son had hidden the upper half of the Venus in their tumbledown shed to use as a kind of bargaining chip for the moment when the price of the statue would be negotiated. At first, they revealed to D'Urville and Matterer only the crude lower torso of the statue and a burlap bag full of fragments. Undeterred, D'Urville described the lower half as a "fine piece of antiquity," and noting that fragments included her detached hand and arm were detached and her hair was coiled into a bun and tied with a ribbon. Then he asked to see the upper half of the Venus, which Yorgos grudgingly presented, later commenting that her face was quite beautiful. D'Urville then turned to Matterer and asked for his judgment, but the officer declined, saying he was no art expert. But he did offer a wonderful observation, saying that the Venus "was something special and powerful, something less like a thing than an event."

His phrasing also reveals what is thrilling about the discovery and often the rediscovery of a work of art. At its best, art revivifies us by reminding us what it means to be alive. First comes the encounter, then, occasionally, the meaning, as with what happened next. Something auspicious and unexpected, which required many years to reveal its meaning.

Stepping outside of the cave, d'Urville noticed that the marble lintel was engraved with a row of weatherworn Greek characters, which he was alert enough to immediately copy letter by letter. His recording provides invaluable evidence about *where* the Venus de Milo was found and why. D'Urville later expanded on his chance observation:

> The entrance to the shed was surmounted by a piece of marble
> four feet and a half long and about six or eight inches wide. It

bore an inscription of which only the first half has been respected by Time. The rest is entirely effaced. This loss is inestimable. At least we might have learned on what occasion and by whom the statues had been dedicated from the stones above the arched entrance... At any rate, I have carefully copied the remaining characters of this inscription and I can guarantee them all except for the defaced part that has been measured in proportion to the letters, which are still legible.

```
∴ΑΚΧΕΟΣΑΤΙΟΥΥΠΟΓΥ..........ΑΣ.
ΤΑΝΤΕΕΞΕΔΡΑΝΚΑΙΤΟ.............
ΕΡΜΑΙΗΡΑΚΛΕΙ
```

The inscription on the lintel of the cave reads:
"Bakchios, son of Atios, the subgymnasiarch [manager] of this gymnasium, has donated this niche and the three statues in it."

While Voutier's sketches gave us clues to the identity and the condition of the Venus, d'Urville's inscriptions provide proof that she was discovered in the ruins of the old gymnasium.

Two nights later, d'Urville wrote a letter to the Comte de Marcellus, secretary to Marquis de Riviere of the French embassy in Constantinople, describing the Venus and asking for written permission to visit Melos to officially acquire the statue. Instead, de Rivière sent his secretary, the Comte de Marcellus. Sailing aboard the *Estafette*, Marcellus arrived on Melos on May 23, along with the returning Voutier. Marcellus gave the order to collect the separate marble parts and sew them into three canvas sacks. Into the first one went the upper torso, into the second went the lower torso, and into the third went the herms, bases, a coiled bun of hair, a left foot, the fragment of an arm, and a left hand holding a stone apple. Then Marcellus and a strange character known as Reverend Oconomos, the village priest, loaded the sacks onto an old donkey cart and transported their treasure down the cobbled, switchbacking Roman road that led to the harbor where the *Estafette* awaited them.

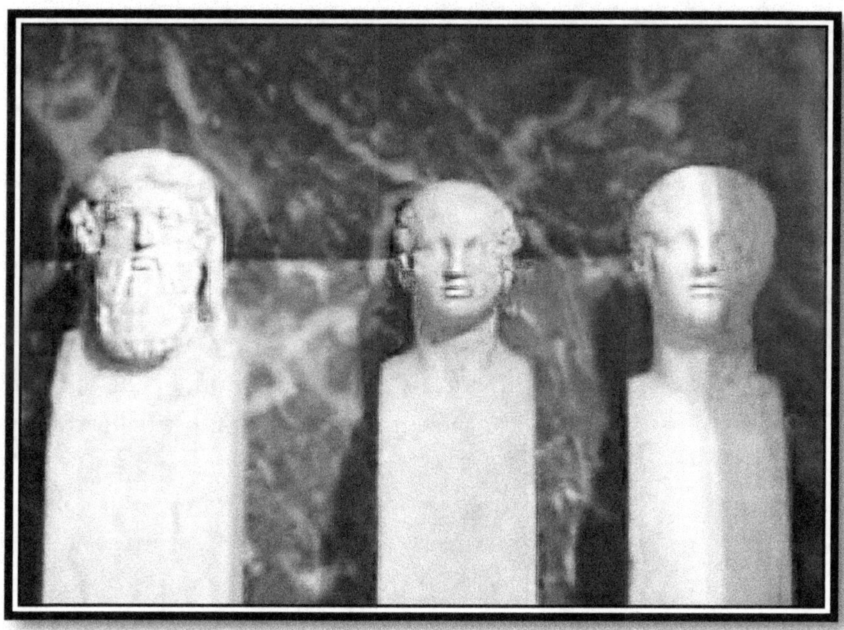

The Two Herms and an Anonymous Third in their New Niche.
Musée du Louvre, Paris, 2010

"Poetry," Frost wrote, "begins as a lump in the throat." *Tendresse* is the beautiful French word to describe the feeling when we sense the precious fragility of life.

Statues are a special kind of poetry. Stone poems. Marble dreams. Be patient. I'm backing into my true subject, the chance flashes of eternity we get at museums if we pay attention. The Sufi poet Rumi wrote that he was a sculptor, a molder, someone who could "rouse a thousand forms / and fill them with spirit." The Fifties poet Kenneth Koch captiously wrote: "The gods take stone / and turn it into men and women. / Men and women take gods and turn them into stone." I turn to the great poets to show me what it takes to understand the spirit of stone; a sculptor reveals to me how stone can show us what it means to be alive.

The herms, strange half-statues, are not incidental to our story. They are an important part of the triptych of meaning, experienced like the three-act structure of a play, the form of drama, the pattern of change. These sculptures featured a head or bust atop a squared pedestal, named after Hermes, the God of Crossroads and Boundaries, where they were often erected in every sense of the word. The most dramatic feature of an ancient herm was the erect phallus that poked out of the pedestal, symbolizing fertility and good luck, the entirety of which was ritually rubbed down with olive oil.

According to the Hungarian classical scholar, Karl Kerényi, a collaborator with Carl Jung, Greek herms served an apotropaic function. They were erected to protect travelers who crossed from one world, as it were, to another. The blue-and-white-stoned "evil eyes" that number in the millions throughout the Mediterranean today act as the rough equivalent. If all this sounds like a bunch of hooey, hoary superstition, consider its modern manifestations: the custom of students rubbing the left shoe of the bronze statue of the French philosopher Montaigne to a fare-thee-well outside the Sorbonne in Paris for good luck on their exams. The tradition of touching the well-burnished shells of stone tortoises in a Hanoi temple for good karma. The tapping of Babe Ruth's bat at Cooperstown by baseball pilgrims hoping some of his prowess will rub off on them.

Knowing all this, what were the herms doing in the niche? What d'Urville had painstakingly copied down, as best he could, was the written evidence for the patron of the new Melos gymnasium, Bakchios, a local dignitary, who then etched his name in the copestones of the niche where the Venus was discovered. Over the past several years, I have run across three different references to this inscription, in a 1904 copy of *The Nation*, in Curtis's *Disarmed*, and Kousser's paper, "Creating the Past: The Venus de Milo," in the *American Journal of Archaeology*.

The latter reading haunts me now.

I needed the information of these half-statues to round out the Venus's story and help me finally realize what these sculptures were trying to tell us about how to live the well-rounded life. Together, the larger-than-life statue and the three herms embodied the three ideals the ancient Greeks believed the visitor to the gymnasium needed to be reminded of while working out: Hermes for cleverness and speed, Herakles for strength and tenacity, and Aphrodite for beauty and desire.

Then came *L'affaire de Venus*, as it has come to be known to scholars, a highly exaggerated and unrelentingly politicized version of a simple skirmish that broke out on the pier when Oconomos left the farmer and the Venus all by her lonesome on the docks rather than load her onto the *Estafette*. There, Oconomos offered bribes to several local boat owners to take the statue on board. Each one turned him down, not wishing to bring on the guns of the French navy. Eventually, Oconomos was able to persuade a certain Captain Pacha of the Albanian (some say Russian) ship to take on the clandestine cargo. Voutier and Marcellus boarded the *Estafette* and stood alongside Captain Robert while the ship's small but armed crew stood ready. They were startled to see their beloved Venus de Milo in the middle of a bobbing rowboat that was advancing toward the *Galaxadi*. The sight was so absurd, they laughed gleefully.

According to his account, written four decades after the events, Voutier shouted, "Look, someone's taking our statue away. This can't be real!"

In his small but informative volume, *La Venus de Milo*, Alain Pasquier, Curator of Greek, Etruscan, and Roman Antiquities at the Louvre, the statue was being loaded onto the *Galaxadi* because its captain "had been bribed by Oconomos to carry the statue to the Arsenal of Constantinople."

What unfolded was a rhapsody on the ancient theme of the mythic struggle over beauty, one that echoes the combustible relationship between Ares and Aphrodite, Mars and Venus. Pasquier observed that the French team was trying to combine diplomacy with the threat of firepower. Voutier and Marcellus reported that they saw Oconomos on horseback galloping across the beach toward the Albanian ship, wildly signaling the ship's captain to open fire on the *Estafette*. With French national pride at stake, Marcellus ordered the *Estafettte's* captain to threaten the use of his soldiers and cannon to stop the Russian ship from leaving with the Venus onboard and to immediately return it—or face the consequences.

The captain of the *Galaxadi* knew that gunplay could be construed as an act of war, but he courted danger by refusing to let the French soldiers board his ship. Thwarted, Marcellus rowed back to the *Estafette*. That night, he claimed, the goddess Venus appeared to him in a dream, a sign that he should pursue the statue for the glory of France, which was underscored by no less than Homer whispering: "What superhuman beauty. What sweet majesty. What shape divine."

The next morning, he conveyed his auspicious dream to three civic leaders of Melos, hoping to appeal to their religious sensibilities. Instead, they insisted the Venus didn't belong to *anyone*. Then Marcellus reminded them about the Muslim "aversion to representations of the human form, especially those that were mutilated." Under Islamic law, any work of art

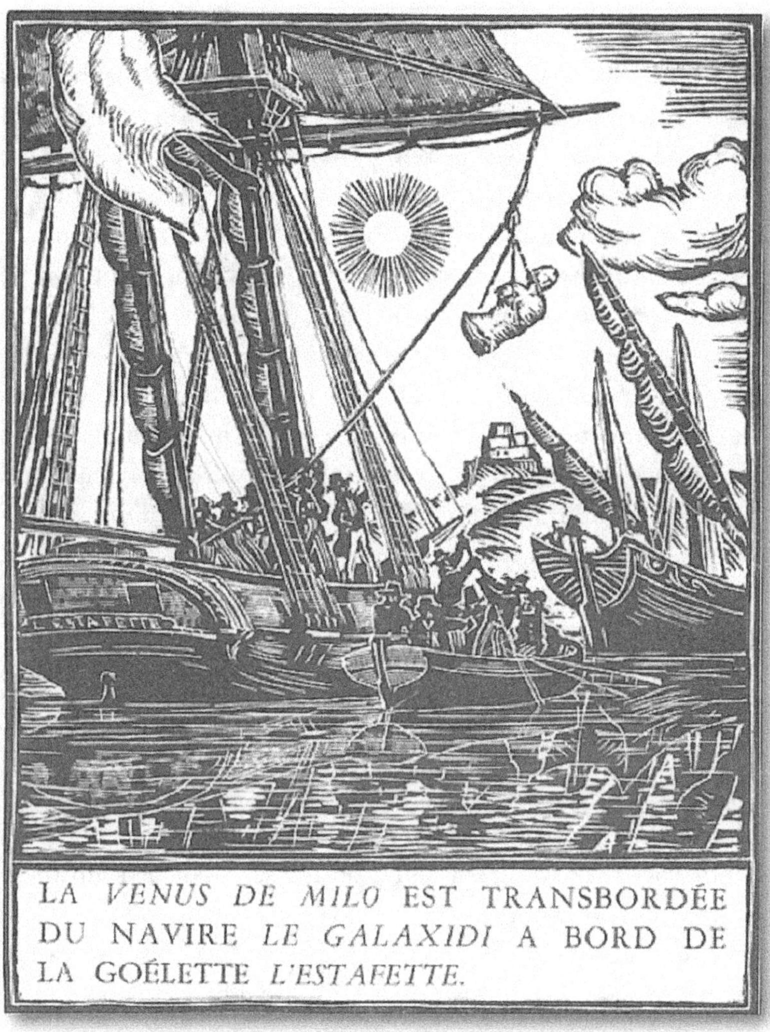

The Venus de Milo is transferred from the Albanian ship
Le Galaxidi to the schooner *L'Estafette*
from Alcaux's *Les Descouvertes de Venus de Milo*

that was not intact was forbidden to be publicly displayed, implying that the Venus might disappear again. Marcellus reminded them that he worked with art restorers in Paris who could repair her. "Wouldn't it be better to sell it to me," he asked, "so I can help repair and restore it properly?"

To avoid the wrath of Greece over a repeat of the humiliating theft of the Parthenon Marbles, Marcellus paid Yorgos 750 French francs and another 250 to the three civic leaders, who were all pleased with the deal. The Louvre's Pasquier is careful to add that the marbles were "duly paid for," becoming the property of the Marquis when the statue was moved from the *Galaxadi* to the *Estafette*. Over the last two hundred years, whenever the thorny question of the Venus's notoriously missing arms has come up, rumors have been heard about how the arms were left behind on the cave floor. Or fell off during the ride in the cart to the waiting ship. The mythomaniacal Marcellus wrote a sensationalized account claiming that the Venus's upper left arm had been intact when the statue was dragged by Yorgos and his son across the harbor beach to the waiting rowboat. The philosopher Paul Carus, underwater archaeologist Jim Thorne, and many modern guidebooks sold today on Melos recount a nonexistent fight breaking out on shore between the Greeks, Turks, and French, replete with clashing swords.

Unfortunately, no arms were ever reported as being attached to the statue, nor have they ever been found on the sea floor beneath the pier despite the efforts of countless divers. However, we have Voutier's sketch taken *in situ*, on the spot, the moment the Venus was first shown to the French officers. No arms, no hands. So, no go with all the loose cannon conspiracy theories regarding piracy and cultural theft. The French soldiers won the hand of the Venus de Milo fair and square.

Not that the missing arms meant the end of the story. Listen to Chuck Berry resurrecting the image in the rollicking "Brown Eyed Handsome Man": "De Milo Venus was a beautiful lass / She had the world in the palm of her hand / But she lost both arms in a wrasslin' match / To meet a brown eyed handsome man." Or maybe the actor John Barrymore had it right: "When archaeologists discover the missing arms of Venus de Milo, they will find she was wearing boxing gloves."

On May 24, 1820, Brest, Marcellus, and Voutier, together with some junior officers, rowed across the harbor to the Russian ship, eager to engage their presumed enemy. The officers were received politely before tumultuous negotiations took place between the Greeks, French, and Russians. Finally, the Russian sailors lowered the statue onto the French lifeboat and hoisted her onto the deck of the Estafette. By virtue of one of those sly winks of fate, a gusty wind arose just as the Russian ship was getting ready to leave, so their sailors were able to safely raise their sails. After fifteen hundred years of the Venus de Milo being hidden inside the walls of the old gymnasium on Melos, she was leaving for her second home via the sea road to Paris by way of Piraeus, Istanbul, and Marseilles.

Later, Dumont d'Urville was nonchalant about his role in the affair. "Upon my return," he wrote, "de Rivière informed me that he had acquired the statue for the museum and that it had been put on board one of the vessels at the landing." The museum, of course, being the one, the only Louvre. Now comes the greatest transformation in the history of art, from a random sculpture for a gymnasium on a remote Greek island to a modern icon, immediately recognizable the world over.

Understood by few, loved by all.

Strange to say, I just heard the words of my first newspaper editor, Roger Turner, at the *Wayne Dispatch*, muttering to me whenever he gave me a late-night sports writing assignment, "Make me care."

INSCRIPT

"The Supreme Sight"
Some say cavalry and others claim
infantry or a fleet of long oars
is the supreme sight on the black earth.
I say it is

the one you love. And easily proved.
Did not Helen who far surpassed all
mortals in beauty desert the best
of men, her kin,

and sail off to Troy and forget
her daughter and dear kinsmen? Merely
the Kyprian's gaze made her bend and led
her from her path;

these things remind me now
of Anaktoria who is far,
and I
for one

would rather see her warm supple step
and the sparkle of her face than watch
all the dazzling chariots and armored
hoplites of Lydia.

Fragment 16, Sappho (630 or 612–582 BCE)
translated by Willis Barnstone

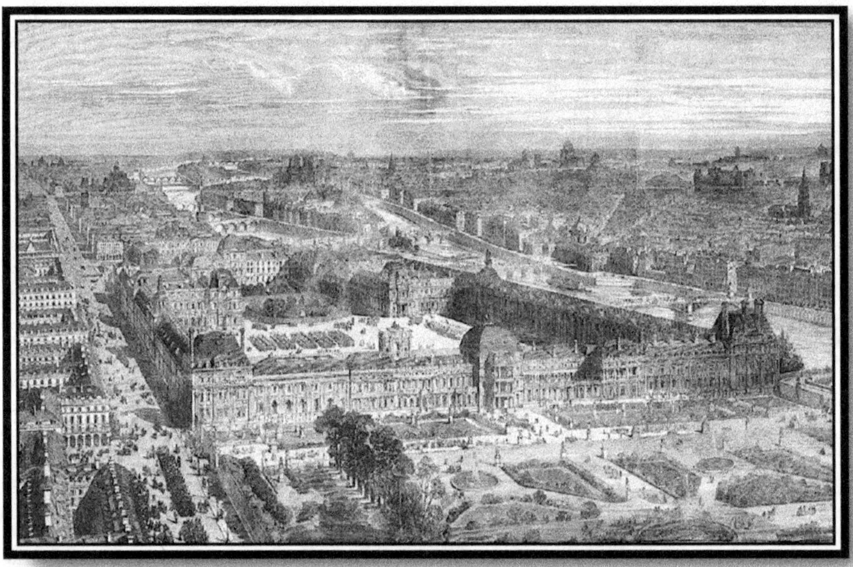

Panoramic or Bird's Eye View of the Louvre and the Rue de Rivoli. Wood engraving published by the London Illustrated News, September 1, 1855.

III.

TURNING AROUND THE VENUS DE MILO

THE HOUSE OF THE MUSES

IN EARLY 1821 THE APHRODITE DE MELOS, OR VENUS DE MILO, WAS transferred from one of the most remote niches in the Old World to one of the most public ones in the New World. After the infamous skirmish on Melos, she was shipped fifteen hundred miles east to Constantinople, then swerved west a thousand miles to Piraeus and Syracuse, before finally traveling another five hundred to the docks of Toulon in southern France. In November, she was loaded onto an elaborately decorated, well-padded royal wagon and pulled by a team of white horses. She wended her way north to Paris, arriving in February 1821. The Venus proved to be a *cause célèbre* on the roughly 430-mile journey, receiving a wildly enthusiastic reception from peasants and nobles alike along the route. The sensation can be likened to that caused by the presentation of moon rocks by the Apollo 11 crew to the Smithsonian Institution in 1969, or the madcap world tour of the Treasures of King Tutankhamun in the late 1970s, or the worldwide craze for exhibitions of Van Gogh's paintings in the early 2000s.

To understand the Venus's impact, it is important to remember that when she arrived in Paris, it wasn't as if the French had never seen a Venus depicted in art before. There already existed dozens of paintings of her by the Old Masters and the recent Impressionists in the halls of the Louvre, plus nearly as many sculptures, as well as representations of her in mosaics, murals, and pottery. But the Venus de Milo filled a different kind of niche, to run with our metaphor. There was, figuratively speaking, an empty hole in the stupendous collection at the Louvre.

After nearly twenty years of immense prestige, the museum, which had opened its doors in 1793, was suddenly a museum bereft of art. In 1815, an estimated 5,000 works of art from Napoleon's expeditions to Egypt and Italy in 1801 were repatriated after the emperor was deposed. For the next five years, the museum's curators were anxious for a return to its former grandeur if only they could replace such cherished—but looted—works. What had been lost was more than marble, wood, and manuscript. The Louvre had been forced to surrender a link to the classical past that many Europeans believed would help revive their moribund cultures. The Louvre had been founded under the ardent belief that seeing and experiencing great art would catalyze creativity. This revealed the heart of the French self-image, which was that it was the most civilized culture in the world. To lose so much of its heritage, however short-lived, was a blow to the French people's dream of its cultural status.

When the Venus arrived, expectations were enormous, even salvific, as if a single work of art, discovered by an educated French sailor on one of their most distant outposts, might save, or at least redeem, their besieged culture. Immediately upon her public unveiling, she was advertised as a *classical* sculpture, meaning from the time of the greatest of all Greek sculptors, Praxiteles, and Phidias; some even bruited that she had been carved by Phidias himself, or at least his school. The well-thought-out propaganda campaign, based on the phenomenon of what the French themselves call "reflected glory," claimed that the Venus was a *classical* work so that it might lift the Louvre above its rivals, the British Museum in London, the Pergamum Museum in Berlin, and the Vatican Museum in Rome.

But what if the Venus wasn't what they claimed it to be? What did it matter that she had arrived incomplete, and that something vital to her origins was missing, or worse, stolen? Could she still be historically significant? Did her beauty need a context, or was it timeless?

The tale's the thing.

On March 1, 1821, eleven months after her discovery or rediscovery on Melos, the Venus de Milo arrived in Paris, a gift of the Goddess of Pleasure for the city of pleasure, an icon of beauty for the city that prided itself as the most beautiful in the world. It seemed to be the perfect marriage of art and politics.

The Comte Forbin, who had recently been named the new head of antiquities at the Louvre, and the Marquis de Riviere were accorded an audience with King Louis XVIII and reported to him that they had legally purchased a classical masterpiece from the Greek islands and were eager to present it to him as a gift. They also reminded him of the role of the museum in cultivating a love of the arts among French citizens and providing easy access to masterpieces to stimulate artists. Their use of the word *classical* was deliberate and their declaration of legality important because of the scandal caused by Lord Elgin's theft of the Parthenon Marbles in Athens only a few years before. The temerity and the scope of the looting had appalled people all over the world, even many British citizens, notably the poet Lord Byron, who called it a brazen act of vandalism. Forbin and de Rivière were counting on the ethical contrast between the French and the English by stressing that theirs was a legal acquisition of a genuine masterpiece.

Nearly ten months after her discovery, the Venus arrived at a turning point in the history of art in Europe. The 1820s were a time when people on every side of the political or social spectrum could find something to admire about her. She was beautiful and she was Greek, and now the French were linked with the Golden Age.

Or so they thought.

The royal viewing of Voutier's prize catch, the Venus, did not take place for a few months. The museum staff had to move the enormous statue up two floors and into a little-used room of the palace-turned-museum. When de Rivière and Forbin formally presented the Venus de Milo to King Louis XVIII, it is apparent by the lithograph that was created at the time that Louis was too incapacitated by gout to move without a wheelchair. When the king finally cast a cold eye upon the statue, he admitted to being baffled about all the fuss and asked why the statue was significant. Forbin's response was as political as it was aesthetic. He carefully reminded the king that the museum's avowed mission was to provide proof of France's "love of the arts and our eagerness to bring together such precious means of study for our artists."

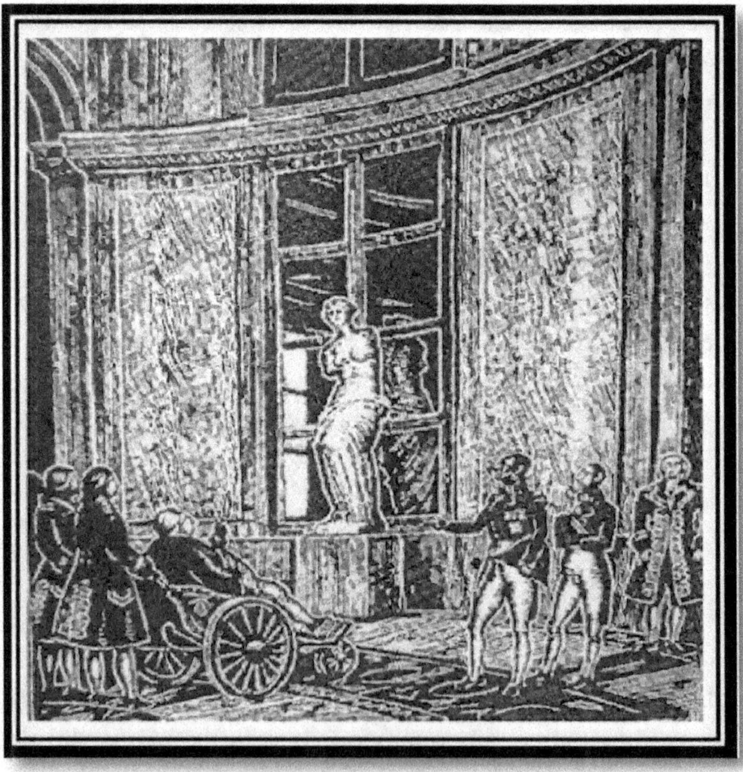

King Louis XVIII appraising the Venus
Musée du Louvre, Paris,1821

As noble as this might sound, the intention was more complicated. When the Comte de Forbin had accompanied the Venus from Constantinople to Athens, he consulted with the French consul, a well-respected authority on antiquities named Fauvel, who described the statue as "a priceless masterpiece from the classical age of Greece." Forbin took this to mean that the Venus came from the chisel of the masters of the fifth century BCE: Phidias, Praxiteles, or even Myron. A Greek original in a world of Roman copies. An example of pure classical art that stood out in a world of degraded Hellenistic works. The Venus entered the museum and art history as a cultural curio installed as political propaganda in the latest skirmish between England and France. Due to the art-shriveled times, Forbin desperately wanted it to be so.

During the Napoleonic Wars, the emperor had plundered Italy, Belgium, Germany, and Egypt, stripping them of thousands of works of art, which he used to stock the Louvre and other French museums. Among the notable works were the *Apollo Belvedere* and the *Laocoon*, looted from the Vatican Museum, and Veronese's *The Marriage of Cana*, stolen from the Monastery of San Giorgio Maggiore in Venice.

After Napoleon's defeat at the Battle of Waterloo in 1815, the formerly conquered countries demanded justice, including history's first recorded case of purloined art being returned to its rightful owners. A high European court agreed. The Louvre was ordered to return five thousand works of art to the countries that France had looted, including Belgium, Germany, Italy, and Egypt. By the end of the year, the museum was denuded and France itself humiliated. A chance visitor, British miniaturist Andrew Robertson, noted that the significantly dismantled museum was "truly doleful to look at now, full of dust, ropes, triangles, and pulleys."

The stage was set for the art world's version of redemption.

The Venus de Milo arrived only six years after the Louvre's loss of scores of masterpieces, landing in an atmosphere of cultural humiliation and aggrievement. After the Great Restitution, the return of the war-torn artwork, many believed the museum had lost its short-lived ascendency to its archrival, the British Museum. For the French, the loss of prestige was intolerable. The Louvre needed to replace the missing marvels with a work of equal or surpassing value. This is why Forbin and others believed they needed an indisputable *classical* work of art, which was defined then as a work from the classical period, not the later Hellenistic, or Roman, era.

The perceived difference was tremendous. Classical Greek art was thought of as pure, while art from the later Hellenic, or Roman, era was considered impure, decadent, and evidence of the serious decline of the Roman Empire when it occupied ancient Greece. Hence, the contemporary belief was Hellenic art was spurious, far less desirable.

At first glance, the Venus de Milo fit the requirements of what curators of the Louvre were longing for. The classicist Mary Beard writes, "It so happened that this damaged beauty appeared on the scene at the very moment when the full flood of Romantic sentiment was cultivation of the nostalgia of the fragment and the ideal of the ruin."

An indisputable masterpiece from classical times was what the Louvre felt was needed to restore its place in the art world. The acquisition of the Venus de Milo was more than the purchase of one more work of art. One more classical statue to adorn her walls would not have made much difference in its collection anyway. She may not have been as historically significant as the museum declared—the equivalent of a Praxiteles, Myron, or Polykleitos—but she didn't need to be. In truth, the Venus de Milo was far more than a statue—and less than a political pawn. She was a mythic image, a work that is inexhaustible in its meanings, one that constellates a culture's self-reflection and values. For Parisians, the Venus was perceived to be as beautiful as the city imagined itself to be. The Venus was a mirror image of what millions of annual visitors imagined they stood for: *love, desire, happiness, surprise, the imperfectly beautiful.*

THE SECRET INSCRIPTION

To paraphrase Mel Brooks, a funny thing happened on the way to the museum. What no one could have foreseen was the accidental appearance of the "third bundle" of marbles that had been discovered when Voutier asked Yorgos to go back inside the cave and look around, which Matterer had packed alongside the crates containing the two halves of the Venus de Milo. The upper and lower parts of the Venus had survived the long journey, more or less intact, suffering only a few minor nicks and scratches. Those were caulked and patched by the art restorers in the basement of the museum, and fortunately, the ill-advised plans to restore the arms of the statue were denied. But to everyone's dismay, the base of the statue had been damaged. A corner had broken off. The restorers tried to fit the broken piece to the left side of the statue, and to their surprise, it fit perfectly. A damaged statue wasn't unusual considering the distances traveled and the harsh conditions of the ships. What *was* startling was the discovery of an inscription that had been etched into the statue's base.

As can be seen in the two-hundred-year-old drawing below, the inscription on the plinth displays five simple Greek words that plainly reveal and honor the names of the sculptor, his father, and the city they hailed from, and qualifies as a revelation:

"Alexandros, son of Menides, citizen of Antioch on the Meander, made this statue."

What should have delighted the museum curators—proof of provenance—proved to be a matter of considerable embarrassment to all involved. No longer could they pretend that the statue was *classical*. Instead, the inscription put a face, a place, and a time on the making of the statue.

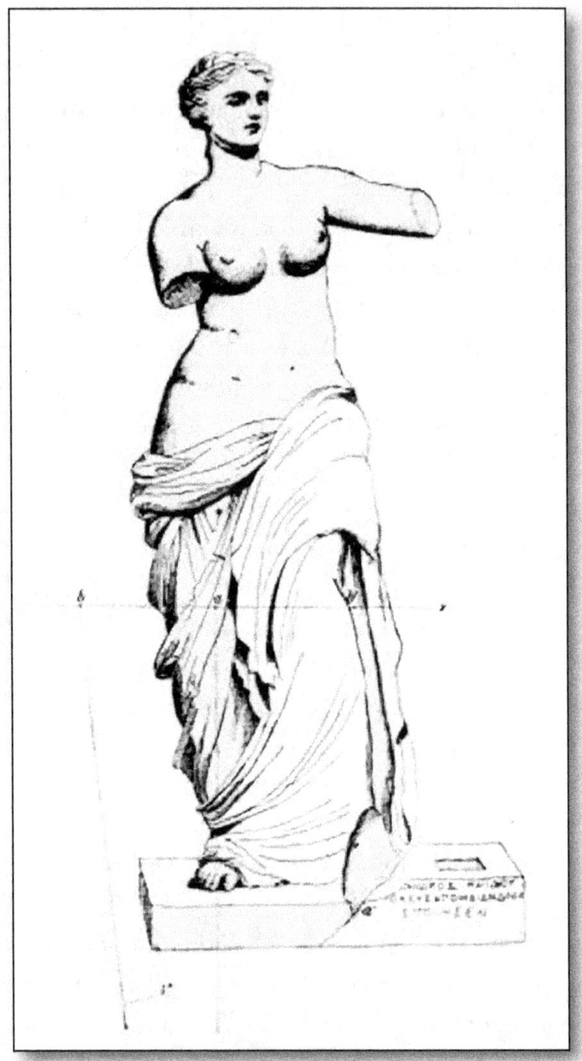

A.Debay's sketch for Jacques David
showing "The Lost Plinth"
Musée du Louvre, 1821

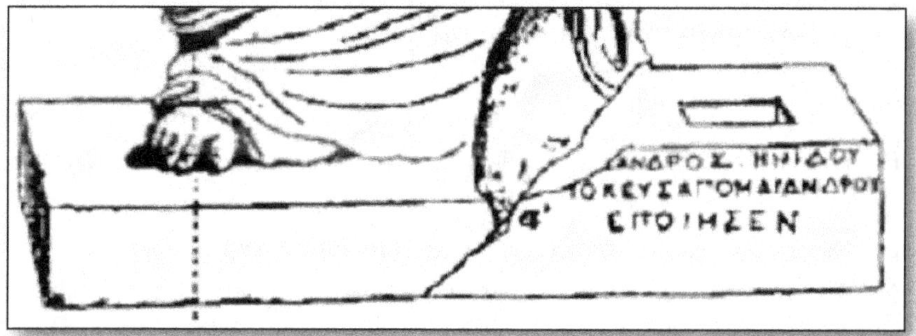

[?]Andros, son of [M]enides of [Ant]ioch-on-the-Maeander, made [it].
[Alexandros, son of Menides of Antioch on the Meander, made this statue.]

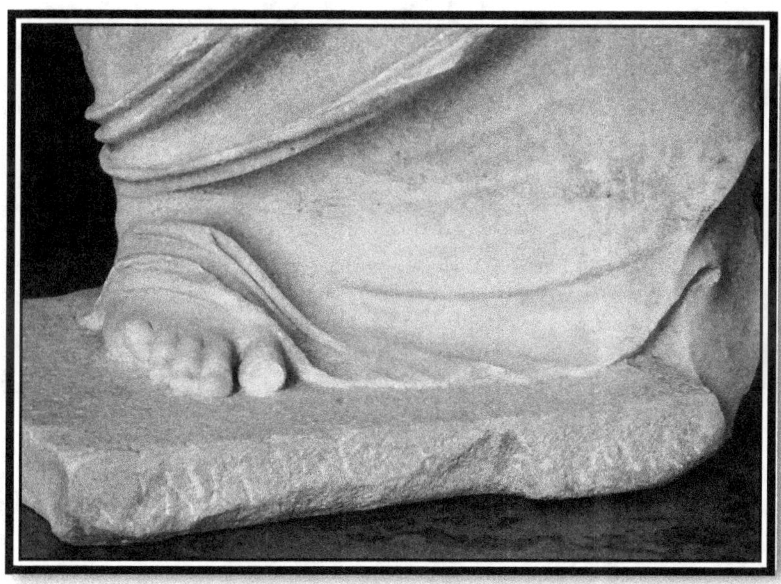

"The Ruined Plinth," missing its original inscription today
Musée du Louvre, 2010

By the early twentieth century, more than seven thousand inscriptions had been discovered by philologists and epigraphers at Delos and Delphi alone. The instinct to inscribe—leave a mark—on bronze and stone was one of the most perdurable practices in the ancient world. Our Greek and Roman ancestors left such words in both public and private. Ancient authors, philosophers, aristocrats, military leaders, and sculptors left their inscriptions often in ceremonial situations to publicize their scholarship, declaim on politics, celebrate victory in athletic competitions, or display their war trophies. The inscriptions were revelatory in context, providing invaluable information, such as when a statue or building survived, but were also invaluable when they disappeared, such as when a building had been razed or the bronze of an Olympic victor melted down for weapons.

What the inscription on the base of the Venus de Milo revealed allowed people then and now to *read* the statue, revealing to us who carved her and when and from where. Significant, exciting, surprising but inconvenient information. Rather than announce the news to the public, the base of the statue vanished. No word of it appeared when the statue went on display. To paraphrase one of France's greatest philosophers, Blaise Pascal, museums have reasons reason does not know. The plinth with the inscription was either lost, destroyed, or misplaced deep in the bowels of the Louvre. And a certain educated ignorance prevailed about the Venus's place in the artistic pantheon because of the feigned historical amnesia, the loss of the inscription.

Nonetheless, for the next two hundred years, the Venus was described vaguely on a placard in the rooms where she has been displayed as simply coming from Melos, created by "Anonymous."

Consider the marvel. In the spring of 1821, only a few months after the arrival of the Venus de Milo at the Louvre, the French Neoclassical painter Jacques-Louis David was languishing in exile in Brussels when he learned of the exciting new addition to the Louvre that some were claiming was the equal of the *Apollo Belvedere.* Today we might ask for a photograph or send a downloaded image or shoot some film footage to see what the ruckus is about. The artist was eager to see what it looked like, so he sent a series of letters from Brussels to Paris in which he requested a sketch of the Venus from his friend Comte Jean-Baptiste-Joseph Debay, a Flemish sculptor and art restorer, who was also serving as the director of the museum. Debay wasn't confident as a draughtsman and turned to his son, an art student, who we only know as "A. Debay," to make a rendering of the statue. Debay the Younger made the drawing, which is efficient and fine, but what is noteworthy, even historical, is how diligently he copied the Greek letters that had been carved into the plinth. The lad's drawing unmistakably reveals a fragmentary but recognizable inscription along the slim side of the plinth, which turned out to be world-tilting, at least in the world of the arts.

As requested, Debay the Elder sent the original sketch to David in Belgium, while copies were circulated among museum staff and throughout Paris as part of the propaganda campaign intended to bring greater glory to the museum. Once the implications of the inscription were understood, the plinth was lost, whether deliberately or accidentally we may never know. Nonetheless, our long-lost hero's name was erased or at least misplaced from the public record. Recapping the sordid affair of the propaganda campaign, Gregory Curtis writes in *Disarmed:* "An inscription in Greek was carved on this broken piece, and in this inscription was the name of a sculptor, a name the Louvre hoped the world would never see."

For those who read it first in the bowels of the Louvre, it could have been happy news because, in true Mark Twain fashion, they "stretched the truth" about the statue. This led to a vast marketing campaign trumpeting the Venus de Milo, the nineteenth-century equivalent of the Egyptian touting the discovery of the tomb of King Tutankhamun in the 1920s. Later, the ungenerous called it flagrant propaganda rather a rhapsody on the theme of *un grand desir*, the great desire for national recognition on the world stage.

So it was that "Alexandros" was replaced by "Anonymous." For the last two centuries, the placard on the wall of the gallery where the Venus has stood and the attributions in art history books, guidebooks, postcards, T-shirts, coffee mugs, and gewgaws of all sorts have all claimed ignorance about the real sculptor. The missing arms are regrettable enough but not as much as the vanishing plinth and the disappearing inscription.

The evidence of the original inscription is proof positive of provenance. Unequivocally, the artist is named, our friend Alexandros, and so is the artist's father and their home in Antioch on the Maeander [Meander] River. The key word for art historians is Antioch, in Asia Minor, which was a Greek city long famed for its school of sculpture as well as being a center of mosaics. The learned scholars at the Louvre were immediately alarmed, knowing that Antioch had not been founded until 300 BCE by Seleucus, one of Alexander the Great's generals. That was at least fifty years after Greece's classical age of sculpture, which has long denoted *perfection*. A belief at least four hundred years in the making, since the rediscovery in the Renaissance of Greek heritage and the belief that the art and literature of antiquity could help stoke a *second* Renaissance, preferably in France. At its best, this is what the Louvre was hoping to acquire in its race with the leading museums of Europe, the longed-for link between Athens and Paris.

One look at the inscription told the scholars that the Venus was Hellenistic, not classical, which ran roughly from the death of Alexander in

323 BCE to the rise of Augustus in Rome in 31 BCE. A minor quibble now, it might be argued, but at the time it was the equivalent of learning that a long-loved Leonardo had been painted not by him but by one of his students or that a newly found Vermeer was a forgery, or that one of Jane Austen's novels had been written by a local schoolteacher. The insinuation was more than what the French call *snobisme*, a perceived defeat in their attempt to reclaim their cultural superiority. The French had not conjured this out of thin cultural air. The much-revered Pliny the Elder had written about the perceived inferiority of the Hellenistic period to the classical era. Pliny believed the earlier art was purer, approaching perfection, the later decadent and imperfect. It was into this fervid atmosphere of political and aesthetic hope that the Venus was unveiled.

Chastened, Forbin and his associates looked closer at the base of the statue and noticed a square hole drilled into the top of the pillar, which they believed was intended to hold a herm with a carved head. This was a common feature of ancient sculptures. What is confusing is why such a master sculptor would carve something that he thought was ugly next to such a showpiece.

After lengthy debate, Forbin and company decided the pillar with the herm was added by a second sculptor or as an awkward way to support her missing left arm that was probably raised and reaching out to some unknown character. Maybe the base of the statue was never meant to stand next to the *Venus*, but then why had it been on display in the cave on Melos? The possibility loomed that the pillar and herm belonged to the statue because it was needed to identify its creator and its origins, which was possible but clumsy. If true, it meant she was created *in the first century* BCE—not the third century—placing her squarely as a Hellenistic work of art, information that offered little cachet for the museum as it would be seen as decadent or derivative. The inscribed base was an inconvenient truth, one that could not be conveniently explained away to a public that was hoping for a link to the "pure" classical past, the Glory that was Greece, which might reflect upon the Glory that was France.

Call it what you will, the statue's base and its mysterious script disappeared. The proof may have been hidden away by Forbin and friends in the vast storage rooms of the Louvre, reminiscent of the looted and auctioned-off art in the thousands of crates in the vast warehouse that stretches to the parallax point in the last shot of *Citizen Kane*. Or it might have been deliberately destroyed by underlings. No one knows, or if they do, they're not talking. The truth is as lost as *Rosebud*, Kane's boyhood sled when it was tossed into the furnace at the end of the movie. In a 2004 interview, Alain Pasquier, the same conservator of the museum and art historian who wrote *Le Venus de Milo*, told Gregory Curtis that he had personally spent many futile hours looking for the base of the Venus through the Louvre's archives and warehouses. When asked if it could have been destroyed, Pasquier replied that the possibility was inconceivable and even refused to comment on the possibility that the base—*if* it even existed—belonged to the Venus. The truth about the disappearance of the missing base of the Venus is as important as the mystery of her missing arms. They are both signifiers of *why we should care* about her.

She is a *celebration*, that's why. Not an ideal, nor a standard, but a calm, cool celebration of female beauty, the source of desire, a stone incarnation of the promise of happiness. Not a guarantee, nor a tease, just a hint of the joyful possibilities.

The poet T. S. Eliot called this the "intersection of a timeless moment."

I say it's that moment you long for in a museum, concert hall, or bookstore when time stands still, and the secret of the universe seems to open for you to see.

And more, as John Berger writes, we go to museums not just to see but to *have seen*. See? We want the experience and the memory, the reminder, the arrow in the quiver. Years ago, I took a train from Oslo up to Narvik, in the Arctic Circle, to see the *aurora borealis*, so I might witness the colors my great-grandfather told my father he had seen in the Yukon, where he had traveled in a birch bark canoe from Ontario as a *voyageur*.

Hearing that, I wanted to see for myself, which I did years later, just as I had wanted to see the Venus, which I did, to know I had lived.

For years I've fantasized about finding the missing book that Alexandros might have been writing, in my artistic reverie, when he sculpted his Venus. Not unlike the dream of finding one of the *portalani*, the sea guides for Pytheas of Massalia, the Greek geographer, at the Athens Flea Market. If I could understand his breakthrough, maybe I could comprehend what the classics scholar Jane Harrison meant when they tried to get to the heart of the transcendent nature of art. In the same spirit, Harrison wrote, "All art springs by way of ritual out of keen emotion toward life, and even the power to appreciate art needs this emotional reality in the spectator." I imagine Alexandros contemplating for the competition on Melos a statue of Aphrodite, perhaps taking to heart one of the seventy-seven "wisdom sayings" displayed at the Temple of Apollo in Delphi: "Strive to Do your Best." Strive to evoke the *life force* itself, *duende, in stone.*

I picture Alexandros walking along the docks of Antioch, looking out to sea at the ships coming and going from Athens, Alexandria, Carthage, Sardinia, and the farthest reaches of the Black Sea. I think of him deciding to study copies of the legendary sculptures of Phidias and Praxiteles and Lysippus so that he might someday join their lustrous ranks. I also think of him making one of the popular pilgrimages to the nearby island of Knidia to see Praxiteles's famous Aphrodite, no doubt hearing that she appeared so lifelike it was rumored that the goddess herself wondered how he had ever seen her as naked as a dove.

THE STONY QUEST

How else, I wonder, could he have succeeded in what Flannagan memorably called the "stony quest in art" by winning the competition on Melos over accomplished sculptors from across the empire, and more, helped him achieve *kleos*, the wide-ranging fame that was the life goal of every Greek? More than anything I can conjure up in my imagination, I like to think that Alexandros must have *loved* the myth that was already a thousand or so years old in his time and already one of the favorite themes for painters, sculptors, poets, and mosaicists, many of whose renderings of the divinely ordained love affair that ignited the Trojan War are still with us today. Loved it enough to make it his own, as all true mentors encourage their students to do. And as he did so, announcing in the fullness of creative perception his singular theme, he shouted a hearty *Yes!* to the cosmos.

Considering the condition in Greece in those years, as Rome was taking control of the ancient Greek empire in the middle of the first century BCE, the young sculptor's resounding *Naí!* (Yes!) was no less impressive than Rembrandt's chiaroscuro depiction of the ultimate affirmation of life despite his withering poverty, or Vermeer's luminous confirmation of light in the midst of the darkness in Delft during the Hundred Years War.

Without Alexandros likewise *loving* his theme and adoring the Aphrodite, who was so central to life in Greek culture, he could not have carved her the way he did, which, ineffably, in a way that defies ordinary language, inspires us to love her all these centuries later, and when gazing upon her gaze, wonder about beauty and the beautiful and what it means to us now.

Then there is the silence. Her silence. The silence of the centuries.

We might ask *What is she trying to say?* Her beguiling power went beyond beauty to the erotic. Christine Mitchell Havelock writes, "The Venus de Milo, both sensuous and distant, these figures are about the sexual impulse, which is common to all mankind and considered divine, and not the nature of woman... [She is] of exceptional beauty... But regardless of her elevation ... she stands apart in sublime indifference."

Stone is, of course, silent. Or is it?

In the late 1980s, I ventured across Paris in a gutter-rattling rainstorm to hear Raymond Carver read his latest collection of short stories and a few poems at the Village Voice Bookstore. Fellow authors Richard Ford and Jonathan Raban sat alongside me, and Carver's wife, the poet Tess Gallagher, leaned against him. I was thirty-five, young enough to know that I needed to know what was loaded into that moment. I took copious notes in a hand-sized spiral notebook as my attention swept the room. The rain drizzled down the steamed-up windows as a hundred people held their breath as he read from "Late Fragment," where he asks himself—and us, "And did you get what / you wanted from this life, even so?" / "I did." / "And what did you want?" / "To call myself beloved." Listening, I felt pummeled by the subtle beauty of his yearning question.

The guttering rain makes it hard to hear his soft-voiced answer to a vague audience question about the purpose of telling stories. A siren sounds down the street. A catfight breaks out in the nearby alley. "Stories are something glimpsed for the—"

A peal of thunder drowns out his answer.

Years later, I found the hand-sized French blue-grid notebook I used that evening. I was inspired to turn the encounter into my own short story but was stymied by the very last line in my notebook, which had been smudged by water and coffee stains, making it indecipherable. I held the page up against the light and was able to make out only the first letter: "m."

Then no more.

My eyes race down the coffee-stain-mottled page, but the last word is indecipherable. Apparently, I had written down something, but what? What's the last word on stories, Ray?

For the what? I can't make out the last word in the dimly lit room, only the letter "m." Music, magic, mana? So, I hold up the thirty-year-old notes to the light and two more letters miraculously appear, to read, "M-a-r—"

And then it comes to me, like missing words restored in old recordings.

Marvel. Stories are glimpsed at it for the marvels within.

A Carveresque word if there ever was one.

I don't think we will ever understand the secret of the Venus de Milo until we understand what Carver was asking of himself, of us, of the world. Not until I know what he was reaching for that night because we need to know what the Venus was reaching for her with her missing arms.

And what was the marvel but to love and be loved, to be beloved.

If asked why I write, I often resort to this image of the need to rekindle my love of words, relearn the words of love art.

"Love is not love until love's vulnerable," wrote the vulnerable Roethke.

This one-liner captures my vulnerability in those moments.

Leave it to the ancient Greeks to have a name for the weighing of love, which they called *Erotostasia*, a word inspired by an ancient statue of Aphrodite where she is depicted holding two Erotes, winged gods of love and sexual intercourse. If we're in a playful mood, we might say that this image is the origin of the folk saying, "She loves me, she loves me not..." Either way, the image gave rise to the suggestion that lovers have a golden scale in their heart, on which they can determine the value and the cost of their turbinating passion, the fire that twists and turns inside them.

Over the years I have come across another way to imagine, if not gauge, the seemingly incalculable power of love and beauty. Of course, the approach just so happens to be inspired by the exquisite charms of Helen of Sparta, who was later described by playwright Christopher Marlowe as having "the face that launched a thousand ships," and in turn ignited the Trojan War. The poetically symmetrical number is based on Homer's description, in Book II of the *Iliad*, where he painstakingly lists the Catalogue of Ships, a gruesomely grand total of 1,186 Achaean (Greek) ships, which sailed to Troy to recapture Helen and bring her home again.

Eventually, the curious exactitude of the number inspired a lovely word, *millihelen*, to fancifully describe how much beauty is required to launch a single ship. As such, Helen has been endowed with a "beauty rating" of 1.186 Helens. Albert Camus beautifully described the hazy origins of the war as a "fight for Helen's beauty," which suggests that she had combustible power, enough to launch 1,186 ships. While this brings what the Greeks called an "Aphroditic Smile" to our faces now, the *millihelen* is also a marvelous metaphor for the endless skirmishes, fights, tussles or battles over "the beauty question," which continues today in virtually every facet of modern life.

But who on earth came up with this crazy but clever approach, you might ask? In his novel *The Rebel Angels*, Robertson Davies attributes the mythopoetic measuring system of beauty to the Cambridge mathematician W.A.H. Rushton. Alternately, the source is the polymath, Isaac Asimov, who claimed in his 1992 collection of jokes, riddles, limericks, and wild words, that he invented the term in a college paper, in the early 1940s.

So, after fighting for Helen's beauty, as Albert Camus explained the origin of the Trojan War, three thousand years later we are fighting over a word to describe the otherwise incomprehensively beautiful around us, or in us.

All told, one *millihelen* is enough beauty to launch one ship.

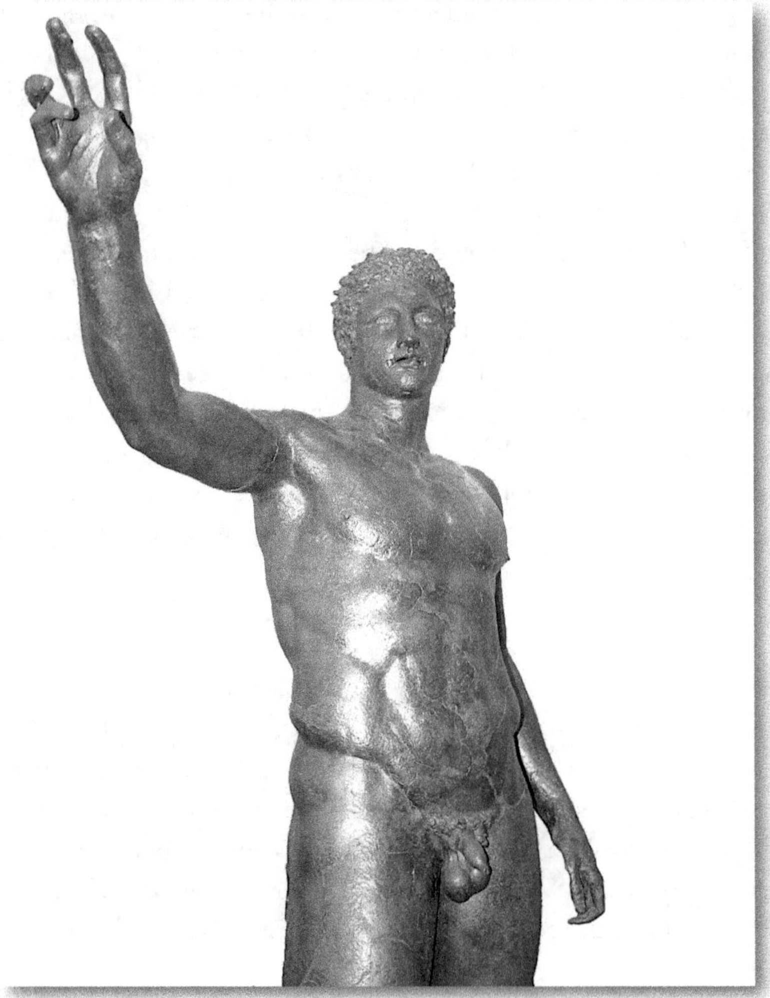

The Ephebe, or The Paris of Troy
National Archaeological Museum, Athens

THE ART IS ALWAYS IN THE SURPRISE

Surprise is what caught me in the summer of 2008 while leading a group of twenty-two sixteen-year-olds from Atlanta around Greece. At the National Archaeological Museum in Athens, I led them into a long room that featured the imposing bronze Poseidon, Myron's bust of the Minotaur, and the stele from Eleusis depicting Aphrodite rising from the sea.

As my young pilgrims surrounded me and impatiently awaited my comments on the Paris bronze, I watch them as they squirmed with teen angst at the sight of the naked Paris. But when I put the statue in the context of the famous story, the kids went quiet, staring at him in awe. Not one of them had *not* felt judged by the beauty wars, as Aphrodite, Hera, and Athena were. Not one of them had not felt exiled, as Paris was. They seemed to understand what it meant to "fall" in love, to be enchanted, and then to be haunted by it.

In a word, they got it. They seemed to understand the ancient connections between love and war, beauty and desire, envy and lust, happiness and unhappiness.

That was the moment I saw something I'd never seen before. Despite the astonishing treasure trove of art in the gallery, my attention was seized by the tall, lean, and pensive bronze statue (c. 340 BCE) in the middle of the gallery. The figure was depicted leaning forward, right arm stretched out with its palm open. I must have passed it by dozens of times over the years and never spent much time with it because the title didn't signify much: "The Ephebe" or "Young Man."

This time I casually glanced down at my new museum guidebook to refresh my memory before addressing the students about its mythic significance. I was startled to find an addition to the description of the statue, which had been hauled by sponge divers from the bottom of the sea in 1901 off the coast of the island of Antikythera, along with the Poseidon, a corroded bronze of a robust Odysseus, and the oft-described world's first computer, the first century Antikythera Mechanism.

For the tall bronze lad, the guidebook read: "The Ephebe, or Paris."

Suddenly, the tumblers in my mind clicked into place, the sealed safe swung open. The secret was out. This wasn't only a common statue depicting the Trojan Prince. It was the sculptor's rendering of "the decisive moment" in the myth of the Judgment of Paris. The anonymous artist had daringly captured him at the very moment he steps forward to award Aphrodite the Apple of Discord after judging her *Kallisteia*, the Most Beautiful. The sight of the statue allowed me to experience the *Pop!*—that movement in the mind when an image seems to leap, to move, to change shape. Think of the eight lines of the Necker Cube that appear to be at first just a simple block, but when stared at, the lines *pop* into a second shape. This thrilling illusion of movement influenced my next thought: the sculpture can be thought of as the other half of a diorama of the Judgment of Paris. The bronze Paris brings together two stories that merge into one. The marble sculpture of the Venus de Milo immortalizes the moment when the startled goddess gazes in amazement at her judge. The bronze Paris is reaching out with his right hand to hand over the prize of the golden apple.

I think the two works of art can be seen as mirror images of one another. Their hands are important, but their eyes are vital. The reaching, the locked gaze, the tension, the implied gifts. The Venus appears to accept her prize in astonishment, which is mirrored in the bafflement of Paris who is startled at being offered the prize of the promised love of Helen, the most beautiful but also most dangerous woman in the world.

Their mystery is doubled as the two statues, Venus and Paris, reveal one moment.

Suddenly but sublimely, the story was complete, as if the two statues had been superimposed on each other. This is my *anagnorisis*, my moment of recognition, as Aristotle named it twenty-five hundred years ago, the point when a character recognizes someone else's true identity—or the truth of their own. Often, when that occurs it is followed by what the Greeks called *thambos*, divine astonishment, amazement, to the point of being rendered immobile.

This is a nuanced way to view the stillness-within-movement of both statues. Venus and Paris both are depicted as being in anticipation of prizes they have been promised. Thambos is the perfect word, *le bon mot*, for the expression on their faces. This wonderful concatenation of thoughts makes me inexplicably happy.

Unfortunately, since the first commentators circulated their opinions about Homeric epics, the more moralistic among them have condemned Paris as a tragic figure—vain, treacherous, oblivious, disdainful of the ancient code of hospitality. But alongside those descriptions have been scores of other readings of the Judgment of Paris, its relationship to the igniting of the Trojan War, and the relationship between fate and free will. If the old Hays Code-like moralism that demands punishment and blames the world's ills for perceived misconduct can be set aside, it is possible to reimagine Paris so that we can conceive of him as being in love with accepting responsibility for his fate. Only then will we come to appreciate the heartstopping beauty of the expression on the face of the Venus de Milo—her surprise, her wistfulness, her sorrow at what is about to unfold.

The vision galvanizes my imagination. It helps me appreciate in a new way the mythic moment of the story that first inspired Alexandros in his depiction of Venus for the Melos gymnasium. Because the bronze Paris had been around for two hundred years by the time Alexandros carved his Venus, surely, he saw copies or at least sketches. It's not too much of a stretch to imagine him conceiving of his Venus because he had seen a version of the Paris bronze.

According to the story that inspired the sculptor, the apple represented two aspects of the same incident: Paris's choice of Aphrodite as the winner of the beauty contest and Aphrodite's victory over the other god-desses in the competition. In this light, the Judgment of Paris was more than a technical decision. Because all three goddesses possessed ethereal beauty, it would have been more than difficult, if not impossible, for Paris to choose one of them.

Instead, as Rachel Kousser has suggested, his judgment focused on the gifts the three goddesses offered him: power, riches, and beauty—or, closer to the core of the story, love. But not just any run-of-the-olive-mill love. No, he is susceptible to the "delight of love" in Kousser's joyful phrase.

It was a bold stroke of genius on Alexandros's part to conceive and execute the already common theme of the Judgment of Paris, but precisely at the moment of Aphrodite's victory, and then imbue in her the moment of desire that she is passing on to her judge, her redeemer, her lover as a kind of gift, a gift that promises not only languorous love but happiness. And then he had to choose the stone and know what to do.

All of which, I conclude, can be seen, if looked at closely, in the Bronze Paris.

"I may not have found the missing arms of the Venus de Milo," I joked to the students, "but I did discover the missing half of her story."

Later, looking at my own photograph of the Paris, I remembered a mighty passage in Eliot's *Sight and Insight:* "The whole point about Greek sculpture is that it was meant to be imitated, not in stone but in flesh. This is what imparts its miraculous life: a life so intense that even an arm-less, legless, headless Greek marble of the best quality shows where the head and limbs would be, upon the air. From the torso, one can strike the stance of the entire figure. The broken statue seems more alive than one's own flesh."

Rereading the first edition of Eliot's book, which I found in my father's library a few days after he died at 56, I fell into reverie, as if I'd just uncovered the secret of art, which is always a new and refreshing way to look at the world, with kinder, more compassionate eyes. I had just encountered a mystery whose source is beyond our comprehension.

INSCRIPT

On a tramp steamer bound for Argentina, the young Eugene O'Neill found himself mesmerized by the rhythm of the waves and deliriously free from the maniacal behavior of his family back in America. Caught in the slipstream between the two, he dropped into reverie and experienced a moment of clarity so real that only the numinous moment on deck existed with no sense of past or future, and in that reeling moment, O'Neill knew who he was and where he belonged and what his life meant. It was the kind of searing moment that is felt as a burning desire to relive the moment again. Writing about it, I do. My father told me with no little awe in his voice, "You writers are lucky. You get to live twice," he said. Years later, the tramp steamer incident inspired O'Neill's definitive play, *Long Day's Journey into Night*, in which he transformed himself into the young poet, Edmund, who says in a sublime reverie:

> I lay on the bowsprit, facing astern, with the water foaming into spume under me, the masts with every sail white in the moonlight, towering high above me. I became drunk with the beauty and singing rhythm of it, and for a moment I lost myself—actually lost my life. I was set free! I dissolved in the sea, became white sails and flying spray, became beauty and rhythm, became moonlight and the ship and the high dim-starred sky! I belonged, without past or future, within peace and unity and a wild joy, within something greater than my own life, or the life of Man, to Life itself! To God, if you want to put it that way... For a second you see—and seeing the secret, are the secret. For a second there is meaning!

For a moment: meaning, significance, value. The goal of a visit to any worthwhile museum is to spend a moment before a masterpiece, a piece of art that I have suddenly discovered *for myself*. Beyond meaning, joy. If only I look close enough. If only. Sometimes the thrill of discovery reminds us there is more to life than meets the eye, which is what meets the heart, and greets the soul.

I'll say it again: Love is the desire for beauty, beauty the need for love.

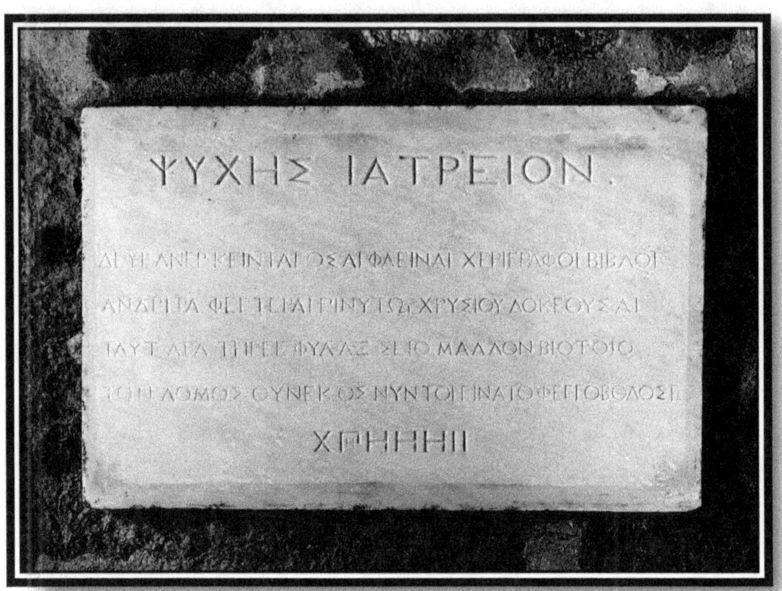

Psyches Iatreion (The Place for the Healing of the Soul)
Slab of marble embedded in lintel above entrance to the library at the
Monastery of Saint John the Theologian, Patmos,
Monastery of Saint John, Patmos
Unknown stone engraver, 1802.

TURNING TO THE MUSES

In April 2018, I led my tenth art and literary tour around Paris, this time with the foreign correspondent Mort Rosenblum. After the group left for home, I stayed behind to conduct what I swore would be one last round of research of the Venus de Milo at the Louvre. After spending seven straight days at the museum, twice changing my flights home, I left Mort's boat on the Seine for one last saunter across the Pont des Artes to say farewell to the Venus. I carried with me my trusty leather satchel packed with my Olympus II, a hand-sized leather notebook from La Coupole, a new edition of *The Goncourt Journal*, and a photocopy of Rodin's essay about the Venus, published a century before in the *New York World*.

At nine a.m., I arrived as the doors were opening, and as I tried to calmly stride inside was jostled by a swarm of bored tourists and elbow-happy culture vultures. After a few annoying minutes, I had to laugh and relax because the mania of the crowds, nearly a religious fervor, brought back memories of the American humorist Art Buchwald's article, "The Five-Minute Louvre," I had read years before in the *International Herald-Tribune*. The Pulitzer Prize-winning columnist had written a satirical piece about a stereotypical American tourist, outfitted in a track suit, and welcomed in by a whistle-blowing guard at the same hour of nine a.m., who then sprinted past the Greatest Hits of the Louvre at a Roger Bannister-like pace for five minutes.

Because this was meant to be my last free day in Paris for a long while, I took my sweet time, passing under one of the many banners advertising the current exhibitions, one of which used the deceptively simple word *museum*. I thought of d'Urville's casual reference in 1821 to the deal that he helped strike for the acquisition of the Venus as a gift to "our museum."

Instantly, the word soared in my mind, with its proud roots in *mouseion*, the House of the Muses, in Ancient Alexandria. As the brainchild of

Ptolemy the Preserver, the collection was founded in the second century BCE as part of the city's famous Library complex. The original museum was a combination research center, cabinet of curiosities, and art institute. As the name indicates, it was named after the nine daughters of Mnemosyne, Goddess of Memory, nine personifications of human creativity from history and oratory to music and dance. Their task was set forth by the classical Greek poet Hesiod in his *Theogony*, where he wrote that the muses inspired bards to sing about the mythic past to help people forget their troubles. As far as I know, this is the first reference to the arts as having such a recognizably human function: *to take our mind off our troubles*. And this task was set in stone.

According to the fourth-century historian Hecataeus of Abdera, in ancient Greece, visitors entered the building under a stone lintel into which was chiseled the balming words, "ΨΥΧΗΣ ΙΑΤΡΕΙΟΝ," "*Psychés Iatreíon*," which translates into the phrase that startles to this day: "This is the Place for the Healing of the Soul." For me, this arresting phrase echoes the Greek belief in the sacredness of books and reverence for libraries. While at a seaside taverna on Crete some years ago, I read *The Vanished Library* by the Italian philologist Luciano Canfora, and was moved enough to pick up pen and paper so I might jot down a few lines of my own, the writer's equivalent of call-and-response in blues music:

> The Place of the Cure of the Soul was a reminder to all who crossed its marble threshold that libraries are portals where the human spirit is stoked by reading spine-tingling words, the heart renewed by sublime images, the imagination stunned by sibilant stories since books are surely the winepress of knowledge.

Traditionally, we think of a museum as a place where we can *see* culturally significant artifacts *for ourselves* rather than through the prism of others' experiences, or only in art books or on videos. But museums are also sacred spaces where we *feel* for ourselves and find or forge some meaning about the larger questions in life. It's not too much to say that museums have been meaning-making machines for the last few thousand years.

Then there is the notion that museums, at least the best of them, are a kind of paradise, a word with roots in *pairidaēza*, ancient Persian for a "walled garden," which leads me to remember Emily Dickinson's observation, "Presence is paradise." Combine the two and you come closer to the palpable power of a museum visit, which is the fulfillment of coming in proximity of the presence of a piece of art that moves you, which offers a moment, a minute, then a lifetime of memories. Paradise by any other name.

In that sensual spirit, I appreciate the French Impressionist Edgar Degas's belief that the museum's central purpose is to provide a place where artists can actively *let us see the world in a new way*. His observation is less obvious than it sounds. One of the truisms of writing is that the truth often lies in what is not said, what is not written, but what is implied, a trick of perspective that allows the reader to *engage* with the text. Degas was repeating what mystics throughout the generations have said—that it is human nature to fall asleep, and the function of the arts is to help yank us out of our stupor.

"In order to awaken, one must first realize that one is in a state of sleep," the Russian mystic Gurdjieff reminded his followers. "Wake up!" according to the legend, were the Buddha's last words. "It is never too late to be what you might have been," said George Eliot.

What we learn from these wisdom quotes is that it is human nature to fall asleep—and then yearn to wake up and see the world anew, which is another way to describe the purpose of museums as being Houses of Seeing, teaching us how to view anew, to see as never before, as if our lives depend on it. Because they do.

The versatile feature writer for the *New Yorker*, Adam Gopnik, breaks down the essential function of a museum as being "a place where we go to look at things." The English art critic John Berger adds the dimension of time, noting that "we go to look at those who once lived." The incisive social critic Camille Paglia comments in her provocative *Sexual Personae*, "The greatest honor that can be paid to the work of art on its pedestal of ritual display is to describe it with sensory completeness... Criticism is ritual revivification."

Revivification. I appreciate the word. That's why I'm here, again, to be restored. Not for mere academic reasons, though I have come to admire art history. There's got to be more than theory; there must be a revival of our inner life. Reanimation. Rejuvenation. Renewal. We must relearn how to refresh ourselves without waiting for it to happen.

Say it again: *We must risk delight.*

I say we go to look at art to experience the invisible, for the soul as much if not more than for the mind. The great Humanist psychologist Rollo May told me as much over a series of meetings in the summer of 1986 at his home in Tiburon on San Francisco Bay. "I used to think people came to me to be *fixed*, then I realized they came to *see* their life in a new way. Creatively. To do that, they needed someone to *listen* to them. I now believe at the end of my career that the source of neurosis is repressed creativity. This makes libraries and museums far more important than we ever imagined." So too with novelist Theodore Dreiser, who described art as "the stored honey of the human soul." The New World satyr Henry Miller remarked that museums "teach nothing but the *significance* of life."

The urge to collect and visit works of art has not faded and is only increasing if you consider the skyrocketing prices for the Old Masters, and the curious fact that far more people visit museums than attend sporting events. The passion for collecting and the desire to see beautiful works of art and historical objects is an ancient one. Our medieval ancestors called their collections Cabinets of Wonder, or *Wunderkammens*, which referred to assembled curiosities, mosaics of marvels. There are now 55,000 museums located in 202 countries around the world. The most famous and influential are longtime rivals: the Louvre, the British Museum, Berlin's Pergamon, the Metropolitan Museum in New York, and the Vatican Collections in Rome. But do we visit them only out of cultural curiosity or social grandstanding, historical interest or sheer boredom?

I believe there is a longer view. The more generous perspective is that we go for a jolt of joy, a dollop of delight, and no small amount of self-satisfaction. I can't forget how one French friend sneered to me with utter disdain, "You Americans go to museums to *improve* yourselves." There is a long precedent for this notion, going all the way back to the ancients. We go to museums as we once went to churches—to learn how to live, to feel something sacred, something beyond the profane. Not all art can do that; some can. I am here to try to learn something from the sweet voluptuousness of the Venus de Milo rather than cultural voyeurism.

Why isn't this aspect of the art experience alluded to more often? This absence leads inevitably to "museum fatigue," the exhaustion that comes with gorging on art rather than digesting it. Why not emphasize the joy of viewing what is ultimately beautiful and significant, what stirs our hearts and moves our souls? The capaciously minded John Berger writes in *The Shape of a Pocket*: "More and more people go to museums to look at paintings and do not come away disappointed. What fascinates them? To answer: Art, or the history of art, or art appreciation, misses, I believe, what is essential. In art museums, we come upon the visible of other periods, and it offers us company. We feel less alone in [the] face of what we ourselves see each day appearing and disappearing."

We feel less alone.

C'est moi. That's me losing my sense of aloneness in a great museum. The last time I visited the Toledo Art Museum, to see the old El Grecos that my father had loved, a line bubbled up from the depths of memory, glittering words I had recently read in a book by Seamus Heaney a few months before in a Clifden bookstore: "*It was my first glimmer of the beautiful.*"

In the early 2000s, I delivered a morning lecture at the Chicago Jung Society, and afterward visited the Art Institute. After a round of casual afternoon viewing, I needed a cup of coffee, which I fetched from the cafeteria. On my way back upstairs to the galleries, my attention was seized by a kaleidoscopically colored stained-glass window set into a wall. When I looked at the placard to identify the artist, I read: Marc Chagall. Underneath was a quote of his: "I paint in order to be surprised." No surprise, I thought. What is essential about a work of art is never obvious, never the received wisdom. The beauty of art is unexpected, a tap on the shoulder, a thrum in the heart, a catch in the throat.

In turn, I have to say that I read and look at art and write about it *in order to be surprised.*

I love these museum moments because they galvanize me. My mind is shocked into thinking new thoughts. At this moment, of all moments, I think of a favorite passage in Read's *Art of Sculpture*: "Every memorable work of art offers a different solution to the so-called 'problem of beauty.'"

Art immortalizes, freeze-frames, preserves. Art helps us get lost so we can find ourselves and offers a rehearsal for recovering after getting lost again and again. And perhaps most important of all, as the cultural commentator Michael Kimmelman writes in his fervid introduction to *The Accidental Masterpiece*, "Art can transform our lives... It provides us clues about how to live our own lives more fully... this book is in part about how creating, collecting, and even just appreciating art can make living a daily masterpiece."

A beautifully written paragraph in a sublime book. One that raises questions about what we are *really* looking for. To say *ourselves* can be fatuous and self-serving. I think there is a finer point, which is the search for how we fit into the wider frame of life.

If I were a more perfectly developed human being, maybe this would come more naturally. But I know I need to be reminded of who I am and what I am looking for. I go to art, in galleries, garrets, or museums, to learn how to see all over again, to feel all over again. I need the jolt, the fix, the story. Especially this one about the previously Unknown Sculptor. The one the Louvre knew about but would not admit to publicly. And yet I am not as concerned, as are few of her visitors, about the arcane issues such as the propaganda campaign. What fascinates and entices me far more is why she *moves* us.

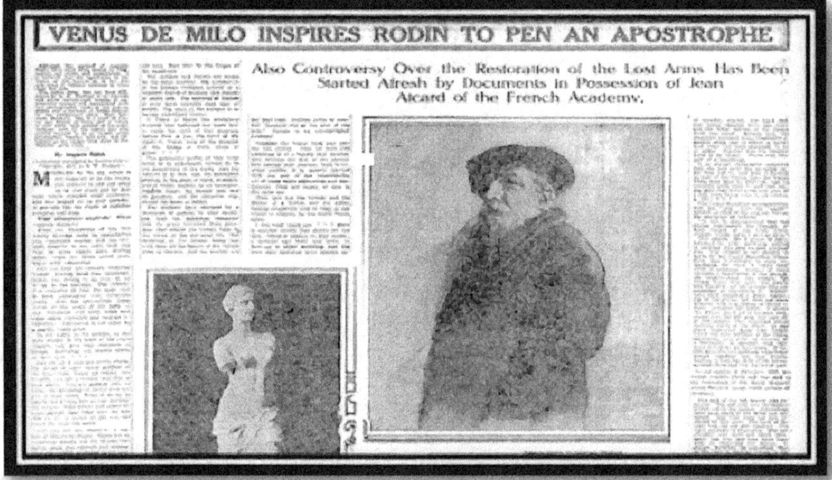

New York World, 1910

WALKING WITH RODIN

In the winter of 1902, Auguste Rodin was suffering through *une crise de confiance*, a crisis of confidence, in his life and work. One morning, he left his stately home in the eighteenth-century Hotel Biron in Paris and walked through the bitterly cold streets to the rue Bonaparte, past the École Nationale superieur des Beaux-Arts, across the Pont des Artes, and entered the Louvre. I imagine him eagerly striding down the long corridors of the Denon wing, named after the museum's first curator, and entering the gallery of ancient Greek and Roman sculptures. There, he paused in front of the Venus de Milo, the "Lady of Beauty," as German poet Heinrich Heine had called her. Then Rodin tumbled headlong into a reverie and began to walk around and around the statue. Circling her, he tried to understand what moved him, why she seemed to tremble with life. In 1910, he wrote about his encounter in an essay for a New York newspaper:

> Modeled by the sea, which is the reservoir of all forces, you enchant us, and you sway us by that grace and by that calm which strength alone possesses and you bestow on us your serenity ... To the poets, to the seekers, to the quiet artists in the heart of the city's tumult, you give long moments of solace ... You breathe, you are a woman. What is divine in you is the infinite love of your sculptor for nature.

A bit breathless to our modern sensibility, but breath as pure spirit. So, I let the words breathe. Despite the purple prose, Rodin manages to say something remarkable. He identifies the essential components of the Venus, such as the force field she exudes, her power to enchant, her strength, divinity, calm, and love—yes, love—and breath.

What is especially moving to me is that salute of *infinite love* to her sculptor, Alexandros of Antioch. Later in his article, Rodin provides some insight into the eternal mystery of how a mere mortal can bring stone to life. He calls attention to what he perceives to be the essence, the "marvel of marvels," in sculpture, delivering a rhapsody on our theme of movement, reminding us often that we come across references to how stone or paint or pages *breathe*, which is to say, how they come alive.

For me, this is the telltale sign of a mighty encounter with the art of arts. The breath that moves from the artist to the viewer. Recently, I mentioned this passage to a friend of mine, the architect and author Anthony Lawlor, and asked him what he thought Rodin meant, to which he thoughtfully replied, "I think he meant *aliveness*."

Aliveness, ah, yes, I thought, smiling at his limber choice of words. What is alive *moves*; what doesn't is dead. What moves is animated, vital, breathtaking, and moves *us*.

At the tail end of my time at the Louvre walking around the Venus de Milo, much like Rodin did, not unlike millions of others who have made the pilgrimage to her shrine, I try to assess my feelings. The first eight days had been a lark. I enjoyed the luxury of the time there, earned by dint of leading one of my annual art and literary tours to great cities and lands. I shot hundreds of photographs with my trusty Olympus II, filled an entire notebook with sketches, wrote poetic descriptions of Paris on the back of vintage postcards and winged them on their way, listened to what Joyce wondrously called "the sounds of manymirth" from the teeming crowds.

But something was missing. Eight days, no big revelation, no essential insight.

At the end of the day, I took a different tack. I turned off my brain. I stashed my notebook away. I snapped the lens cap back on my camera. Then I just walked around her for the last precious hour the museum was open. No agenda, no lofty goal, just the pleasure of sauntering around a great museum. To every statue, *turn, turn, turn.* Turn till you get it right, like the twisting of a kaleidoscope that creates new patterns from the colored objects inside with the simple motion of your rotating hand.

I walked around her like Rodin on his morning visits to the Louvre, Yeats turning with his gyres, Rilke circling his ancient tower, Pete Seeger turn, turn, turning with the seasons.

Art affects me less than a fantasy and more as a *quickening* of my spirit.

Walking in Rodin's footsteps, I strain to keep my sense of humor as tourists elbow me out of the way to take selfies of themselves with her as if it would make them more beautiful. The most recent iteration of the "reflected glory" phenomenon. Other visitors scowl in confusion when they read the bland placard that states "Anonymous." I overhear one visitor with a cockney accent share his disappointment in the Venus with his wife, sneering, "I thought the damned thing was carved by Michelangelo. It can't be any good if it wasn't made by Michelangelo. You know, I mean, well, somebody famous." An art gawker in a University of Texas T-shirt sneered to his friend out of the side of his mouth, "Geez, Harold, my mother-in-law is more beautiful than her—and she ain't no prize."

After an hour of sketching and journaling in the former royal chamber that now houses the Venus and snapping a hundred photographs, I had to catch my breath after the intense focus. I leaned against the back wall of the gallery and relaxed into a long stretch of silence. While doing so, I glanced at the simple mounted placard meant to describe the Venus in the center of the room. I bent over to read it and was disappointed to find only an ordinary description of the extraordinary work of art:

The Venus de Milo Artist: Unknown
Discovered: 1820, installed 1821
Site: Melos, Greece

As if the Louvre didn't know better. As if we never deserved to know the truth about the artist who made her and where she came from. As if we shouldn't see her with our eyes, feel her with our hearts. As if. The very stuff of drama. The question that pries open a million mysteries.

Strange and wonderful how our minds work. Mulling over these memories, I can hear in my third ear the lyrics to Cole Porter's "All of You," from the first time I played Ella Fitzgerald's version for my wife Jo in my old apartment near Golden Gate Park in the early days of our dating:

> I love the looks of you, the lure of you
> I'd love to make a tour of you
> The eyes, the arms, the mouth of you
> The east, west, north and the south of you...

Turning back to the Venus, I take a tour of her so that I might see something I've never seen before. I have a theory that we have a choice about how closely we pay attention—to our breakfast cereal, the noon whistle from a distant factory, the cry for help from an empty warehouse. If we do, and don't turn away, the world will pay us back with magnificence. These hours and days at the Louvre are only my latest experiment in attention. I've been playing the deep attention game since playing ball in my youth, again in my world travels, and in the thirty-plus documentary films I worked on. The closer I looked, even in dire circumstances, such as while working on war films, the more perplexing but also astonishing the world became. I didn't always solve the problems I was probing, such as trying to get to the bottom of the Spanish Civil War, such as the documentary I co-wrote, *Forever Activists: Stories from the Abraham Lincoln Brigade*, but always the mystery grew deeper. Eventually, I learned that the secret meaning lay in the mystery itself.

Why else visit a museum but to deepen the unknowns of our own lives?

Still, it's painfully clear how much I missed in my earlier visits. Was I distracted with other things to do in Paris, too cerebral, or too pleased with myself for learning so many mere facts about her? What did I miss? The essentials, the incidentals, the hype?

The story behind the story, the emotion beyond the emotion?

I think again of Pessoa's haunting thought about the great *besides* that accompanies everything. The poet Mark Strand described the elusive quality of Edward Hopper's incandescent *Cape Cod Morning*: "In Hopper, it seems there is always something beyond."

This concern about the mysterious origins of a work of art amazed Tom Stoppard. In his play *Voyage*, he suggests that the wider meaning of art lies not in the thing itself but in the moment of creation. Between the inspiration and the movement of the sculptor's chisel, the poet's pen, or the artist's paintbrush, something uncanny is occurring. The Spanish poet Antonio Machado called it "the third thing," the force that compels us to make something. T. S. Eliot described in Four Quartets as the moment where the dancer and the dance are one.

"Where do we go in that moment we create," Stoppard asks, "or experience a great work of art?"

The question simmers. I've been asking about origins and beyonds all my life. Where do I go when I write? Why do I have to come back?

Art is the greatest transportation system ever devised, carrying away the artist and then the audience. I have traveled the world to feel that sense of emotional freefall before great works of art, such as Rothko's "No. 14, 1960" at SFMOMA; Correggio's *The Assumption* in Orvieto, Italy; Frida Kahlo's *Self-Portrait with Thorn Necklace* and *Hummingbird* at the Harry Ransom Center in Austin; Rembrandt's *Self-Portrait* at the Rijksmuseum in Amsterdam; and Joan Mitchell's four-panel *Minnesota* in the Minnesota

Museum of Modern Art. And when I do, I feel a great wave of giddy happiness, as when I went skydiving during my college years in the early 1970s and pushed off from the wing of an airplane flying at twenty-five hundred feet above the Irish Hills outside Ann Arbor, Michigan. A clawing of terror was followed by euphoria, then sheer timelessness, as I fell, swaddled in near silence. I was so entranced by the beauty of the moment, I almost forgot to pull the ripcord. The *whoosh* of the *ground rush* coming at me reminded me. Then the chute blossomed open above me. White, sunlit, heavenly. Falling, falling, falling. Weightless, timeless, until the last possible moment, when I tucked into myself and hit the ground with a *thump* and rolled to a safe landing. And then back into the plane before I could change my mind, and then again, and again, for emphasis.

While contemplating the Venus, I often think of the three jumps I made that day. I needed to take a leap into the unknown. Exhilarated, frightened, somehow more alive than ever before. What was I trying to prove? What was I hoping to accomplish? Sometimes I think I was trying to recapture the original innocence of those hours with my father at the Detroit Institute of Arts, or the following flares of emotion I felt in those early museum encounters on my American Grand Tour of Europe.

I've come to regard these as my Camusian moments, inspired by the passage in his essay, "Between Yes and No," where he writes, "A person's life purpose is nothing but this slow trek to rediscover, through the detours of art or love or passionate work, those one or two simple images in whose presence his heart first opened."

Still, what is it that is more than a feeling, less than an idea? Remembering that everything else in my young life was asleep, I was most alive in a museum, reading a book, playing ball, walking along a beach. *Dreaming with my eyes open.*

Today, if you wish to make the art pilgrimage to the Louvre so you might share a personal moment with the Venus de Milo, as an estimated three million visitors a year do (as a museum guard told me), you need to enter through I. M. Pei's Pyramid, meander through the main hall, serpentine your way through the frenetic crowds in the hall, and then swagger your way up two flights of stairs to reach the gallery of Roman and Greek sculpture.

There you will find a rogue's gallery of Greek and Roman statues, including the *Apollo of Mantua*, the *Borghese Gladiator*, the *Diana of Gabii*, the *Venus Genetrix*, and the *Lady of Auxerre*, that give some vital context to the Venus you are about to encounter. By far the most significant of these Greco-Roman statues is Praxiteles's *Aphrodite of Knidos*. The masterpiece was the most celebrated work of sculpture in antiquity, carved around 364-361 BCE, and most scholars agree it likely inspired Alexandros's vision of our Venus.

Walk on and you reach her gallery, the former royal chambers, appropriately enough, of the Queen of France, refurbished for, if you will, the Queen of Melos. With an elegant touch, the Louvre's architects used marble from the same quarry on Paros that provided Alexandros with his stone when he sculpted her roughly two hundred years after Praxiteles carved his in the early first century BCE.

Today, I try to key in on something I hadn't noticed before, an always rewarding practice. There is a wonderful symmetry to the Venus being framed by a beautiful arch of red marble as if an echo of the niche in which she was found by Yorgos and Voutier. No sooner do I enter the chamber than I feel the centripetal force of the statue and find myself circumambulating her. I can sense what is *there*, the size and technical virtuosity, but also what is *not there*, the ethereal *besides* and *beyond*, which is another way of getting closer to the mystery of why her infamously missing arms are as famous as what's left of her.

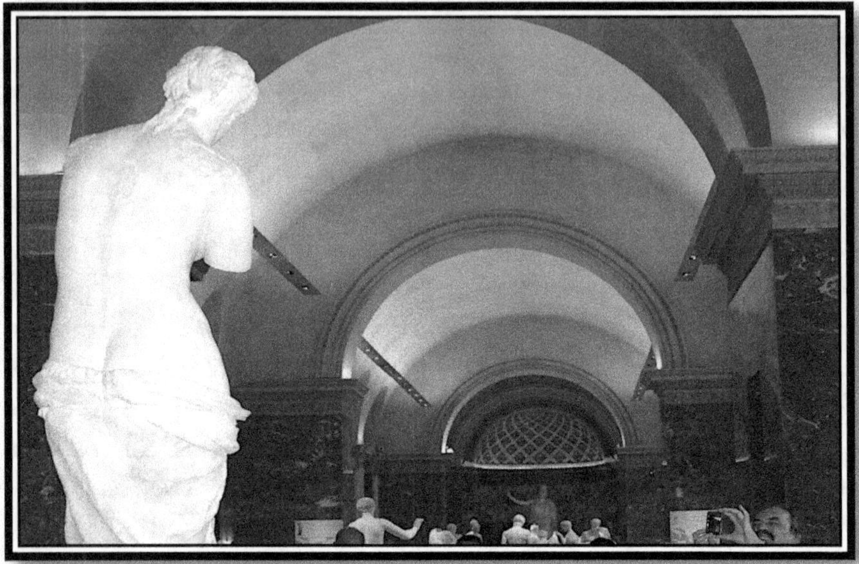

The Venus gazes out over the Greco-Roman Hall of Sculpture.
Musée du Louvre, 2010

What is it, I wonder?

There is her magical stillness and her serenity in stone, comparable to Vermeer's *Woman in Blue Reading a Letter*. While the Dutch painter was drawing on his memory of a husband or lover half a world away, the sculptor of the Venus de Milo was carving an early version of what the Surrealists and later the Italian designer Luigi Nono deftly regarded as nostalgia for the future. An infinite moment. Transportive. Quivering.

Hers is more than a smile, a gentle phenomenon.

Inspired, I look, I gaze, I regard, I absorb, I remember.

I felt vindicated for this occasionally obsessive practice when I read the words of the very first art historian, Giorgio Vasari, in his magisterial three-volume *Lives of the Artists*: "I confess, I confirm, I learn, I marvel." Poring over the pages of Edith Hamilton's *The Greek Way*, I smiled to see, "The Greeks were realists. They saw the beauty of common things and were content with it." I can taste the words of Rilke, in a letter to his wife in 1906 after spending a day with Cezanne's paintings in Paris: "It's as if every part were aware of all the others."

Seeing, hearing, absorbing these voices from decades of reading and museum-going, I pause to really look at the Venus, and as occasionally happens in the presence of masterpieces, I sense she is looking back at me. Sure, that may be impossible on the literal level, but not on the level of truly experiencing a work of art, what we might call the mysticism of direct encounter. It has to do with the deft move from glancing to witnessing to what poet Donald Hall, in his interview with the sculptor Henry Moore, called "absorption," the uncanny ability to will ourselves into a deep state of concentration.

Whenever I remember to take a breath and gaze on art this way, it's as if I need to find a secret resting place to gather my thoughts and feelings. As I do now, I am turning, slightly changed, but also, frankly, *slightly disappointed* in myself, seeing the obvious, missing the necessary.

Gazing, it seems to me, at her thousand-yard stare is more than technique, closer to wistfulness. There is something *annunciatory* about her this afternoon, evocative for me of Correggio's sky-swirling *Assumption* on the dome of the Cathedral of Parma. Something haloed, such as Hopper's *Woman in the Sun*, whose porch-straddling figure stares into the back of beyond, Vermeer's opalescent *Girl with a Pearl Earring*, Toulouse-Lautrec's green-eyed *The Absinthe Drinker*, and Mark Rothko's glow-from-within portal painting, *Number 14*.

I could look at these works forever. Sometimes it feels as if I do. Time stops. I drop into a kind of rambunctious reverie. Through great art, I catch a glimpse of eternity as an experience of intensity more than duration, devotion more than aesthetics.

I'm a dweller on the threshold of the moment. I just wish I could keep my thoughts only on the Venus, but my tendency to free-associate gets the best of me. Each detail of her reminds me of her story or other works of art. It is dizzying, thrilling. Eventually, I come back to myself, back into the room, back to the Venus.

I've been returning her gaze since I was twelve. The statue is something we usually associate with preternatural beauty, her sheer confidence that her mere presence ignites desire in all who come near her. I look again at her face, utterly beautiful but breathless, defiant but humbled, as if knowing something a second before it changed her, changed the world. I am walking around her to see her and myself more fully, as I would around a garden, a ballpark, a megalithic site, a library, a friend. I am writing to remind myself what I am looking for: art with wings, beauty with soul, life with meaning. I am writing to bring myself back to life. What I don't see informs what I do see, see?

"One cannot divine nor forecast the conditions that will make happiness," wrote Willa Cather in *Le Lavandou*. "One only stumbles upon them, by chance, in a lucky hour, at the world's end somewhere, and holds fast to the days, as to fortune or to fame."

"A circle whose circumference is everywhere and center nowhere" was the alchemists' aphorism about the ineffable mystery of God, a startling line that came to me while realizing that the Venus's arms are nowhere to be seen but everywhere to be found.

Clearly, there is a story here, but it's hiding within a myth inside an enigma. Getting to the heart of the mystery will take some time, some prying apart. I need to believe the story is right in front of me, a sculpture in the center of the room, with a tribute to the niche in which she was found, flaring out behind her in the rear wall. Why not a pedestal, a colonnade, a garden folly, a pool in a villa?

The Venus de Milo was found at the entrance to the island's gymnasium.

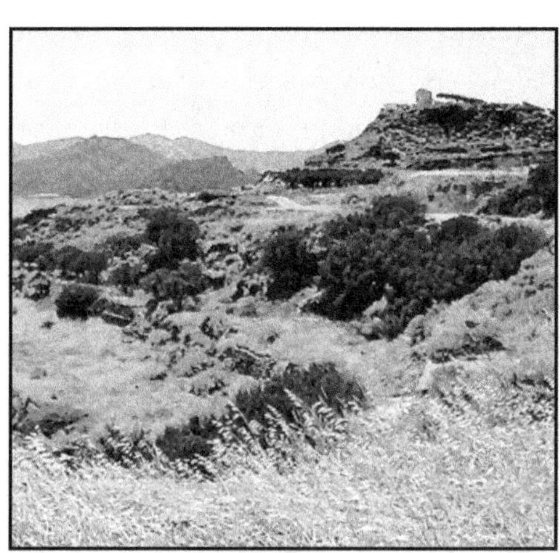

The ruins of the Old Running Track of the Gymnasium, Melos, Greece.

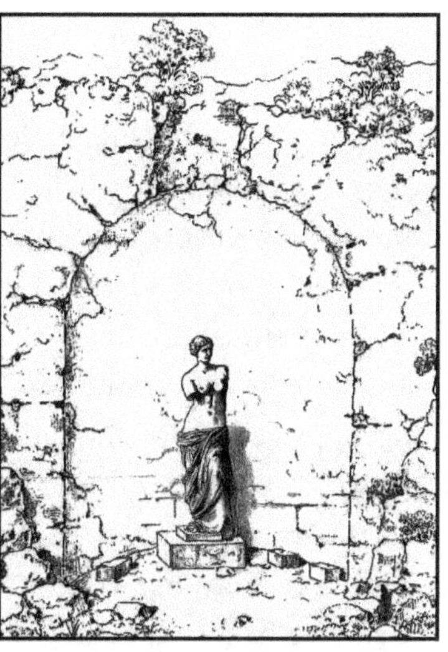

A. Debay sketch based on Brest's description of the niche on Melos. Musée du Louvre, 1821

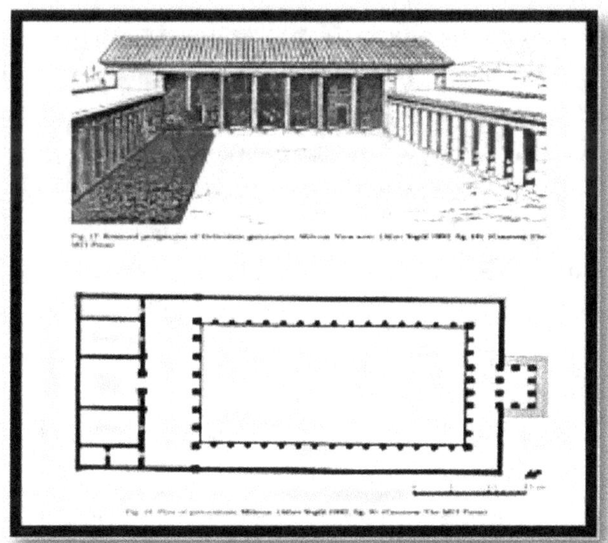

The plan of a typical Greek gym

THE NICHE

Niche, n., is from the French for "recess" and from the Italian *nicchia*, nest, nook, from *niechio*, seashell. The latter association seems appropriate for Venus, goddess of myriad things, including seashells. Its verb form is *nichier*, to nestle, or build, which is doubly meaningful because that is where the Venus ended up, in a place of rest, where she was a good fit. The word itself situates our statue and our story. The Venus had been nestled, lodged, placed in a niche on Ancient Melos.

Of course, neither Yorgos nor Voutier had any way of knowing any of this. Art scholars and historians wouldn't know the truth for another hundred years. What was common knowledge was that thousands of marble statues had disappeared across the ancient world, their niches sealed or buried under landslides, and thousands of bronzes had been melted down into weapons or lost at sea. Why was this one, our Venus, languishing in the middle of nowhere, a farmer's field on one of the more remote Cyclades islands? Had the niche been carved out of the side of the hill simply to hold a little votive statue, as you see in grottoes from Portugal to Ireland, France to Turkey? Or was this niche part of something greater, far more glorious? The question isn't academic at all. We need to know where she fit into ancient life so that we know how she fits into ours. If we don't, we'll never understand her carefully carved expression of desire.

Well, at least I need to know. I need to know her back story to understand why she has moved the hearts of art lovers and tourists alike over the last two centuries, and who knows how many Greek athletes and warriors worked out there.

Walking into the gallery today brings some of the confusion into focus. The doubling of the niche motif evokes the very site where the farmer and the soldier were digging, which we now know was not located in a meaningless field. *The niche was recessed in the back wall of the entrance to the ancient gymnasium on Melos,* fitted in between the herms of Herakles and Hermes to form a curious triad of mythic statues intended to inspire the training athlete or soldier. The massive building had been part of a complex that included a wrestling school and a running track. Together, they comprised the main social center on the island, which was also where young men between the ages of eighteen and twenty rigorously trained in athletics, dialectics, history, and war games.

The very word *gym* raises the hair on my arms, bringing on butterflies and a pounding heart. A huge part of my youth was spent in gyms. While friends were itching to break out of school, I was breaking into ours—well, specifically, the gym. Often, my buddies and I played late-night basketball that went on into the early morning hours, our version of what's now called Midnight Basketball in many urban centers. We improved our shooting and passing while deepening our friendships, many of which have lasted us a lifetime. In college, I worked out at the university gym and scrimmaged with the basketball team, and once with Spencer Haywood, the freshman who vaulted straight into the NBA, and Owen Wells, a future All-American, and working out alongside Alex Karras, Dick LeBeau, and Milt Plum of the Detroit Lions. Later, while crisscrossing Europe, I played basketball on courts from England to France, Germany to Italy, Greece to Israel, one of the great, undiluted joys of my life. For me, gyms have long been a holy and winged thing, the place where I lost myself to find myself.

All this is to explain why I was giddy when I discovered that during classical times, every city in Greece boasted a vast gymnasium complex. They consisted of hot and cold baths, training rooms, classrooms, running tracks, wrestling pits, banquet halls, hotels for visitors. The gymnasiums/athletic centers were not only situated in the center of each city. They were deliberately placed near each city's main temple and theatre. Together, they formed an uncanny architectural Golden Triangle to reflect in stone the ideal of mind, body, and soul.

Together, they presented the outward manifestation and daily physical reminders of the spiritual ideal of perfecting the well-lived life, which taught citizens to attend to mind, body, and soul in the theater, gymnasium, and temple, respectively. Cities vied with one another for the most magnificent training grounds and often held festivals that the scholar Rachel Voussar says were "associated with the gymnasia [and] grew to major civic affairs, with processions, sacrifices, contests, and banquets." Every significant town had a well-appointed gymnasium. To enter a Greek gym was to enter an ideal world in which the training, teaching, and artwork were designed to encourage the well-lived life. At the entrance, there would have been a niche for a statue. When a student, athlete, trainer, or teacher proceeded toward the *palaestra* (the athletic area and baths), they would pass a series of sculptures of former Olympians, local athletes, or patrons of the gymnasium—or the gods. The first statue would be of Hermes, who symbolized cleverness and speed and was often the patron of runners. The second was Hercules, the embodiment of strength and endurance, the patron god of warriors. The third was Aphrodite, the personification of love, beauty, and desire.

Passing her every day in the gymnasium must have been a visual aphrodisiac, a tonic for the superstition-saturated ancient world, where women were thought to have testicles, capable of making men pregnant if they laid on top during lovemaking. An athlete or warrior, mentor or philosopher who entered the athletic complex would have passed the Venus every day, pondering her beauty and nudity, reminding them of all the glorious gifts of the gods and prompting them to wonder about the relationship between her combustible beauty and masculine strength. Art moves us in this way. If we perceive motion, there will be a corresponding movement in us, a necessary one.

On every visit I have made to her chambers over the long and winding years, she appears as sudden as a specter. The first thing you notice is how she looms over everyone. She is much larger than seems possible from all the postcards and the replicas found around the world. Appropriately, she is larger than life, standing a startling six foot, eight inches, which is why she looms over the crowd. In the close encounter, you notice a certain resoluteness bordering on toughness that dissolves into tenderness edging into seductiveness.

How many visitors today know they are walking in the footsteps of those who, over the centuries, made pilgrimages to mythic statues? Often, the first impression is *recognition*, the thrill we've all felt rising in us that comes from seeing anything famous, the delicious *Aha!* moment provoked by the realization that something we've seen in books or movies still exists, and more than that, this one has *survived*. The Venus is a beautiful survivor. She is there and she isn't. She's missing her arms, but she is somehow complete. It's uncanny, and as Freud noted, we can suddenly appreciate the "strangeness of the ordinary." The Venus has outlasted the ravages of time and the scourges of the Church-ordered destruction of thousands of ancient sites.

After the rapacious Roman emperor Theodosius demolished the ancient pagan sites at the end of the fourth century, the Venus and the two herms were left in their respective niches, forgotten, forlorn. Over the next twenty-one centuries, the site was used as a quarry. The marble and bricks were hauled away or burned in lime kilns. Earthquakes probably toppled whatever was left. By the time Yorgos inherited the property, the wall had been sealed up for more than two thousand years.

Today, the Venus suffers the dubious distinction of having her image emblazoned on coffee mugs and T-shirts, and we succumb to a numbing familiarity. But it remains one of the first lessons of art appreciation to learn how to see her all over again, which is becoming more and more uncomfortable to admit. How many visits have I had the great luck to enjoy her—a dozen, two dozen? And if I'm honest with myself, I have looked at her a great deal but still haven't *seen* her. I am talking myself into accepting all the unknowns, to live in the mystery, but I am haunted by Don Henley's plaintive voice singing, "But I know what's been on your mind / You're afraid it's all been wasted time." Once, when I was wasting mine, I played that song forty-two times in a row. It was not a waste of time.

Neither was coming to the Louvre nine days in a row.

I can't be deterred, can't be stopped, although I may need to change my point of view. I need to refine the *way of seeing.* I am shifting my head at odd angles, bending down, standing on my tiptoes, turning around the Venus to gaze at her from every possible angle. Inevitably, a few comparable exercises come to mind, such as the Wallace Stevens poem, "Thirteen Ways of Looking at a Blackbird," and Claude Monet's views of the Rouen Cathedral, Kurosawa's *Rashomon* with its seven different storylines, and Glen Gould's thirty-plus versions of Bach's Goldberg Variations. This visit feels like a natural progression of all my museum visits and my obsessive riffling through hundreds of art books. The more angles the better, the more emotions evoked, the finer.

Then I recall the reflections of the Chicago Art Institute scholar, James Elkins, who wrote that it is advisable to let your memory run wild at a museum so you can free-associate and probe your deepest feelings about what you're looking at. How else can art get into our souls and alter our chemistry? Rather than art being the result of a cultural conspiracy to force certain political ideas on people, I identify more with Tolstoy's suggestion that art and literature are the "transmission of feeling." Not sentiment but feeling, the release of honest emotion.

Then again, I feel my forehead wrinkling, a surefire sign I am trying too hard.

A thought from Herbert Read's *A Letter to a Young Painter*: "The shock of pleasure one gets from a painting [or sculpture] is the shock of a revived experience, of a communicated sensation. One must feel the sensation along the nerves, in the brain." Read goes on to say to his earnest art student and correspondent, another piece of beautiful advice that pierces me to the quick, "The one thing all art must aim for is a certain enhancement of the purpose of being, the affirmation of life, and of the significance of human destiny."

Enhancement, purpose, affirmation, significance.

If this isn't what we yearn for in a work of art, what is?

A painting or sculpture, poem, song, or novel that doesn't provide the qualities that make our hearts pound faster—works that merely entertain or distract or waste our time or mock what is truly beautiful—are examples of who or what stole the arms of the Venus de Milo. There are stolen moments and there are stolen infinite moments. This is the province of cynicism, sarcasm, and snarkiness when it comes to how much we are or are not moved.

The philosopher in Herbert Read was suggesting far more than a career move to the callow young painter. He was offering a way of life. He was rendering a statement that creates a moment of horripilation, the telltale tingling of hair on your arms or scalp. We don't go to *see* beauty in the abstract, we go to *feel* the physical and spiritual *sensations* of the beautiful, specific works or objects that are radiant, harmonious, and uplifting. They allow us to practice two things: first, the elegant reminder of the Canadian poet-astronomer Rebecca Elson to live up to "our responsibility to awe," and beyond to what Einstein believed was the greatest pursuit of all, "to awaken joy."

Joy and the rebirth of my waning wonder may be why I am at the Louvre.

Penedo, Portugal, 1991. Living in an old village along the Atlantic, alone in a two-hundred-year-old stone house, trying desperately to write. Knowing that the Dave Brubeck band had stayed in the house the month before me and completed an album there should have helped but didn't. I was stuck, down and out, feeling as splintered as Pessoa, the national poet, known for writing under four different names because he experienced four different personalities. One night, under an El Greco sky, blue and black thunderclouds passing in front of a near-full moon, I felt the need for a walk down to the ocean. When I reached the beach, I started down a long wooden staircase. The moon came out from behind the thunderheads, shining a sudden light on the high granite wall to my left. I smiled as I craned my neck to see the beautiful light—then was stunned to see colossal footprints imprinted on the wall, dinosaur tracks climbing into the night sky. Paleolithic footprints striding high into the heavens.

A vertiginous moment. I am reeling and need to reach for the wooden railing to steady myself. The beauty is maddening, though the image made no sense—how could fossilized footprints rise into the air? Slowly, I realized that the ground had somehow tilted over the last sixty million years, probably because of an earthquake, shifting the ground from horizontal to vertical. The tectonic details didn't matter as much as the emotion. The sheer beauty of moonlight on stone, the night's spotlight on the tracks of ancient beasts, brought joy into my heart. The uplift of my spirit aligned with the uplift of the ancient ground. Something cracked open in me, the emotion that comes with being surprised by—what else—the joy of what the poet Robinson Jeffers called "divinely superfluous beauty."

Since I learned the identity of the creator of the Venus de Milo, I have enjoyed imagining the sculptor's studio in Antioch-on-the-Meander. Toiling away is a marble-dusted, concupiscent, competitive young man, Alexandros, who strove to do something new with stone, hoping to update or refurbish the very idea of Aphrodite. No mean feat, this. His attempt to advance what was known and what had been attempted in his field, a penchant for originality, is the first level of being a *genius*. The second is an extraordinary attendant spirit, an indwelling *genius*, a supernatural *daemon*, what Socrates deemed to be the second soul. I see Alexandros, the Michelangelo of the ancient world, working in a continuum that stretched back four centuries to Praxiteles, but one that he infused with his own style so he might achieve a breakthrough that people intuit but rarely attribute to him. His version of Venus is one he envisioned in the two Parian marble blocks he chose. The top half stone is carved to reveal her sensual attributes and her emotional depths, while the lower half stone reveals her indomitable strength and her boundless generativity.

It is a miraculous accomplishment.

By doing so, Alexandros anticipated by two thousand years what Read would declare in *History of Sculpture* to be the qualities of greatness in carving: *Interiority, Inwardness, Integrity.*

One night, while staying on Ithaka, only a few hundred yards away from the tumbledown ruins of the reputed palace of Odysseus and Penelope, I dreamt of something strange happening to Alexandros while he was carving his Venus. I imagined him carving away in his studio, a passionate young man, adept in many fields, a victor in a local singing competition, and not unfamiliar with gymnasium life. There he was chiseling away at his block of stone when a wandering bard arrives drunk and regales him with a far different version of the Judgment of Paris story that allowed him to grasp and then carve the spiritual essence of the mythological story.

❂

I stand before her now. The Venus de Milo, impervious to the circling crowds, the inane tourists, and the weeping lovers alike. As I moved around her, it occurrs to me that her creator must have had the heart of a poet to be able to infuse something resembling a personality into a goddess while she was clearly based on the sumptuous curves of a real-life woman he must have hired to sit for him in his studio. But we reserve the word for geniuses like him who went beyond the realistic to do just what the Greek poet Posidippus of Pella envisioned in one of his beautiful epigrams, which was that a sculptor would someday *make marble come alive*. Not unlike what happened in the myth of Pygmalion and Galatea, or in the avowed wish of the modern sculptor John B. Flannagan, who described his own work as a lifelong journey to capture the human spirit in stone by "thinking with my hands," a phrase I have come to love.

Naturally, the ancient Greeks even had a word for it, coined by no less an observer than Socrates: *zotikoterans*, to come alive. The marvel of making the spirit move from one human being to another through a work of original creation. The miracle of allowing someone else to feel what you felt a moment or a thousand years from now. What could be more miraculous than that—to have felt for a moment what the sculptor felt as he carved this miraculous face? Tolstoy went as far as calling it an "infection," a disturbing but accurate description that perfectly conveys the transmission of feeling from an artist to an observer, which may very well be the sibilant source of the shiver up the spine, saying, "What a strange illusion it is to suppose that beauty is goodness."

This reflects the age-old secret of what we have always wanted, if not demanded, from our artists: vitality, movement, radiance. All of which require a certain wizardry on the part of the sculptor. Not just technique. Magic. We cannot shy away from this element in the art of sculpture because it always reveals that wondrous ingredient, the joy-in-creating that we secretly long for.

How else could Alexandros have won the competition against the other great sculptors from the studios of Pergamum, Paros, Naxos, and Athens except by daring to be original? In this sense, he did for sculpture what Homer did for poetry when the bard had made the gods seem human. Through his work, we know better our own humanity. What Rodin recognized is evidence of what the German psychologist Rudolf Otto, in *The Idea of the Holy*, called the "numinous," after the Latin *numen*, which originally referred to the "nod of the gods," or what we today might call divine approval. The numinous is the display or revelation of a power or presence that is somehow *other*, and some would say divine. Others would say these are the works of genius, which is often another form of mystification. A contemporary of Rodin's, the poet Paul Valery, looked at work like this as the very definition of art. It is not just an idea, it is an *action*, such as the making of a poem, a song, or a sculpture with the intention of creating something beautiful—and succeeding.

There is always something invisible at play in the fields of art, a presence pulsing beyond the visible, as Mark Strand pointed out in the most haunting of Edward Hopper's paintings as if he had witnessed invisible forces working on him in every waking moment, chanting that the past is here, always here, the ghost in the marble, and it's beautiful anyway. Strand helped me to reimagine Alexandros. I began to think of him witnessing a magical moment in Antioch, in a temple, a theater, a park, a grove, and turning it into Aphrodite. I pictured him as a young man who was after the *deeper mysteries* in the way I have long imagined the trances of the painter Mark Tobey, which he described to the journalist Selden Rodman as the mystical moments when his soul guided his hand. The corollary is the sculptor in Asia Minor gazing out over the Aegean and imagining himself on Melos, thinking, *I have something in me*, and then sculpting his feelings. As the painter Franz Kline once said, "I paint not the things I see but the feelings they arouse in me." Or, as Paul Klee observed, "One eye sees; the other feels." While the German poet Rilke was living in Paris, he became paralyzed with writer's block and took a job as Rodin's secretary. What he learned from his mentor was that if he worked hard, he would enjoy "the grace of great things." So awestruck was Rilke by the *le maître's* work ethic that he described his mentor as a "very knowledgeable man who pours souls into his marble statues, which quiver with life…" There's that shudder again.

Speaking of Rodin, I experienced that quirky quickening when my father took me downtown to what he was fond of calling the DIA, the Detroit Institute of Arts, and introduced me to his most famous statue, *Le Penseur*, which we call *The Thinker*. I felt pride in my father's voice when he said "we," as in "we Detroiters," had been awarded one of only twelve copies created from the original molds from Rodin's own foundry. My father may have identified with the fevered brow the sculptor had carved into the character's forehead, a signifier of his deep thinking, a resemblance I see now in old yellowing photographs he left behind. That display of pride has never left me.

Walk on, write on through the writing of a vision of what she is missing, what she is holding. An apple, a ball, an offering, a gift? Whatever it was, and all the evidence points to the golden apple, it was a *quickening* in the hands of Paris, then Aphrodite, which I read in her startled face. What I am seeing is far from an *ideal*, an unfair image that no one can live up to, a depiction of unrealistic beauty. No, I am imagining the apple in her hand, her extended arm, her look of utter surprise as she gazes into the eyes of the young buck, Paris, who chose her. I am *feeling* the gush of art, the transference of feeling from the artist to the viewer. Alexandros to the marble, the marble to me, some twenty-one hundred years later. This is the fulfillment of a moment written about by Homer himself when he said, daringly for the times, that human beings invented the gods in order to know themselves better.

What I am proposing is this: The Venus is a vision inspired by the myths and then personified by a beautiful but relatable model from Antioch who was far from the rather inhuman ideal that inspired Praxiteles and Phidias and other sculptors who first immortalized mortal beauty. Their sculptures may have been remarkable but weren't as relatable as the work of the sculptor from Antioch.

For me, Alexandros' great accomplishment was that he brought beauty from its ethereal heights back down to earth. His Venus was not a lamentation about unfair ideals, but a celebration. His Venus de Milo was an ode to love, beauty, and desire.

Coming to this moment was worth the waiting, the reading of this atlas of desire and beauty. I live inside a mystery too marvelous to be comprehended, too beautiful to miss. Every encounter gives me traction for the life that follows.

Don't tell me to look away.

I might miss what's missing.

INSCRIPT

At the Mill Valley Film Festival in 1984, the two-time Oscar-winning screen-writer Waldo Salt told me that he was inspired to write the flashbacks for "Midnight Cowboy" as "flash-presents" because he came to realize that he didn't want the action to go backwards. "There was something missing in the way we use flashbacks now," he said gently. "I needed to honor the nuances of time." By this, he meant he wanted to show that important memories were entering the head of Joe Buck (Jon Voight) at the moment he was depicted moving across the silver screen. The memories didn't come only once, long ago; they were happening now to the haunted gigolo and to us as we watched him.

Strange how I thought of Waldo on my last day of nine at the Louvre in 2018. It was the moment of the quiver when I had the sensation that the Venus had always existed and always would, that Alexandros just chiseled away what distracted from her beauty, cutting into the cut, as one recent sculptor put it, which in turn brought to mind a passage by the Swiss sculptor and painter Alberto Giacometti, who wrote, "The more I work, the more I see things differently, that is, the grandeur becomes more and more unknown and more and more beautiful. The closer I come, the grander it gets, the more remote it is."

Simultaneity. Life comes at us all at once and we ask ourselves if we are quick enough to catch it. A zoetrope of stone, a spin of ancient stories, the movement of life itself. If I look again, what can I catch?

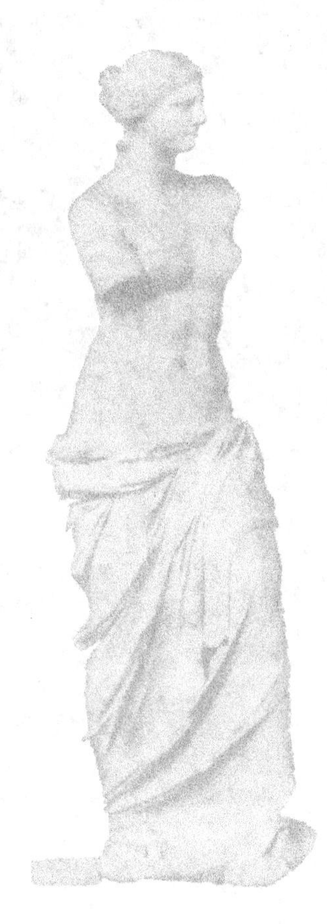

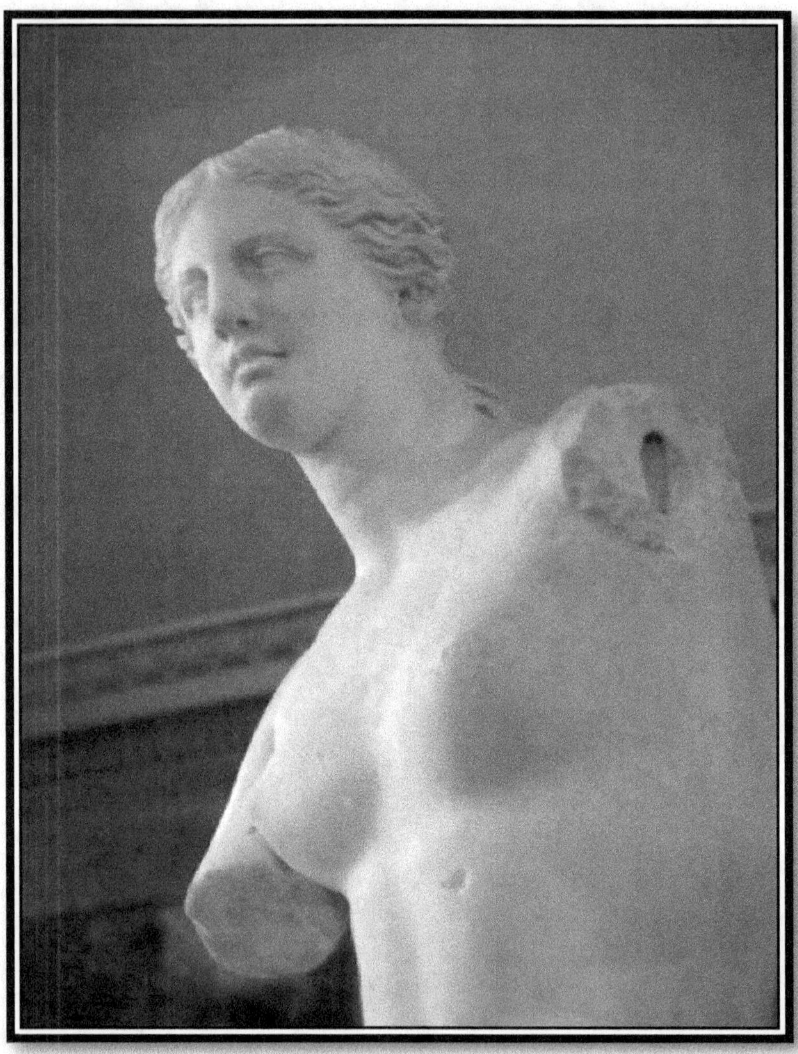

"How long are we to heed your call, / O armless sculpture?"
—Marina Tsvetaeva, translated by Nina Kossman
Musée du Louvre, Paris

THOSE MISSING ARMS

On my Cole Porter tour of her, I smile. Never before had I noticed how much she looms over the room; never before had I felt how strongly she commands the space. It could be a trick of the light as it slices through the tall windows or the way the crowds are moving in and out of the room like the tide at Gaspé Bay in Nova Scotia, which seems strangely appropriate because she is able to give off that illusion of movement. Walking around her, it occurs to me that's why her sculptor twisted her voluptuous hips. The scholars call this *contrapposto*, counterpoised, so she appears to shift her weight into a lean on one foot. The innovation allows the sculptor to achieve a posture that is not passive, as it is in so many earlier versions of Venus/Aphrodite sculptures, including, to my eyes, the groundbreaking Praxiteles's Aphrodite. Nor does the Venus de Milo appear weak or timid, a pose that is not only tiresome to observe but wrong. The Aphrodite of the poets and bards is powerful. Active. Leaning into the moment of love, desire, beauty. Then there is the slight tilt of her strong chin that draws your attention to the strange stump on her left shoulder. Other statues from antiquity are missing limbs, heads, and other features, but few have this effect on the viewer. The viewer's imagination is likewise challenged to *feel* the *absence*, and through a bold act of imagination, sense the *presence* of the missing arms. "I'm missing you," weeps Bruce Springsteen in "The Rising," and Blink 182 moans about the ghostly presence of an absent lover in "I Miss You," describing the memory as a painful voice "inside my head." Bill Withers intones "Ain't No Sunshine," his soulful ballad about missing his lover, which was one of the anthems played over and over again in the Detroit factory where I worked in the early Seventies. Looking back, it seems that the song stood in for the life we were all missing by working sixty hours a week at a job that brought little joy. And in recent years, the achy-breaky voice required for these plaintive songs came to us by way of

Adele and her ballad, "Someone Like You."

Missing. Every time I spend a few moments or a few days with her, I am riddled with missing memories, memories of what's gone missing in my own life.

Then I let them go and recall a warm memory of John O'Donogue telling me one morning at a hostel near Dun Aengus, the Iron Age fort on Inis Mor, as we rejoiced over a breakfast of Irish oatmeal and whiskey, "You know I've been thinking, Phil, that absence is the sister of presence."

✺

In the early Seventies, it was my task to train a war veteran only two weeks out of the rice paddies of Vietnam in the Detroit factory where I worked to put myself through college and support my family. Let's call him Rick. He couldn't have been more than nineteen. Slicked-back hair slathered with Vitalis. Permanent sneer on his face. Hard-working, no nonsense. Never showed an ounce of self-pity about the hand grenade accident that blew off his left hand and forearm up to the elbow. At most, he shrugged, then said, "Let's get on with it" as I taught him how to drive a forklift with one hand. No mean feat. He learned in an hour. Late one night, about six months along, Rick was rattled by the backfire of the forklift, or "Hi-Lo," as we called it, that I was deft at driving around the plant. The gunfire-like noise terrified him, and he impulsively reached out with the stub of his left arm for the steering wheel—then hit the brake. Screeching to a halt next to one of the steel-tapping machines, he sat there trembling, smiled feebly, shrugged, and carried on.

In those benighted years, it was my phantom memory of that Detroit factory that came to me night after night for years in dreams that I had failed in everything and been lured back home, back to the pounding, putrid steel presses to make enough money to support my family. I was overwrought with fear that I had failed because I had left my mother, who told me she had been afflicted (her word) with cancer; concern over my college girlfriend, Sagata, whose mother had been murdered in a hit instigated by her father; and empathy for my younger brother, who joined the Air Force to escape the soul-storms of his life in Michigan.

Night after night for seven years, I woke up with my right hand clenching a phantom pen as if my soul was prompting me to go straight to my old rattan rolltop desk and redeem myself by writing. The dream of many a besotted poet. What was missing was my soul. There was a cannonball-sized hole where my soul should have been. It must have gone into hiding, to protect itself, and it hadn't come out of hiding for a long time. Who knows, maybe that's why I have identified for so long with the Venus and her missing bits. At the very least, I admit that thinking about her fills a hole in my life, a gap about the size of her missing limbs, and when I can imagine or visualize her and her story, I feel more whole.

THE ARMS RACE

Arms. The whereabouts of the missing arms of the Venus de Milo is one of the more tantalizing mysteries in art history, haunting scholars, tourists, archaeologists, artists, sculptors, and psychologists alike. *National Geographic magazine*, Jacques Cousteau, Jim Thorne of the Adventurers Club, and many other stellar investigators have spent great swatches of time on Melos searching the harbor for her arms. Countless others, including fishermen, farmers, and romantic tourists, are also acutely aware of the fame and fortune that awaits whoever discovers the most famous missing arms in the world.

Arms. One version I was told on Melos was that there was a fight, a battle, a skirmish, on the pier on the southern half of the island when Marcellus was trying to haul the statue off to the waiting ship, the Albanian

Galaxia, bound for Constantinople. The baker in Adamas told me his family traded in the story that the French soldiers became entangled with the Russians who were manning the ship, and they broke off her arms, which fell into the sea.

"I am sure of it," he said in a thick accent. His grandfather had told him so.

Many believe that if only we can find those missing arms, maybe we'll know the truth of the mystery of one of the world's most famous statues, not unlike those who hover around the body of a dying person hoping against hope that he or she will finally reveal the truth about themselves as they utter their last words. Maybe we will finally know what her missing left arm was reaching for and what her surviving right hand held: a shield, an apple, a ball, or a mirror. There is an enduring connection between her being an ideal of perfection and a nadir of imperfection, as she is a ruin.

On the other hand, we can say she is a beautiful survivor.

What is so important about the arms *anyway*? What do they symbolize? According to *The Herder Dictionary of Symbols*, "an arm is a symbol of strength...frequently a symbol of the power of justice... Various Indian deities possess more than two arms, thus expressing their omnipotence. In Christian liturgy the raised arms signify the plea for grace. In medieval Christian paintings, the arm—or hand—that reaches out of heaven is a symbol of God, and raised arms are a gesture of subordinates signifying the renunciation of self-defense. An arm is a bridge between hand and shoulder, an extension, a means of reaching. Arms at our side are considered passive; arms angled to our hips are called akimbo. Arms are a euphemism for weapons." We keep people at arm's length, but we also embrace and are embraced by arms. And we miss them if we can't use or see them or realize they are gone, as with a mutilated soldier whose arms have gone missing. In the case of the Venus de Milo, her arms have taken on legendary importance *in absentia*.

Occasionally, I have pondered the plight of her missing arms. My imagination leaps around when I try to imagine what may have happened. Looters? A misguided attempt to haul her out of the cave and stuff her into a nearby lime kiln? Who knows? As with most human encounters, there is often a moment of confusion. What do you look at, what do you focus on? Usually someone's eyes, but sometimes, in the case of those with missing limbs, how can we help but stare? And then that encounter becomes a story.

Outsized myths, tall tales, languorous legends. Stories magnetized by the floating filaments of storytelling. You never know who will become attracted to them or why. I would look at those arms and wonder how I had offended Aphrodite, and what I could do personally to restore her embrace?! If art isn't personal, it doesn't move us to ask the probing questions that nudge us toward demanding of ourselves, "You must change your life."

Whether subtly or dramatically, it is up to us. We are always editing our stories.

To change or at least adapt our lives.

This Venus *knows* something about change and adaptation. Not just anything, maybe everything. That is why she is the one goddess all the other gods fear. Her power to inspire—or inflict—love is considered greater than all the other powers. This Venus knows her offer to the gallant Paris of the hand of Helen would have world-tilting consequences. But beauty is what beauty does, often drunk on its own power. With all that foresight, she still "glamoured," as the Scottish say, both Paris and Helen, and, as we still say, all hell broke loose.

Thinking about this, I am shifting my focus from her missing arms to her newfound gaze, back and forth, until I feel something essential. Her secret message floated across the universe and only now lands on the shore of our modern consciousness. If you look long enough to see, you uncork the bottle and read a message from our Greek friends who reached out to us from long, long ago: *Love is a divine gift that has untold consequences. We love through the pain; we love anyway.*

✿

In the spring of 1984, I was leading a mythological study group around Ireland with the rapscallion poet Robert Bly and storyteller Gioia Timpanelli. On the last night of the tour, we gathered in front of the old fireplace in the library of Dublin's Shelbourne Hotel. The white-maned poet from Minnesota had invited Seamus Heaney, the tousle-haired Belfast poet and future Nobel Prize winner, and promptly launched into what the ancient Irish would have called a bardic challenge.

"Seamus, give us some Yeats," blustered Bly. Leaning back in his chair, Heaney crossed his legs, which allowed me to see a gaping hole the size of a half-dollar in the bottom of his shoe. Tousling his hair with his oversized farm hands, he mused for a minute then recited "The Song of Wandering Aengus" by heart.

"Beautiful, Seamus," purred Bly. "Just beautiful." I do mean *purred*. The man was in awe.

Smiling, Heaney nodded and returned the challenge: "Now give us some Whitman."

Bly repaid him with a few stanzas from "Song of Myself."

Heaney rocked back and forth in his overstuffed chair to Whitman's rhythms.

Slowly, as if watching a sunset over Belfast, he echoed Bly's "Beautiful, just beautiful."

The turf fire crackled and smelled sweet. Bly smiled to beat the band and asked Heaney to recite his most famous poem at the time, "Digging," which he did with a tender ferocity, ending with the whiplash line, "I'll do my digging with a pen." Then he softly asked Bly to recite his translation of Rilke's iconic poem, "The Ancient Tower," beginning with these spiraling lines:

> I have been circling around God, the ancient tower,
> and I have been circling for a million years
> and, still, I don't know
> if I am falcon, a storm, or a great song.

I am beside myself with happiness at the utter good fortune of being able to spend all this time alone here with the Venus at the Louvre. According to the loose chronology found in my travel journals, it is my first visit here since the late Nineties, but it feels significantly different. I may not be circling a god, as Rilke invoked, but I am turning around a goddess. The metaphor holds.

Soon, I am wrapped in reverie and not ashamed to admit it. Once again, I conjure up a thrilling art conversation with Alexander Eliot. We were at the Getty Villa Museum, in Malibu, and he was confessing to me how numb he felt after fifteen years of writing art criticism for *Time* magazine. For him, there was a kind of soul sign, a signal from deep within him to come up with some of his own original conclusions about art—or move on. Being unmoved by the usual charms of art alarmed him. He decided to pare down his museum visits to one painter at a time—Picasso, Matisse, or Hopper, artists he had interviewed, or Breughel, the painter who most intrigued him. Soon, he said over a glass of Chardonnay in his Venice, California apartment, he had tightened the lens of his attention to one room. Then one painter, then one painting at a time. "Until I could finally *see* what I was seeing," he explained.

The Blackfoot scholar Jamake Highwater came to the same conclusion, telling me in the late 1980s, while we were exploring Delos, the most sacred of Aegean islands, "Look until you see, see until you *feel*." I remember him standing with arms akimbo, the wind blowing in his hair, as he stared out at the sea and mischievously pronounced the word *feel* with glee. But, he added, you need to learn how to see and feel as First or Native Peoples do, "which we did instinctively because we grant consciousness to all things. For us, *everything* is alive, as it is for great artists."

Something in the way I have been circling the Venus has dredged up those Rilke verses from the musty memory vaults, as well as distant reminiscences of art discussions with Eliot. It occurs to me this is one of the secret powers of museum ramblings. Concatenation. Chains of associations. Links of emotions and feelings. Inside-out moves among intense moments of focusing on a single work of art. Lambent memories of aunts and uncles giving me art books, my parents taking me to art museums, stolen moments with friends in front of unforgettable paintings that forged life-long bonds. As I am now, gazing at the Venus, scribbling notes, then slowly floating back to myself like a marooned astronaut being rescued.

How I *feel* about the Venus this time surprises me. I am cosmically alone. Now, in the practically abandoned gallery, the distance in her eyes signals to me her surprise at the recognition from Paris of her own beauty. If you take the time, you might also notice the uncanny knowledge of what she has unleashed.

Out of the depths of my mythic memory, I dredge up a green-tinted photograph of a diver swimming in the sea near Alexandria, Egypt, and coming across a timid statue of Venus standing on the floor of the ocean. She is the very picture of modesty, covering her private parts, as surprised by her first visitor in a couple of thousand years as he is by her. His bulging eyes, visible through his mask, are giveaways. That's how I feel today: startled, awash in awe, lost in wonder.

It only takes one work of art to become your portal to the other world you long to enter.

July 2002. An email appeared on my laptop from a mysterious character who claimed to be the owner of the submersible called the Deepsea Challenger that film director James Cameron used, in 1995, to discover the *Titanic*. The mystery man had read that I was on a quest to find the missing arms of the Venus de Milo. He wondered if I could share my secret with him and tell him where they were. Bemused, I replied, "Sorry, no, I haven't found the arms. As a matter of fact, I'd only mentioned the arms as a mighty metaphor for what's missing in our lives." His quick response was to the effect that he didn't quite believe me, but he'd be happy to put his submarine at my disposal if only I'd tell him where to find the arms. I shot back another email. "Her arms were lost fifteen hundred years ago! I'm interested in them now as a symbol for the lost world, the lost aspects of ourselves, for what is *always* missing in life and what we must learn to love." After a third email about how easy it is to miss the meaning of words, and then a few more futile exchanges, I lost touch with him.

Fall 1987, Paris at dawn. I thought I had solved the mystery of the missing arms of the Venus de Milo. I had just left my room above Shakespeare and Company bookstore, a labyrinthine cave of books and magazines, and gone jogging along the Seine when I passed a young art student walking across the Pont des Artes with a large, matted print of the Venus de Milo. There were two holes where the statue's arms ended—and the student had thrust her bare right arm through the hole where the Venus's right arm would have dangled. For one fugacious moment, she was reaching down with her arm, clutching the billowing drapery falling over her hips. A beautiful sight! I reached for my camera bag—and was mortified that I had left it behind in my friends' houseboat on the Seine. The surreal sight made me think of my college art teacher insisting that what negative space reveals is not missing as much as momentarily hidden, and it was our job to *imply* what was there by drawing the border between them. So much goes missing so often in our lives. Reading Emerson helped me, especially when the news of the day stung like a paper cut: "The poet knows the missing link by the joy that it brings." In *Confabulations*, John Berger pursued this theme by putting his arms around the negative space in writing: "Songs are journeys sung to an absence." It might help to remember the words of writer Havelock Ellis: "The absence of flaw in beauty is itself a flaw."

For me, the infamously missing arms once held some semblance of an answer to the mystery of beauty itself. Recent research tells us that her left arm was once extended, probably resting on a pillar, with her left hand holding the golden apple in its upturned palm. I could have saved myself a lot of time if I had just gone to an encyclopedia. The *American Heritage Dictionary* condenses the story: "An ancient Greek statue of Venus, famous for its beauty, *though its arms were broken off centuries ago*." Technically correct but aesthetically bereft because it doesn't allude to the power of *presence*. If absence makes the heart grow fonder, it also tantalizes the imagination. Perhaps we need to express our eternal gratitude that the art restorers on staff at the Louvre in 1821, who had been faithful to the practice of the time by cementing missing heads and limbs back onto mutilated ancient statuary for the previous century, in the case of the Venus de Milo, let her be.

This is proof of the adage that absence in her current state makes the heart grow fonder.

"There is one pain I often feel," wrote Shakespeare, "which you will never know. It is caused by the absence of you." This is the heart of the matter, our longing for wholeness, the pang of being able to fill the void. What I feel when I am traveling abroad is that I miss my father, who would have loved Paris, London, and Athens, and sometimes my son, with whom I long to share the world. And yet each one slips away, in his own way.

In *Sound and Insight*, Alexander Eliot helps fill in the gaps, which is what writers are for, isn't it? "The broken statue can seem more alive than one's own flesh," he writes. "This gives rise to one's shame over one's own lethargy combined with pride in the shaping spirit of mankind, and, finally, an urge to godliness, as was intended."

Fascinating stuff, but I must admit I've never been certain what he was referring to. A cosmic guilt, an existential lack of meaning, an inability to see more deeply, feel more thoroughly? After Alex's death, at the dandy old age, as he would have said, of ninety-seven, I asked our mutual friend Richard Beban, who raised his eyebrows, sighed, and said, "That's him, alright, feeling as if he had never done enough as the grandson of the founder of Harvard and T. S. Eliot's great-nephew. Guilt over the undone, shame over the time he missed with his wife and children." Richard drew a deep breath and added, "Time. Never enough time, he used to say to me after several whiskeys. Never enough."

In Alex and Richard's honor, I want to include here the opening lines of T. S. Eliot's "Burnt Norton": "Time present and time past / Are both perhaps present in time future / And time future contained in time past. / If all time is eternally present / All time is unredeemable."

Still, laden with all this history, a part of us wants to know what *really* happened to the Venus's missing arms. Or, as the little Irish girl asked so plaintively, "Who stole her arms?" But let's not get ahead or behind ourselves. What *are* arms anyway? Ladders to our hands, extensions for our wrists so that we might reach further for the beloved?

There are still thousands of "disappeared ones" in Argentina, victims of the junta in the late 1980s, many of them pushed out of airplanes without parachutes. So much goes missing, we tend to fixate on the things that stand in for them—missing keys, missing pets, missing letters or typos in newspapers that drive some people crazy, and worse, what the stout-hearted Zen monk, Jon Kabat-Zinn, warned us: "*If you miss the moment you miss your life.*" Missing, missing, missing. Writing those words, I think of the actor Jack Lemmon's mournful face, playing Edmund Horman in Costa-Gavras's 1982 film, *Missing*, when he is informed by the dastardly secret police that his son, Charles (John Shea), has been "disappeared" during the "Dirty War" in Chile.

Yes, the young adventurer was *disappeared*, a term invented to make the missing visible.

Turning back to the statue, I feel a pang of disappointment but don't feel thwarted by such minimalism. I feel challenged to fill in the missing gaps in her story, and mine. What am I looking for? Nine straight days here. I have filled two leather notebooks with scribblings, interviewed a dozen tourists, snapped hundreds of photographs, made several pencil sketches. What do I need from this statue, with these pilgrimages to beauty? I am caught in the grip of an obsession. I am trying to get at the heart of a very great thing: art's lived truth.

Walking around her, reveling, wondering, remembering. My mind going orthogonal, this way and that, sideways, up and down, conjuring up lines of poetry, other sculptures, the beautiful bodies of the women I've loved, and songs. I wonder now if it's still fair to ask who *stole* the arms of the Venus de Milo. Closer to the point would be to ask *what happened to them*, and then *why would missing arms be so important anyway?* Why does it matter, why bother, why think about it? Precisely because she is flawed, incomplete. Perfectly imperfect. Like me, like you, like everyone who has ever gazed at her.

Long ago conversations about art roll around in my mind, reminders that the arts being the great consolation of the world. I pause behind the

Imaginative Reconstructions of the Venus de Milo

How she might have appeared with her arms, seducing Ares, primping, posing, holding an apple, writing on a shield, holding up her drapery as she emerges from her bath.

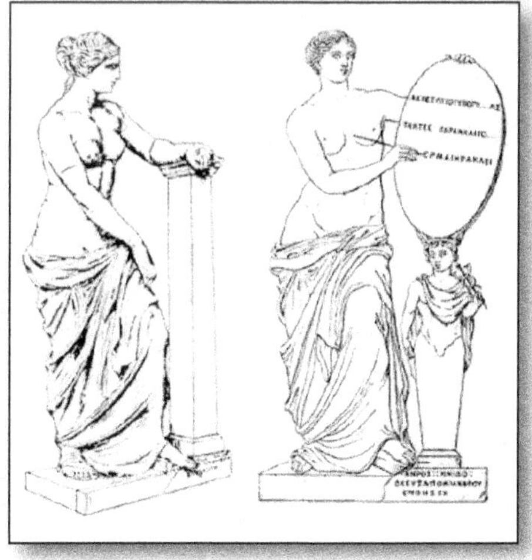

Venus, astonished at the waterfall roar of gasps from the crowd in front of her. Grateful for the recognition. I no longer miss her missing arms. I am focusing on what is there rather than what's not. To my mind, she's no longer an absence; she's a presence. I leave the gallery and head toward the cafeteria for the classic French *le petit dejeuner*: coffee, croissants, and a copy of the *International Herald-Tribune*. If Balzac could drink forty cups of coffee a day and Voltaire imbibed fifty cups, surely, I deserve a coffee break. Braced for a few more hours of statue-gazing, braced by the double espresso, I stroll back into the Venus's gallery. Late afternoon light arrives in the room like a sun flare. Everything appears intensified. Could be the light, could be the caffeine. My sweat-burning leather satchel feels like a burden, filled as it is with books, camera, journals, memories. I set it down on a bench against the back wall and look ahead.

Suddenly, I feel, like Rilke before the Cezannes, that I have the *right eyes*, the feeling ones. At this blading moment, the Venus looks on fire, *enflared*, like Garbo when she was backlit by Clarence Sinclair Bull, who took more than four thousand glamorizing photographs of her. Moments later, everything in the gallery seems haloed, as if in a Rembrandt painting. I gaze at her in the great French tradition of my ancestors *wanting to know*.

Have patience. I am trying to get to the heart of something essential but unfathomable, which I need to make fathomable.

Is that asking too much out of my life?

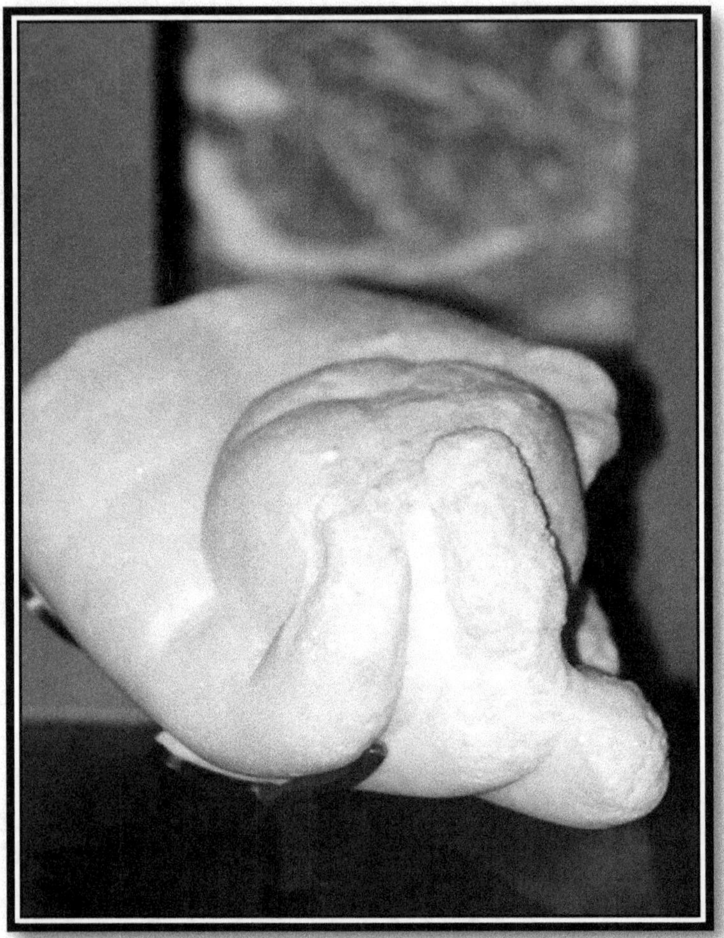

The missing left hand of the Venus
holding the Apple of Discord
Musée du Louvre, Paris, 2023

HER HANDS

The Greek mythographers tell us that Aphrodite's hands are worthy of our attention. The goddess used hers to hold doves, myrtle, roses, sparrows, rabbits, and swans. Her ever-loving hands tenderly touch her son, Eros, her husband, Hephaestus, and her myriad lovers, such as Ares, Adonis, and Hermes. Those hands hypnotized all who came and laid eyes on her.

According to legend, Menelaus won the hand of Helen, as we used to say, though a closer reading reveals that he too had abducted her, and some claim he raped her when she was no more than twelve. An ancient way to say it would be that he "earned" her, or he was awarded her hand, or that she proffered her hand in marriage. After the initial signal in the story, we know that Venus 'influenced' or enchanted the Queen of Sparta to fall truly, madly, deeply in love with the shepherd of Mount Ida, the wayward Prince of Troy.

Of course, this is *mythspeak*, code for the common experience of not being able to control who we fall in love with. So symbolically important is this notion of the sanctity of the hand that near the end of the sacking of Troy, when Menelaus discovers her when she is mad with the desire for vengeance, he wants to slay her and have it done with.

Later, it was the discovery of her hand, clasped around a stone apple or ball, that clinched the deal of who she was and why she was there in the sealed cave on Melos. Caves. Mysterious hollows, the inversion of mountains, they are places of retreat, initiation, and hiding. When Paris awards the prize to Aphrodite, he *hands it over* to the outstretched hand of the goddess, which inspired Alexandros's admittedly crude carving that now sits in a vitrine ten yards away from his Venus. To understand why, let's recall d'Urville's poetic and precise description when he first saw the statue outside the niche on Yorgos's land: "It represented a nude woman whose left hand was raised and held an apple and the right supported a garment draped in easy folds and falling carelessly from her loins to her feet."

Of course, Aphrodite's sensual touch is also associated with love potions, found all over the world, and named *aphrodisiacs* after her. According to *The Encyclopedia of Aphrodisiacs*, the goddess's potions are sensual and sensory, erotic and playful, a link to a world of once sexy games of love. The apple that Paris awards Aphrodite in the beauty contest is a wink to these ancient love games and to the fruit itself as the apple has long been associated with temptation and heightened desire.

Today, she has only one hand, which remains unattached, suspended in a vitrine a few yards away. If you examine it closely, as I did recently, two observations come to mind. The hand is more crudely carved than the sumptuous body it once belonged to, but the true source of astonishment is the round object in her hand, *"la pomme d'accord,"* the notorious Apple of Discord, as d'Urville described it in a letter to Brest. Next to the hand is a segment of her left forearm, a small but significant portion of the famed missing arms. Most visitors walk right past the "marble bits," as I heard a guide describe them, in the vitrine near the back window. The few who do stop tend to stare stolidly, mutter to themselves, and move on with the disdain of the uninformed.

Every culture known to history has naturally used the human hand for touching things but also for being touched, and beyond that for symbolic purposes. In various traditions, hands symbolize power, force, dominance, action, and strength. The proffered open hand represents friendship and marriage, while the clenched hand signals anger, animus, or impending violence. In religious iconography, God's hand appears from the clouds, the Buddha's hand has the spiritual eye, and the hand in ancient Egypt symbolized fertility. There is the laying of hands, which purports miracles, the waving of the hand as a greeting, the lifting of the right hand to grant mercy and the left to issue justice. There is the hand of fate, raised and lowered thumbs for killing or mercy, the reading of hands by palm readers. We raise our hand in question or to deny something. An old proverb says, "An empty hand is no lure for a hawk."

Venus's hand that holds the apple is the hand of love.

I love hands, the touch of them, the look of them. As it happens for all of us, I will never forget the first time I touched the hand of the girl I was infatuated with in high school, Colleen at a sophomore dance at Wayne St. Mary's while one of our rotating bands played a slow dance number for us. I vaguely remember it was "Tell It Like It Is" by New Orleans's own Aaron Neville, but I could be wrong; I was distracted. The moment of truth came when she responded to my casual tightening of my grip on her hand by clenched mine then stroking the back of my hand, my fingers, then the small of my neck. All while we swayed to Neville's incantatory song. For three minutes, we danced across the newly varnished gym floor, her hands intertwined in mine. I felt like a million bucks.

Twenty-five years later, in 1985, I hung out with Neville backstage at the Grateful Dead concert where I had taken Joseph Campbell and his wife Jean Erdman so they might enjoy what he deemed to be "a modern Dionysian rite." Casually, I mentioned the clutched hands at the same high school dance to Aaron himself. He grinned like a jack o'lantern, took a long toke, strummed his guitar strings, then muttered, "That's the real deal, man."

Then there was the time my basketball coach shouted, "Great hands, Cousineau," during my sophomore year when I stole a pass from Matt Piscopink, our star senior center. On my first visit to the Le Musée Rodin, I was thunderstruck by the "Hands" sculpture of Rodin's student and lover, Camille Claudel. I can't help but think of the supple hands of Dr. Kenneth Akisuki, the San Francisco Giants' team doctor, who performed knee surgery on me with a tough-and-tender touch, as he did with the ankle of Buster Posey, the Giants' catcher. And the hands of the three Russell Brothers at O'Connor's Pub in Doolin, Ireland, that astonished me for a month of evenings in the winter of 1974. The swift fingers of local farmer Micho, the country healer, storyteller, and greatest tin whistle player in the

West Country, who was able to evoke the legendary *one note*, as Seamus Heaney described the ethereal music brought from the Back of Beyond. Packie, who flicked the keys of his concertina so quickly they blurred. And the stonecutter Gussie, who played his traditional flute with his quarry-toughened hands that belied the tenderness needed to carry the melody.

And then the most scorched memory of all is the one from my last visit with my eighty-nine-year-old mother when I massaged her arthritic hands, steepled in wrinkled prayer, as she relaxed into her long freefall into what I lovingly refer to as her *forgettery*.

How I miss those hands now that they're gone.

Hands. I've fixated on the handsome fact, if you will, that Alfred Stieglitz took exactly 325 photographs of his wife, painter Georgia O'Keefe, two dozen of them of her hands. I am awestruck that Leonardo made more than six hundred drawings, forty of them of human hands, which he deliberately made with his *right* hand. He did so out of an ardent belief that using his usual *left* hand would have been too easy, intuiting that it would be more impressive if he used his secondary hand. Of course, it helped that he was naturally ambidextrous.

To carry on with our metaphor, I have to *hand it* to my favorite poet-gardener, Stanley Kunitz, who wrote a love poem to his wife of sixty years when he turned an even 100, a tribute that ended with seven devastatingly tender words: "Touch me, remind me who I am." And I can barely breathe when I read Ida Limon's poem, "The End of Poetry," which ends with this sensorial line: "I am asking you to touch me."

Why carry on so long about hands other than they point us toward the function of art, which is to touch and be touched? Even if by the "invisible hands" that appear in so many fairy tales from so many eras and cultures? At least that's what the Venus says to me this morning, moving as she does in my mind with her invisible hands.

❁

Turning and turning, my gaze tours the statue, roaming from her face to her eyes, smile, shoulders, breasts, and back to that yawningly empty space at the end of the stump where her shoulders used to reach down to her long-gone arms and hands. It's not that hard to imagine what once hung there. All we need to do is sneak a peek at the surviving Judgment of Paris Venuses, which feature her left arm raised in the air, holding a certain round object in her hand. Here I defer to Rachel Kousser, who accounts for several versions, such as the Capitoline Venus, the Venus Genetrix, the Knidian Aphrodite. She writes in the *American Journal of Archaeology*:

> As Aphrodite held out her prize of victory [the golden apple or ball inscribed with "most beautiful"], she encouraged the viewer to reflect upon the decision faced by Paris: What is best—political power, military success, or love?

Those divine hands, then, have the power to ignite love and desire, as well as envy and jealousy. The goddess held the uncanny power to urge lovers to unite their hands, and fold or even tie them together, so that they might "tie the knot," for she is the goddess of marriage as well as unbridled lust. Renaissance artists by the pallet load tell us something similar. In Botticelli's iconic *The Birth of Venus*, her left hand is stretched across her breast and touches her heart, while her left hand holds a gold drape across her loins in the famed Venus *pudica gesture*. What these touchings, as we might call the gestures, signify is that she is an intimate goddess, in touch with her sexuality and the sexuality of others, mortal and immortal. She has the power to inflame love or lust with the mere touch of her hands, and I submit, with a simple gaze. The look of love, as we call it now. In the British Museum is a small fragment of sculpture called *The Hand of Aphrodite*. No one knows where it's from or how it got there. The hands are everywhere and nowhere, and none are more mysterious, except perhaps Rodin's and Claudel's hands, in the history of art.

Hands hold apples or balls or fans, or in one case, sandals, with which she is about to swat away the advances of a leering Pan. Handprints are left behind on the walls of those painted cave temples found all over the world when Paleolithic people "marked their passage" through the world about forty thousand years ago by leaving their painted dreams on cave walls. Galloping horses, charging mammoths, dancing shamans. Geometric designs. Black and red stencils of their own hands.

There is more than one way to say, *"I was here."*

Now I wander away to a shadowed corner of the gallery in the shadows of the otherwise brightly lit room. There must be five hundred visitors here, gasping, guffawing, marveling, objecting, issuing every imaginable response to this iconic work. The whole gamut of art tourists, not completely unlike me because we share one thing in common—a desire to know what the fuss is all about. How different was their urge to leave a mark in their world than our urge to make art? Our impulse to leave works of art behind is our equivalent of those handprints, proof that we were here, that we saw, that we felt, that we imagined, that we *made images.* Hands, handprints, hand signs. There exists an entire language of hands.

The spell has been cast. The mute stone has spoken.

Once upon a time, I took a guided tour of Walt Whitman's home in Camden, New Jersey. Afterward, as I stepped onto the sidewalk, I noticed a remarkable sight. Across the street was a prison where many of the windows were open. When I squinted, I could see the hazy image of inmates flashing hand signs to their girlfriends or wives who were clinging to the chain link fence that ran alongside the prison. Tentatively, I approached one of the women and watched her weeping face and dancing hands as she communicated with one of the prisoners. Her hands whirled in the air, like those of the young Cambodian dancers I had seen perform in Phnom Penh as they mimicked the Apsaras, who churned the world into existence, and again in Delhi. I remembered, too, a performance of the Mahabharata in Benares where the young Indian dancers flashed *mudras*, or symbolic hand gestures, to help make the old epics alive in the eyes of the audience.

And then there was the day I went to an Oakland A's ballgame with Bruce Bochte, who used to play first base for them. I thought I knew the game fairly well. Then the former All-Star began pointing out to me one baseball sign after the other, from the manager in the dugout to the first and third base coaches, the outfielders to each other, the catcher to the pitcher. When he noticed me startled by what had been invisible hand signs to me up until then, I asked how many—roughly—hand signs were flashed in an average game.

"Oh, about a thousand," he said calmly, using his hands like an umpire to signal "*Safe!*"

Watching, appreciating, free-associating, seeing hand signs I had missed.

Not unlike the way I respond to art, looking again and again until I see.

Making the invisible visible.

Beauty laid bare.

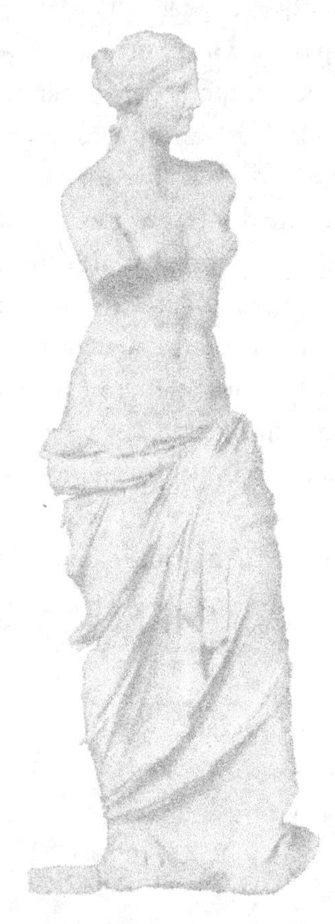

INSCRIPTS

Four Songs of Love

This is Venus' love,
For she loves to smile at the bright sea
And make sailors happy.
All around her the sea trembles,
Seeing her loveliness.
—Anyte of Tegea, third-century BCE Greek female poet
(trans. Burton Raffels)

I wonder, wonder who, who-oo-ooh, who
Who wrote the book of love?
—The Monotones, "Book of Love," 1958

Thus art, thus beauty. Therefore concealed.
The word itself used carefully.
—Andrew Hudgins, *The Joker*, 2013

You've got the look of love on your face,
a look that time can't erase.
—Lyrics sung by a sensual bossa nova singer in a smoky
  Rio de Janeiro wine bar, 1993. From "The Look of Love,"
  lyrics by Burt Bacharach and Hal David

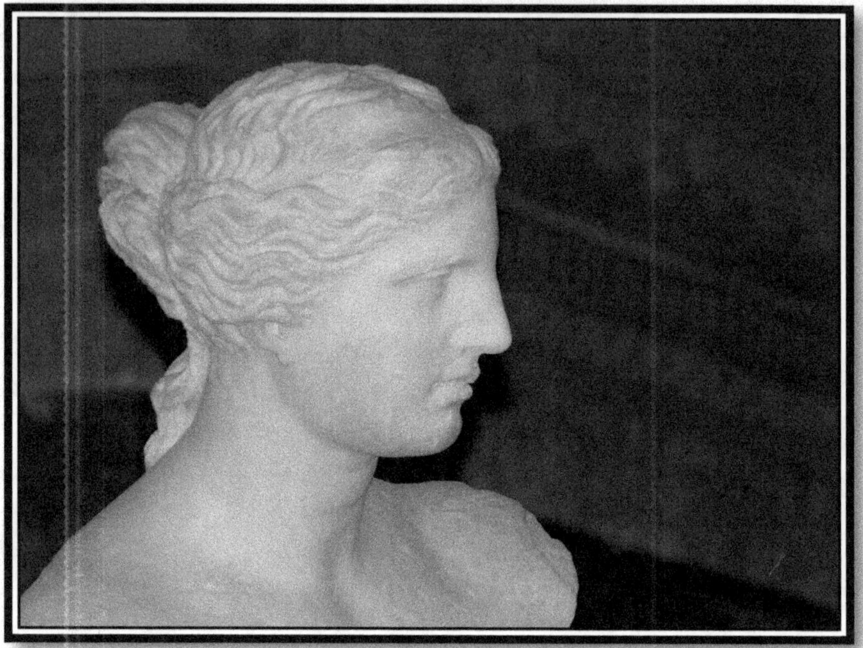

The Golden One's Radiant Face.
Musée du Louvre, Paris, 2023

THE FIRST TIME EVER I SAW HER FACE

The moment I slip back into Venus' intimate chamber, I can't help eaves-dropping on a brief conversation between two visitors with Yorkshire ac-cents. The chap in the argyle cap says to his friend, "Did ye hear what that clown John Cleese said on the Beeb the other night? The poser says the brain recognizes a caricature faster than a human face. Says that's how the brain works." Scoffing at such a thought, his mate harrumphs, "What a wanker. I knows a pretty face when I see one. Not when my *brain* sees one."

Shrugging, I push through the madding crowd in the gallery. Slowly, in no hurry, I turn sideways like a running back and squirm through the defense. When I reach the rope cord that encircles the statue, I take out my sketchbook and make a few simple line drawings of my own. Satisfied, I thrust the hand-size book back into my leather satchel and replace it with my journal, where I have logged a few pertinent quotes from experts and savants, phrases I use for inspiration, words to move me closer to the elusive truth of art. I feel like I'm trying to prove to myself that I've taken my visit seriously, by sheer dint of will, and no little squinting.

I jot down Pessoa's haunted adverb *besides* just as one of the suspicious museum guards sidles up next to me, eyeing me suspiciously. I wonder what I could have possibly done to make her want to search through my satchel. Was it the intensity of my gaze or the perception of danger in my sketches or notes taken over the course of the long morning? The guard has the self-important sneer of someone who watched the 2014 documen-tary *The Missing Piece: The Mona Lisa, Her Thief, the True Story*, one too many times. I turn to the guard and show her my journal and manage a weak smile. She frowns with disdain and snarls, "*Tourists*," and walks away, her voice fading as she addresses an invisible boss on the small security radio perched on her shoulder. Her attitude reminds me of the old saw about the traveler who broke an ankle when she was caught in a tourist trap.

Turning back to the Venus, I admit I'm not getting any closer to her mystery. I need to reorient myself. I need to let her teach me. A frown frizzles my face. I crane my neck to the side, trying to see something different in her this time, a kind of timidness, the insecurity of the beautiful bordering on astonishment as she casts her thousand-yard stare. There is something ineffable happening, yes, right now, in her face. Let's call it *love*, the look of love, or as I heard Sergio Mendes sing long ago in a quiet nightclub in Sao Paulo, *"The look that time can't erase."*

The mythographers of old agreed on one thing: Love was there at the beginning. According to Homer, Aphrodite wasn't born out of the foam of the sea but was the daughter of Zeus and Dione. In another version of the myth, recounted by the Italian publisher and mythologist Roberto Calasso in *The Marriage of Cadmus and Harmony*, the goddess Ananke is her mother, a deft suggestion as this potent goddess personifies inevitability, compulsion, and *necessity*. I read this as "Necessity is the mother of love," the cosmos telling us, *We need love*. The old poets and most new ones are telling us that love has been built into us from the beginning—not as an indulgence but as a deep human need.

Mythically, the ancient Greeks were also saying, *We need beauty*.

I am struck by one of the rare surviving depictions of Ananke, on an urn painting, which shows her as a winged, helmeted goddess holding a lit torch in front of her as she strides into the future. Beside her is Aphrodite, her daughter. Together, they embody the Necessity of Love, its fire and its light. Ananke's appearance in the ancient Greek myths also reveals her as often being erotically entwined with Kronos, the God of Time. A creative reading of the myth suggests that the original forces are *fate* and *time*, which makes necessary the qualities of love and beauty if we are to endure the sorrows of the world.

In turn, I have come to believe it is these ineffable traits that Alexandros chose to infuse into his Venus, the traits that set her apart from all the other Venuses that had been carved in the centuries before he set up his studio in Antioch.

At last, I am content to call his accomplishment a mystery.

In his ambrosial study of Greek myth, Calasso chose the oldest of Venus/Aphrodite's origin stories for his meditation on her personal mythology. Out of the myriad versions, Calasso chose the curious one of the goddess Nemesis being ravaged by Apollo to become the mother of Helen, which provides a plausible motivation for the revenge that ran in the blood of the goddess. Nemesis was the daughter of Nyx, Goddess of Pitch-black Night, depicted as winged and wielding a dagger and whip. She was also the Goddess of Unstinting Revenge and Divine Retribution, especially against those deemed guilty of hubris. As always in Greek myth, her meaning is rooted in her name. Nemesis comes from *nemein*, to distribute, to move around the punishment that has come due. In this sense, the dreaded nemesis is a psychological necessity, and its existence is one Aphrodite or Venus challenges us to see so that we don't obsess about the loneliness of life.

If we add up the mythic messages about Venus/Aphrodite, we arrive at a startling total. We *need* to begin with love, but then find it *necessary* to add that it inevitably proves to be a nemesis. We learn more about the complexity of love in a single lyric by Smokey Robinson than from all the self-help books on the market: "The promise of love was written on your face..."

As Epictetus, the Stoic philosopher, wrote in the first century: "What troubles men / are not things / but rather the judgments / they make about things." And trouble it was that was triggered by the choice, which was a judgment, which wreaked havoc. Curiously, the word *judge* is related to the Old English *deman*, from which we get *demand* but also *doom*. The long tongue of linguistics is telling us that justice is *demanded* by life, and we risk *doom* if we do not judge wisely.

Was it even a choice, that demand thrust on Paris by Zeus and Hermes? Was it fair to choose who was fairest of all? Was devastating jealousy at the heart of the very first beauty contest? Would it be fairer to say it is the choice that is no choice? The choice that reappears again and again, age after age?

We are still wrestling with these themes. *In The English Patient*, the Sri Lankan/Canadian author Michael Ondaatje's 1996 award-winning epic novel and 1997 movie, the difficult choices about love and desire are recognizable. In a complex series of flashbacks, we learn that the main character is a Hungarian cartographer, Count Lazlo de Almásy (Ralph Fiennes), mistaken for a fallen Englishman, Peter Madox. Despite his best attempts at resisting an affair, Almásy falls in love with a beautiful married Englishwoman, Katherine Clifton (Kristin Scott Thomas), who has fallen in love with the beauty of the desert. Told through a daring series of forty different temporal transitions, flashbacks, and flashforwards, we learn that she crashed with her husband in his plane near the Egypt-Libyan border. When Almásy discovers them, her husband has died, and she is mortally wounded. The enchantment has held. Caught in an anguishing bind, Almásy decides he must save her by carrying her through the hot Saharan Desert to the Cave of the Swimmers, the ancient site in the Gilf Kebir that features achingly beautiful cave art. The cartographer leaves his lover with a kit of provisions and his beloved copy of Herodotus's *Histories*, promising to return with help. When he does, it is too late. She has died. Soon after, he crashes his rescue plane, nearly burning to death, turning his once handsome face into a horrifying mask of scars. The movie ends with another character, the kind-hearted nurse, Hana (Juliette Binoche), reading aloud to the dying Almásy a letter Katherine wrote to him before she died:

My darling, I'm waiting for you. How long is a day in the dark? Or a week? The fire is gone now and I'm horribly cold. 1 really ought to drag myself outside but then there'd be the sun. I'm afraid 1 waste the light on the paintings and on writing these words. We die. We die. We die rich with lovers and tribes. Tastes we have swallowed, bodies we have entered and swum up like rivers. Fears we have hidden in like this wretched cave. I want all this marked on my body. We are the real countries, not the boundaries drawn on maps with the names of powerful men. I know you will come and carry me out into the palace of winds, the rumors of water. That's all I've wanted—to walk in such a place with you, with friends, on earth without maps. The lamp's gone out and I'm writing in the darkness.

According to the ancients, Aphrodite knew—and envied—the curious fact that human beings were willing to die for love, perish from desire, sacrifice everything for beauty. All they needed was to be cast under the spell of love, be offered the chance to tumble into the arms of the beloved, between the white thighs of love, for the pleasure that makes us immortal. He needed to choose, he needed love, he needed a chance at happiness. He chose, he loved, he took a chance. This cannot be said too often as it is too often forgotten. What Aphrodite unleashed with her "look of love" was a gift, not just the hand but the guaranteed love of the most beautiful woman in the world. Helen, Queen of Sparta.

Love, desire, and satisfaction, to be sure, are accompanied by grief, despair, and broken hearts in this tragic romance. The myth personifies the untrammeled desire that is the source of all sorrow, as the Buddha later warned. The ecstasy and the heartache lay side by side, like entwined lovers on satin sheets. Strange to say, sweet love often brings bitter war, as depicted in the odd tale of the dark cave where the arrows of Eros became tragically mixed up with those of Thanatos. Now you know why the ancient Greek fabulists said that love and death are found in the same quiver.

❃

Today, if you gaze into the startled and startling face of the Venus de Milo, as I am doing in her presence, you can discern the secret that lives in her gaze. There is a wistfulness in her face, the liquid eyes, the pulsing longing, the genuine surprise that I feel in my ribs when I'm in her presence, paying attention, feeling her vitality. While trying to meet the heavenward gaze of the Venus, I am whisked away, transported back to my youth, gazing at the pictures more than reading the perplexing text of Kenneth Clark's classic, *The Nude,* in our modest living room library. While I have fond memories of learning some of life's mysteries in those pages, I also have the dreadful memory of a gaggle of my mother's coffee-klatch friends and neighbors visiting her one day and urging her to hide "those books" in our hall closet. When my mother asked why, they said the books embarrassed them. She refused. Never spoke to them again. A contemporary example, I suppose, of forbidden beauty, an issue that has burdened us since our time in the Paleolithic caves.

Cicero's reflection comes to mind: "The face is a picture of the mind with the eyes as its interpreter." Remembering those words, I think back to the first time, as Roberta Flack sang, rather unforgettably, ever I saw her face. Wistful or taboo, there isn't much distance between them. They link up, eventually, in the way Alexandros of Antioch carved the Venus's face. One that haunts and taunts me. Now we come to the crux of the controversy: Why did he carve it with such tenderness when the tradition up to the time, the first century BCE, was to render the faces of the Venuses in either some semblance of ideal beauty or as harmless, boring, lifeless, listless. To me, even the much-vaunted Praxiteles's Venus seems fey, sexless, and coy in contrast.

Famously, Albert Camus said, "Alas, after a certain age every man is responsible for his face." The aphorism could just as easily have come from Mrs. Keaney, my red-haired, matronly neighbor in Ballyconneely, Connemara, where I lived in the early 1980s, who used to say of the beauty of her elderly neighbors, "Ah, she has a *lived-in* face."

What a contrast to our culture that vaunts the seven-billion-dollars-a-year cosmetic surgery industry, which shames women into believing that aging is a wretched process, one that should be halted or even reversed if possible. My French friend, Anne Stellio, from the Savoie region of France, zeroed in on this when she visited me some years ago. After a week in the States, she asked, "Why do American women want to have faces that pretend they're innocent and have never had life experience at all? Do they think their baby faces make them less threatening to the men they're trying to attract?"

A lived-in face boldly announces that beauty is more than skin-deep; beauty is in the lines, the creases, the grooves, the ruts—the evidence that a lived life leaves behind.

"To watch her face is like contemplating a masterwork," wrote Greta Garbo's biographer, John Bainbridge. "It becomes an experience that strikes both the heart and mind." He relishes riffing on how others described her: "She is as beautiful as the aurora borealis," or "It needs a work of fiction to invent a face to approach hers," or "Garbo manages, because she is a supremely beautiful woman, to make beauty look like a mark of religion." He concludes, "Garbo, like any other thing of beauty, is indescribable." But her beauty was so hypnotic, she withered underneath for the twisting effect it had on her fans.

The power of faces, always a mystery, an inexhaustible source of inspiration.

Contemplation, invention, religion, hypnosis. These are the marks of the magic spell: inspiring, musing, but not as close to the mark as Ralph Ellison, who came as close to describing the knee-buckling, soul-rattling beauty of Aphrodite as anyone I've ever read. In his novel *Battle Royale*, he observes that the perils of beauty cut to the quick: "Had the price of looking been blindness, I would have looked." Those words could very well have come from Paris, the Trojan prince, when he awarded the apple to Aphrodite, knowing full well what would happen when he laid his eyes on Helen, when his heart would be wedged open. Her beauty was blinding, her love so overwhelming that he was willing to risk death. This is the secret strength of the Venus de Milo. The goddess's face tells us she knows he knows and is willing to look, to love, and perhaps *to be loved in return*. This is what infuses her blinding power of love.

One of the original Monuments Men who rescued several hundred thousand looted works of art as World War II wound down, Sgt. Kenneth C. Lindsay of Milwaukee, recalled them being derided as effete "Venus Fixers" by fellow soldiers. "The Painted Queen is here. She's safe!" he heard a worker cry out while he was unpacking crates of looted art. "I'm suddenly looking into Nefertiti's face, just as beautiful as when she lived in the eighteenth dynasty. I lifted her out, and that is when every man in the room fell in love with her. I know I did... We knew the circumstances that had brought those things in. You couldn't sleep at night."

Let's face it, the fame of the Venus de Milo endures because of a quality far beyond her missing arms. Her seductively beautiful face. If that look didn't strike the flint in the hearts of visitors who were on Beauty Pilgrimages, the public would have abandoned her long ago. But, given a chance, she might fill you with the kind of ardor that made an anonymous Renaissance poet's heart overflow when he declared his lover's smile could reveal six paradises:

I see your face before me
Crowding my every dream
There is your face before me
You are my only theme...

Circling and circling the statue and gazing at her face and thinking about the strong heart that sculpted her, my mind moves of its own accord to John Berger's book of essays, *And Our Faces, My Heart, Brief as Photos*: "The existence of pleasure is the first mystery."

How can this be? How can it *not* be?

The pilgrim paying homage to the Venus de Milo is generally happy to have made the effort; the scores of artists who have created homages to her must be pleased to have spent time thinking about her. Otherwise, a visit to a museum, poring over a book, sending postcards of great art, verges on the voyeuristic.

Aphrodite did have her opposite side, embodied as Aphrodite Pornos, usually depicted as a languorous woman waiting to be ravished. Generally, she invites us to *enjoy* the pleasures of life, which isn't encouraged as much as we would like or disguised as the reward for consuming more and more *stuff*, including sex. The myths that surround her are as bountiful as marble dust in a sculptor's studio, part of a long and venerable tradition of worship of her; she has decorated homes, shrines, gardens, fountains, baths, palaces, and even tombs. Her fate has been to come here to be idealized, worshiped and idolized, mocked and satirized, and copied and reproduced, not unlike her predecessors from Babylon to Jerusalem, Angkor Wat to Easter Island, Michelangelo to Canova, who flocked like art pilgrims to be *in the presence of living stone* in the house of the muses, to witness, as we read in the ancient chronicles, stone or wood or metal *come to life*. This is the backdrop for such stories as Daedalus, the inventor of the labyrinth on Crete, who also created toys that purportedly moved; or Hephaestus, god of the forge, who made lifelike robots. It's been called the Pygmalion effect, the ancient urge to make the inanimate animate. It inspired Ovid, George Bernard Shaw, Mary Shelley, and Stephen Spielberg, who wrote the creepily beautiful movie *A. I.*, a prescient story about an animatronic boy whose parents look to him to bring a spark of human love into their lives.

As Dante wrote, love is the power that moves the sun, the moon, and the stars. But how does it move us, and what does it reveal to us about how we should live our lives? How can we hope to transform the torture of love and desire into the rapture of selfless happiness? Can the Venus de Milo point the way, even without her arms but with her eyes, gazing out at the world she helped create and destroy—and created again, infusing it with passion and pleasure? If there is indeed a profound wisdom of love, as every known tradition has proclaimed, what is the wisdom of beauty?

For the first time, I seem to detect in her mouth a hint of what the French call a *moue*, and the ancient Greeks called the "Smile of Aphrodite," referring to the *inner radiance* of all things that are beautiful and full of eros. Whatever we see that is ultimately life-affirming, whether a finely made painting, an exquisite bracelet, a lovely vase, an awe-inspiring athletic performance, or the expression on the face of the one we love, embodies that smile of the goddess. Long have we been mystified by this power. One of Greece's legendary female poets, Anyte, from the third-century BCE, described her feeling of rapture in Burton Raffel's translation, "This is Venus' love, / For she loves to smile at the bright sea / And make sailors happy / All around her the sea trembles, / Seeing her loveliness."

Similarly, I remember my Grandma Dora after my Grandpa Sydney died playing "Smile" by the chronically melancholic Charlie Chaplin, which he had composed for his movie *Modern Times*, over and over again on her vintage Victrola record player. She needed to hear the memorable lines, "Smile though your heart is aching / Smile even though it's breaking / When there are clouds in the sky, / you'll get by / If you smile through your fear and sorrow…"

Love and sorrow, intertwined as ever, stoking each other's fires, balming the soul.

Years ago, when I found myself scavenging for unusual manuscripts about the history of storytelling in the San Francisco Library, I stumbled across a dusty folder in the classics section that contained a tattered reprint of an 1868 essay by Heinrich Grimm, son of Wilhelm, one of the Brothers Grimm. He describes a visit to the Berlin State Museum to view an exact copy of the Venus de Milo. Making copies was a common nineteenth-century practice, and this one had been made shortly after the original arrived in Paris:

> All that adorns and elevates a woman, in our eyes, seems to me united in these features... I think of the bewildering smile...it hovers round this mouth. See the graceful outline of these lips... in the corners of the mouth nestles a smile, possible only to the goddess who gave herself to men, and yet was never frail and mortal...she seems to have imprisoned a spark of immortal love to bestow it upon the race that look up to her with reverence.

It's time to explore the barest hint of a smile that creases the face of the Venus de Milo, the feature that for me ties together the threads of her mystery. Smiling, I look at her smile, as if for the first time—perplexed, confused, determined. Slowly, a phrase from Paul Valery's essay *Seashells* arrives in my mind, which he used to describe growth: "A seashell emanates from a mollusk." *Emanate* strikes me as the right verb here. Gazing at the Venus now, gratitude emanates from me.

I feel glad to be alive.

What do we do with these tinctures of insight from the ancients? Aphrodite is variously described as a goddess with a seductive face, quick-blinking, sweet-smiling, a singer of seductive songs, lover of laughter, gold-crowned, one who awakens pleasant yearning in immortals and mortals alike, fills mortal hearts with sweet longing, and from whose cheeks shines an ambrosial beauty.

Her attendants are the Graces, the personifications of Beauty, Grace, Flowering, Joy, and Radiance. They are depicted as perpetually crowning her with myrtle and laying rose petals at her feet. Her desire is unpredictable, often surprising even her, such as when her heart is attracted to the mortal Anchises, revealing to him how strong and irresistible the force was that brought her to him, sometimes experienced as a terrible anguish. But she often felt joy in her heart when desire rose like color in her cheeks.

Still, I wonder, *Who is she, this goddess to whom the ancients dedicated so many statues, so many temples, and who lives on in our sex goddesses?* The English scholar and poet Geoffrey Grigson concludes that the Venus is a thesaurus, a treasury, in stone. Her power over us has lasted for thousands of years because we still can't fathom the depths of our own hearts, and we're still surprised when love breaks our hearts. So, we listen to Ella Fitzgerald and Van Morrison, gaze into the portals of Rothko's red squares, ponder the mysteries of Vermeer's wistful women, fall into reverie over Calatrava's bridges, trying to see the roots of our great and our wretched desires.

Originally, Venus/Aphrodite descended from the heavens dancing on the foam of the sea, came ashore, and made men and women crazy with desire. We spend our lives talking around and around things like this—where beauty comes from, how desire overwhelms us, how much happiness comes from that vision coming ashore. I'm not sure why. Why is it so difficult to simply describe her?

In *Frank Sinatra and the Lost Art of Livin': The Way You Wear Your Hat,* the biographer Bill Zehme tells a touching story that would have been welcome in the banquet halls of King Priam's Troy. He quotes the Hoboken crooner as saying, "A fella came up to me the other day in a bar with a nice story. He was in a bar somewhere and it was the quiet time of the night. Everybody's staring down at the sauce and one of my saloon songs comes on the jukebox, 'One for My Baby,' and after a while a drunk at the end of the bar looks up and says, jerking his thumb toward the jukebox, 'I wonder who *he* listens to?'"

As for me, I've long wondered who the Aphrodite de Melos is listening to or watching, who she is reaching for with her invisible arms. This is nearly impossible to comprehend until we remember that in the long run, as Théodore Jouffroy suggests, "We are moved only by that which is invisible." Power and money, glory and fame, or love and beauty, happiness and desire.

Fall 2018, Paris. This afternoon, it starts to rain. A week of research into her seemingly fathomless history is not too much to ask of myself. I've demanded more. I've enjoyed my raptures. But here I've also become mystified, exasperated by the teeming, steaming crowds. What does it mean that someone wants to be photographed next to or in front of a famous work of art and holds a camera at arm's length to take a photo of herself?

Shortly before leaving, I overhear three unusually attentive young women talking about the Venus. As opposed to the snap-and-run tourists, they have been completely captivated by the statue. Overhearing that they are from Traverse City, Michigan, my home state, I approach them and ask what they are thinking about the Venus. I trust them; they look reflective. I ask whether they think the Venus is truly beautiful or overrated, or worse, an unfair, patriarchal ideal. They shake off my objections and sing her praises, like a Sixties doo-wop group from Philadelphia or a Motown girl group.

"Yes," they chime in together, agreeing that she is as wonderful as they'd hoped she'd be.

"Wonderful," murmurs Sharon, the tallest of the group.

"What's her story?" asks the third.

For a few minutes, I regale them with the Judgment of Paris story that inspired the statue, a tale they are unfamiliar with but are avidly listening to. As they are about to leave, I ask Sharon one last question. I am interested in an aspect of the Venus that I'd always felt was inextricably connected with that long moaning look, that pensive gaze, those magnetic eyes. A phrase from the maverick culture critic Camille Paglia comes to mind, "the interest [and] the promise of sexual pleasure and constant devotion," but I kept it to myself.

Instead, I asked, "What do you think she's thinking about? What's on her mind?" We were standing together only a few feet from the statue. The three young Michiganders paused to look at her pensively, appearing to me for a moment like the Three Graces, the attendants to Aphrodite. Then tall, dark-haired Sharon turned to me and said like someone who was confident in what she felt about the world: "She knows what's about to happen."

Of course, she does. And now so do I. And soon, so will you.

INSCRIPT

Words matter, stories mean, myths imply. Etymologically, Venus is electrifying. Geoffrey Grigson masterfully tracked her Latin name down, in *The Goddess of Love*, to its most distant roots through the conceptual rebuilding of our reputed ancestral language, [PIE], Proto Indo-European. By this method we can track down the prefix of *Venus* to *win-*, which originally meant *strive, want* or *desire*. Primal forces at the heart of life. Since the Venus was discovered in a Greek gymnasium, it is curious that "Venus" entered the English language as *win*, our word for victory.

Through its offshoot *venia*, we find a significant secondary meaning, the grace or favor of the gods, *venerari*, the ritual of asking for divine grace. Over time, Venus and Aphrodite represent the goddess who yields favors, satisfies desires, and illuminates beauty.

Our word *beauty* derives from the Latin *bellum* and the Old French *bealte*, for fair, and earlier, the Greek *kallos*, from *kaleo*, a pointed verb meaning to provoke. As ugly is an ugsome word, beauty is a beautiful, provocative, and melodic word that reaches back to the red dawn of time. It's all there, dimly remembered in the halls of our memory, that beauty arouses the desire for both love and war, desire being the operative word.

The jawbreaker of a word *concupiscible* means "worthy of being desired." Matisse uses the word in a startling way to describe his drawing: "One must always search the desire of the line, where it wishes to enter, where to die away." The prolific diarist and delineator of desire, Anais Nin, writes, "We are like sculptors, constantly carving out of others the image we long for, need, love, desire..." Wordplay helps us close in on the mystery of the Venus, who was less an ideal of beauty, as later described, than a reflection of the *moment of desire*, or as the great Ovid later wrote, the *moment of offering* "the gift of love."

Why is Venus important? She puts a face on the forces of love, desire, happiness, selflessness, and other, darker desires, which are alluded to by, of all people, Charles Baudelaire, who wrote in his *Intimate Journals*, "A last, general rule: in love, beware of the moon and the stars, beware of the Venus de Milo, of lakes, guitars, rope-ladders, and most of all, love stories — yes, even the most beautiful in the world, were it written by Apollo himself!"

The incomparable images of the goddess remind us that beauty isn't skin-deep, desire isn't superficial, and love isn't here from the force of our will, but arrives from the unfathomable depths of life itself. Venus represents the divine way to deal with the illusion of the lack-love, lack-beauty, lack-language nature of the universe by revealing the gift of cosmic beauty that is constantly being offered to those who look closely.

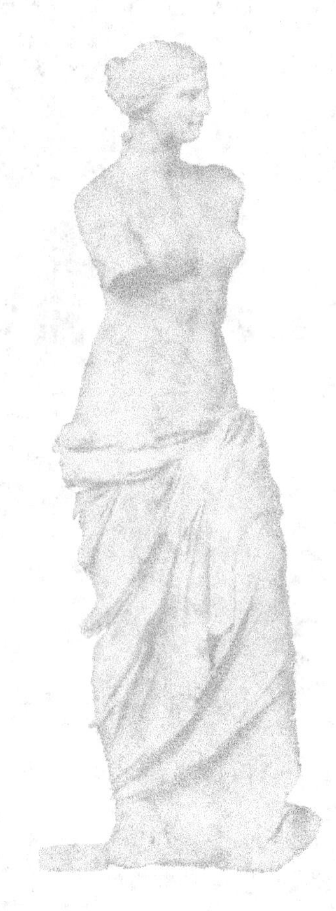

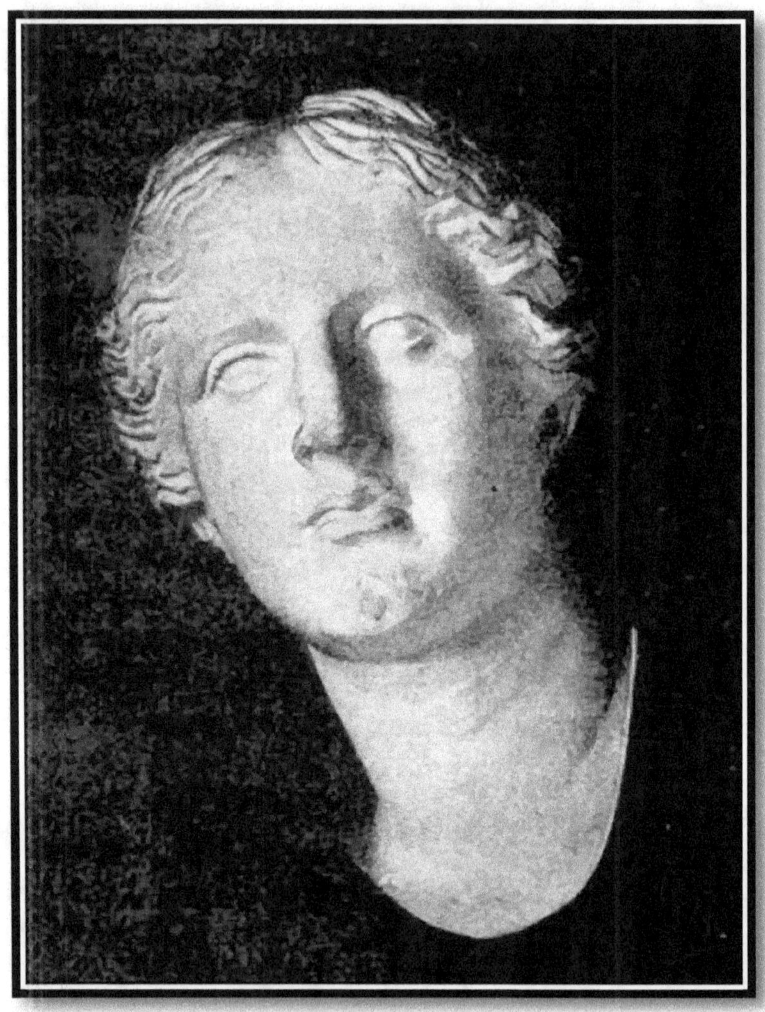

Nineteenth-century photograph of the head of the Venus de Milo, *Century* magazine, 1888

THE EYES HAVE IT

Turning around the Venus, enjoying her incomparable beauty, the ever-green freshness of her desirability, the subtle suggestion of lust, my gaze moves from her breasts and waist up to her face and then finds a home in her eyes. What a wonderful word, home, which gives rise to *homing in,* the inward move, the tectonic pull that brings us back to where we began.

Around three in the afternoon on my last day at the Louvre, I relax into my gaze. This time, her thousand-yard stare meets mine. It's as if we are aware of each other. I see her *seeing.* I stare at her staring into the distance, into eternity, and want to meet her there. I find myself reveling in every part of the Venus, coming back to her face to try to detect her thoughts, the spirit that moves through her, the story that informs her, and sense that I had stumbled across one of the great secrets in art history: how the Greeks learned to *see* their world.

"The Greeks began to use their eyes," wrote E. H. Gombrich in his classic study, *The Story of Art.* "Once this revolution began, there was no stopping it." Of course, they even had a mellifluous word to describe the love of seeing, *philotheamon,* and another for the love of statues, *agalmato-philia.* What can these arcane words add to our appreciation in helping our search for the meaning of the Venus de Milo? Intensity, reverence, awe, and wonder at the ability to see within and without. It can be found in the eyes, as Emerson expressed in his shimmering thought, "The eyes indicate the antiquity of the soul."

Until now, I have been viewing the fine-grained marble of the Venus as strange and wonderful, unknown and unknowable, but necessary and desirable. But now, encouraged by her scintillating smile, I look into her eyes then look again, remembering the daring words that Rilke penned to his wife Clara after seeing a Cezanne painting at the Grand Palais: "Suddenly I had the right eyes." As if he had found Shangri-La, Valhalla, or

Timbuktu. What did he mean? Think, man, think.

Then I am transported to a memory of seeing the *shimmer* of life in the rice terraces of the Philippines after a torrential monsoon had cleansed the skies and revealed the glistening green mountainsides and desert brown nipa huts, a sight as *alive* as anything I'd ever viewed in my life.

All the arts are rhapsodies on the theme of seeing more clearly.

"In love, the eyes are the guides," wrote the first-century Roman Propertius, one of Ovid's mentors, though it sounds like it could have been written yesterday, let's say by Emily Dickinson or Leonard Cohen, which just goes to prove what we mean by immortal.

Similarly, the German French painter Jean Arp once said that he hoped his work might encourage viewers to dream with their eyes open. Paul Klee said as much in his *Diaries*: "One eye sees; one eye feels." The novelist Joseph Conrad once wrote, "I am only here to make you see." Art critic John Berger echoes all of them when he announced in his BBC series, "What we need is a new way of seeing."

Gazing at her now, I think about that startling line in the Homeric scholar Michael Finley's analysis of Odysseus, that the Greeks invented the gods so we might know ourselves better. And when I connect this insight to this infinite moment at the Louvre, the not-so-obvious occurs to me. We need to take our time with great art, *so we might know ourselves better.*

Yes, a new kind of Venus is gazing across time and space, as her creator, Alexandros of Antioch, conceived her, to accept the infamous Apple of Discord from Paris. The Trojan Prince stands just off-stage, off-screen, off-dream. He is there, but he isn't. To understand her, you need to see him. The Venus and the Paris sculptures are two halves of the same story. He has just chosen her as the most beautiful woman in the world, as Zeus commanded him to decide. But as we know from other mythographers, she also chose him. She is looking at him, not in an overly romanticized or idealized way, not in the least. She is surely not the tepid Venus portrayed in scores of other paintings and sculptures, staring into an abstract distance, conveying no emotion.

No. Our Venus is *wonderstruck.*

Alexandros captured the *mythic* moment when the goddess is surprised. Stunned. Stupefied. She is taken by the sudden realization that a price must be paid for the tryst she has arranged, for the love she has made possible, for the sorrow to come. As powerful as she is in the pantheon of gods and goddesses, she reveals a shade of insecurity and will do anything to win the beauty contest over Hera and Athena. So, she has offered a gift of love, as if it doesn't come with a price to be paid. Or at least not a financial price. The price is pain, heartache, regret, disappointment, and violent conflict. Again and again throughout history, this is symbolized by lovers' quarrels, fighting, battle, or, worse, war. Consider the relationship between Aphrodite and Ares, Venus and Mars, Love and War.

If you peer closely at the Venus, you will see in her face the expression of a woman, a goddess, in the moment she realizes she has unleashed a bloodthirsty war, the most famous one of all in ancient times, the Trojan War. Surely, this is one of the most transcendent moments in the history of art. But how can anyone relate to those mythic moments today other than to talk to veterans who have endured the scourge of battle, the guilt of survival? Or to think about those battles of love we have endured. This afternoon, I am ashamed to admit, I think back to a grueling dinner in San Francisco I endured with my then-girlfriend's parents. After scouring me with questions about what I was going to do after I gave up my "cute" desire to write for a living, I was steamed as we drove home back to her apartment in the Marina, where she reported that her mom and dad agreed I was a "diamond in the rough." What followed was a furious argument, when I became red-faced with rage, as Ares is described in the myths, and had to fight off her attempts to seduce me, like the diaphanously draped

Aphrodite in so many of her love stories. As my old friend, Joseph Campbell, used to joke, "Yes, the myths are alive and well. *Beauty and the Beast* are on the corner of 42nd Street and 5th Avenue waiting for the lights to change."

Our sculptor, Alexandros, made the Venus de Milo one of the first existential works of art. The previous carvings of Aphrodite, including the epoch-making Knidian by Praxiteles, offer a few innovations but are timid in comparison. The focus is on the goddess contemplating herself, eyes lowered demurely, hands coyly holding onto her chiton so it doesn't slip away. There is no hint of the profound *conflict* that is at the heart of the Judgment of Paris. The Knidian and the Capua and others are lovely without being profound. What makes Alexandros's Venus existential is that it insists on you, the viewer, filling in the blanks, answering the riddles at the heart of the story: If the gods and goddesses cast a spell over us, how can we have free will? Is love a conscious or unconscious act? If Aphrodite enchanted both Paris and Helen by promising that each would love the other, knowing how impossible that is to resist, what does that say about the human condition?

Of course, it's the function of art to encourage us to *do*, and of mythic art, in particular the Venus de Milo, to lure us into the *sensation* of feeling *alive*, that phenomenon of *aliveness* that is the difference between art and entertainment.

Regarding, literally *looking again*, at the Venus de Milo has helped me see everything else I have come across in a deeper, kinder, truer light. It is not too much to say that for years I have been trying to *see* her—in the flesh-like stone, in the Louvre, but also in hundreds of books and magazines—as if my life depended on it. Trying to see what she might have meant to the ancient Greeks, then to the French soldiers who rediscovered her, and nowadays to the reams of visitors who are now trying to see her through the distorting filter of pop culture.

The more I visit her, the more I think about her, the more intrigued I am about what she is focused on, with what the Quakers lovingly call "quiet eyes," the soft glances that look inward and outward at the same time.

Do you *see* what I am trying to get at? Essentially, to see through her eyes, which are focused on the infinite moment, as I believe it is the intensity of her gaze that makes her beautiful. Not her svelte shape, nor her bountiful breasts, and not even the yearning of her missing arms. The beauty of her thousand-yard gaze, which in turn *leads to the love of life itself,* as Vincent puts it in a letter to his brother Theo, from Etten, Netherlands, March 9, 1881. There he describes the three stages of love as a kind of oscillating seeing, a process he learned from his relationship with a young woman named Kee Vos:

> The more she disappears, the more she appears. Theo, aren't you in love too, at times? I wish you were, for believe me, the 'petty miseries' of it are also of some value. Sometimes one is desolate, there are moments when one is in hell, as it were, but... There are three stages, first not loving and not being loved, second loving and not being loved (the case in question), third loving and being loved. I'd say that the second stage is better than the first, but the third! That's it.

Love has levels is what the ancient Greeks were telling us in their personification of it as the goddess Aphrodite, who is aware of her life-changing beauty and the power that implies, and unduly proud of being the one who provides the spark. She knows ahead of time both the passion and the tragedy that her gift of Helen to Paris will unleash. Hers is the gaze of knowledge of the power of beauty that even the gods are afraid of and that mortals fear but cannot live without. The long gaze of Aphrodite looks through you and me to the end of time. She is happy—for the moment. That's all that the gods will allow. The difference between her and us is that we know she knows. In her autobiography, the deaf and blind Helen Keller described her visit to the Louvre:

> Museums and art stores are also sources of pleasure and inspiration... Doubtless it will seem strange to many that the hand unaided by sight can feel action, sentiment, beauty in the cold marble; and yet it is true that I derive genuine pleasure from touching great works of art... My soul delights in the repose and gracious curves of the Venus; and in Barré's bronzes the secrets of the jungle are revealed to me.

It bears repeating that the original intention behind the founding of the Louvre was a combination of providing a grand place to *see* great art but also to help visitors learn to *see* for themselves.

"The meaning of life is to see," said the seventh-century Chinese monk Hui Neng. Thirteen hundred years later, novelist Saul Bellow wrote, "What is art but a way of seeing?" And not just literal sight. Keller also described her visit to Rodin's studio, where she "saw" with her fingertips and "heard" with her heart. When Rodin guided her fingers across the forehead of his bust of Balzac, Keller exclaimed, "I feel the throes of the emerging mind."

Once, in the late Nineties, I was enjoying a silvery swirl of Pernod at Le Select in Paris. At closing time, I shut my notebook and walked down Rue du Montparnasse to the corner, where the lights of La Rotonde still shone. I wanted to see the bigger-than-life bronze Balzac by Rodin, which stood on a pedestal. I reached as high as I could so I might run my fingers across his metallic brow. I too felt the throes, felt alive, as I often did in my midnight rambles around the City of Light.

As Alexandros of Antioch made visible something far more potent than supernatural beauty, he helped us see and hear and feel the bittersweet power of enchantment.

Once, at the National Gallery in Dublin, I spoke with a young visitor named Colette, who told me that her job as a flight attendant for Aer Lingus was so stressful, she began to have eye problems. Her doctor recommended going once a week to the local museums so she could learn all over again how to see. That will help your eyes more than all the eyedrops in the world.

When questioned about how he was able to appreciate his years of globetrotting despite being blinded in World War I, James Holman said, "I see with my feet."

What we are talking about when we talk about an encounter with a work of art that inspires or jars us is the art of seeing. The English poet Denise Levertov wrote, "Where the eye is rapt, every word is a rapture." What we are doing here is taking in the power of the Venus inch by inch, detail by detail, until it feels natural to walk around her while piecing her together. I am trying to appreciate her as Stieglitz appreciated O'Keefe, taking photographs of her sensuous body—not out of voyeurism—but out of a desire to see her in her entirety. Not just body parts and her flesh, however beautiful, but her body as one part of the whole of her, mind, body, and spirit.

And when the Venus *reached out*, what did she find?

In *Helen of Troy*, Bettany Hughes writes, "Where love travels, Eris or Strife or deadly conflict, gutsy, delectable, deadly will follow..." Priam says, "I don't blame you, so Greeks and Trojans will fight to possess the ultimate beauty." Hughes cites the Roman writer Lucian's little-known book, *The Judgment of the Goddesses*, and the dialogue he created between Paris and Aphrodite that reflects his unrest and her vanity:

> Paris: [It is] downright incredible to me that she would be willing to abandon her husband and sail away with a foreigner and stranger.
>
> Aphrodite: Be easy on that score! I have two beautiful pages [assistants], Desire and Love, that I will give to you on your journey.

Her two intensifiers, if you will, are there to enforce her entrancing gift. The roots of the ardent belief in the power of Western love lie here, suggesting smooth sailing for people if only they trust desire and love and the happiness that is meant to accompany those two emotions. What she doesn't account for is what the actress Halle Berry has called "the strife of beauty" (evoking the goddess Eris), shorthand for the price exacted by envy, jealousy, and ill will.

I insist on looking elsewhere. The word choice is not accidental, it's serendipitous.

The nineteenth-century French poets often referred to life being elsewhere—not here, but there. The Irish literary critic Hugh Kenner wrote a wonderful series of essays with the evocative title *The Elsewhere Community* to help illuminate the long tradition of creative souls feeling not-quite-at-home in their own homes and seeking kindred spirits in places like Paris, London, Dublin, Berlin, New York, San Francisco. To do what? To become themselves. To what effect? To learn or relearn how to see for ourselves, inspired to do so by the example of her tender gaze?

All this from the power of a glance. That's the beauty of it, the point of a museum visit, the time spent with a work of art we more than admire. A work we love.

Turning around the Venus de Milo feels like strolling through a waking dream. I am trying to see where love, the sweetbitter gift, emerges and have come to admire Anne Carson's insight:

"Where Eros is lack, its activism calls for three structural components—lover, beloved, and that which comes between them. The lover wants what he does not have. It is, by definition, impossible for him to have what he wants if, as soon as it is had, it is no longer wanting. This is more than wordplay. There is a dilemma within eros that has been thought crucial by thinkers from Sappho to the present day."

What is the cost of that illusion? That she can be so easily bedded? Are we looking at her in a superficial way? Then you can talk about how she is the alpha and omega of the human story. In Hesiod's version of the origin story, Eros was there from the beginning, born in the World Egg. Without the God of Love, says the story, nothing else would exist. He is a wild child worthy of Francois Truffaut who slings "barbed arrows of desire," and "wantonly setting hearts on fire with dreadful torches," in Graves' description. No one, not even Zeus, can resist the sweet wounds left by his arrows, though they put panic in the lover's heart.

Aphrodite's bribe offers to fill in what's missing in the lives of both Paris and Helen, and ever since in the hearts of all of us who have been temporarily or permanently exiled from love. What is missing is the tenderness of human touch, the desire that brings home happiness. If they had been in love with someone else, if they had been happy, if they had felt any joy, if their souls hadn't swooned, there would be no dilemma, no *frisson*. This could also be read as one of the first cultural myths about the temptation of forbidden love.

There would also be no story, or at least not the full story, which has gone missing for two thousand years. If so, there would never be any real choice, no knee-buckling story about the irresistible force of love. But they weren't satisfied with their lot in life. Something essential was missing in them, making them vulnerable to what the poet calls "the promise of happiness."

Do I have to spell it out?

Love is a spark in the tinderbox, a flicker of light, a burst of heat, a conflagration. But sometimes we must be persuaded to open our hearts to the possibilities. This goes for me, as well. Every day, I reproach myself: *Write what you love. Love what you write.* What choice do I have other than the choice that is no choice? The one Paris had to make about beauty, the one Aphrodite chose to make in return, with him and with Helen. Not unlike the choice Odysseus was forced to make with Circe: immortality with her or mortality with Penelope. Or Rick's bold choice with Ilsa in *Casablanca* to sacrifice his love, his happiness, for hers.

Over the past twenty years, I have been circling the Venus de Milo to see her as if for the first time. The most curious emotions come over me as the very movement sparks muscle memories of my old turn-and-shoot moves on the basketball court when I was younger or the long, slow, deliberate way I have encircled beautiful things I've photographed, from my wife's body when she was pregnant with our son to the Easter Island statues and the Calatrava Olympic Stadium in Athens. Turning like Stieglitz around the undulating body of his wife, Georgia O'Keefe, seeing as beautiful each distinct part of her body so that we could see her in the whole. And so to turn around the Venus is to turn around yourself, which if done well is a form of self-reconciliation.

One night at the Boom Boom Room in San Francisco, I heard its owner, the legendary bluesman John Lee Hooker, mumbling to himself in between songs, "People always asking, 'John Lee, John Lee, what are the blues?' John Lee always say, 'The blues ain't nothin' more than three minutes of triumph over sorrow.'"

All significant art is the result of a great battle.

A real work of art also reveals an innovation, a breakthrough, and often a leap to the transcendental, achieving what the Swiss painter Paul Klee described in an aphorism from his essay, "Creative Credo," in 1920, "Art does not reproduce the visible but makes the visible."

Nothing is as it seems, and it's the artist's job to reveal why not and show us what it is.

The Parisian sun is dipping down. I look out through the mullioned window of the chamber of the Venus de Milo. The light changes color, subtly, from butterscotch to lemon. The stone poem of a sculpture is in the center of the gallery, a work produced by a sensual imagination, and I circle her, by my count, for the thirty-third time today. I am still mystified by what she evokes what Joyce called, oxymoronically, "love's bitter mystery"—the sweetbitter mystery of finding the glint in someone's eyes, even the eyes of a statue, that reveals the mystery of the universe.

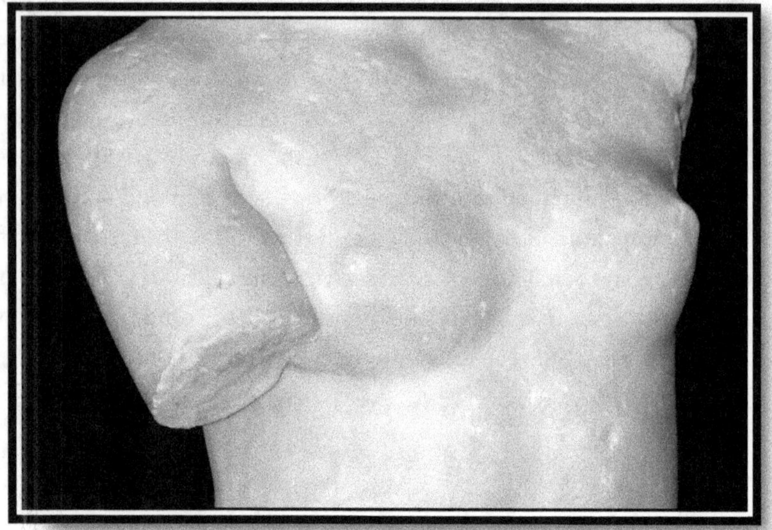

The Quietude,
Musée du Louvre, 2010

TRUTH HATH A QUIET BREAST

I have borrowed my subheading from Shakespeare's *Richard II* because the phrase came to me on a soft breeze as I admired the legendary breasts of the Venus de Milo. Of course, when the Bard penned those lines, the Venus was still immured in the cave on Melos, but we know he loved his Ovid, and the Roman poet had waxed eloquently about the goddess's attributes. For me, the poet was using the word in the figurative sense, one that had developed over millennia, conjuring up the nurturing quality of the archetypal mother or the nourishing aspect of the goddess, as well as a sexual signal, courtesy of evolution, sometimes a point of pride, sometimes of defiance.

Walking around again, aware now of the flickering sunlight in the museum and that there were only a few hours to go before the museum closed at six p.m. Looking up now from my notebook, my eyes rove to the Venus's beautiful breasts. One of her finest attributes, as the mythographers described the qualities of the gods and goddesses. I can barely conceal my smile of recognition, remembering my father's black-framed *Life* magazine cover hanging from the nail on our basement's cement wall. My mind ricochets to *The Schmulowitz Collection of Wit & Humor* at the San Francisco Library, where I was researching my book, *Riddle Me This* and happily discovered this puzzler in an anthology called *The Exeter Book*, composed around 975 CE:

"You come from the depths of the breast; you make the world *move*."

What could those old Anglo-Saxon riddlers have been on about?

The riddlic answer: *Love*.

It took hours for me to crack the mystery when I first read this thousand-year-old puzzler. The answer is the same word—love—that Sophocles used when he compared it to the melting of ice in the hands of children: love, beauty, desire, and the poet's promise of happiness, compressed into the Venus's beautiful marble breasts, which is less a case of leering than a testimony to the archetypal power of the goddess.

Twenty-five thousand or so years ago, human beings began carving large-breasted, full-vulvaed idols to represent robust female fertility. Throughout the history of art, we have seen a bevy of breasts depicted from every imaginable perspective. There are Artemis's multiple egg-shaped breasts, Hera's imperious breasts, the tender breasts of the Madonna, the apple-shaped breasts of Eve, and the lifelike breasts of the Venus de Milo. These are no gratuitous details, no voyeuristic anecdotes. These are appreciations. Enthusiasms. Treasurings. Speculations about the breast, or the heart below it, as the birthplace of love, desire, affection, nourishment.

Gazing at the Venus now, I think of the myriad words and expressions associated with what the Greeks called her "divine attributes," such as the way a child or love is taken to the breast, the place where hope springs eternal. Turning around her, I review in the reading carrel of my mind various accounts I've come across, from Hesiod to Ovid, H. D. (Hilda Dolittle) to Roberto Calasso. What I like to think of as the gods' stenographers recount how Aphrodite took the initiative in the beauty contest against Hera and Athena. She took the lead over the other goddesses by baring her breasts, knowing the hypnotic effect the gesture would have on the strapping young Trojan prince, Paris. The mythologem reveals one of the sources of her enchanting powers and those of her second most-famous spellbinding work, Helen of Troy.

When Helen was hiding during the Siege of Troy, her infuriated and cuckolded husband, Menelaus, fights his way into her quarters with the overheated intention of slaying her. The moment the king eyes his wife's beautiful breasts, however, the bloodlust in him is quelled. The beast within is softened by the beauty without. With his blood-seeking sword poised above his wife's neck, Menelaus feels the desire for revenge weaken. He spares her life.

The historian Marilyn Yalom writes in her classic study, *A History of the Breast*, "In ancient times, the breast was viewed as an object of veneration, of sustenance. In early Christian imagery, it had transmogrified [into] a threat to spiritual life, purity... During [the] Middle Ages, comforting and nourishing figured in art from Florentine Madonna paintings to Vermeer's *Procuress*, Delacroix to Mary Cassatt and Louise Bourgeois, Shakespeare to Tolstoy (who famously advocated breastfeeding), Calvino to Adrienne Rich."

Through a similar lens of veneration, art historian Kenneth Clark described her in *The Nude*: "The visitor's gaze moves easily from her gorgeous face down her neck, across her shoulders, and down to her legendarily beautiful breasts." Clark goes on to say, "No nude, however abstract, should fail to arouse in the spectator some vestige of erotic feeling, even if it be only the faintest shadow—and if it does not do so it is bad art and false morals." Beyond this description is the distinction he draws between *nude* and *naked*, which helps illuminate the genius of our Venus. Then he unties the unfortunate knot of misunderstanding:

The English language with its elaborate generosity distinguishes between the naked and the nude. To be naked is to be deprived of our clothes, and the word implies some of the embarrassment most of us feel in that condition. The word *nude*, on the other hand, carries, in educated usage, no uncomfortable overtone. The vague image it projects into the mind is not of a huddled and defenseless body but of a balanced, prosperous, and confident body: the body re-formed. In fact, the word was forced into our vocabulary by critics of the early eighteenth century to persuade the artless islanders [of the UK] that, in countries where painting and sculpture were practiced and valued as they should be, the naked human body was the central subject of art.

With those distinctions in mind, we can consider the sculpted breasts of the Venus de Milo as a reflection of the ideals of her creator, Alexandros of Antioch, who would have been aware of the fabled goddess's power to arouse the natural desire for beauty in the eyes of the young shepherd Paris. This was long considered one of her attributes, the capacity for stimulating the desire for love and sex, but also for marriage and companionship. The genius of his masterwork is revealed in the way he depicts how Aphrodite "presents" herself to her callow young judge, Paris. The pride of Antioch doesn't depict her as sentimental or as an exhibitionist, nor does he present her as vainglorious or, as Clark points out, deprived of anything, which was the style preferred at the time. Instead, the goddess is convincingly portrayed as proud in the tilt of her head, the swivel of her hips, and the tilt of her beautiful breasts. She is, as they used to say in the Irish legends, *presenting* herself, fully and truthfully. She is beyond hiding because she wants her beauty to speak for itself. When you consider the intensity of the returned gaze from the Antikythera statue of Paris, it is apparent how moved to the point of being stunned he is.

Naturally, symbolism abounds. In Celtic mythology, bare-breasted women were symbolic of defiance and submission during wartime. The Irish "lady pirate," Grace O'Malley, dodged her English pursuers for years until she was caught and sent to the Tower of London. Queen Elizabeth I asked to see her before her execution, and when O'Malley approached her, she bared her breasts, spoke Latin, recited poetry—and won a reprieve. During the French Revolution, the bare-breasted Marianne became the symbol of Liberty, Reason, and the Homeland, the great mother who would defy the enemy and nurture the citizens. In Jerusalem, thousands of tiny clay votive offerings have been discovered that depict women—possibly copies of the Great Mother goddess—in a "breast-displaying" attitude. In the fourth century BCE, a famous courtesan and lover of the widely loved sculptor Praxiteles, Phryne, went on trial, accused of blasphemy by one of her lovers. She was influential enough to hire the orator Hypereides as her lawyer, and it is said he "was making no progress in his pleas, and it became apparent that the judges meant to condemn her; he caused her to be brought where all could see her; tearing off her undervests he laid bare her bosom..."

Havelock describes the breast-baring rituals of the Amazons but also the Irish priestesses and female pirates. Romans used to spice the breasts of their courtesans. All over the ancient world, powerful women *displayed* their breasts in tender acts of nurturing but also of defiance or independence from men who claimed to possess them like chattel. The psychologist Melanie Klein writes about those obscure objects of desire: "The infant does not respond to the mother as a whole person but simply as a 'breast,' a supplier of its needs. In turn, the breast becomes an object of desire in its own right." Read in that context, Homer writes that Paris was totally smitten when he saw Helen's "milky white breasts," code for her staggering beauty, which enthralls him, literally makes him her slave, and once again we understand how defenseless the ancient Greek men felt about the sudden exposure of luxuriousness. Her breasts sealed the deal and let loose the dogs of war.

No wonder, no art. No art, no wonder. No wonder, no eye-caress.

The sun is starting to sink, sending shadows across the gallery. I walk on, hoping to see her more fully, as I would a botanical garden with newly blooming roses, a ballpark with freshly painted seats and newly planted outfield grass, a megalithic site, an old sequoia, or, figuratively, Mozart's Clarinet Concerto, Henry VI's speech at Agincourt, Louise Bourgeoise's spider sculptures. For the pleasure of seeing and the solace of art whose parts are in harmony, which is one of the oldest descriptions of the beautiful.

And what do I see? What do *you* see reading about what I see?

There is a calm before the storm of war, as gentle beauty always disrupts the peace and brings war. Still, I need a break, which for me is often in a bookstore. I saunter out of the Denon Wing and head downstairs to the capacious museum gift shop. I look around for a book solely dedicated to the Venus. None can be found. Strange. The Venus is one of the symbols of the Louvre; her image is iconic. She is omnipresent. Yet no major French books or studies have been published about her. Numerous works are available that honor several other of the Louvre's prized masterpieces, such as the *Winged Victory*, the *Rosetta Stone*, Van Gogh's *Starry Night*, and the Egyptian sculpture, *The Seated Scribe*. Nothing in depth is available about the Venus de Milo. The curious museum goer can only find a few scant references in the general histories of the museum's immense collection of some nine million works of art.

An inexplicable silence still surrounds her, approaching loneliness, and suggesting abandonment. Strange bedfellows are beauty and isolation and shame. The unexpected feelings conjure brooding memories of Sinatra's midnight voice, crooning, "What is this funny thing called...love... What is its mystery?"

I strive to understand the source of the mysterious power of the song, which may lie in the way he enunciates those two words, *funny* and *love*. Whole worlds are packed into those two words, and more, such as the mere fact that he's asking humbly, as if love is one of the greatest mysteries. What we discover here is that the Venus de Milo is far more than a poster child for famous artifacts. She is a one-woman *thesaurus* of mythological meanings, a treasury of desire, a gallery of goddess faces, a glossary of stone rendering the full palette of *human* possibilities, ranging from love and desire to passion and lust, envy and jealousy, pathos and ecstasy.

That's the beauty of it.

Every image changes as you move around it, or it remains lifeless. Circling for the last time, I feel the pull of the Venus's uncanny centripetal force. I edge closer, coming nearer to the central mystery of her generativity, believing more than ever that the beauty is understood not through preconceptions, theory, or studies, such as the velvet cage of aesthetics, but through deliberate contemplation. What is beautiful about the Venus is the tremendous force of nature that Greeks believed was the goddess of the ultimate source, the generative power of all that lives. The Japanese call the mysterious quality that pervades the Venus de Milo *shibui*, restrained elegance. Art teachers and historians call it *contraposto*, the torque-filled turning of her hips that suggests movement, promises intimacy, surges with the life force, and detonates what Gerald Manley Hopkins called "the green fuse." The Venus de Milo personifies the source of ecstasy, embodies the seductiveness of beauty, and suggests the havoc in the heart of all sensuality.

Where does this life force come from? Who knows? No one except the artist.

To me, it is as real as rain, tangible as stone, true as the moon.

So, we make myths, from the powers of Athena to the spells of Yoda in *Star Wars*. Can we tap into the life force? We want to know what moves us and why so that we can make this force the center of our lives. We *need* to know. I need to know. Where does this energy come from, the force that Aristotle called *energeia* (the root of "energy"), the force in the core of art, and what Henry Moore described, paradoxically, when he said, "If I set out to sculpt a standing man and it becomes a lying woman, I know I am making art."

They are tapping into the generative force.

I like to think that this is why we are *energized* by the real thing. She energizes the universe, enlivens the world, generates life, honors mother-hood. The Romans called her Venus Genetrix, the Guardian of Domes-ticity, a personal ancestress of the Julian lineage. In 46 BCE, Julius Caesar dedicated a Temple of Venus Genetrix, which is celebrated every Sep-tember 26.

There is a sculpture of her, to illustrate this aspect of her only a jave-lin's throw away from the Venus de Milo, in the nearby Greco-Roman sculpture galley. There you can see a shift of focus between the two views or renditions of the goddess is revealed by the position of her right hand, which demurely covers her private parts in the *pudica gesture*. For the last two thousand plus years, this tender placement has reflected myriad mean-ings, from the numinous quality of female genitals and the phenomenon of birth, to emotional healing, seduction, or the unambiguous promise of sensual pleasure.

In *The Aphrodite of Knidos and Her Successors*, Christine Mitchell Have-lock provides us with a tantalizing thread that we might follow. She writes, "The autonomous and proud bearing of the half-draped Aphrodite of Melos does not make a pathetic appeal to our sympathies; the figure is both sensuous and distant. But in the long run, these statues are state-ments about the sexual impulse, which is common to all mankind and is considered divine."

To signal this, her hips are turning toward the left, helping the left arm reach forward. Over her hips, the waterfall of her tumbling chiton. Whether it's falling or being pulled up in a gesture of modesty is difficult to tell because her hand is missing. But it does tantalize, it hints, it prom-ises, and it asks, *When does love begin? When does it end? What role does beauty play in our lives?* This is not a mystery that can be solved; it plays out as an eternal drama.

WRITING DOWN THE BEAUTY In the fall of 2019 I found myself spiraling down into a fugue state while working on an earlier draft of this book. To yank myself out of the funk, I wrote down a few quotes about the width and breadth of beauty and the beautiful from memory, if for no other reason than to feel the *energeia* in them, as the man described the life-charge. I did. I felt the jizz, the vibe, the frisson, the throb.

"An *insistence* of beauty," as the poet Stephen Dunn calls the force.

"A magnitude of beauty that leaves me no peace," writes Jack Gilbert.

"The purpose of beauty is to wash the bitter taste from the eyes," says Susan Mitchell in *Erotikon*.

Together the descriptions jarred something loose in me. An odd thing happened. I was visited by an image of my first newspaper editor, Roger Turner, like a just-developed photograph from our darkroom that he used to slide onto the mock-up of the front page. I leaned into the memory, saw him poring over an early draft of a profile I had written about Ernie Unson, a Filipino exchange student at my high school. A sorry story, Roger told me, and far from finished. "Start over," he harumphed, blowing cigar smoke over my story. "Write as if you just woke up."

To this day, I can feel the tremors from that advice.

Now I think it as, "Write, don't think, write again."

Smiling now, in the way of dreaming with our eyes wide open, I am moved to say we may not need the myth of beauty anymore, no more of the beauty myth. Instead, these observations point beyond the charges of beauty being an indulgence and back and down to its primal necessity, where love is born, desire felt, happiness touched.

The Shakers have a wonderful proverb, "The beauty of the world around us, only according to what we already bring to it." I take this to mean that intention and attention change everything when we deeply look upon the world around us; otherwise, we miss the beauty that can make life worthwhile.

"Everything has its beauty," Confucius reminds us, "but not everyone sees it."

I've come to believe that's the purpose of art, poetry, and myth—to remind us, revive our imaginations, reintegrate beauty in our lives, and truly see and feel that beauty is one of the first and most important pleasures. Its very existence is baffling to many, obvious to others, such as the "politically correct *anti-pleasure* [my italics] school of art people" in the beating-heart prose of critic Janet Malcolm. A great work of art is a self-sufficient world that we revolve around looking for pleasure, seeking beauty, longing for genius, and occasionally finding ourselves staring back.

Not for nothing did the essayist and diarist Anais Nin name her revelatory and revolutionary collection of fourteen erotic short stories *Delta of Venus*. Literary critics panned the collection at first but now say they capture the spirit of female sexuality in a world where only romantic love carries much meaning.

The Venus de Milo miraculously captures both essences with her beautiful face, shoulders, and breasts, her torso resting atop the sublimely twisting lower half, presenting herself to her judge. That's the beauty of it, we say in everyday life. Then again, to speak like that happens to beg the question of what beauty or the beautiful is or attempts to be. The mystery is creativity, the power to conceive. I return once again to the mystery of *aliveness* in stone, *animation* in words, *vibrancy* in painting, *vertigo* of love. And to the conundrum expressed by the twenty-five-year-old James Joyce in his short story, "The Dead," where he asks, "Why am I feeling this riot of emotion?"

This is what I ask myself in front of every work of art that makes me *gasp* (the original meaning of aesthetics) or brings me to my knees. The first one I recall was Edward Hopper's *Montauk*, which my father took me to see at the Met in New York a few days after we had vacationed at Long Island's Montauk Point. For the first time, it was a miracle to see the breathtaking lighthouse rendered in luminous paint and framed on a canvas. I don't think I ever got over that. Later, it was the Vermeers in Amsterdam, Morandis at a small gallery near where I was living in Paris in the late 1990s, O'Keefes in New Mexico. And yet, as keen as the memories are, I have learned again and again that the greatest gift of the greatest art is to see the startlingly beautiful everywhere.

While living in the West of Ireland in the '80s, I was hushed at dusk by a murmuration of swirling, swooping starlings above the Connemara bogs. On a rainy winter night in the '90s I rattled the chain-link fence surrounding the cemetery in Dearborn where my father is buried and was shaken by three bolts of lightning that lit up his gravestone so I could read the carved letters of his name and rank. Leaning over the guardrail of the ferry to Palawan, in the Philippines, I was greeted by a half dozen dolphins who squealed with delight.

For reasons reason cannot tell, I credit my infatuation with the Venus de Milo for sensitizing me to art for the rest of my life. I don't need any other reason. I just need the "singular sensation" that nineteen dancers in *A Chorus Line* sing about, that shivery feeling that comes from being one with the art before me, even if only for a few moments.

A feeling that allows me to come back from the dead and love life anew.

THE DIVINE DRAPERY

Turning, turning, turning. Noticing details that help the reader appreciate art and beauty. So beautiful are the wave-like folds of the drapery that covers the loins of the Venus de Milo, it's as if an invisible wind is fluttering the folds until they slip down her right hip. This must have been a source of boundless fascination for the ancient Greeks because it is such a common feature of how the Venus is depicted in both sculpture and painting. By the time Alexandros displayed his Venus de Milo to visitors in his Antioch studio, such as the judges from Melos or other sculptors in the art school that had become famous across the Mediterranean, I like to think that he earned a reputation for creating something original, a Venus that was both sublime *and* beautiful.

Uncannily, I found a passage in a letter from the sculptor John B. Flannagan to his agent, Carl Zigrosser, in which he reveals a refreshing alternative to the agony of the artistic struggle. "My aim is to produce a sculpture with such ease, freedom, and simplicity that it hardly seems carved but rather to have always been that way... You once called it inevitable."

That is how I view the Venus de Milo. Unforced, unavoidable, inevitable.

One of the greatest effects of art is how one work leads you to another, then another and another, the viewer's appreciation increasing and intensifying.

I suspect that something very strange happened to Alexandros. He might have owned a print of a fellow sculptor's Venus that was ruined or smudged, or a wandering bard got drunk and emphasized the smuttier aspects of the story, igniting a spark in his mind that caught fire. I would even venture to say that he grasped the spiritual essence of the mythological story. So, I can see him chiseling away at his block of stone, resolving his stony quest for a fresh way of seeing the goddess who everyone in his world would have worshipped, Aphrodite.

Surely there must have been a measure of pride in Antioch that one of their own had won the faraway competition. Such was the devotion to Aphrodite that art lovers and devotees made long-distance journeys to the island of Knidia to see Praxiteles's masterpiece and to Olympia to see his Dionysus and Hermes. In the anonymous seventh-century BCE Greek epic

Kypria, it is written of Aphrodite, "She clothed herself with garments which the Graces and Hours [her lovely attendants] had made for her and dyed in flowers of spring—such flowers as the Seasons wear—in crocus and hyacinth and flourishing violet and the rose's lovely bloom, so sweet and delicious, and heavenly buds, the flowers of the narcissus and lily. In such perfumed garments is Aphrodite clothed at all seasons. Then laughter-loving Aphrodite and her handmaidens wove sweet-smelling crowns of flowers of the earth and put them upon their heads—the bright-coiffed goddesses, the Nymphs and Graces, and golden Aphrodite too, while they sang sweetly on the mount of many-fountained Ida."

It may take a few turns around her and a few wonders, but slowly you can feel the accretion of detail of what has made her so *seductively beautiful,* so erotically charged with seeming effortlessness. After dozens of visits one day, the light flickering in from the southern windows of the room struck her just right, so it provided the illusion that her robe was *falling* from behind and insinuated for the first time to me, at least in a visceral way, that her right arm was probably holding onto the hem of the robe as it fell—or hovered just above to catch it.

What a touching gesture, so reminiscent of Pierre Bonnard's paintings of his wife Marie reaching for a robe as she stepped out of their bathtub. Touching is the operative word here. Now look again, with feeling and more closely, just above the coil of robe around her waist, slightly off center left. The sculptor makes you look for it, knowing you will. There is the slightest of Y-shaped lines, carved there ingeniously by Alexandros to suggest what art historians call the *pubis,* the first hint of her body's parting between her waist, legs, and loins, what Anais Nin called "the delta of Venus." The hint of her irresistible sex appeal is evoked through a miraculously delicate sculpting of her robe. For many observers over the last two hundred years, the beauty of this Aphrodite is reflected in her remarkable proportions and the seductive power of what scholars call her *mouillee draperie*, the seeming transparency of her clothing. Of course, the Irish have something to say about that clothing detail in their traditional limerick:

> There once was a sculptor named Phidias
> Whose manners in art were invidious.
> He carved Aphrodite without any nightie—
> Which startled the ultrafastidious.

Of course, this is the kind of poetry you recite, as the Irish say, at silly o'clock. If you are still up at midnight, or burning the midnight oil at 3 a.m., or up at the crack of dawn, you might want to contemplate Rilke's "Archaic Torso of Apollo." There he performs a similar visual exploration as I have modestly attempted to do here, scanning the god's legendary head, rippling torso, gently gleaming gaze, curved breast, placid hips and thighs, flaring loins, cascading shoulders, and downy fur.

For, as I have tried to reveal, in Stephen Mitchell's translation, "there is no place that does not see you." And is this not true of all stupendous art? And is not his whiplashing last line true of all great encounters with it, a white-water rush of words in the original German that make you catch your breath, "Du mußt dein Leben ändern," and in English makes you gasp, *"You must change your life."*

By this, I don't think the poet meant you need to change addresses, professions, lovers, or wardrobes, but something far more fundamental. We need to change *how we see*, change how we feel. This injunction has been echoed from Aristotle to Da Vinci, Austen to Van Gogh, Twyla Tharp to John Berger and Minor White, philosophers to artists, and scientists insisting that there is an *art of seeing well* and it is worthwhile to practice it.

Far afield we must travel to understand the immensity of meaning in the Venus de Milo.

The torque, twist, and turn in her torso are suggestive to me that she is turning in anticipation, that she is waiting to either receive the apple or has just taken it in her hand from Paris, having won the question: "Who is the most beautiful?"

Call this the erotics of art. Desire speaking to desire.

When the Louvre purchased one of Frida Kahlo's paintings at an exhibition of her sublime art in the mid-1930s, the Russian Wassily Kandinsky, one of the pioneers of abstract painting, kissed her hand in gratitude, a beautiful gesture, an expression of his desire for beauty. One of the nine lauded female poets from classical times, Anyte of Tegerea, the sexy Arcadian poet, wrote:

> If you could see Kallistion naked, stranger,
> you'd suggest we switch the "th" in thighs
> to an "s."

As in the "s" in our lusty word *desire*.

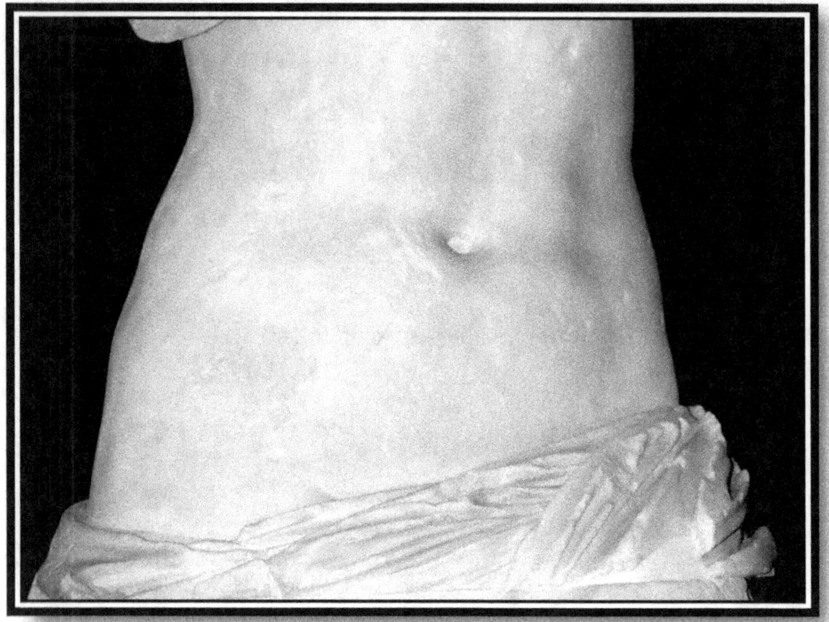

Venus' Desire Line
Musée du Louvre, 2010

THE DESIRE LINE

There is an elusive quality that is achieved by Voutier by virtue of his quick contour sketches of the Venus de Milo. I like to think the swift and clean lines came from the desire he felt to act quickly if he was going to save her. What he lacks in details he makes up for in clarity, along with a certain *je ne sais quoi*, an animating spirit, that he captures from the original intent of the sculptor. He reveals the beauty of her subtly parted lips, the shadow of her smile, the confidence of her presentation of her breasts, an echo of archaic rituals of pride or submission. Her belly is slightly but sensuously turned, revealing an erotic torsion, and hint of expectation. The lower portion of her belly is just visible, a hint of the tremendous fecund energy of the goddess of childbirth. Together, they reveal in stone the generative power of the Spanish proverb "Desire beautifies what is ugly." Without this slight sense of menace, of a kind of dulcet duende, there may be illustration and technique, but no art.

Looking at these sketches again, I thought once more about Matisse's *line of desire:* "One must always search the desire of the line, where it wishes to enter, where to die away." This *desire line* is the saving grace of the drawing. It saves the artist from mere illustration and saves the viewer from boredom. The line desired resembles what art critic John Berger cannily describes in his essay on the legendary lost sketchbook of philosopher Barach Spinoza, as the contours of reality that "harass" the very act of drawing. The verb cuts like a diamond-tipped drill down to the essence of a hard truth. As curious as the verb might be, Berger picked up on it in his own book about sketching, "If the lines of a drawing don't convey this harassment, the drawing remains a mere sign."

So, we can hazard to say that the forces of the real world *harass* the lines of a work like the gravitational forces of time, the pressures of the history of art, market forces, expectations of friends and foes. If we're not careful, they push us down like a pneumatic drill.

The tectonic force of this torment lies in the simple rendering of the just discovered Venus de Milo. Her arms were already missing, laying low the suspicion of theft because of the rising theft of antiquities across the Mediterranean. If this drawing had been made public from the day the statue was unveiled at the Louvre, a little more than a year later, a lot of heartache could have been avoided. But Voutier didn't show his sketches to another soul for decades. Whatever happened to the arms we will never know—unless they eventually turn up in the still abandoned field, or in another cave, or even in the burlap bags filled with the fragments the soldiers had been gathering, which Voutier ordered buried. Those bags have likewise never been found. What's missing here is part of her essential mystery, not just literally but figuratively, as the little Irish girl illuminated for me. The arms of beauty are missing but often feel stolen, in the largely unvoiced concern over how much beauty has been cut off, severed, stolen from us—in ugly architecture, stolen art, torn-down ballparks, megalithic sites torn down for shopping malls, battlefield sites paved over for parking lots.

What goes missing often feels like it has been robbed.

As the man said, rather than dwell on what's gone, *make* what's missing.

Curious how what goes missing stimulates the imagination more than what turns up. This longing for what we can't quite reach or will never find is at the core of the story of Tantalus and the vivid verb it inspired, *tantalize*, to be up to our chin in water, but unable to drink. That describes our efforts to drink in the beauty of the world while we can in the stunningly short time that we have here on earth to enjoy it.

Unquestionably beautiful, the Venus de Milo is also sublime.

Far beyond pretty, far less than dowdy, as some have charged, the Venus is shattering, a form of beauty that is perceived as terrible, even threatening. Both beauty and the sublime can provide a numinous experience, a revelation of the divine in the middle of everyday life. But in significantly different ways. The Venus de Milo provides us with that rare example that contains both the sublime and the beautiful. These two qualities are two often pitted against each other like fiercely competitive wrestlers, or the two halves of a single centaur.

Her erotic, soulful lower body evokes the dark sublime, while her more attractive upper body and her spiritualized face reveal the traditionally beautiful. The play of tension between the two, upper and lower, spirit and soul, sacred and profane, is the genius of the statue. At once, this is Alexandros' personal genius in action, forging the sublime and the beautiful together in unprecedented ways. Still, it is as famed script analyst Robert McKee says in his foreword to *The War of Art*, "It's called talent: the innate power to discover the hidden connection between two things—images, ideas, words—that no one else has seen before, linked them, created a third utterly unique work."

If the first sketch of the Venus' upper body, appears classically beautiful that's no accident. All is calm, in balance, harmonious. The chiseler's equivalent of literary quoting, an act of homage to his teachers and the great sculptors who came before him. With a few confident strokes, Voutier captures the coolness, impassiveness, contemplative qualities of the classical goddess. In contrast, the second sketch is the lower body revealing the essential nature of the later Hellenistic, which is corrupt to some, human to others.

However, the lower half subtly suggests the sublime forces of erotic tension, powers greater than you and me, forces that reflect the very source of life. The sublime is more than just puissant, powerful, overwhelming, as if that weren't enough. The sublime is, as art curator James Elkins writes, a storm, an attack during war, a vision of something that "transcends the human." In the case of the Venus, her eyes, face, shoulders, back, hands, breasts, and belly are recognizably human. Beautiful. But if your gaze wanders lower, as Alexandros tempts us to do with the way he sculpts her robe, your attention hovers just above her loins. This method inexplicably connects us with what is divine in her. The illusion in stone is created by slightly flexing her left knee, and the modesty that overcame her as she draped her cloak across her hips and legs. These lines practically rustle under his pencil. Her left foot is rendered slightly out of perspective, but captures the shift of weight, which occurs when she lifts her left knee so she can reach forward—what?

The prize, the gift, the boon, that which changes everything.

For Alexandros, the achievement was an ingenious balance of the upper and lower body, the intellectual and the sexual, the Classical and the Hellenistic. Out of that alchemical mix arises the erotic tension in the *desire line* that has stunned and disturbed viewers ever since. What this original flash of genius also provides is an uncanny image of an idea that transcends ordinary language.

Looking closer, we see that *the entire base is intact*, a deceptively simple fact that will be shown to have profound implications. Finally, there are the herms, columns or pedestals, with the busts of an older and a younger man riding atop each one. Who they represent leads to our understanding of their original purpose, flanking the Venus as they do. By all reckoning the figure on the left is Herakles, god of strength and loyalty; the figure on right is Hermes, god of speed, cunning, and the crossroads.

What fascinates me most is that taken together, the three sketches of Hermes, Aphrodite, and Herakles, serve as a kind of triptych of the three *excellences* in Greek culture—mind, body, and soul—the noble pursuit of which makes possible the well-lived life. This is the crux of our search, the revelation of a kind of syzygy of Greek genius that has influenced the Western world for the last twenty-five centuries.

Beyond her sensual features, it is the drapery that is the unacknowledged carrier of the sublime here. Its folds cover and tease the imagination, conveying modesty and sensuality at the same time. Giacometti described his approach in his *Art History Writings*, and his answer created a parallax of words: "The more I work, the more I see things differently, that is, the grandeur becomes more and more unknown and more and more beautiful. The closer I come, the grander it gets, the more remote it is." Rodgers and Hammerstein lyricized the loveliest of impulses this way:

> Do I love you because you're beautiful,
> Or are you beautiful because I love you?
> Do we have to choose, or is it enough to be in your presence?

Turning from pusillanimous cynicism of the post-modern art world back to heart-restoring praise just may help us remember how to appreciate the world around us.

"To exalt the human spirit," artist Clifford Still said, "practice praise singing."

Why bother, you ask. I say it is because those among us who do not find something to praise every day are thieves of beauty. Look no further if you want to know who stole the arms of the Venus de Milo.

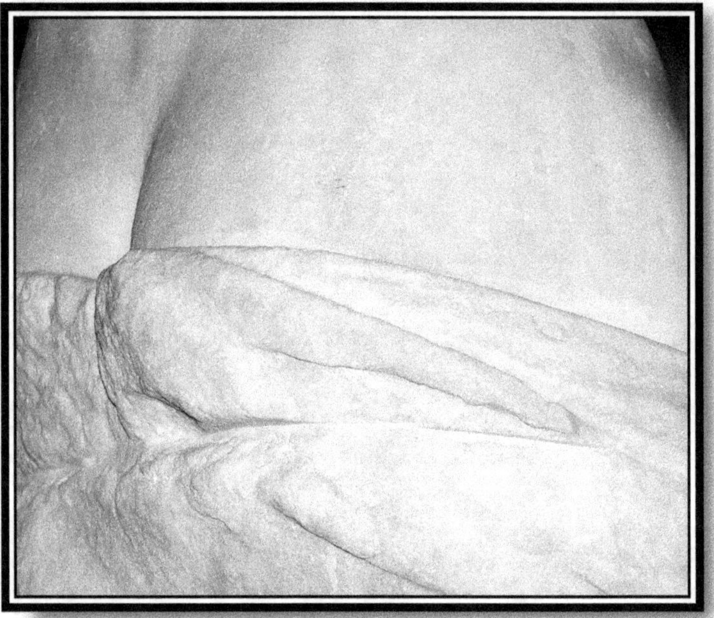

The Venus from the Rear
Musée du Louvre, 2010

IN PRAISE OF HER BACKSIDE

Callipygian has always been one of my favorite words. *Beautiful buttocks*, as the Greeks of Alexandros's time would've said. Turning and turning around his Venus, I finally understand the reason and the motivation for the Cult of the Callipygian, the many Venuses with prominent posteriors that are rounded, curvaceous, and proud, statues that didn't shy away from a proud display of beautiful buttocks. Instead, they signal a voluptuous ideal of beauty.

The ancients used to praise her backside; now we sing hip-hop songs about her booty.

The long-enduring division between the sublime and the beautiful is signaled right there in the drapery that covers the separation of the two halves of the torso. All the more seductive because she was never meant to be seen in the round if her lifespan as a statue in the niche of a gym consisted of facing outward toward the passing athletes, soldiers, and trainers who visited every day. Why so much tender attention lavished there when she was ensconced in a niche? A visitor would never have enjoyed her back or her rear end. Did Alexandros have in mind that his masterpiece would be displayed in a gallery similar to the one in a round temple, a rotunda that the proud citizens of Knidia commissioned to display Praxiteles's Venus? Not really. The plan to display it only in the gym seemed to be a common one in that era when upwards of three hundred gymnasia were being built across Hellas, Greece as we now know it. Each required a foyer with the requisite three statues of Hermes, Aphrodite, and Herakles for the usual three niches in the entrance.

She is raising or lowering her *peplos*, the lovely Greek word for robe, to uncover her hips and buttocks. Again, it is the suggestion of movement, the motion of lifting a skirt to arouse either affection, awe, or even fear, as in warfare. Naturally, the Greeks had a name—*anasyrma*—for this beautiful gesture of depicting a slightly draped or slowly *undraping* woman or goddess. Leave it to the often smutty-minded musical genius, Wolfgang Amadeus Mozart, to provide us with one of our finest anatomical wishes: "Our arses should be signs of peace."

The upper crack of her cheeks, which signifies *exposure*, vulnerability, an integral part of her *allure*, is accentuated by what is happening in front, which is the way for Langston Hughes, "Beauty for some provides escape who gain a happiness in eyeing the gorgeous buttocks of the ape of Autumn exquisitely dying."

John Updike wrote provocatively about the backside in his marvelous collection of art essays, *Still Looking*: "A woman's beauty lies not in any exaggeration of the specialized zones, nor in any general harmony that could be worked out by means of the *sectio aurea* or a similar aesthetic superstition, but in the arabesque of the spine. The curve by which the back modulates into the buttocks. It is here that grace sits and rides a woman's body."

My father's favorite painter was Pierre-Auguste Renoir. In the French artist's honor he framed three of his prints and hung them on our living room walls, and was known to be fond of quoting *le maître* to guests in our home that Renoir knew one of his portraits was finished when he created the impulse in his viewers to reach and touch her buttocks. Later, I read in Renoir's memoir: "A painter who has the feel of breasts and buttocks is saved." So, my dad got it half-right, the right half.

Peter-Paul Rubens said something similar: "I paint a woman's big, rounded buttocks so that I want to reach out and stroke the dimpled flesh." The arch-feminist and author Germaine Greer once remarked, "The most popular image of the female despite the exigencies of the clothing trade is all boobs and buttocks, a hallucinating sequence of parabola and bulges." The Australian actress Kate Winslet offers a contrarian view:

"It's true that you need much time to get rid of the fat girl you once were, but you know, I am sincerely grateful for my buttocks."

Why carve her "in the round," as detailed from behind as in front? What was the sculptor trying to say? Was it a ploy to overwhelm the judges back on Melos? Was it his way of honoring Aphrodite, as Praxiteles was famously devoted to her when he carved the Knidian? Or was it simply necessary due to the standards of the day to provide a rear-view mirror of desire itself, or as the editors of the photographic collection, *In Praise of the Buttocks*, take pains to point out in the introduction, "The classical object of libidinousness was the posterior."

In *Studies in the Psychology of Sex*, published in 1927, British physician and social reformer Havelock Ellis describes cultural sexual characteristics of the buttocks. He wrote: "Thus we find, among most of the peoples of Europe, Asia, and Africa, the chief continents of the world, that the large hips and buttocks of women are commonly regarded as an important feature of beauty, a deviation demanded by the reproductive function of women, and in the admiration it arouses, sexual selection is thus working alongside natural selection." He adds that the European artist frequently seeks to attenuate rather than accentuate the protuberant lines of the feminine hips, and it is noteworthy that the Japanese also regard small hips as beautiful. Nearly everywhere else, large hips and buttocks are regarded as a mark of beauty, and the average man is of this opinion even in the most aesthetic countries. Ellis also claims that corsets and bustles are meant to emphasize the buttocks. Emphasis on the female buttocks as a sexual characteristic has increased in recent times according to Ray B. Browne, who attributes the change to the popularization of denim jeans:

[E]mphasis on the upper female torso has recently given way to the lower area of the body, specifically the buttocks. Such a change happened quite recently when denim jeans became fashionable.

In order to emphasize fit, jeans manufacturers accentuated hips. And after brand-name jeans became so popular with the designer's name on the hip pocket, even more accentuation was given to the posterior. The more jeans sales increased, the more ads were used which emphasized the derriere, to such an extent, in fact, that this particular area may eventually surpass breasts as the number one sexual image of the female body.

A more generous and aesthetic view, embraced by those who are charmed rather than repelled by this most tremulous part of the body—curvy, rippling, sometimes dimpled, always reminiscent of *l'oeuf Paques*, veritable Easter eggs—the buttocks are as beautiful as the mind that gazes upon them.

Looking upon the backside of the Venus de Milo brings to mind the words of the Italian poet Aretino, who described "the opening of the white pages of a missal," and the anonymous Victorian poet who winkingly described the "decolletage of the buttocks."

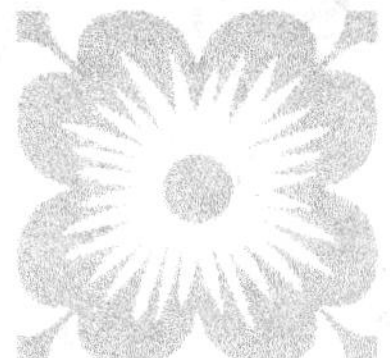

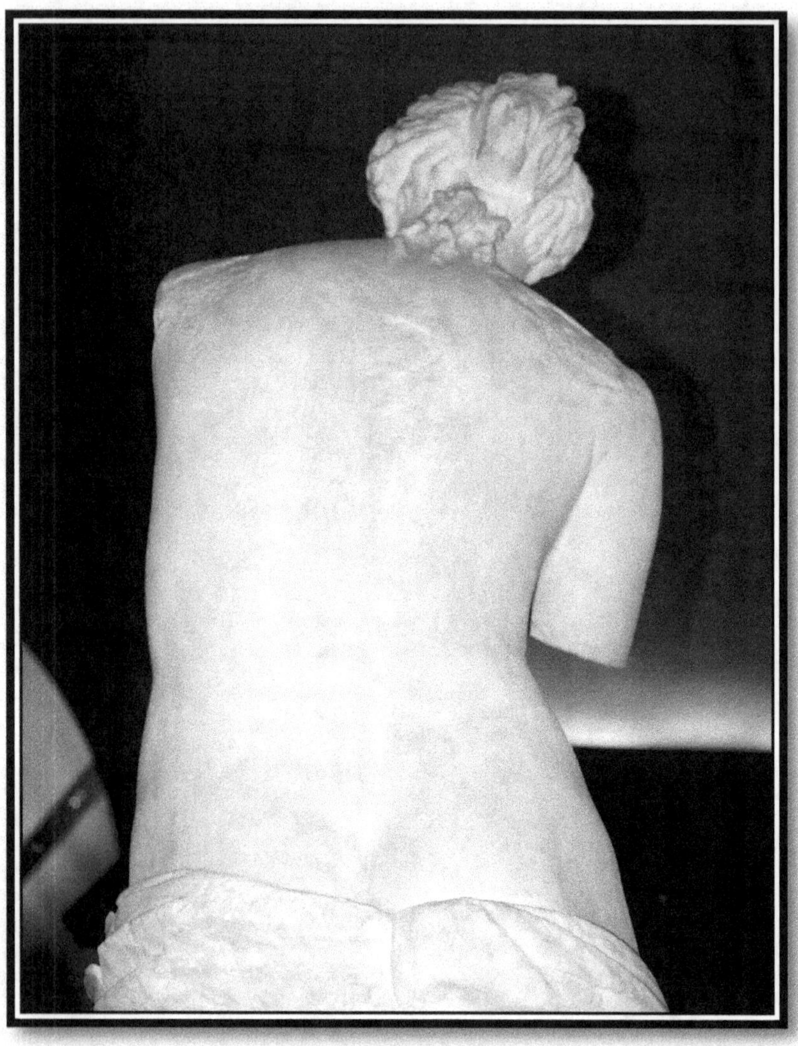

"The most beautiful back in the world."
—Auguste Rodin
Musée du Louvre, 2023

GOD HAS YOUR BACK

Walking around the Venus, a random thought comes to me from the Ramayana: "There are only three things that are Real: God, human folly, and laughter. The first two are beyond our comprehension, so we must do what we can with the third." One of the hallmarks of Greek art is the absence of struggle and the presence of a very real power. I marvel at that sense of calm the sculptor was able to achieve, evoked by the constant search for balance in Greek culture. I turn around her and feel the quickening of her beauty the moment I see nothing but her beautiful back.

Today, I see her back as if for the first time. Startled, I remember that haunting line from *The Talmud*, "God loves the back." I've been pondering this holy-of-holies saying for years. What can this possibly mean? Spend a day at the Louvre and gaze at the back of the Venus de Milo and the meaning may become clear to the perceptive visitor.

In the afternoon, I took the above photograph. I spent an hour in the gallery gazing at her back. I tried to feel my way in, as Kant suggested we do with significant works of art, and eventually was able to sense my own back muscles flex, as if in support of hers.

How curious the composition must have been for Alexandros, the entranced sculptor. I appreciate how he carved her as broad-shouldered, which is innovative. Remember the tender but timid shoulders of the common Venuses of the time and you'll appreciate what a leap forward this was. See how visible her back muscles are, straining as if against fate itself. Symbolically, the back signifies support, and today it seems to me she could hold up the world, a female counterpart to Atlas and his rippling back and shoulder muscles carrying the weight of the world.

Her lower back is the foundation "on which everything is built." Often, this part of the body is considered the basis for physical support and emotional security. A strong back symbolizes strength, fortitude, determination, and hard work. When we say, "Put your back into it," we mean use everything at your command, give it your all.

In the Judgment of Paris, Aphrodite is the only one of the three goddesses to gaze at herself in the bronze mirror, the only one to primp, the only one to attempt to *attract* the young prince. According to Ovid and others, Paris asked her to disrobe. In many paintings, such as those by Rubens, Titian, and Munch, Aphrodite is half-turned, as if she wants him to see her back as well as her front, the strength of her spine, and her surprisingly muscular back—not just her beautiful breasts, long angling neck, and strong shoulders. It's as if Alexandros is saying she knew something about men and the power of love to render them weak. By signaling how strong she was as the goddess of love and beauty, she is saying, "Look upon my beautiful front—my display—but don't miss my back. *My love is strong.*" Inevitably when you gaze at art, you start an unstoppable train of associations.

One day gazing at her back, I thought of Louise Brooks' cello-shaped back in *Pandora's Box*, sometimes called the most beautiful woman's back in the history of movies. There is an ancient Indian concept called *rasa*, which is alternately translated as *taste*, *savor*, or *quality*, of which there are nine. They offer the most sophisticated approach to the deliberation of art in the world. Essentially, it is about distilled *essences*, "aesthetic delight produced by the emotions and the *excellences*."

At her resting place in Yorgos's field, the ancient gym on Melos, the Venus faced out toward her viewers and admirers. No one would have seen her back, and yet Alexandros carved intimate details in her back as well as her front, in the small bun of hair as well as in her front curls. Why? To please the gods, I suspect he would have said.

"I have your back," we say to good friends, and then if our friendship is true, we back them up. There is another aspect of the word and concept, the notion of *looking* back, over our shoulder, usually signifying regret or doubt, or at best taking a glance in hopes of catching a pattern. That is not happening here. The Venus is looking forward to the next moment, the *infinite moment*, which is the core meaning of the sculpture.

And this is the bigger frame that's needed here—after all the details of the historical creation, original context, and unearthing. As the light shifted in the gallery, I noticed the sheer angle of her forward lean, which accentuated the way she accepted the notorious Apple of Discord. Her back reveals strength, not softness—tensile character but also a sense of anticipation.

In my mind, only one other artwork can vie for the place of beauty that the Louvre's Venus holds and that is the bust of Nefertiti in the Neues Museum in Berlin. Like Nefertiti, stolen from the warmth of Egypt and transported to the northern climes of Germany, the Venus de Milo still carries the insouciance of the Mediterranean. The warmth of the Hellenic sun can still be sensed on her marble flesh. It is the warmth of that sun upon her back that calls forth the memories of summer and the brown flesh of languid days on the shore. When I look at the Venus de Milo, I can feel the warmth of the afternoon sun, I can see the light bouncing off the Aegean Sea, and I can taste the salt air and dream of an evening of wine and passion.

The Venus is breathtakingly beautiful from the front but equally attractive and mysteriously alluring from the back. This lustrous back, painstakingly rendered by Alexandros, *would never be seen* in her niche in the Melos gymnasium because she faced out toward the foyer, which the athletes and warriors in training passed through every day. From the day she was installed, except for the occasional statue-rubbers (those employed to keep them clean), would see her? It is a curiosity of art and architecture that reappeared in the age of cathedral building when the craftsmen spent a devoted but decidedly irrational amount of time carving detail into statues hundreds of meters above ground level that nobody but the occasional angel or God Himself would ever see.

The irresistible possibility is that this deep devotion is rooted in the belief that there should be no skimping on the details in art. The gods are watching, artists may have believed, carefully noting their attention to detail. What it amounts to isn't irrational or superstitious as much an explanation for the creation of an irrefutable sense of *presence*, of divine power, which hits the viewer or devotee in the solar plexus, taking the breath away. In this sense, the Venus de Milo never turns her back on us. Like several other famous statues in antiquity that were intended to be seen *in the round*, she needs to be walked around, circumambulated, encircled if she is to be embraced.

At the fever dream moment in *Bull Durham*, the seduction of the minor league catcher Crash Davis (Kevin Costner), he declares his passionate beliefs to the sexy baseball groupie Annie Savoy (Susan Sarandon): "I believe in the Soul, the small of a woman's back, the hanging curveball, high fiber, [and] good scotch…" She swoons at his sensitive man routine, eyes dilating with desire, a gasp rising from her.

I recall another of my father's favorite painters, Thomas Eakins, who painted rough-and-tumble boxing scenes, river scenes, and a study of "A Woman's Back" with similar fervor, and more, with that secret attention to what Janet Malcolm calls "defamiliarization." Write, paint, sculpt something that plants the idea in the viewer's mind that they have never seen that object before.

In the early 2000s, before a book signing at Book Soup, I was in a Sunset Boulevard café with my friend, the painter Gregg Chadwick, and asked him about his fascination with women's backs. I later enjoyed my modest summary of our afternoon's musings: "Art at its best brings forth the most human of feelings. To approach another from the back in a spirit of love is a privileged introduction. The first hidden gaze allows for a moment of voyeurism that perhaps will lead to lust before either party is aware of deeper feelings. And then there is the touch and embrace. The back of the Venus de Milo combines both strength and femininity in an almost painful display of eroticism. Venus's back seems to will us to caress her skin and ease her tired muscles with firm hands. From the front, she plays demure. But, held in a romantic embrace from the rear, Venus allows herself to reveal the goddess of love. Breasts seduce the suitor but also speak of maternity and motherhood, while a woman's back calls only to the lover. It is fitting that the Venus de Milo was taken from the Greek island of Melos to Paris, where her beauty can be encountered 'in the round.'"

Twenty-five hundred years ago, Plato described the encounter with the gods this way: "First a shudder runs through you, and then the old awe creeps over you." The great love poet, Sappho, who was the first to describe Eros as the impish son of Aphrodite, suggested, "I am seized by a sudden shuddering," a feeling all lovers live for. The original Greek word was *phrisso*, a tremble but also a cringe, which was used to describe Aphrodite's double-edged effect on lovers. Over time, the word evolved into the modern French word *frisson*, the shiver down the spine Nabokov used to describe the shock of recognition in a work of art.

The telltale shiver, the shudder, is what we commonly associate with *coup de foudre*, the lightning-bolt experience of love at first sight, implying a serpentining movement going up and down your spine. The snake of love is captured in "Shakin' All Over," the 1959 rock-and-roll song by Johnny and the Pirates: "When you move in right up close to me / That's when I get the shakes all over me. / Quivers down my backbone / I got the shakes down my knee bone / Ye-ah, the tremors in my thigh bone / Shakin' all over..."

Similarly, the ancient Greeks described the moment of truth in love, cosmic desire, as the infamous "limb-loosener." Eros was by any other name an impish love child but was also regarded as "the tyrant of men," in the words of Euripides. Widely considered the most beautiful of creatures and the very personification of passionate longing, not just for the beloved but for victory, accomplishment, and excellence, Eros (Cupid to the Romans) taunts us with the promise that pricks us with the sweetbitter possibility that love may lead to happiness. This may be what we are afraid of because it takes away our last excuse, that we don't have a choice, that all is fated—yesterday by the gods, today by our genes.

The painter Jean Arp once said that he hoped his work might encourage viewers to dream with their eyes open. That's what all art and all myth encourage us to do. Live in the waking dream, even if it's a nightmare. This rarely happens on its own. So, how do we move past voyeurism or culture-vulturism? How do we find the dream in the art?

Herbert Read cites the obscure German word *einfuhlung*, as "one of those culturally untranslatable words that has proved useful to suggest a certain *feeling into*, not just with, but into... We project ourselves into a work of art and feel accordingly."

If we can cultivate this sensibility, we might empathize with the spirit of the work, which offers an opportunity to *experience* the work and in turn allow it to surprise us. If it doesn't startle, it ain't art. More paintings have been created about the Judgment of Paris, the freeze-frame moment and one of the most elemental choices men and women can be offered, than any other. And yet, maybe this is the way it is supposed to be for lovers—swinging like a metronome between agony and ecstasy, paying and yet not paying a price for a taste of golden honeyed love. The invitation to lose ourselves in bliss is hard to resist.

"When the partner assumes an incandescent beauty," writes the mythologist Ginette Paris, "the moment achieves a peaceful perfection, for one has been granted a vision of eternity by Aphrodite." That incandescence didn't just flare once, on the slopes of Mount Ida some three thousand years ago. It flares on, which is the essence of a mythic image. Recall novelist Saul Bellow's description of Marilyn Monroe, that she had "a sort of incandescence under her skin." The story that lights up the Venus de Milo like an inner lantern isn't about sexual helplessness The mythology that inspired the story of the Judgment of Paris is about more than the *seductive power of beauty*, and if that weren't enough, *the sweet desire for happiness*, as elusive and transitory as it may be for those who seldom or never enjoyed it. Aphrodite was the Goddess of Love and Beauty whom none could resist, Paris a fair prince in search of love, and Helen a desperately unhappy, thrice-violated young queen born of the goddess Necessity, which is to say that *beauty is born out of necessity and love out of the desire for happiness*, all of which Aphrodite knew all along. Men would blame them and not themselves for the horror of the Trojan War, as men always find someone else to blame. The war was born out of lust alright, but it was the lust for land and trade, or fame and glory, which is why the myth is truer than the facts.

One night, long ago, I was walking home through Grace Cathedral Park in San Francisco just in time to hear Tony Bennett's "Fly Me to the Moon" playing from a car radio in an open window, soaring across the night sky, stopping me in my tracks by the infinite...pause... between the imploring words "Hold...my...hand." Of all the songs I've ever heard, I don't think I've ever heard gentler or more touching phrasing. The great crooner held each word tenderly, stretching them like a bow. I remember hearing the biographer of the cabaret composer Bart Howard aboard the QE2 remarking that Howard's original title of the song had been "In Other Words," but everyone remembered it as "Fly Me to the Moon." Of all the lectures I've ever attended, why do I recall that one? Perhaps because the lecturer reminded me about the art of the *pause*, the time when your breath is taken away. The moment of transport is everything in art and in life, the flight from the one to the One, from the terror to the wonder and back again. Over and over, if we're lucky. If we're blessed by the gods, the world's beauty is more than enough.

Whatever beauty is—or isn't—is ultimately less important than what is beautiful to us, the simplest but most elegant and natural expression of our pleasure. To say, "It's beautiful" or "You're beautiful" is inevitably accompanied by a sigh, a smile, an assurance that all is well despite it all. Writing in his hermitage on the Greek island of Patmos, the poet-mystic Robert Lax reminds us, "God wants you to *enjoy* life." To which I would add *goddess*, especially our Venus/Aphrodite, who has your back, your heart, your desires in mind. She is the very embodiment of the promise of happiness. No guarantee, just a promise. That's the beauty of it.

While visiting the Musée Marmottan, in Paris, I was asked by a guard, "*Monsieur, q'uest-ce vous cherchez?*" What are you looking for?" I thought it was the most preposterous question because the Marmottan features the work of only one painter, Claude Monet, and one kind of his paintings, the famous Water Lilies. I mumbled something, wandered away, and promptly got lost trying to find the exit. Only then did I realize how close to *lost* it can seem when you have been *transported* by a work of art, whether it's a great movie, dance, play, or a *Water Lily*. And that is, I believe, what we are looking for when we look at art—not just paint and canvas, not only the presence of the artist, which somehow dwells in the very molecules of the work, but the transport it promises, like the eyes of the Venus de Milo as she stares into the eyes of Paris, Prince of Troy.

If so, what else are we looking for when we walk through the corridors of a museum? Distraction? Education? Cultural status? A dear friend of my mine from Sauvignon, Anne Stellio, once told me that the difference between Americans and French in museums is that Americans are looking for self-improvement and the French are looking for transcendence.

Not more theories, but stories, or beauty shots in the movies, and nineteenth-century pastor, Coventry Patmore, that illustrate how art is relevant to our everyday lives.

Tonight, I am thinking of the beautiful passage in Milan Kundera's *The Unbearable Lightness of Being* when he wrote of his heroine, "It was a sense of beauty that conquered her depression." Not the beauty of beauty pageants, beauty parlors, or beauty shots in the movies but the beauty that keeps us alive, willing to risk everything, even ruin.

What the discoverers of the Venus saw was the consummate *yes to life.* Arms or no arms. They are nowhere to be seen but everywhere to be found. Look inside for what is missing in yourself and in the world around you. Then tell me a story of deep delight, the story behind the story, the time-defying messages, like this one from the nineteenth-century pastor Coventry Patmore: "Let those who never loved love now; / Let those who loved love again." Don't you just love it?

"Can you feel it," as the Detroit preacher sang, "can you feel the mystery?" I am searching for the *secret strength* of the Venus, the what-it-is that gives her her charm and power. Maybe it will explain her paradox, a cool statue that sets its admirers on fire, which is a hallmark of all great art. I wouldn't trade my search for anything.

Now I know what I would say to the Irishwoman and her daughter if by chance I were to bump into them again at the Louvre or on Grafton Street in Dublin or at home in San Francisco. "Who stole the Venus's arms?" they might inquire, and I would demur again. I would say no single person stole them; we all did, or are doing now, every time we choose something ugly in the world over something beautiful, life-affirming, heart-pounding—anything that doesn't contribute to our sense of *aliveness*, as Alexandros did in creating her.

✹

The last time I saw my friend, Alexander Eliot, he proudly led me to the back of his small bungalow in Venice, California, and picked up the hefty manuscript of his final book, his long-awaited memoir, which he titled *Because It's Beautiful*. Smiling, the crusty art critic read from a single page where he describes his own last mentor encounter with famed art critic Bernard Berenson, in Venice, Italy. "This encounter has helped me stay on the path of beauty," Alex said in his gravelly voice. "The master was looking at snowflakes after studying museum drawings. He revealed to me his realization that every great encounter with art *is a means of experiencing further beauty.*"

And so it is. As glorious as the Venus de Milo is to me, as moved as I am by Turner's "Ships of Fire" and Vermeer's "The Lacemaker" and Hopper's "Movie Theater," the ultimate gift is how the rendering of the beautiful in those works has inspired me to find it elsewhere and everywhere, such as the Little League field in my North Beach neighborhood, the frosting of fog on Telegraph Hill when I get up at dawn to walk down to my local café, the look of joy on my wife's face when she comes home at night and sees the Greek takeout food I've laid out on the table.

Recently, I was having my morning coffee in a small redwood grove in the town of San Anselmo in Marin County and reading John Berger's probing essay on the relationship between love and art in the work of Van Gogh. Berger's prose nudged my mind into a swerve after reading, "Why write more—his capacity to love, his ability to *achieve* love with art." The tough Marxist social critic finds himself in awe of the Dutch painter's ability to write and paint despite crippling depression, financial problems, and declining health. What carried him through, Berger concludes, as if to convince himself, was what the painter called his "intense witnessing." In writing to his brother, Van Gogh says, "And then I have nature, art, and poetry. And then if that is not enough, what is enough?"

In *A Letter to a Young Painter*, Herbert Read writes, "First the inner silence, in between the notes; then the outer silence which is added, where the descent is one of love. She found the same *double descending movement in Greek sculpture* [my italics] and suggested that this double descent of silences is the key to all art... Art creates the moment when some notion of a transcendental reality becomes possible...a harmony which some people call beauty and others love."

There they are again, those kissing cousins, love and beauty.

I probe the world for stories so I might make my own. They allow me to go on living.

The beautiful isn't a concept or a theory. It's an experience, an encounter. The beautiful makes us more human. It's inhuman to act as if we are beyond it. I'll say again what the poets have been saying for millennia: Beauty is the promise of happiness, love the desire for beauty, necessity the mother of love.

Something beautiful this way comes.

We need to let it in.

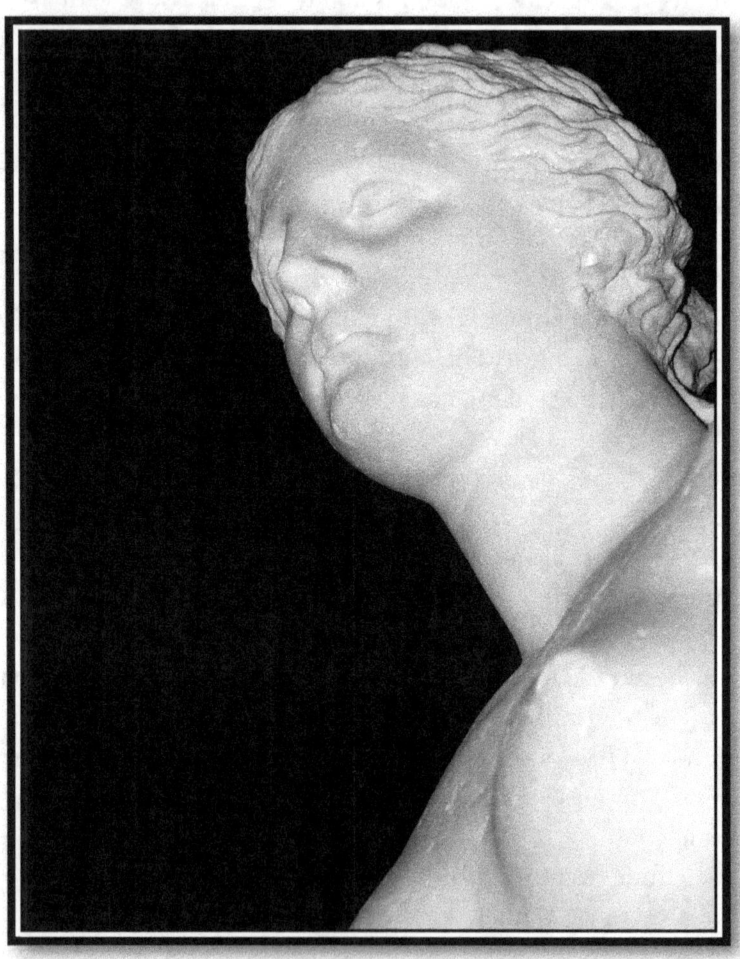

Looming Beauty
Musée du Louvre, 2018

EPILOGUE

"But just when we are beginning to despair of the human race,
we remember Vézelay or Chartres, Raphael's *School of Athens*
or Titian's *Sacred and Profane Love*, and once more
we are proud of our equivalent humanity."

–Kenneth Clark, *What is a Masterpiece?*

Often have I wondered about where the urge to make art comes from and why we bother to care when we know how much struggle is involved with creating it. The answer is nebulous. Still, we try because the reasons we need to leave a mark on the cave wall are beyond the scope of ordinary language. We tell stories, conjure up myths and legends. Here is one about the origins of the urge to paint.

Listen. Lean in. Get it.

This is as unexpected as it is beautiful, as all true origin stories are.

Case in point, Pliny the Elder's retelling of a venerable old story, in his 37-volume *Natural History*, about the mythical beginning of painting. According to the personifying ways of folklore, there was a certain artist named Butades of Corinth who was the first to have the idea of modeling clay in relief. The artist had been inspired by his beautiful daughter, Kora, who had fallen for a handsome local youth. Pliny wrote, "She was deeply in love with a young man who was about to depart on a long journey, and so traced the profile of his face as thrown upon the wall by the light of the lamp." Motivated by the desire to preserve his memory, she drew an outline of his shadow. Upon the sketch, her father created a clay model of his face, which he then baked in his oven next to the decorative clay tiles that he had also invented. And by such legerdemain, the trick of her hand, young Kora was able to keep the image of her lover alive in her heart, and on the wall of her home.

How can I not think about what happened to Alexandros when he paused over his marble block, as Stoppard wondered about where the poet went between inspiration and creation, and decided to carve the Venus the way he did, which was with a chisel that fused together the sublime and the beautiful. The meaning of his art is there. Where did he go in the moment the idea came to him? When did he finally move his chisel? Did he decide how to carve his Venus or did the times dictate how far his impulse would take him, or did his audience in faraway Melos shape his vision? And where do we go when we gaze at her?

If we can find that moment and name it, we will know who stole her arms.

If we aren't transported somewhere, to some other place and time, the work we've encountered may be well-crafted or socially interesting, but it isn't art, which hits us deep down in inside, which Ray Charles intones when he sings, "I believe to my soul." I have been trying to honor that *movement* with the discursive nature of this book, the flicker of my own life. Baudelaire called it "the double nature of beauty," which features both an eternal element and a circumstantial one. We might even say the movement works both ways.

Years ago, I was collaborating with the great philosopher and historian of religion Huston Smith on a book for the University of California Press, *The Way Things Are.* One day, I accompanied him to a radio interview at KQED in San Francisco, where he was interviewed along with Grateful Dead drummer Mickey Hart. The steadfast host, Michael Krasny, opened with an unexpected but clever question: "What do the two of you *possibly* have in common?" he inquired with cheerful emphasis.

Spontaneously, as if jumping in on a drum solo, Mickey said, "We're both in the transportation business." Later, on the ride home to Berkeley, the delighted Professor Smith took up the prompt, "Yes, yes," he said, "Mickey was right. I would just like to add that while music carries us away, religion spirits us away. That answer makes me very happy."

The relationship between art, beauty, religion, meaning, and happiness is a curious one.

"Of one thing I am certain," wrote the mystic monk-poet Thomas Merton. "My life must have meaning." That's all, not a lot to ask, I thought when I visited his cabin at the hermitage in Gethsemane, Kentucky, where he wrote seven books in the last three years of his life. That's what I've been striving for here, the mining of the seams of our great stories about the Venus for their meaning. I am trying to tell you that the best stories hover outside of time and space. Let's call them life's imponderables. Stories about art, beauty, desire, happiness, dreams, death, redemption, resolution, restoration. Royal roads to meaning.

"Meaning is not instantaneous," wrote the art critic and political activist John Berger. "Meaning is discovered in what connects and cannot exist without development. Without a story, without an unfolding, there is no meaning."

In the thumpingly moody "Hypnotized," by Fleetwood Mac, there are two lines that have haunted me for years, and more, they often play in the jukebox of my mind when I fall into a trance over art, music, poetry, or great sporting events:

It's not a meaningless question to ask if those stories are right,
What matters most is the feeling you get when you're hypnotized.

Every time I hear that melody, sense that heavy base line thumping in my bones, I believe again in the importance of transport to that silver-platter moon and the planet Venus rising in the spring sky, and it is enough. What matters most about our dreamlike encounters with any work of art is the feeling we get when we're hypnotized. If we're not entranced, enspelled, or ensorcelled, the work might be entertaining, it might be trendy, but if doesn't transport us, it ain't art.

✺

Art counts, beauty matters, desire lures, happiness happens. These are among the life lessons I've learned from my years of study and research on the Venus de Milo. Every encounter, every book, every conversation about her led me somewhere else, to more art, more myths, more travel, and ideally, more self-expression. Without exception, each great encounter with the Venus or Vermeer, Blake or Turner, Angelou or Malick stoked my creative fires, and I feel an adrenaline rush that inspires me to want to create something of my own.

Art helps ratchet forth the gears in our hearts. Just being around it. Witnessing it. Making it. Sharing it with others. Learning how to see all over again, then again and again. Art helps us remember what we love, shows us how we might preserve the infinite moment.

✺

Contemplating the Venus de Milo has taught me that everything in my everyday ordinary life has been enriched because of the deeper attention I have learned to pay to life, and I'm led to believe that it is *a means of experiencing further beauty*. What did the great poet Jack Gilbert, whose vision was sharpened by living in the Greek islands for ten years, say to me over a glass of white wine at San Francisco's Fort Mason after one of his last poetry readings? He furrowed his brow, asked if he was "okay" that night, and then began talking about how Venus, or Aphrodite as the Greeks knew her, was a jealous mistress. He repeated a phrase from one of the poems he read that night, "A magnitude of beauty that allows me no peace."

A magnitude of beauty. The phrase bears repeating, like a chorus in a memorable song. So, no, in case you're wondering, I wouldn't trade any of the time I've spent with the Venus or any other works I love, from Hopper to Mozart, Rodin to Beethoven, Bach to Miles Davis, Ella Fitzgerald to Leonard Cohen. Not for all the marble in Greece.

One work leads to another.

That's the beauty of it.

Believing in the beautiful has taught me to practice the art of what Henri Bergson called "*the duree*," the duration, the elongation of the moment that outlasts the original encounter. I've learned how to stretch time, and that has changed everything in my life: the way I write, film, listen to music, cultivate friendships, and devote myself to family life.

I have learned how art has a way of sharpening the knife edge of our seeing so that we are more alert, aware, and grateful about what is meaningful in the world beyond the museum or gallery or concert hall—until we see the beautiful in our own backyards. Without that aspect, that intensification of experience, art risks being self-indulgent, a luxury, and I hesitate to say, irrelevant. Art is a way to help us endure and glean some joy out of life. Art is a whetstone for our senses, and as the poets have long promised, the experience, if even for fleeting moments, of happiness.

The prolific Japanese author Yasunari Kawabata said in his gorgeous book, *The Existence and Discovery of Beauty*, "I have been led to consider the happiness arising" from the recognition and exclamation of beauty everywhere. For himself, it was an ordinary moment in a hotel, the Kahala Hilton, when he happened to notice "the beauty of an assortment of drinking glasses gleaming the morning sunshine on a long table in the corner of the restaurant." Out of such a mundane moment, he remembered for the rest of his life the way the parade of glasses "gave off sparkling stars... gleaming points of light." Later, Kawabata cited the the beloved poet Issa, who had exclaimed "How beautiful!" in one of his haiku, the use of which, Kawabata suggests, reveals that the master not only discovered something beautiful—but in that sublime moment *created* beauty. His colleague John Young wrote that the eloquence of Kawabata's speeches rivaled the moon in beauty and inspired in his listeners to follow his example in seeing beauty everywhere, until "We too wish to become such a person."

I love this observation. The fable within the fable reveals an admirable goal, that of *developing* the capacity to see the beautiful everywhere *anyway*—despite the despair that ancient and modern observers have warned us about, the loss of hope, from Kierkegaard and Haruki Murakami to Anne Sexton, Lydia Millet, and Walker Percy.

Speaking of Percy, he writes in his novel of spiritual redemption, *The Moviegoer*, "To become aware of the search is to be onto something. Not to be onto something is to be in despair." For Millet, in an interview for The *New York Times*, it is hopelessness that rankles, "If nothing matters, then nothing matters and you can just sit around," she said. "Where really what is hopeful is always to act." But act on what, you wonder, and she answers on our sense of awe and wonder, such as for the natural world. There are arguments galore about the need to protect endangered species, to which she responds, "We're here because we love them, and they matter because they're beautiful."

Not the facile and manipulative kind of beauty that infamously contorts our minds and bodies, but what psychologist James Hillman pinpoints as *kallos*, as in Helen of Troy's own *deep beauty*, "which proved to be more bane than bounty." The beauty, so to speak, of reclaiming these words that bring together the transcendental aspect of beauty with the elusive component of erotic desire, until the tension between the two is resolved in *the desire to see beautifully*.

These final fables are rhapsodies on the theme of the secret strength of the Venus de Milo, which are necessary because every exploration and discussion of the statue brings us back to a paradox: She is a cool statue that offers to set her viewers on fire.

In the late Nineties, I was part of a team in Taiwan shooting a documentary that became *The Meaning of Tea*. One rainy afternoon, I had drinks with a local tea maven who regaled me with the marvelous tale of the seventeenth-century Chinese playwright, Chin Shêng-t'an. The beloved writer was stranded by a rainstorm in a temple for ten days and used his time, more diligently than most of us would, to write down a list of thirty-three moments of happiness in his life. His examples are the essence of simplicity. He briefly described the most deceptively simple of moments, such as a noonday meal during a thunderstorm, entertaining a friend he hadn't seen for decades, making a bonfire of debts to him he had been holding onto, and watching a friend display his talent for calligraphy, swirling tall characters.

After each vignette, Shêng-t'an simply wrote, "Ah, is this not happiness?"

What an elegantly simple question. No theory, no posturing, no spiritual one-upmanship. The honorable writer was only listing his actual *experiences*, not *theories* or aphorisms, which in turn brought me *joy*, three centuries after he composed the list. It is the joy of encountering a well-lived life, further proof of my emerging belief that my fascination with the Venus de Milo has led to my ever-deepening appreciation of other art, but also the beautiful in nature, urban life, design, and most importantly and mysteriously, the people in my life.

✿

One last time, let's turn around her. Let's remember her story.. Let's look again at her face, her eyes, her composure. She has just offered Paris, Prince of Troy, the hand of Helen, the most beautiful woman in the world, and then upped the ante by promising him that Helen will love him. The goddess has offered the *promise of happiness.* Not the guarantee but the possibility, which is at the heart of the enchantment, the promise of love. Her sculptor sways her hips so that she can lean forward to accept the Golden Apple; her drapery slips, tantalizingly; her stomach muscles tighten; a shadow comes over her face. At that precise moment, Alexandros of Antioch, son of Menides, had rendered from his revolutionary reading of the myth that Venus/Aphrodite knows she has sparked young love—but also released the the dogs of war. Helen was married. Odysseus cleverly had all the captains of Greece pledge an oath to come to the side of her husband Menelaus if she was ever in danger. There it is, the ever-entangled myths of love and war.

The secret strength of the Venus de Milo is that her genius creator captured, in marble, the moment of realization that love and war are found in the same gaze.

She says, *Choose love, anyway.*

✿

My gut tells me this is true. I think back to the moment my father took me to the Detroit Institute of Art to show me some paintings by Renoir, stunning me with his story. Call it the three-act structure of every dramatic encounter with a significant work of art. Miraculously, I can detect a path from there to the old oak dining room table at Ansel Adams' old home in Carmel, California, where I learned from Edward Weston's son, Cole, that his father had heard Alfred Stieglitz once say, "Beauty is the universal seen."

And that has been the thrust of my life since I punched the time clock at the Detroit factory where I worked for four years and went out to see the world and wound up going in to see myself. My hero in college where I studied photography was Henri Cartier-Bresson, who, I learned, walked and stalked the back streets of Paris, his Leica tucked almost imperceptibly inside his trench coat, looking until he could see, seeing until he could love. The images that he captured—a bicyclist casting a long shadow, a boy jumping from one puddle to the next, Matisse lost in a room of white birds—do what all great art does: surprises you, making you feel as if you've never seen these things before.

In that way, art *strangifies* the world, making even the most familiar seem unfamiliar, if even for a moment. That slippage is a shock, a *frisson*, a shiver down the spine. To my eyes, there is no art without a shiver of strange running through it. The shiver and the surprise that seizes the breath and stops time, the glimpse that shakes us to the core, as if to say, *Look what you missed the first time around; look what's been all around you.*

"Reel away the real world," in the words of movie-obsessed James Joyce, who opened the first cinema in Dublin.

Reeling away here on Ithaka, floating above the Ionian Sea, I remember in filmlike flickers the blue tiles of Claude Monet's kitchen in Giverny. Beautiful. Victor Hugo's writing room in a glass-walled cupola on Guernsey in the Channel Islands. Beautiful. The Waimpi warriors deep in the Amazon applying fire-ash whiskers at dawn, then using their bows and arrows to shoot monkeys out of the sky-scraping trees. Beautiful. Beautiful. The northern lights in Narvik, Norway, and my encounter with three staggering moose with clattering antlers at dawn in Ontario's Algonquin Park. Beautiful, beautiful. I think of the black-caped, blue-hatted Rudolf Nureyev sitting on a tree stump in Muir Woods, returning my surprised gaze with his bull-black eyes. Beautiful. I can see her now, the black-shrouded widow bringing blue flowers to her husband's grave in soft-stoned Assisi, Italy, and the haunted widow in Nuremberg, Germany, who took me in out of a violent rainstorm, warmed me before her blazing fire, and then brought out framed photographs of her Nazi officer husband. Strangely beautiful. The revolutionary performer Jean Erdman Campbell *danced her answers* to my questions about her working relationship with Martha Graham while we were filming her in Honolulu. Beautiful. Beautiful, too, the day I was hiking on a beach near Clifden Castle in Connemara, when I saw a *fulgurite*, an otherworldly glassy piece of petrified lightning, and the afternoon I swam in the Red Sea, along the Negev, and saw millions of kaleidoscopically-colored fish moving in and around me, ribboning through the water, and then gasped when I saw the light blue water turn darker and darker blue as the sea dropped 9,927 feet into the canyons below. Beyond beautiful.

Ah, is this not happiness? Is this not beauty?

Beauty leads to beauty, desire to desire, happiness to happiness. The quest for beauty, beautiful moments, life-affirming encounters, never ends. It is the fall of 1989. Slate-blue skies. The smell of coffee, croissants, and easels wet with paint. I am *flaneuring* around Paris. Reaching the Marais, I come across a gallery featuring three sandy-colored bottles on a simple wooden table, three still lifes by the seraphic Giorgio Morandi. The Italian painter was a simple man who stayed out of the spotlight, content to practice what his contemporary, philosopher Gaston Bachelard, described in his works as the "poetics of stillness." I am too shoddily dressed to step inside. Instead, I hover, standing on the cobbled street, losing myself in the beauty Morandi wrested from what he felt was a wanton world. Spotting a few free pamphlets inside an old letterbox, I read an announcement of the small exhibition. On one is written a Morandi quote, a kind of credo:

"Everything is a mystery, ourselves and all things both simple and humble. A half dozen pictures would just about be enough for the life of an artist, for my life."

It's all still a mystery. I can easily imagine Alexandros of Antioch writing something similar about his sculpture, the Venus de Milo, perhaps to his teacher, maybe his model, or perhaps the committee on Melos that arranged the competition.

Suddener. The world is suddener than I ever imagined. We need the *thump* of that word to get the world. The word is choiceworthy. Worth our effort to suddenly learn. I learned this, too, from the strange gaze of the Venus de Milo. The more you look at her looking out at the world, the more you, too, will learn about the curious relationship between love, beauty, and happiness.

This mosaic of meditations is about many things, including a treatise on the virtues of observation, a life lesson about the quality of our attention, the realization that nothing that we do will matter unless it touches the human heart. This is one of the most important things I've learned about life while studying the Venus de Milo. If art is the lie that tells the truth, then mythic art tells a greater lie to reveal a deeper truth. If we are alert, there is something in the world beautiful enough to save us *anyway.*

One night in the winter of 1973, ensconced with my college girlfriend in the gymnasium at the University of Detroit to listen to the white-maned, black-hatted, flickering-fingered Leon Russell, I was astonished to watch him transform from rocker to ballad singer, sitting down at his long gleaming black piano to croon, "A Song for You." When he reached the chorus, he sang the first line with a depth of unsparing truth that pierced me: "I love you in a place beyond space and time." A lapidary moment, we might call it, both beautiful and painful, informing me that I *didn't* love the one

I was with the way he loved his woman. A part of me decided then and there that I needed to find someone to love with that degree of certitude, and evidently, tenderness. I've never forgotten the tenderness. It took me seventeen years to do so, but because it happened in a place beyond space and time, who's counting? Only me, counting the days till I found the love I could call my own.

ART'S AFFIRMATION

Late fall, 2019, San Francisco. I have just returned from a long lecture tour around Europe and feel the need to ritually celebrate my homecoming with my wife Jo. Together, we climb up our metal spiral staircase to our roof overlooking San Francisco Bay. I carry a glass of Glenlivet Scotch and Jo totes a bottle of her favorite Cabernet. We gaze out over the city, reveling in the sunset, and toast, which feels like a benediction. We go quiet, silenced by the sunset. I take a few steps out to the railing and watch the night sky spilling stars over the city and the starlight glistening on the bay. Again, we clink glasses, and I am at a loss for something to say, other than wanting it to be real. "I missed you," I say, and hope it hits the mark.

My gaze flies like a bright white seagull over the bay, and a warm feeling of contentment comes over me. There is no end of beauty for anyone who is awake, and I laugh to myself when I remember one of my Greek friends, from Crete, telling me that his ancestors were right, that *acting* happy sometimes takes us halfway there. Without beauty, there is no joy in the world, and even if the acting and noticing are difficult, it feels true to think it was meant to be this way. We are meant to dwell on the threshold, to exist in two infinities at once.

"Yes" is all I can manage to say, lifting my glass to the sunset and hugging my wife, and as I do, I feel the wings of happiness fly past me, realizing this is the *What it is of all that is*, the holding of someone in your arms and feeling as if you are holding onto the universe.

Saying yes to life *anyway*. If there's a trick to life, that's it, its saving grace.

In his memoir, *Markings*, Dag Hammarskjöld, the second Secretary-General of the United Nations, wrote, "I don't know Who, or what, put the question, I don't know when it was put. I don't even remember answering. But at some moment I did answer *Yes* to Someone—and from that hour I was certain that existence is meaningful and that, therefore, my life, in self-surrender, had a goal."

This depth of conviction, despite the tragic facts of life, can also be seen in Vermeer's response to life during war and plagues when he rendered exquisite tenderness on canvas, or in Eugene O'Neill's embrace of the long-buried truth of his life that allowed him to pen *Long Day's Journey into Night*.

I think now of the Greek poet Yannis Ritsos, who wrote, "Ah, yes, the world is beautiful. A man beneath the trees wept from the joy of love. He was stronger than death, that man—which is why we sing... No one will silence our song. We sing on. The world is beautiful, we insist."

Ah, is this not beautiful? The revelation of *what shines through* and saves us from despair? Is this not *it*, what it is, the thing we are up against and the thing that shores us up?

The question always returns to what to do about the truth as we see it. The answer always returns to whether or not the work is beautiful enough to inspire us to experience further beauty. Yes or no? No mind, no matter. I say yes, anyway, like Wallace Stevens in "The Well-Dressed Man with a Beard," where he writes, "After the final no there comes a yes / And on that yes the world depends."

Closer to home, I recall the sound of my father's voice when I surprised him with a phone call from the Beverly Hills house of the drummer of a legendary L. A. rock band, where I was working on the book about his life in the music business. We hadn't spoken in years for the stupidest of reasons, and I wanted to make up for lost time. We spoke for an hour and a half while I listened and stared at the wall of gold records while the Wurlitzer played hits from the sixties.

"When you recover, Dad, we'll finally travel together," I vowed, hoping against hope he would get over the nerve disease that was racking him. "We'll go to France and track down our ancestors, or maybe we'll go to Greece because of your love of Homer, or Cambodia because, well, I remember the first book you ever gave me, when I was about ten, was about Angkor Wat. Anywhere you want to go, Dad."

"Son, I can't believe you remember that book. Yes, a thousand times yes, buddy."

Ah, is this not the what it is of all that is?

Yes, *anyway*.

At the Musée National Eugène Delacroix in Paris,
I open to a random page in the French painter's *Journals* and read:

"The last word on beauty can never be said."

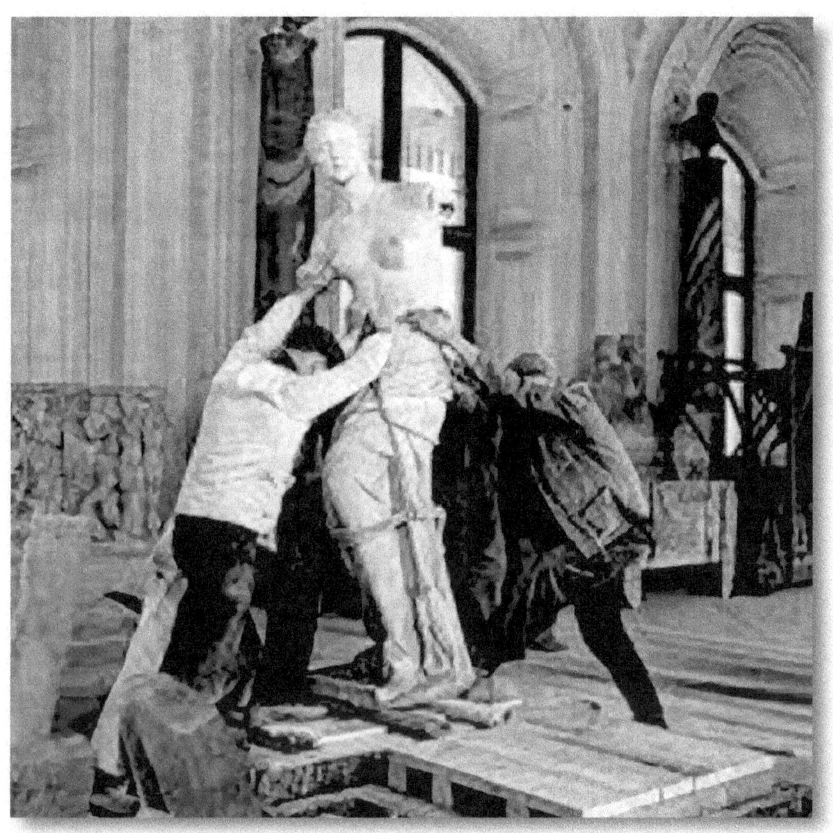

Returning the *Venus de Milo* to the Louvre after
the four-year German Occupation of Paris, 1945
Unknown photographer

RECOMMENDED READING

Adams, Robert. *Beauty in Photography*. New York: Aperture, 1996.

Acts of Love: Ancient Poetry from Aphrodite's Garden. Translated by George Economou. New York: Modern Library, 2006.

Alaux, Jean-Paul. *La Venus de Milo et Olivier Voutier. The Discovery of the Venus de Milo*. Paris: Editions du Galion d'or, 1939.

Barfield, Owen. *History in English Words*. Herdon, VA.: Lindisfarne Books, 2002.

Barnstone, Willis. Edited and translated by. *Sweetbitter Love: Poems of Sappho*. London & New York: Shambhala Press, 2006.

Barolsky, Paul. *Why Mona Lisa Smiles and Other Tales*. Ann Arbor: University of Michigan Press, 1991.

Belavnakis, Gregory. *Brief Illustrated History of Melos*. Translated by Geoffrey Cox. Athens: S & B Industrial Minerals, S. A., 2006.

Berger, John. *About Looking*. New York: Penguin Books, 2000.

Berger, John. *Ways of Seeing*. New York: Penguin Books, 1990.

Bloom, Paul. *How Pleasure Works: The New Science of Why We Like What We Like*. New York: W. W. Norton & Company, 2010.

Boelte, Kyle. *The Beautiful Unseen*. New York: Penguin Random House, 2015.

Calasso, Roberto. *The Marriage of Cadmus and Harmony*. New York: Vintage International, 2013.

Canfora, Luciano. *The Vanished Library*. Translated by Martin Ryle. Berkeley: University of California Press, 1990.

Carson, Anne. *Eros: The Bittersweet*. Princeton, N. J.: Princeton University Classics, 2023.

Carus, Paul. *The Venus de Milo: An Archaeological Study of Woman*. Chicago and London: The Open Court Publishing Company and the Theosophical Society, 1916.

Chardin de, Pierre Teilhard. *Hymns of the Universe.* New York Harper & Row, 1961.

Clark, Kenneth. *The Nude: A Study in Ideal Form.* Princeton, N. J.: Princeton University Press, 1972.

Connolly Cyril. *The Unquiet Grave: A Word Cycle.* New York and London: Harper and Brothers, 1945.

Cousineau, Phil. *Once and Future Myths: The Power of Ancient Stories in Modern Times.* Berkeley: Conari Press, 2001.

Cousineau, Phil. *The Blue Museum.* San Francisco: Sisyphus Press, 2004.

Curtis, Gregory. *Disarmed: the Venus de Milo.* New York: Vintage Books, 2004.

Dillard, Annie. *For the Time Being.* New York: Vintage Books, 2000.

Dunn, Stephen. *The Insistence of Beauty: Poems.* New York: W. W. Norton & Company, 2004.

Eliot, Alexander. *Because it was Beautiful: My Life and Loves.* Venice, CA: WriteSpa, 2016.

Eliot, Alexander. *Sight and Insight.* Venice, CA: WriteSpa, 2010.

Elson, Rebecca. *A Responsibility to Awe.* Manchester, England: Carcanet Classics, 2018.

Encyclopedia of Aphrodisiacs.

Euripides. *Helen* (a dramatic play). New York: Scribe Books, 2017.

Febbraro, Flavio. *How to Read Erotic Art.* New York: Henry A. Abrams, 2011.

Felch, Jason and Ralph Frammolino. *Chasing Aphrodite: The Hunt for Looted Antiquities at the World's Largest Museum.* New York: Houghton Mifflin Publishing Company, 2011.

Finley, Moses. *The World of Odysseus.* New York: New York Review of Books Classics, 2002.

Flannagan, John B. *The Sculpture of John B. Flannagan.* New York: Plantin Press, 1942.

Frankl, Victor. *Yes to Life: In Spite of Everything.* Boston: Beacon Books, 2021.

Giono, Jean. *The Man Who Planted Trees.* Chelsea, VT: Chelsea Green Publishing, 2007.

Gombrich, Emile. *The Story of Art.* London and New York: Phaidon Press, 1995.

Graves, Robert. *The Greek Myths.* New York: Viking Books, 2018.

Grigson, Geoffrey. *The Goddess of Love: The Birth, Triumph, Death and Return of Aphrodite.* London: Stein and Day, 1977.

Grimm, Heinrich. *The Venus de Milo.* Translated by Alice M. Hawes. Boston: J. J. Hawes, 1868.

Grudin, Robert. *Time and the Art of Living.* Boston: Mariner Books, 1997.

Gutzwiller, Kathyrn. *The New Posidippus: A Hellenistic Poetry Book.* Oxford: Oxford University Press, 2005.

Hamill, Sam. Editor and translator. *The Infinite Moment: Poems from Ancient Greek.* New York: New Directions Books, 1991.

Hamilton, Edith. *The Greek Way.* New York: W. W. Norton & Company, 2017.

Hamlyn, Paul. *Aphrodisiacs: An Encyclopedia of Erotic Wisdom.* London: Hamlyn Publishing, 1990.

Havelock, Christine Mitchell. *The Aphrodite of Knidos and Her Successors.* Ann Arbor, MI: University of Michigan Press, 1995.

Hersey, George. L. *The Evolution of Allure: Sexual Selection from the Medici Venus to the Incredible Hulk.* Cambridge, MA: MIT Press, 1996.

Hickey, Dave. *The Invisible Dragon: Essays on Beauty.* Chicago: The University of Chicago Press, 2009.

Hughes, Bettany. *Helen of Troy: The Story Behind the Most Beautiful Woman in the World.* New York: Vintage Books, 2007.

Hughes, Bettany. *Venus and Aphrodite: A Biography of Desire.* New York: Basic Books, 2020.

Hyde, Lewis. *The Gift: How the Creative Spirit Transforms the World.* New York: Vintage Books, 2019.

Jung, Carl. *Memories, Dreams, and Reflections.* Translated by Aniela Jaffe, ed. Clara Winston. New York: Vintage Books, 1989.

Kawabata, Yusanari. *The Existence and Discovery of Beauty.* Translated by V. H. Viglielmo. Tokyo: Mainichi, 1969.

Kimmelman, Michael. *The Accidental Masterpiece: On the Art of Life and Vice Versa.* New York: Penguin Books, 2006.

Kousser, Rachel. "Creating the Past: The Venus de Milo." *American Journal of Archaeology*: 109, 2005.

Kousser, Rachel. *Hellenistic and Roman Ideal Sculpture: The Allure of the Classical.* Cambridge: Cambridge University Press, 2008.

Macaulay, Dame Rose. *Pleasure of Ruins.* New York: Holt, Rinehart & Winston, 1977.

May, Rollo. *My Quest for Beauty.* New York: W. W. Norton & Co., 1985.

May, Rollo. *The Cry for Myth.* New York: W. W. Norton & Co., 1991.

Milosz, Czeslaw. *Unattainable Earth.* New York: Harper Collins, 1986.

Mitchell, Susan. *Erotikon: Poems.* New York: Harper Collins, 2005.

Needleman, Jacob. *The Wisdom of Love: Toward a Shared Inner Life.* Indianapolis, IN: Morning Light Press, 2005.

Nehamas, Alexander. *Only a Promise of Happiness: The Place of Beauty in a World of Art.* Princeton, NJ: Princeton University Press, 2010.

O'Donohue, John. *Beauty: The Invisible Embrace.* New York: Harper Perennial, 2005.

Ondaatje, Michael. *The English Patient.* New York: Vintage Books, 1993.

Orlean, Susan. *The Orchid Thief: A True Story of Beauty and Obsession.* New York: Ballantine Books, 2005.

Otto, Rudolph. *The Idea of the Holy: Second Edition.* Oxford: Oxford University Press, 1958.

Ovid, *Metamorphoses.* Translated by Rolfe Humphries. New York: Penguin Classics, 2004.

Ovid. *Heroides*. Translated by Harold Isbell. New York: Penguin Classics, 1990

Paglia, Camille. *Sexual Personae: Art and Decadence from Nefertiti to Emily Dickinson*. New York: Vintage Books, 1991.

Paris, Ginette. *Pagan Meditations: The Worlds of Aphrodite, Artemis, and Hestia*. Dallas: Spring Publications, 2022.

Pasquier, Alain. *Le Venus de Milo*. French Edition. Editions de la Reunion des musees nationaux; HORS COLLECTION edition, 1985.

Pessoa, Fernando. *Always Astonished*. Translated by Edwin Honig. San Francisco: City Lights Publishers, 2001.

Pindar, *The Odes*. Translated by C. M. Bowra. New York: Penguin Classics, 1982.

Prettejean, Elizabeth. *Aphrodite*. Ann Arbor, MI: University of Michigan Press.

Read, Herbert. *A Letter to a Young Painter*. New York: Horizon Press, 1962.

Read, Herbert. *The Art of Sculpture*. Princeton, NJ: Princeton University Press, 1961.

Rexroth, Kenneth. *Poems from the Greek Anthology: Expanded Edition*. Ann Arbor, MI: Ann Arbor Paperbacks, 1999.

Rilke, Rainer Marie. *Letters on Cezanne*. Translated by Joel Agee. Berkeley, CA: North Point Press, 2002.

Ritsos, Yannis. Selected Poems. Trans. Nikos Stangos. Athens: Efstathiadis Group, 1971.

Rodin, Auguste. *Venus*. Translated by Dorothy Dudley. New York: B. W. Huebesch, 1912.

Rovelli, Claudio. *The Order of Time*. New York: Riverhead Books, 2019.

Salmon, Dimitri. *La Venus de Milo: Un Mythe*. Paris: Gallimard, 2000.

Santayana, George. *The Sense of Beauty*. New York: Dover Publishing, 1956. Original edition: Charles Scribner's Sons, 1896.

Sappho. *The Songs of Sappho: In English Translation by Many Poets*. Mount Vernon, NY: The Peter Pauper Press, 1962.

Scarry, Elaine. *On Beauty and Being Just.* Princeton, NJ: Princeton University Press, 2001.

Smith, Huston, and Phil Cousineau. *The Way Things Are.* Berkeley, CA: University of California Press, 2003.

Spivey, Nigel. *Songs of Bronze: The Greek Myths Made Real.* New York: Farrar Straus Giroux, 2005.

Strand, Mark. *Hopper.* New York: Alfred A. Knopf, 2011.

Stevens, Wallace. *Harmonium.* London: Faber & Faber, 2001.

Stoppard, Tom. *The Coast of Utopia: Voyage, Shipwreck, Salvage.* New York: Grove Press, 2007.

Swami, Viren. *The Missing Arms of the Venus de Milo: Reflections on the Science of Attraction.* Brighton, UK: Book Guild, 2007.

Thorne, Jim. *Adventures Under the Sea.* New York: Walker and Company, 1965.

Tolstoy, Leopold. *What is Art?* Translated by Richard Pevear. New York Penguin Classics, 1996.

Updike, John. *Still Looking: Essays on American Art.* New York: Knopf, 2005.

Vasari, Georgio. *The Lives of the Artists.* First published as *The Lives of the Most Excellent Painters, Sculptors, and Architects,* 1550. New York: Penguin Books, 2004.

Voutier, Colonel Olivier. *Decouverte et Acquisition de la Venus de Milo.* Paris: Hyere, 1874.

Villa, Daniele. *Terrence Malick: Rehearsing the Unexpected.* London: Faber & Faber, 2020.

Weil, Simone. *War and the Iliad, or the Poem of Force: A Critical Edition.* Translated by Mary McCarthy. New York: New York Review of Books, 2006.

Weschler, Lawrence. *Vermeer in Bosnia: Selected Writings.* New York: Vintage Books, 2005.

Woolf, Virginia. *To the Lighthouse.* London: Warbler Classics Editions, 2023.

Zehme, Bill. *Frank Sinatra and the Lost Art of Livin': The Way You Wear Your Hat.* New York: Harper, 1997.

ILLUSTRATIONS

Cover. The Venus de Milo, Louvre. Photograph by Phil Cousineau, 2010.

Frontispiece. The Venus de Milo, Infrared photograph by Phil Cousineau, 2010.

4. Life magazine, January 4, 1963. Collection of Stanley H. Cousineau, Detroit, Michigan.

42. The Island of Melos in the Cyclades, from Century Magazine, 1881.

51. Captain Olivier Voutier. Unknown painter. c. 1821.

55. The Ruins of the Ancient Roman Theater of Melos. Photograph by Phil Cousineau, 2004. (Above) Anonymous Engraving, The Ancient Roman theater of Melos, 1869. (Below)

60. The Wall of the Ancient Gymnasium, Yorgos' field, Melos, Greece. Century Magazine, 1913.

72. The Face of Venus. Photograph by Phil Cousineau, 2010.

88. The Lower Half of the Venus. Photograph by Phil Cousineau, 2010.

98. The Gaze. Photograph by Phil Cousineau, 2010.

109. The Findspot, Melos, Greece. Photograph by Phil Cousineau, 2004.

122. Olivier Voutier draws the Venus de Milo. Engraving by Gustave Alaux, 1939.

123. The upper and lower halves of the Venus de Milo and herms of Herakles and Hermes. Sketches by Olivier Voutier, April 1820.

139. The Apple of Discord in Venus' right hand, Louvre Vitrine. Photograph by Phil Cousineau, 2010.

152. The Judgment of Paris. Fresco. House of Jupiter, Pompeii. Public domain.

196. "Mars and Venus United by Love," by Paolo Veronese, created 1570. Metropolitan Art Museum, New York.

311. Imaginative reconstructions of the Venus. Source: The Venus de Milo by Paul Carus, 1910.

314. The left hand of the Venus holding the Apple of Discord. Musee du Louvre, Paris. Photograph by Phil Cousineau, 2010.

324. The Pensive Venus. Musee du Louvre, Paris. Photograph by Phil Cousineau, 2019.

342. The Eyes Have It. Nineteenth-century photograph. Source: The Venus de Milo by Paul Carus, 1910.

354: The Quietude of the Venus de Milo. Musee du Louvre, Paris. Photograph by Phil Cousineau, 2010.

370: Venus' Desire Line. Musee du Louvre, Paris. Photograph by Phil Cousineau, 2010.

376: The Callypygian Venus. Musee du Louvre, Paris. Photograph by Phil Cousineau, 2010.

382: The Most Beautiful Back in the World. Musee du Louvre, Paris. Photograph by Phil Cousineau, 2010.

394. The Looming Beauty. Musee du Louvre, Paris. Photograph by Phil Cousineau, 2010.

418: Returning the Venus de Milo to the Musee du Louvre, 1945. Unknown photographer.

422: The Author, Café Aphrodite, Melos, Greece. Photograph by Jo Beaton Cousineau, Melos, 2008.

425: Engraving original nineteenth-century tile work. City Hall, Adamas, Melos, Greece. 2008.

ACKNOWLEDGMENTS

My deepest gratitude goes to Jo and Jack, my wife and son, fellow Dwellers on the Threshold, in our Cloud Cottage on Telegraph Hill, San Francisco. Incalculable thanks to Sir Geoffrey Ashe of Glastonbury, England, Willis Barnstone, and Alexander Eliot for their encouragement after reading early drafts of this book. Special and heartfelt thanks to Valerie Andrews, publisher of the indispensable online magazine "Reinventing Home," for her prodigious editorial advice, soulful counsel, and savvy literary mentoring, and to Dennis Slattery for his input about the mythology behind the creation of Alexandros' statue. A hearty *epharisto poli*, many thanks, to my friends in Greece who read various sections of this manuscript: Agamemnon Dasis, of Mycenae; Spyros Couvras, of Ithaka; and Georgios Spiradakis, of Iraklion. Special thanks to Palma Puzzuoli for her French translations of Jean-Paul Alcaux's about the rediscovery of the Venus and her help deciphering Oliver Voutier's memoir, and to Irene Kometseli for her Greek translations, as well as the great scholar Thanasis Maskaleris, from Arcadia, Greece, who shared my passion for Homer and early Greek sculpture. Thanks to those other Great Hearts who read various drafts or sections of this book over the last two decades, including Alexander and Jane Eliot, who read the penultimate draft of the book shortly before they passed away in 2015, likewise with Robert A. Johnson, Angeles Arrien, Theodore Rozak, Jacob Needleman, who provided me with unwavering support, anyway. I wish to offer a handshake of thanks to Brian Swimme, who provided unstinting moral support when the going got tough with the completion of the final, final draft when I was sorely tempted to put down my chisel and hide the manuscript away. Not unlike how the statue herself was hidden for centuries.

Thanks, too, to Joyce Jenkins of Poetry Flash for providing me with the original text from Robert Haas' lecture on art's "raid on the inarticulate," James Norwood Pratt for his gift of Gregory Grigson's book on our Aphrodite, and his deft translation of Virgil's *vera incessu patuit dea.* Thanks too to Fr. Gary Young for his special insight into the spirituality of art when we sauntered around the Louvre a few years ago, and to my long-time friend Gregg Chadwick for years of exhilarating discussions about arts. A nod as well to fellow art lovers John Borton, Richard Beban, Lisa Sonora, Salley Stewart, and Joanne Warfield. And I wish to sing the praises of the alchemically gifted copy editor Stuart Balcomb, who helped transform my lead into gold.

Furthermore, I am grateful as well to those I interviewed for this book, including Ray Bradbury, Alexander Eliot, Valerie Andrews, Roger Walsh, Chris Franek, Mort Rosenblum, Jeanne Adams, Goody Cable, Leigh Carpenter, John Nance, and the late photographer Alison Wright, who provided spirited advice about the need to capture the world's beauty while we still can.

"Tell it true, but tell it slant," as Emily Dickinson said, so here I would like to acknowledge the Venus de Milo herself. Her strange allure has provided me with the means of experiencing beauty over a lifetime of closely observing and appreciating the beautiful in both ordinary and extraordinary realms and as a curious cautionary tale to never forget the love that lingers everywhere if we only pay attention.

If.

ABOUT THE AUTHOR

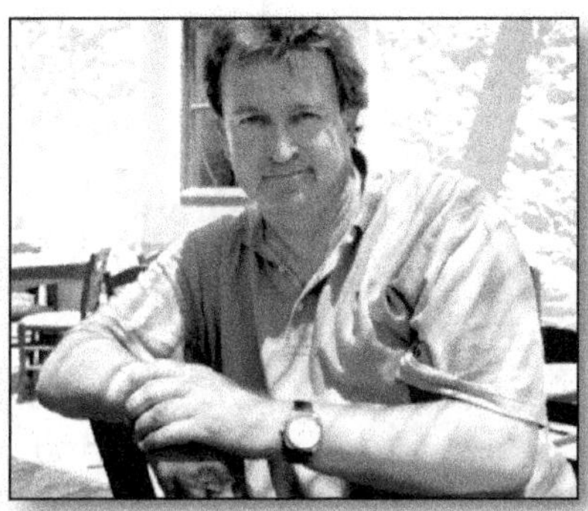
The author on Melos, Greece, 2008

Since punching out his timecard at Industrial and Automotive Fasteners, a steel factory in Detroit, on June 17, 1974, and graduating from the University of Detroit that same week, Phil Cousineau has chosen to strike out on his own as a freelance writer, independent filmmaker, maverick photographer, and mythographer. Over the course of his writing career, he has produced a body of more than 100 original works, including 42 books, 25 documentary films scripts, 20 television scripts, scores of newspaper and magazine articles, and contributed to 80 other books. His published works range from *The Hero's Journey: The Life and Work of Joseph Campbell, Once and Future Myths*, and *Stoking the Creative Fires*, to *Once and Future Myths, The Book of Roads*, and *The Lost Notebooks of Sisyphus*. His documentary films have won more than 50 international awards and he has thrived as a mythology consultant for dozens of feature films at Warner Brothers, Twentieth-Century Fox, Lucas Films, and Pixar. For ten years he was the host and cowriter of *Global Spirit*, which ran on PBS and Link TV, and he has been honored as Writer-in-Residence at Shakespeare and Company Bookstore in Paris, The James Thurber House in Columbus, Ohio, and Brush Creek Ranch, in Wyoming. He lives with his wife Jo, son Jack, and Stella, a Golden Doodle, on Telegraph Hill in San Francisco, where he doffs his hat daily to the beauty of the world and writes at a rattan roll top desk outfitted with a miniature marble statue of the Venus de Milo.

PRAISE FOR PHIL COUSINEAU

"I've read Phil Cousineau's *The Accidental Aphorist* with great interest, admiration, and fascination. Two aphorisms caught my attention: 'Time is the insomnia of infinity' and 'God created the world in six days, and on the seventh, wondered why.' These wisdom sayings are quite worthy of William Blake."

—Geoffrey Ashe, author, *King Arthur's England.*

"How few writers realize the gift of the complete freedom of speech and the colossal spiritual gift of poetry. Phil Cousineau's new poems here are ingenious, wondrous, and delightful. *Night Train* has stunning glimpses of the world and a cosmic planet citizen appeal."

—Antler, author of *Factory* and *Last Words.*

"Phil Cousineau has a nose for what can touch the soul, warm it, tickle it, and inspire it. I turn to his books with pleasure and appetite. There's *The Oldest Story in the World, Rasa,* his marvelous photographs from India, his poems in *The Blue Museum,* and his book of hours, *The Soul of the World.* Lucky me."

—Joanna Macy, author of *Active Hope* and *A Wild Love.*

"Phil Cousineau, one of the most mythically-attuned people I know, writes in *Once and Future Myths,* 'This much I know: Unless we search for ways to become aware of the myths that are unfolding in our lives, we run the risk of being controlled by them... In this book, I will tell you things I myself have lived and learned about myth.' In that last sentence, we can feel a story or series of stories warming up on the front burner."

—Dennis Slattery, author of *The Daily Odyssey.*

"*The Painted Word* stakes out a claim to the standard dictionary for this soulful companion. It contains fewer words but more fireworks, sending out Fourth of July skyrockets on every page. But caveat emptor, readers beware! Cousineau's love affair with words is contagious, and you are likely to end up lovesick with words yourself! His prolific output amazes me."
—Huston Smith, author of The World's Religions.

"*Wordcatcher* is a book that allows us to remember the genius of language—to see, feel and, it seems, even 'taste' the livingness and poetry hidden within these many common and uncommon words.
A delicious book."
—Jacob Needleman, author of What Is God?

"Phil Cousineau's *Wordcatcher* is a wonderful meditation on words that can be read from beginning to end if you are obsessed with speech, greedy for mountain air, and into enlightened verbal play. Not a dry lexical listing, each word Cousineau chooses sings with cellos, vagabonds through tongues and history, and bounces like a balloon on the moon, as high as his quirky imagination takes us. Compelled reading for residence in the ancient synagogue of the word."
—Willis Barnstone, author of Ancient Greek Lyrics.

"Deadlines is superb, a new genre, in fact, combining the pleasures of list-making with that of last-minute eavesdropping."
— Alberto Manguel, author of The History of Reading

"The Soul of the World is a human gift—thank you for caring so much."
—Elie Wiesel, author of Night, and winner
of the Nobel Peace Prize

"Phil Cousineau is a word wizard, and his book *Wordcatcher* is a delightful adventure into a magical world. As I read his amazing etymological explanations of words from eldritch to floccinaucinihilipilification to lagniappe, I marveled at his range of literary knowledge, humor, and sense of wonder."

—Deepak Chopra, author of *Quantum Healing*

"Phil Cousineau's work on the mythic origins of beauty deeply influenced my own thoughts on this timeless subject. His magnum opus, *The Art of Pilgrimage*, is widely considered to be a classic on the virtues of deep travel."

— John O'Donohue, author of *Anam Cara and Beauty: The Invisible Embrace*

"Phil Cousineau's beautifully written *The Book of Roads* has a true current that carries fragrances and faces, landscapes and stories, rooms carved out of rock and the sudden jolt of perception sharp as a sail-driven wagon wheel covering hitherto untraveled ground."

— Jane Hirshfield, author of *The Lives of the Heart*

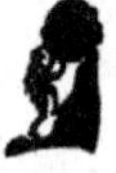

SISYPHUS PRESS
P. O. BOX 330098

SAN FRANCISCO, CALIFORNIA 94133
PILGRIMAGE@EARTHLINK.NET

COLOPHON

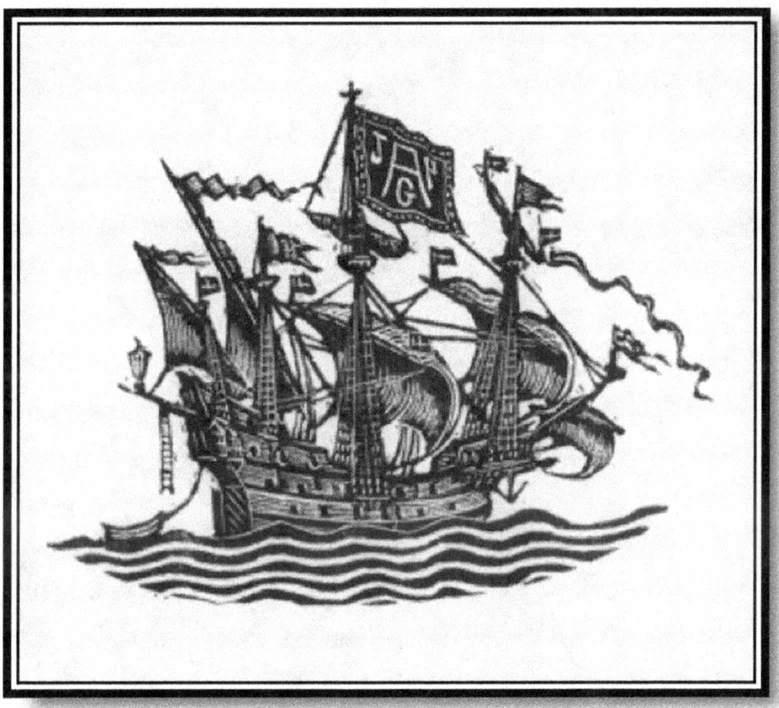

This book was written with a quill pen on ancient parchment from Pergamum, etched in pure Parian marble, then illustrated with woodcuts created from blocks cut from the Roman workshop of Piranesi. It has been published in an edition of one hundred million copies, all of which have been personally autographed by the grateful author while in residence in the Clonmacnoise Scriptorium, in Tir Na Nog, Ireland.